THE LEE BROS.
SOUTHERN COOKBOOK

THE LEE BROS.
SOUTHERN COOKBOOK

❊ *STORIES AND RECIPES FOR SOUTHERNERS* ❊
AND WOULD-BE SOUTHERNERS

MATT LEE AND TED LEE

Color photography by Gentl & Hyers

W. W. NORTON & COMPANY
New York · London

For information about permission to reproduce selections from this book, write to
Permissions, W. W. Norton & Company, Inc., 500 Fifth Avenue, New York, NY 10110

Manufacturing by The Maple-Vail Book Manufacturing Group
Book design by Jean Orlebeke
Production manager: Andrew Marasia

Library of Congress Cataloging-in-Publication Data

Lee, Matt.
The Lee Bros. southern cookbook : stories and recipes for southerners
and would-be southerners / Matt Lee and Ted Lee.
p. cm.
Includes index.
ISBN-13: 978-0-393-05781-2 (hardcover)
ISBN-10: 0-393-05781-X (hardcover)
1. Cookery, American—Southern style. I. Lee, Ted. II. Title.
TX715.2.S68L446 2006
641.5′975—dc22
2006022745

W. W. Norton & Company, Inc., 500 Fifth Avenue, New York, N.Y. 10110
www.wwnorton.com

W. W. Norton & Company Ltd., Castle House, 75/76 Wells Street, London W1T 3QT

1 2 3 4 5 6 7 8 9 0

To the memory of
Dennis Croteau, Gordon Huskey, James Kearney, Michael Lee, Hazel Miracle, Rose Mitchell,
Ted Phillips, Phil Powell, DuPre Sassard, Dan Stevens, William Washington, and Bill
Williams, and our grandparents Charlotte Lee, Arthur Lee, and Charles Maxwell, Jr.,

and in tribute to
our loyal customers and readers,

and to
Elizabeth Scheuer Maxwell—Gran—who is always game
and always the best of company.

❋ CONTENTS ❋

❈ ACKNOWLEDGMENTS ❈

It is an absolute thrill to be able to thank in print the generous souls who gave their time, astute advice, good taste, and hard labor to the making of this book, and we will attempt to name them all—aware that even with two of us on the task, our faulty memories may cause us to miss a deserving few in the process.

Those who nurtured us with their love, encouragement, and counsel include David Rawle and Carol Perkins Rawle, Carl Palazzolo and Vance Muse, Melinda Muse, Conley Rollins and Meredith Kahn Rollins, Lucy Wethers, Ginny Deerin, Joyce Gooden, the Hutcheson, Guckenberger, and Humphreys families, Adrian, Caroline, Magda, and Tony Jones, Susan and William Frost, the Kesslers, the Youngs, the Geers, the Wyricks, the Lefers, Janet Hopkins, Alice Phillips and Sarah Phillips, Peter Milewicz, Mayor Joseph Riley, Jr., Jean-Marie Mauclet and Gwylene Gallimard and the staff of G&M, Susan Simons and John Hagerty, Elisabeth Biondi, Alice Gordon, Alexander Smalls, Trish Richman, Terry Gillis, Gigi Guerra, Kiwon and Dan Standen, Erin and Thomas Moore, Mary Caldwell, Myra Mayman, Nils Schlebusch and Lisa Preston, David Tsay, Alma Montague, Tanya Atkins, Betty Bass, Carolyn Green, Betty Hill, Martha Jackson, Judy Kaplan, Margaret MacMillan, Ann Patrick, Mary Ellen Rickenbaker, Renée Skory, Marguerite Stoddard, Betty Taylor, Mary Welch, Ben Wizner, Carey Monserrate, Catherine Eng and Mark Helmuth, Whitney Lawson, Jennifer Rubell and Daniel Kim, and especially Elizabeth Verity Day, Louise Elliott Holt, Mom, Dad, Caroline, Gran, Uncle John, Pudge Pie, and Pickle.

Those who have also generously shared their expertise, opened their homes to us, or have patiently suffered our questions (and often all of the above) on culinary and other topics include Owen Lee, Bobo and Pamela Lee, Ronni Lundy, John T Edge, John Egerton, Nathalie Dupree, Lolis Eric Elie, Carol Daly, Damon Lee Fowler, Mindy Merrell, Elizabeth Sims, Jessica Harris, Joe Dabney, Mary Beth Lasseter, Leah Chase, Nancy Newsome Mahaffey, Fritz Blank, Robert Stehling and Nunally Kersh, Kathy Starr, Lynn Winter, Sara Gibbs, Karen and Ben Barker, Mike Riley and Family, the Southern Foodways Alliance, Bill, Bertie and Michael Best, Nichole Green, Dale, Ted and Rafael Rosengarten, Ben Moise, John Williams, The Fields Family of Johns Island, Mary Jo Wannamaker, Francisco Torres, Stephen Leong, Sam Calagione, Helen and Harry Spell, Ann and Ken Hutchins, Limehouse Produce, Gertrude, Allen, and Dayna Sassard, Austin McKenna and Windsor Beaver McKenna, Toby Bryce and Biz Mitchell, Hawes Bostic and Sherri Chambers, Hunter Kennedy and Maggie Brett, Trey Beck, Susan and Thomas Sully, Mason and Anne Pope, Isaac Templeton, Mary Calhoun, John Ziegler, Nina Liu, Billy Vandiver, Steve Hanson, Dora Keogh, Ponniah Vijeyaratnam, Randall Lanthier, Miss Linda Brackman, Bryan Simmons and Ralph Vetters, Charlie and Heidi Parnell, Annie Laura Perdue, Martha Lou Gadsden and Family, Sam and Jan VanNorte, Valerie VanNorte, Robert and Zedia Ellis, Paul Blanchard, Carver Blanchard and Laura Lawton, Dorothy Blanchard, Langhorne Howard, Dodie Condon, Frank Marvin, James Miracle, Marcus Samuelsson, Bill Wharton, Fred Scott, The Yavarkovsky Family, Rosaleen Poole, Margaret Braun, Robert and Julianna Layfield, Kurt and Pam Hirabara, Mark Ritchie, Frances and Neal Smith, Jim and Bonnie Swartzenberg, Rona and Dale Scott, Mannie Berk, Hamburg Inn No. 2, Linda Gadson and The Rural Mission, Kirk Pomper, John Kay, Stephen Foster Folklife Center, Nancy Morgan, Hilward Morgan, Helen Cribbs, Woody Woodard and Family, Mary Harris, Ruby Shaw, and Thisbe Nissen.

And for actually moving things forward, for keeping the world supplied with boiled peanuts, we thank Patrick Brantley, our shipping manager, and the alumni of his position: Octavia Peck, Corinne Cayce, Cecilia Post, John Dorfman, Todd Giacometti, Glenn Dickson, Charles Dickson, Jennifer Bryan, Emily Choi, Sinai Choi, Young Choi, Shannon Atkins, Alan Bielsky, Sasha Adams, Will Milner, and the family members or friends who valiantly stepped in to make a shipping deadline. And a heartfelt thanks also to the Board of The Confederate Home and College, Matthew Butterick, David Black, Robert Bruno, John H. Warren III, Elizabeth Broadwin, and Stirling Kelso.

Nancy Novogrod and Margot Guralnick at *Travel + Leisure* assigned us our first story, and we're deeply grateful to them for encouraging us to put down the tape gun and hit the road. Others who've nurtured that impulse over the years were Dana Cowin, Pam Kaufman, Kate Krader, Pete Wells, Jane Margolies, Regina Schrambling, Michalene Busico, Adam Rapoport, Sam Sifton, Kathleen McElroy, Nick Fox, Kris Ensminger, Charles Klaveness, Howard Goldberg, Niloufar Motamed, Salma Abdelnour, Michelle Shih, Gillian Blake, Geoff Kloske, Sara James, Sarah Gray Miller, Jennifer Cole, Darcy Shankland, Marion Sullivan, Scott Jones, Donna Florio, Charles Walton IV, Kim Sunee, Marialisa Calta, Colman Andrews, Margo True, Lucinda Scala Quinn, Lynne

Rossetto Kasper, Dean Olsher, Jane Daniels Lear, Laura Heon, Betsy Bradley, Joe Zee, Jonathan Paul, Debra Puchalla, and Margaret Roach.

And in the production of these very pages we owe our utmost gratitude to our agent David McCormick, Matthew Cole, David Lawrence Mitchell, and Hunter Lewis (ace cooks all, without whom this book would have taken a decade more to complete), Lela Rose, Andre Glover, Bobby Fisher, Kate Hays, Sally Anne McCartin, Jacqui Daniels, Jean Orlebecke, Liz Duvall, Andrea Gentl & Marty Hyers, Kate Sears and Daniel Hakkanson, Michael Pedersen, Sabine Tucker and Yuko Yamamoto, Alice Patrick and Croghans Jewel Box, Capers White, and especially the folks at Norton: our dear editor Maria Guarnaschelli, Debra Morton Hoyt, Sarah Rothbard, Robin Muller, Erik Johnson, Aaron Lammer, Nancy Palmquist, Susan Sanfrey, Louise Brockett, Samantha Choy, Starling Lawrence, Bill Rusin, Jeannie Luciano, Morgen Van Vorst, Wanda Bazemore, and Karen Walker.

We cannot thank you enough.

THE LEE BROS.
SOUTHERN COOKBOOK

Hanging out in Hollywood, South Carolina.
(*Photo by Bobby Fisher*)

WELCOME. THE BOOK YOU HOLD IN YOUR HANDS BEGAN WITH TEN POUNDS OF RAW PEANUTS,

five gallons of salted water, and a thirty-three-quart enameled-tin stockpot that spanned all four burners of the stove in a tiny tenement apartment on the Lower East Side of Manhattan. It might seem odd for a southern cookbook to begin in New York City, but that's where, emerging from the long blizzard of 1994, we tested our first recipe for boiled peanuts. We'd both recently moved from Charleston, South Carolina, our hometown, and we were homesick: for sea spray and sand, and for something as soothingly simple as boiled peanuts—the raw, unroasted peanuts boiled in salted water that are sold by casual vendors along roadsides throughout the Southeast. But where to find raw peanuts in New York?

Next door to our apartment was a broker of dried fruit and roasted nuts. He didn't stock raw peanuts, but he pointed us toward the Hunts Point Terminal Market, the wholesale produce market in the Bronx where we eventually found our quarry: a fifty-pound yellow mesh bag of them, as big as a small refrigerator. Within minutes of our return, the apartment began to fill with steam that smelled like hay, sweet potatoes, and tea; about eight hours later, we were cracking the peanut shells, with brine running over our hands, and slurping the nuts down. Their earthy, beanlike flavor, in that cramped room overlooking the heroin dealers and hipsters on Ludlow Street, conjured up the creek banks and marshes south of Charleston. The feeling of having cheated geography through food was exhilarating.

And the peanuts tasted so good we thought we should share them with the big city. We knew that the flavor of boiled peanuts fresh from the pot—to say nothing of their wet, mushy texture—often alarms people who've tasted only roasted peanuts, but it didn't make sense that in New York, the city with the most adventurous palates on the planet, no restaurant or bar—not even the southern ones—were serving boiled peanuts.

At the time Ted was logging close to sixty hours a week at a prominent New York publishing house but only getting paid for thirty. Matt was demoralized, trying to parlay his college degree into a bottom-rung job at Christie's or Sotheby's.

Soon after we'd eaten our fill, we arranged with a stationer on Grand Street to print business cards ("Lee Bros. Boiled Peanuts: 'The Snack of the 90s,'" they read in 8-point copperplate type), and as soon as they were in hand, we spent a week knocking on restaurant doors with resealable sandwich bags full of the salty, wet treat.

We might as well have been selling lobster traps in Montana.

"Who are you *really*?" one chef wanted to know. "Is this a hidden-camera-type thing?"

"That's wet—I'm not touching that," a bartender told us.

But at most establishments we didn't even get beyond the host's stand, so we left off our bags of peanuts and business cards. We received not a single call.

This development was music to our parents' ears. Our mom is a former private-school English teacher and headmistress; our dad's a gastroenterologist and medical professor. They're safety-seeking academics, and in the South, being a boiled peanuts vendor is either a vocation of convenience—*Heck, you own the gas station, why not offer boiled peanuts?*—or a venture of last resort. Our parents adopted a tone of tolerant skepticism, and didn't care that President Jimmy Carter had been a boiled peanuts vendor. Carter was six years old when he sold boiled peanuts. We were twenty-one and twenty-three and we'd just graduated from Amherst and Harvard, where we'd studied English (Ted) and art history (Matt).

Still, we were undaunted and undeterred. Lugging the peanuts across Manhattan pavement, we'd learned a very important lesson: that regional foods hold fast to their geographical roots. But instead of being utterly dejected by that truth, we got to thinking about how its culinary corollary—that regional folk cling tenaciously to their hometown delicacies—meant there must be other expatriate southerners like us out there. We made it our mission to find them.

A letter we mailed the following week to a food writer at the *New York Times* garnered us a miraculous response: she phoned us, intrigued, and the next day we delivered a bag of boiled peanuts to her apartment building on the Upper West Side. She called back to give us the news: she hated them, but a friend from Virginia had explained them to her, and so she understood them for what they were. Two weeks later a short note appeared in the *Times*, to the effect that boiled peanuts were available, via mail-order, from us.

When the calls came in—over a hundred that same day—they were from Park Avenue in

Manhattan and Flatbush Avenue in Brooklyn, but also from places like Anchorage and San Antonio. People wanted boiled peanuts, and they wanted them soon, even if the FedEx charges (boiled peanuts are perishable) cost more than the peanuts themselves. But almost more than anything, they wanted to converse about southern food—about their grandmothers' recipes, about how their fathers had sold boiled peanuts, about the obstacles that stood in the way when they tried to locate raw peanuts in Lincoln, Nebraska. As long as we were sending the peanuts, they wondered, couldn't we find them a jar of fig preserves, the kind made with whole figs and with paper-thin slices of lemon mixed in? Couldn't we ship them sorghum syrup—pure, undiluted sorghum? And while we were at it, wouldn't we track down some stone-ground grits?

We had a business on our hands, and a reason for being. So we loaded up the car, returned to Charleston, and began seeking out sources. A couple weeks later, with a jury-rigged laser printer (Ted's graduation gift, which Matt had dropped on the floor) and an old Singer sewing machine, we printed and bound the first Lee Bros. Boiled Peanuts Catalogue. Since then, without ever advertising, we've built a loyal following of nearly 15,000 customers and shipped southern pantry staples around the globe to satisfy their cravings. In 1999, the same year *Saveur* named the Lee Bros. Boiled Peanuts Catalogue one of its first "100 Things We Love About Food," a longtime customer called to say she thought what we did in our business lives—road-tripping the Southeast in search of foods for the catalogue—would make a great travel story. She was an editor at *Travel + Leisure*, and she gave us our first journalistic assignment, 3,500 words about a road trip through upstate South Carolina. *Food & Wine* called shortly thereafter; the editors there wanted us to take on the wilds of northern Florida.

Traveling and writing changed our lives in a number of ways. Some days, there's nothing more satisfying than hearing the screech of the tape gun as we seal a packed box of pickles shut, or watching those boxes stack up and then disappear out the door when Hal, our current FedEx guy, comes around. But we're thankful that writing has afforded us some quality time on the road, exploring unfamiliar regions of the South, like Kentucky, Florida, and Tennessee, and meeting a few of the growers, cooks, and sages who create exceptional southern food. Over the years, they've inspired us to perfect some delicious recipes in our own kitchen, and this cookbook is our attempt to share the flavors—as well as the fun and the sense of possibility we experience on the road.

When we return from our travels and file our stories, our editors often ask us to develop

Makes 2 catalogues

TIME: 15 minutes

EQUIPMENT

A sewing machine threaded with white thread

4 sheets 8½-×-11-inch plain white or yellow paper

1 sheet 8½-×-11-inch colored construction paper

1 sheet 8½-×-11-inch brown kraft paper

1. Fold each of the 4 plain white or yellow sheets in half across their longest dimension and then in half again across the longest dimension. You will have 4 "signatures" measuring 4¼ x 5 inches. Stand them upright along the 4¼-inch seam and nest 1 signature inside the other. Do the same for the remaining 2 and reserve.

2. Crease the kraft paper in half lengthwise and then slice or cut across its width with scissors. Wrap these 2 "covers" around the nested signatures.

3. Cut two ½-inch strips of construction paper from the longest edge of the sheet. Fold the strips in half lengthwise to make the bindings.

4.   Insert the 4¼-inch seam of 1 unbound catalogue into 1 construction-paper binding. Place the leading edge under the foot of the sewing machine and stitch a straight seam through both the binding and the catalogue, trying as best you can to bisect the strip and pierce both signatures with the needle. Repeat with the second unbound catalogue and binding.

5.   With scissors, trim the top and bottom ends of the spines. Using a sharp knife, slit the bottoms of the signatures so the pages turn freely. Although the string ends are left loose, the binding will not unravel.

In the Lee Bros. Boiled Peanuts Catalogue headquarters, downtown Charleston, South Carolina. (*Photo by Bobby Fisher*)

recipes that distill the experience of the journey, and though the quest may already be over, this is always a giddy and rewarding part of the trip. What they're asking us to do, in essence, is to repeat the experience of boiling those first peanuts on Ludlow Street—to conjure up through food the sensations of a place, a time, and a people. Recipes provide a wonderful third dimension to travel writing, and our best writing often emerges from these kitchen sessions.

While the recipes in this book roam from the mountains of eastern Kentucky to Florida's beachy panhandle, the roots of our cookbook are firmly planted in Charleston, South Carolina, and the surrounding coastal plain, called the Lowcountry. The Lowcountry is where we learned to cook, the place we call home, and where, in 1980—exactly fourteen years before we tried peddling boiled peanuts in New York City—we first got turned on to regional food, when our parents left the Big Apple for Charleston. Yes, folks, we were born in New York.

There are striking parallels between Manhattan and Charleston. Both are Atlantic port cities situated on a peninsula between two rivers, at the mouth of a harbor. The architecture of both is stunning, historic, and noteworthy (in its own fashion), and the streets of both towns are laid out on a grid. But we were preteens the year our parents moved there—Ted was eight and Matt was eleven—and such similarities paled in comparison to the differences. Most sociological differences we weren't old enough to comprehend. Instead, what we found most compelling were the sensory differences.

We left a cramped, dark apartment in a prewar building that stretched an entire city block and contained literally hundreds of apartments. We landed in Charleston in a tall, pastel-yellow townhouse on a two-block stretch of similar stucco houses painted in faded pinks, yellows, greens, and blues that locals call Rainbow Row. East Bay Street ran parallel to the harborfront, so along with visual changes came new sounds, like the thrumming engines of the harbor pilot's boat docked a block away, which cut through the nighttime silence. The wind off the water whipped halyards against the masts of boats parked at the Carolina Yacht Club, an urgent rhythmic peal like tiny bells ringing. And the smells—like the sulfuric aroma of low tide, which wasn't so different from the smell of the paper mills outside the city. The thickness of the humid air made breathing almost difficult, especially when summer arrived.

But some of the most acute differences were in the grocery stores and restaurants. In New York, we had accompanied Mom and Dad on trips to the Daitch Shopwell, a supermarket at 90th Street and Broadway, to the butcher a few doors down who gave out free slices of bologna to kids, and to H&H, two blocks from our school, a place that made yeasty-sweet, pillowy bagels with a crisp outer shell. Within weeks of moving to Charleston, we dearly missed H&H, but by then we'd already discovered new and yummy foods and cool ways to acquire them ourselves. Our new friends, the brothers Simmons and Rutledge Young, taught us to throw a cast net and catch shrimp in the creeks behind Seabrook Island, a barrier island outside Charleston. We learned to tie butcher's twine around a chicken neck and drop it into the creek to lure crabs, which we then scooped up with a long-handled net. Other kids in Charleston showed us the places downtown where boughs of loquat, fig, and mulberry trees hung low enough over the street for us to reach the fruit.

Food was a big part of life in the Lowcountry. Hunters lived for the return of venison and quail season, fishermen for the shrimp, bass, and flounder of the estuaries and the deep-sea grouper and shark. To our peers, such pursuits weren't especially exotic, except insofar as they were adult sport; to us, they were irresistible.

There is something about discovering a cuisine at the brink of adolescence that causes you never to take its ingredients for granted; that spark of elation at first tasting a stolen mulberry is always accessible. The more we learned about the Lowcountry's food traditions, the more we became keenly aware of what food existed *here* and not *there*—produce like scuppernong grapes and crowder peas and cymling squash, dishes like shrimp and grits and she-crab soup, even sugary grocery-store treats like Cheerwine soda and MoonPies. And the more we journeyed outside Charleston, the *there* we compared our new home to was no longer New York but often another southern region, sometimes only a county or two away from Rainbow Row.

We were both fascinated with the new culture we encountered, but we were rapidly growing into two very different people. Ted increasingly spent his time hanging around the Prism, a punk record store on King Street, and skateboarding in the empty pool behind a dilapidated mansion on George Street (now headquarters of the Spoleto Festival USA, a performing arts festival) until the police came. Matt whiled away his early adolescence by setting off model rockets in the East Bay Playground, role-playing in games like Kingmaker, and especially sitting in front of the screen of the family's Apple II Plus, acquiring skills that at the time seemed esoteric.

For years we didn't have a kind word to say to each other. Two things forced a rapprochement. The first was a beautiful 1951 Jaguar named Belle that our uncle drove down from

Toronto on Christmas Day 1986 (thus infuriating our mother, his older sister, who shunned anything ostentatious), and the second was cooking.

We learned to work together in the kitchen because we had to. Our mother, who never managed to find a job in Charleston as inspiring as the one she'd left behind in New York, began to commute to her former workplace, the Brearley School, a private school for girls in Manhattan. She spent her weeks in New York at the tiny apartment she sublet from a friend, flying home only on weekends. Our father came home from the hospital most nights at seven or later, which left open the matter of who was going to put dinner on the table.

Meals in our family (which included our little sister, Caroline) weren't terribly ambitious, but they were an essential element of Lee family life, and we all ate together. There was always a protein, a starch, and a green vegetable. Sometimes we took shortcuts, like frozen vegetables or marinara sauce from a jar, but more often than not everything was made from scratch.

So we became Dad's prep cooks on weeknights, and we did a decent amount of the food shopping, too—a skill we value today as the unsung ingredient in successful cooking. Mom and Dad were adventuresome cooks on weekends, but nothing particularly imaginative came out of our weekday meals except that we ate well and we learned the basics: chopping vegetables, cooking rice, peeling shrimp. And we were fortunate, just when we were getting comfortable in the kitchen, to be inspired by a few characters in our lives for whom food *was* life.

The foremost of these was our uncle, John Maxwell, a restaurateur in Toronto. As soon as we'd both turned fifteen and acquired our driver's licenses, we headed up to Uncle John's for a month or a summer at a time and worked in his restaurants, washing pots and pans, bearding mussels, doing all the tasks of a bottom-rung kitchen steward.

But we did whatever it took to spend time with the guy, an inexhaustible, pint-sized maverick and elbows-deep food enthusiast. Uncle John was also a great teacher, and relished the opportunity to articulate the pleasures of a ballpark bratwurst as much as he did a glass of the Super Tuscan wine Sassicaia (and he introduced us to both). He was hip to the dawn of the fresh-seasonal-local renaissance—in the late eighties, he contracted with a farmer outside Toronto to raise organic Highland cattle for the carpaccio on his menu—but he also had a good-taste-be-damned streak, which occasionally served him well. Just when the Cajun food craze had peaked and no one wanted to see the word "blackened" on a menu ever again, he developed a recipe for blackened potato salad—a smoky, dizzyingly delicious variation on the classic—that may be the single best use of a Cajun spice blend. It remains on his restaurant menu to this day (and because it is, in its own way, inspired by the South, we've included it here).

Uncle John endeared himself to us forever by driving the old Jag to Charleston. But his gift to us in the realm of food—making us recognize that every weeknight pork chop or roast potato can be treated as an indulgence and a delight to prepare—was an insight we've been dining out on ever since.

Folks who haven't done much exploring in the South tend to see its cuisine as monolithic and singular. But what immediately became apparent as we traveled throughout the southeastern United States is just how differently people eat from place to place. And it's not simply the expected—that states along the coast are seafood-centric and the mountain South has more pork and beef. Tastes can differ from county to county. South Carolina is said to have three barbecue belts, each representing a different style of sauce, and Orangeburg County claims to have its own, fourth, distinct style (distinguished by the use of mayonnaise and pickle juice). Even from town to town, things change. In Charleston, you can live to be thirty without ever eating a shrimp burger, but in the shrimping town of McClellanville, just a half-hour up the road, you'll probably acquire the taste for shrimp burgers before you're thirty months old. Around Berea, Kentucky, so many different varieties of heirloom beans are growing in such confined geographical spaces that they're often named for the family on whose property they were found. Whether it's beans, barbecue, shrimp burgers, or corn bread, southerners maintain strong allegiances to the specific places where their food traditions originated, and they thrill to their defense in the face of any pressure to assimilate (even if they themselves have moved to Los Angeles). This may partly explain why we so often find in southern food lore and literature the language of the exclusive, the *this, not that* of folks yearning to define the most traditional recipe, the most authentic recipe, the Horry County recipe, the "best" recipe.

We firmly believe that the diversity of southern cuisine should *always* be cause for celebration, never a call to choose sides. When you tip a sacred cow like gumbo, its fall reverberates not just in New Orleans and Charleston but in Philadelphia and Senegal, and that fact should be a clarion call to cook—to study and learn about different techniques, to borrow, to experiment, and above all to create something delicious.

Southern food really can't afford to be wistful or obsessed with its past. Otherwise, it risks becoming a curiosity, a genre to dip into now and again rather than what it is—food born from a spirited resourcefulness, of the kind that informs so much daily decisionmaking in the kitchen. It reflects a desire to get the most from the ingredients you've got, to take every opportunity you have to enhance flavor and add dimension without giving a fig for what the neighbors might think—to see the roiling broth for your Sunday greens as a chance to whip up some quick dumplings.

There has never been a better time to cook southern. Great collards are grown by the truckload in New Jersey, and rare southern ingredients are shipped far and wide. The long-held perception that southern food is a pinch-of-this, pinch-of-that cuisine inspired only by poverty and hardship—that it is all about lard—is history. These days you have a former war correspondent writing a front-page story about a Mississippi barbecue symposium and a four-star French chef proffering pickled peaches. We all should know by now that lard was never the demon it was made out to be, that it's the key to flaky pie crust and great fried chicken. Southern food stands on its own merits, and that's exciting.

Our book aims to demystify southern food for folks who may not have tried it. But for the seen-it, done-it southern epicure, we offer incisive, updated southern standards that remain true to the spirit of the originals. Of course we'd be laughed out of St. Helena Island's Shrimp Shack for the lemon zest and ginger we put in our own shrimp burger, but we also know that those ingredients make all the difference when you want to knock your guests' socks off. (We blind-tested ten different recipes on a gathering of twenty to discover that one.) And you'll find recipes here that you've never seen before, like Boiled Peanut and Sorghum Swirl Ice Cream, which came about as happy accidents or flights of fancy. No matter what your background, we hope you'll catch the spirit and decide to become a southerner by choice. The kitchen is a great place to begin.

We began developing and testing recipes in earnest when we started writing, six years ago, and the effect that has had on our cooking is to liberate us from our habits, to show us new ways of approaching our "best" recipes. Think you know all there is to know about gumbo? Try testing six different gumbos for a Monday deadline, and you can bet by Sunday you'll see your favorite recipe in a new light. You might discover an opportunity to add flavor to roux that you haven't considered before; you might find that adding a few blue crab claws gives so much shellfish flavor that you can skip the shrimp stock. And as long as you're skipping the shrimp stock, do you want to spend the shrimp money on more oysters?

Recipes are suggestive architecture, and understanding the basic structure of a well-designed recipe frees you to make informed choices based on what you like, how much time you've got, what's in your pantry, what's within your budget, and who's coming to dinner. That unbound spirit is among the many insights we hope to provide in this cookbook, so you'll often find a variation or two following a recipe. Occasionally, a variation will take the dish in a totally different direction, turning a pork tenderloin from a hot-'n'-spicy barbecue into a honey-and-sour-orange version. Other times, the variation may be a simple change that makes a dish a tad more ambitious, for those times when you're cooking for friends who would be thrilled that you'd thickened a classic crab soup with a puree of Jerusalem artichoke. We call a change like that the Downtown Touch—and we're using "downtown" in the Charleston sense of the word, that is, "fancy" (or at least trying to be). Changes in the other direction we call Rustic Touches, and they are steps we take for friends who would be happy to find a gizzard at the bottom of a bowl of gumbo or a whole crab to crack open in their Frogmore stew.

One of the most astute things we ever heard said about food, southern or otherwise, was offered at the Southern Foodways Symposium in Oxford, Mississippi. The late Bill Williams, a cofounder of Glory Foods (the southern-style canned goods company he helped build into a multimillion-dollar business), said that when he launched the company with seasoned collard greens in a can, a friend told him he'd never succeed. No one would buy canned greens, the friend said, because they'd be comparing them to the greens they cook on Sundays, when they have the time to slow-simmer them with a smoked hog jowl. "I'm not selling Sunday greens," Williams replied. "I'm selling Tuesday greens."

It's a point that gets lost by so many cookbook authors, rattling their test-kitchen pots to get the "best" recipe. Sometimes you simply don't have time to brine your chicken for a day. Sometimes the craving for tasty fried chicken hits on a weekday, and you want to put some on your table anyway. Though we use few cans when we cook, you will find two recipes here for fried chicken, one for Sunday Fried Chicken and one for Tuesday Fried Chicken. They are both terrific, and both will give you juicy chicken with a crisp, delicate crust. Once you've read our recipe for Sunday Collards, you'll know not just how to prepare a pot of delicious, slowly simmered, meaty collards but also how to make Sneaky Collards—braised greens that cook up with just as much smoky richness but that use no meat whatsoever. And you'll know how to prepare Tuesday Collards—smoky, spicy greens that take just a half-hour to wash and cook.

Along with our own takes on classic southern dishes like shrimp and grits, chicken and dumplings, and red velvet cake, we've included plenty of rare, underappreciated dishes you're likely to find only in southern homes: pickled oysters, shad roe with madeira and onion gravy, creamed mushrooms over cornmeal waffles. Home cooks take particular pride in making these dishes for company. They're comfort food in many ways, and yet they seem fresh and original against the backdrop of familiar southern standards.

Throughout this book you'll notice we refer to pantry items and pickles whenever we can. Such foods are always perceived to be an afterthought to the main dish, but we've come to realize over the years that a relish, preserves, or even something as simple as a cruet of pepper vinegar can determine what we're going to prepare. That half cup of Jerusalem artichoke relish left in the jar gets us thinking: mixing it with some mayo would make a terrific tartar sauce for shrimp burgers. That quarter cup of scuppernong preserves? A great glaze for a slow-roasted duck. And if it's not enough for glaze, why not a topping for buttermilk ice cream? Condiments and relishes play a much more important role in the kitchen than people think, so make them as good as they can be—give them the attention they deserve, the extra care or flourish that makes you excited to use them. Out with that forlorn jar of marmalade and the ketchup going brown at the back of the fridge! Get some real live relishes and condiments in your cooking, ones that stay on the top shelf of the fridge, at the front.

Another thing: drinks. Go to old southern cookbooks and you'll find recipes for various fruit wines, for alluring punches made with such ingredients as green tea and Madeira, rice wine, and the kernels inside peach pits. Given the phenomenal range and diversity of beverage history in the South, it's unconscionable that, with a few choice exceptions, contemporary southern drinking culture, with its chocolate martinis, light beers, and sour apple cosmopolitans, seems to be trying its damnedest to ape the global lounge culture. Our drinks chapter is an attempt to change that, and we think you'll find it compelling.

There are plenty of excuses not to cook southern food: because you don't have that glistening seasoned skillet that your college roommate from Georgia's grandmother had, or because your grits have been sitting in the freezer too long. There are always reasons not to go into the kitchen, so do whatever gets you there as often as possible. One way to accomplish that is to have some *quick knockout* (QKO) southern dishes in your repertoire that are morale boosters, that psych you up and make you want to cook for friends and relatives—things like creamed corn and hot slaw, which use just a few ingredients and take less than half an hour to prepare. Another way to make the most of your kitchen time is to get creative with left-overs, so at the end of a number of the recipes in this book you'll find our *killer leftover* (KLO) ideas. We feel leftovers go underexplored in most cookbooks—they're perceived to be defla-tionary, an embarrassment to serve, when in reality they may taste better than they did the night before!

Last, the deepest reverence that you can give southern food is to cook it with such fre-quency that it becomes your own. Sure, we spent a lot of time on our recipe for fry dredge, get-ting the right balance of cornmeal and flour, so the corn flavor doesn't overpower the delicate sweetness of your fish or your green tomatoes, but it would thrill us to know that a cook with a taste for heat spiced it up with a teaspoon of ancho chile powder or Ethiopian berbere spice. We hope you'll use this cookbook like a comfortable second home, with familiar rooms, where you feel free to rearrange the lamps and change the drapes to suit your taste, and where you are always welcome. Come on in.

DRINKS

BY THE LOOKS OF IT, YOU'D NEVER GUESS CHARLESTON'S A HEAVY DRINKING TOWN;

the liquor stores blend effortlessly into the residential scenery. Flashing neon LIQUORS signs—any illuminated signs, for that matter—are discouraged in the historic district, so the stores are discreetly marked with a red spot, about the size of a large pizza, painted directly on a wall near the entrance. When you're stepping out for a bottle of bourbon, you say you're going to the "red dot."

But there are clues elsewhere. The seminal Lowcountry cookbook, *Charleston Receipts*, begins with a chapter on drinks. Of course drinks precede most meals, but we think in this case the chapter's placement is a bolder statement about the Holy City's priorities. The cocktail party rules here, even more than the elaborate dinners that made Charleston's reputation. And why not? There's nothing like a few hours of drinking to take the edge off the humidity and the formality of downtown life.

But Charleston's drinking culture has changed significantly in the past fifty years. Many of the recipes in *Charleston Receipts* are nineteenth-century punches and "cups"— often the house drinks of various clubs—that make elaborate use of the imports of the eighteenth and nineteenth centuries: brandy, green tea, champagne, rum, sauternes, sherry, and Madeira, the fortified wine from the Portuguese island of the same name. Madeira was so much the rage in Charleston in the 1800s that one brand was named Two-Bottle Rutledge, after a thirsty gent from a Charleston family better known as the kin of Edward Rutledge, whose signature appears on the Declaration of Independence.

Some of the punches in *Charleston Receipts* are quite simple to prepare, like William A. Hutchinson's Legare Street Punch, made of Sauternes, champagne, cognac, and soda. Others, like Mrs. A. H. Mazyck's circa 1830 recipe for Ratifia, which calls for a thousand peach pits steeped for a month in a two-gallon brew of brandy, Madeira, rosewater, orange-flower water, and sugar, are quite laborious. But neither of these concoctions would be present at a Charleston party nowadays, where tastes run more to generic (if refreshing) vodka tonics, rum and Cokes, and gin and tonics. And the city's restaurants certainly don't seem to be doing a whole lot to make things more interesting. "What's your house drink?" we recently asked the bartender of a spanking new place with entrées in the thirty-dollar range. His reply: "What does my house drink? I'm not quite sure what you're asking."

This chapter is our own house-drinks list. The beverages here take their inspiration not just from Lowcountry traditions but from travels throughout Tennessee, Florida, Kentucky, North Carolina. Cocktails should deliver flavor but also fun, and a little bit of a mad-scientist element. Taken as a collection, they show, we hope, that drinks paying homage to southern drinking traditions can feel contemporary and fresh.

❈ ST. CECILIA PUNCH ❈

THE EARLIEST PROMOTERS OF LIVE MUSIC IN THE HOLY CITY WEREN'T THE FOLKS AT MYSKYN'S TAVERN OR THE MUSIC Farm (late-twentieth-century institutions) but the thirty-seven Charleston aristocrats who founded the St. Cecilia Society in 1767. For decades St. Cecilia concerts were the town's most celebrated gigs, but in 1822, the society's musical mission went social. Grand balls took the place of concerts, and because membership was strictly hereditary, the dances enhanced the society's aura of mystery. To this day, the St. Cecilia Ball, held at Hibernian Hall each January, is the most exclusive event on Charleston's social calendar.

But even nonmembers like us can enjoy St. Cecilia's most lasting gift to society: a fruity, fizzy, brandy- and rum-powered punch. In 1934, Helen Woodward published in *Two Hundred Years of Charleston Cooking* a recipe for St. Cecilia punch that had been given to her by a member of the society's board of managers. An elegant concoction of lemon brandy, peach brandy, green tea, champagne, rum, and soda, the recipe appeared again (in nearly identical form) in 1950 in the Charleston Junior League cookbook, *Charleston Receipts*, where it remains the very first recipe in the book.

Woodward writes in her notes: "Is it possible that St. Cecilia punch contributes to the glamour of [the balls]?" Whatever its effect on the dance (which is now reputed to be alcohol-free), we do know that the punch adds luster to our most casual parties. With respectful irreverence—imagine a tuxedoed young Rutledge with a full dance card and a pierced nose—we offer our variation on the original, adapted for smaller gatherings, in tribute to the patron saint of music. It's deliciously complex, fruity, and even spicy.

Makes 3½ quarts, enough for 10 people to have two drinks

TIME: 2 hours to steep, 30 minutes to prepare

2 teaspoons grated peeled fresh ginger (about one 2-inch-long piece)

2 lemons, ends trimmed, thinly sliced

3 ripe peaches, skins on, sliced ¼-inch thick

3 cups brandy

¾ cup dark rum, such as Mount Gay or Barbancourt

1 small ripe pineapple (about 3–3½ pounds)

3 cups cold, strongly-brewed Lee Bros. Sweet Tea (page 23)

1 bottle cold champagne or other sparkling wine

1 quart cold seltzer water or club soda

1 round block of ice, made by freezing water in a 4½-cup ring mold or a 6-cup bowl

1. Wrap the ginger in a piece of cheesecloth or a strong paper towel folded like an envelope and seal with string or a large paper clip. Place the ginger, lemons, and peaches in the bottom of a 2-quart bowl. Pour the brandy and rum into the bowl, cover with plastic wrap, and steep in the refrigerator for at least 2 hours, twice that if possible.

2. When ready to serve, discard the ginger and the peaches and transfer the lemons and the brandy and rum mixture to a 6-quart punch bowl.

3. With a sharp knife, trim the ends of the pineapple, carefully slice off the rind, and cut it in half lengthwise. Cut the core out of each side, slice each half crosswise into ¼-inch-thick demilunes (half moons), and add them to the bowl. Pour the sweet iced tea, champagne, and seltzer into the bowl and float the ice ring in the punch.

4. Ladle the punch into punch glasses or teacups and serve.

CHARLESTON IS FUNDAMENTALLY A WALKING TOWN. The house we grew up in stood midway between the Carolina Yacht Club, watering hole of preference for most old-line Charleston families (also the host of informal regattas called "the beer races" on Friday afternoons), and the "red dot" at the corner of Exchange Street—an axis of the tipsy, you might say. We had one neighbor whose progress on a Saturday night could be marked by her enthusiastic rendition of "Onward, Christian Soldiers," a hymn she belted out as she marched herself home. Our parents thought she was trying to give the neighbors the impression that she'd been rehearsing for church on Sunday morning. Not even our sister, age five at the time, was fooled, but we all appreciated the lady's brassy alto.

✻ ICED TEA ✻

GROWING UP, WE DRANK PITCHER UPON PITCHER OF ORANGE PEKOE TEA LACED WITH PLENTY OF SUGAR AND CHILLED. Coke wasn't permitted in our house, but we don't recall missing it terribly. Today we drink the same iced tea. We still like it sweet, but instead of adding sugar to the pitcher, we sweeten it by the glass, with simple syrup, so our guests don't have to abide by our own sweet teeth.

When our sister, Caroline, was in first grade, she sold this iced tea outside the front door of our house, on East Bay Street, where she exhibited a precocious understanding of human nature. When she made change for dollar bills, she'd fumble around in her change box, pick up a nickel, and ask the customer, "Is this a quarter?" "Keep the change, dear" was most often the answer to that question. Not surprisingly, Caroline has grown up to be a sociology professor!

Makes 1½ quarts; or about 6 drinks

TIME: 15 minutes to prepare, 1 hour to cool

6 cups (1½ quarts) cold water
6 bags Orange Pekoe tea or 6 teaspoons loose tea, such as Lipton
½ cup sugar (optional)

1. Pour the water into a kettle and bring to a boil over high heat. Let rest for 2 minutes.

2. Strip the paper tags from the tea bags, gather the strings together, and knot them around the handle of a ladle or long-handled spoon. Place the ladle and bags in a heatproof 2-quart pitcher. (If using loose tea, simply put the tea in the pitcher.) Pour the hot water into the pitcher and let steep 10 minutes.

3. Remove the tea bags (or strain the tea). To sweeten the entire pitcher, add the sugar and stir to dissolve. Let cool about ½ hour, then transfer to refrigerator to cool completely another ½ hour. Serve in tall glasses filled ⅔ to the rim with ice.

❧ LEE BROS. SWEET TEA ❧

Makes 1 serving

1 tablespoon Simple Syrup (page 24) or Mint
      Simple Syrup (page 25)
1 cup (8 ounces) Iced Tea (page 21)

1 wedge lemon
1 sprig mint

1.   Pour the simple syrup into a tall, 14-ounce glass filled two thirds to the rim with ice. Pour the tea into the glass and stir vigorously with a spoon.

2.   Squeeze the lemon wedge into the tea glass and drop the wedge into the drink. Garnish with the mint.

❋ SIMPLE SYRUP ❋

THIS IS AN EASY WAY TO SWEETEN ICED TEA, LEMONADE, AND MYRIAD COCKTAILS WITHOUT CHANGING THEIR TEXTURE. WE keep Mason jars of simple syrup in our fridge because they're so useful at cocktail hour.

Makes 1 cup (8 ounces) simple syrup

TIME: 3 minutes

1 cup sugar
½ cup (4 ounces) water

In a small saucepan, combine the sugar and water and cook over low heat, stirring with a wooden spoon, until the sugar is completely dissolved, about 2 minutes. Pour into a glass jar or a vessel with a tight-fitting lid, cool to room temperature, and store in the refrigerator. The syrup keeps for 1 month.

☀ MINT SIMPLE SYRUP ☀

"MUDDLING" MINT WITH SUGAR IS THE WAY TO MAKE A TRADITIONAL MINT JULEP (PAGE 26), BUT IT TAKES TIME, AND then some folks don't love having bits of mint in their teeth quite like we do. This syrup gets sweet mint flavor into a drink quickly, with a minimum of leaf litter. A must for Derby Day, or any day you plan to serve mint juleps to a crowd. It's terrific for sweetening iced tea and lemonade, too.

Makes 1 cup (8 ounces) mint simple syrup

TIME: 2 minutes to prepare, ½ hour to steep

1 cup sugar
½ cup (4 ounces) water

½ cup tightly packed fresh mint leaves (from about 12 to 14 stems, or a bunch weighing 1½ ounces)

1. In a small saucepan, combine the sugar, water, and mint leaves and heat over a low flame, alternately stirring with a wooden spoon and pressing the mint leaves against the sugar on the bottom of the pan with the spoon (the leaves will darken and wilt). When the sugar has completely dissolved, about 2 minutes, turn off the flame, cover the pan, and let steep for ½ hour.

2. Strain into a glass jar or a vessel with a tight-fitting lid and store in the refrigerator. The syrup will keep 2 weeks.

⚜ MINT JULEP ⚜

FOR THE PAST FIVE YEARS WE'VE SPENT KENTUCKY DERBY DAY IN A LOFT IN WILLIAMSBURG, BROOKLYN, WHERE OUR pals Austin, Hawes, and Toby—southern guys, from Virginia and North Carolina—host a derby party for about a hundred people. It's not quite Louisville, but it could be, for all the seersucker suits, the wagering, and the mint juleps flowing.

We make mint juleps for most of our early-summer cocktail parties and dinners, and we make them simply, "muddling" fresh mint with a spoonful of sugar and bourbon. But the Williamsburg guys taught us a great trick for serving a crowd: they infuse a whole pitcher of simple syrup with mint the day before, so they can pour out a dozen mint juleps in a flash. When all eyes are on the race, nobody wants to be muddling mint to order. Here we offer two recipes, one for a single cocktail, for more intimate occasions, and one pitcher-sized recipe for a rowdy, cheering crowd.

Makes 1 drink

2 stems fresh mint

2 teaspoons sugar

½ cup crushed or cracked ice

¼ cup (2 ounces) bourbon

Strip the leaves from one of the mint stems; you should have 8 to 12 leaves. Using a pestle, muddle (crush) the mint with the sugar in the bottom of an 8-ounce julep cup or rocks glass. Add the crushed ice and bourbon and stir vigorously with a spoon. Garnish with the top sprig of the remaining mint stem.

❅ A PITCHER OF MINT JULEPS ❅

Makes about 1 quart, or about 18 drinks

½ cup (4 ounces) Mint Simple Syrup
    (page 25)
4 cups (32 ounces) bourbon

2 stems plus 18 sprigs fresh mint
9 cups crushed or cracked ice
cold water or cold seltzer (optional)

1. In a two-quart pitcher, combine the Mint Simple Syrup and bourbon and stir with a long-handled spoon until thoroughly mixed. Add the stems of mint.

2. For each julep, put ½ cup ice in an 8-ounce julep cup or rocks glass and pour 2 ounces of the drink over it. Garnish with a sprig of fresh mint, and, if desired, add a splash of cold water or seltzer.

PORTRAIT: GORDON HUSKEY

OVER THE YEARS WE'VE BEEN WRITING, WE'VE LOST more than a few of the people who've inspired us, and while every one of these losses is tragic, these friends are often very much alive for us, thanks to the foods and flavors they left behind. Take Gordon Huskey, who showed us the ropes of country winemaking for a story we wrote for *Gourmet* and who inspired our recipe for corncob wine that appears in this chapter.

Since 1999, when we met him, one of our favorite things to do after a successful dinner party has been to bring out one of Gordon's wines. We often have on hand a corncob wine or a vintage muscadine wine, bottled in a glass milk jug or a Bacardi bottle and labeled in ballpoint pen "Muscadine, 1976" or "Corncob, 2001." Invariably, our guests are amazed at how smooth, easy drinking, and downright delicious these wines are. Knowing that a wine brewed in a dark closet in a general store in the shadow of the Great Smoky Mountains during the early days of the Carter administration is being enjoyed by a bunch of young adults in the Bush II era has given us much delight, and it would have tickled Gordon's fancy, too.

Gordon died in early 2003, aged ninety, of complications resulting from a tractor accident. We've finally drunk the last of the wines he gave us, but we toast his longevity and tenacity with every sip of our own brew. Make it and serve it to company, and you might crack a smile like plucky Gordon, who always seemed amazed by what he could do.

✺ CORNCOB WINE ✺

"I EAT THE TAR OUT OF THIS STUFF," THE LATE GORDON HUSKEY TOLD US, REFERRING TO THE FRESH CORN HE'D HAULED IN from the acre and a half behind his home, a former gas station he operated until 1987 in Pigeon Forge, Tennessee. Until his ninetieth year, Huskey attacked this end-of-summer harvest ritual with gusto, hand-cutting the kernels from each cob and packing them in resealable plastic bags to freeze for the year to come.

But the next few steps in the process were what really got Huskey's heart racing (we'll say nothing of his collection of *Maxim* magazines, stacked by his recliner). Since it's difficult to shear all the kernels clean off the rounded cob, a fraction of sweet kernel gets left behind. Rather than send this residue to the compost pile, Huskey put it to a higher use, making wine by packing the half-naked cobs into a water-filled pail. Airborne wild yeasts did the work of extracting the remaining sugar from the cobs and converting it into alcohol. Corncob wine has a nice balance of sweet and tart and a nutty, unmistakably corny flavor.

For centuries southern home winemakers have added granulated sugar to their wild grape, plum, berry, or peach wine preparations, to boost the alcohol level and make the wines more drinkable (few old-timers were exposed to the vinifera wines favored today, and most never developed a taste for the drier style of contemporary winemaking). Huskey's corncob cuvée is no exception, though in some years the unpredictable yeasts did a more efficient job and the wine ended up drier and more elegant than usual. Either way, corncob wine offers a smooth sip and a pleasant buzz either before or after dinner; it is as welcome in our house as Dom Perignon when we're out of the professionally made stuff.

This wine makes a great gift and is also a useful all-purpose tonic in the kitchen, good for deglazing a pan or beginning a risotto with a mysterious and yet familiar corn flavor. We often pour a pearly-white shot of corncob wine into short glasses after a satisfying southern dinner—because its sweetness and slight effervescence suit the occasion, but also because it's such a fun conversation piece. We've stumped 100 percent of the guests we've introduced to it.

Makes 1 gallon; enough for 15 to 20 drinks
TIME: 30 minutes to prepare, 2 weeks to ferment, 1 week to settle

EQUIPMENT

One 1-gallon-size plastic milk jug with cap

8 corncobs, kernels cut off and reserved for another use
2 cups plus 1 teaspoon sugar
1 teaspoon active dry yeast or brewer's yeast

1. Orient the handle of the milk jug at 12 o'clock. Using a short sharp knife or scissors, cut five sixths of the way around the neck of the jug an inch below the cap, from 1 o'clock to 11 o'clock, leaving the strip of plastic nearest the handle uncut. You now have a hinged lid to the jug that snaps back into place (leave the cap on the original spout). The new opening should be just large enough to admit a corncob. Wash the jug thoroughly and pack it with the corncobs.

2. In a small bowl, dissolve 1 teaspoon sugar in 2 tablespoons warm water and then dissolve the yeast in the water, stirring once or twice, until the water is cloudy. Allow to sit for 3 or 4 minutes in a warm place, until the yeast begins to generate minute bubbles.

3. In a 4-quart stockpot, heat 3 quarts water over high heat until it boils. Turn off the heat, add 2 cups sugar, and stir until dissolved. Allow the water to cool until cool enough to touch, then fill the jug with sugar water until the level is ½ inch below the new mouth of the jug.

4. Add the yeast to the jug and set it in a cool, dark place for about 2 weeks, until it appears to have stopped bubbling. The wine will be a cloudy white with a tinge of yellow. It should smell pleasantly yeasty and like corn.

5. Decant the wine and then filter it through a mesh sieve to remove errant corn hulls. Bottle it any way you like, in a sterilized glass or plastic bottle—or in a Mason jar, for best visual effect. Set the containers in the refrigerator for a week to allow the yeast to settle before serving. Keep refrigerated and consume within 2 months.

One of many well-maintained vintage neon signs to be seen in Louisville, Kentucky, a town with superb southern food (and drink!).

☀ PLANTERS' PUNCH ☀

THE SMOKY, BITTERSWEET CARAMEL NOTES OF A REAL
RUM—A DARK CARIBBEAN RUM, LIKE MOUNT GAY OR BARBAN-
court—put to shame all those denatured clear versions invented by large distillers in the mid-
twentieth century to serve as innocuous mixers for soda-based drinks. Dark rums, while not much
more expensive, have a thousand times more personality than clear rums, because when they are
distilled, a small proportion of the caramelized sugarcane compounds and flavors is allowed to
sneak through. Additionally, real rums are aged in oak casks to enhance and mellow their personality. They are delicious and refreshing on their own, on the rocks with a twist of lime. But their
rich flavor and hint of sweetness pair beautifully with a variety of tropical fruits. In fact, they're
robust enough to work well with the most chaotic blend of tart and sweet juices—in a punch.

Of course, a conventional planters' punch (a cruise-ship and southern country-club staple) is
built around pineapple juice from a can—tinny, acidic, cooked-tasting stuff that doesn't do justice
to this amazing fruit. A ripe pineapple breaks down to a luscious puree after just a minute in the
blender or food processor, and it gives our version a terrific flavor and a pulpy, velvety texture that
seems to suit a drink with two feet in the sand. Serve Planters' Punch in a super-tall glass with a
tacky garnish of a maraschino cherry and orange and pineapple slices (if you care enough to drink
classy rum, you can let all the other stuff hang out). This Planters' Punch is perfect at a barbecue
or fish fry or with any spicy, peppery food that needs a cooling companion.

6 tablespoons (3 ounces) dark Caribbean rum

2 tablespoons (1 ounce) freshly squeezed lime juice

2 tablespoons (1 ounce) freshly squeezed orange juice

¼ cup (2 ounces) pureed pineapple (see note below)

1 tablespoon orange liqueur, such as Triple Sec, Grand Marnier, or curaçao

1 tablespoon light or dark brown sugar

2 quick dashes Angostura bitters

1 tablespoon egg white (from 1 small egg) for body and froth

1 maraschino cherry, for garnish

1 slice orange or pineapple, for garnish

Mix all the ingredients in a large cocktail shaker with a couple of ice cubes and shake vigorously. Strain into a tall glass filled two-thirds full with ice cubes. Garnish with a cherry and an orange or pineapple slice.

Note: To make pineapple puree, trim the ends from a very fresh pineapple, carefully slice off the rind with a sharp knife, and cut it in half. Cut the core out of each half, cut each half into chunks, and place the chunks in a food processor. Pulse until pureed, about 1 minute. One 3-pound pineapple makes approximately 3 cups puree, enough for 12 glasses of punch.

❋ GRAN'S MIMOSA ❋

THIS LIGHT CHAMPAGNE COCKTAIL IS THE FAVORITE
SATURDAY EYE-OPENER OF OUR GRANDMOTHER, ELIZABETH MAXWELL.
In 1982, two years after our parents moved to Charleston, she decided she wanted to watch her
grandchildren grow up, so Gran (as we call her)—an eleventh-generation New Yorker and a lifelong atheist—quit her job as a receptionist and moved to the Holy City, renting a small house a
few blocks away from ours.

Gran had never owned a car, so she walked the city streets in her spike heels and short skirts,
and before long had a larger coterie of friends and a busier social schedule than she'd ever had in
Manhattan. For nearly twenty-five years she lived in Charleston, threw epic parties, and was a constant inspiration to us. But her taste for adventure is as keen as her taste in great food and beverages; in 2005, at the age of ninety-three, she applied for Canadian citizenship and moved to
Toronto to spend more time with her son.

Orange juice (especially freshly squeezed) and champagne combine well in almost any proportion, but we concocted a recipe that takes this sprightly brunch cooler to a new level of sophis-
tication. Our ideal mimosa hovers between sweet and bitter, just like an expensive piece of
candied orange peel. We like drinking tart, fizzy mimosas for brunch with decadently rich
Creamed Mushrooms on Cornmeal Waffles (page 229).

½ teaspoon Grand Marnier, Triple Sec, or other orange liqueur

4 tablespoons (2 ounces) fresh orange juice from ½ navel orange

6 tablespoons (3 ounces) champagne or other dry bubbly wine

Sugar, for garnish (optional)

Pour the Grand Marnier into the bottom of a champagne flute. Add the orange juice and then the champagne. If you prefer your mimosa a shade sweeter, dip the rim of the glass in orange juice and then a saucer of sugar to coat before making the drink.

Our grandmother, Elizabeth Maxwell, standing outside the gate to her landlady's house, dressed for a night on the town.

☀ LEMONADE ☀

THE PERFECT SUMMER COOLER, THIS NOT-TOO-SWEET
AND NOT-TOO-ACIDIC LEMONADE IS ALSO TED'S NIGHTCAP OF
choice in any season.

Makes about 1⅝ quarts; enough for 6 drinks

TIME: 5 minutes

½ cup (4 ounces) lemon juice (juice of 4–5 lemons)

½ cup plus 2 tablespoons (5 ounces) Simple Syrup (page 24) or Mint Simple Syrup (page 25)

6 cups (48 ounces) cold seltzer water, club soda, or still water

Six 1-inch-long pieces lemon peel

1. In a 2-quart pitcher, mix the lemon juice, simple syrup, and seltzer and stir thoroughly with a spoon.

2. For each glass of lemonade, fill a tall, 14-ounce glass ⅔ to the rim with ice cubes. Pour the lemonade into the glass, then twist 1 lemon peel over the drink to release the oil and toss the peel into the glass.

CHEERWINE COCKTAILS

Cheerwine is a burgundy-colored cherry soda bottled in North Carolina and sold only in the Southeast. Although it contains not a drop of wine or alcohol, when we were preteens it somehow felt more grown-up than other flavored sodas. Mark Ritchie, the fourth generation of the Ritchie-Peeler family to bottle Cheerwine since its founding in 1917, explained to us the naming logic of his ancestors. The names of other soft drinks of the time, like gingerale and root beer, combined a flavor description with the name of an alcoholic beverage. It made sense, then, to call an effervescent cherry-flavored red beverage Cheerwine. Simple, right?

Ritchie once boasted to us that Cheerwine outsells Pepsi in Rowan County, North Carolina, ten to one. We were skeptical until we spent a couple hours eavesdropping on customers at Hap's Grill, a terrific burger-and-dog joint in downtown Salisbury that serves both Pepsi and Cheerwine in bottles, and found that Ritchie had underestimated the count. Our research, however informal, reported eleven-to-one.

❋ CHEERWINE COCKTAIL NO. 1 ❋

CHEERWINE GOES GREAT WITH GIN AND LIME, LIKE A CHERRY-LIME RICKEY. IT'S ONLY MODERATELY EFFERVESCENT AND is rather sweet for a cocktail, so a blast of seltzer helps round out the drink. If you can't get Cheerwine in your area, you can substitute for flavor's sake any black cherry soda.

Makes one 8-ounce cocktail

2 tablespoons (1 ounce) gin
Juice from ½ small lime
¾ cup (6 ounces, ½ can or bottle) Cheerwine
    or other black cherry soda

3 tablespoons (1½ ounces, 1 jigger) seltzer
    water or club soda

Fill a tall, 14-ounce cocktail glass ⅔ to the rim with ice cubes. Pour the gin into the glass and squeeze the lime juice into it. Toss the lime into the drink, followed by the Cheerwine. Top up the glass with the seltzer and stir.

❋ CHEERWINE COCKTAIL NO. 2 ❋ (AMERICANO EDITION)

THIS COCKTAIL, A TRIBUTE TO SPOLETO, CHARLESTON'S ITALIAN SISTER CITY, BRINGS IN THE BITTERNESS OF THE CLASSIC Italian aperitifs Campari and vermouth to counter the sweetness of the soda.

Makes one 8-ounce cocktail

¼ cup (2 ounces) Campari
¼ cup (2 ounces) sweet vermouth
¾ cup (6 ounces, ½ can) Cheerwine or other
    black cherry soda

1 slice orange or orange peel, for garnish

Fill a tall, 14-ounce cocktail glass ⅔ of the way to the rim with ice. Pour the Campari and vermouth into the glass and top up the glass with the Cheerwine. Garnish with the orange slice or peel.

DUPLIN WINERY, IN ROSE HILL, NORTH CAROLINA, MAKES scuppernong and muscadine wines with the kind of care that goes into the best California wines. They taste smooth and as richly flavored as the fresh grapes themselves, without any of the off flavors we've come to associate with country wines that are less scrupulously made. Duplin's scuppernong wine is sweeter than the wines it makes from early-harvest Carlos and late-harvest Magnolia muscadine varieties, but any of these wines are terrifically suited to making Johns Island Iced Tea. Duplin Winery, 505 N. Sycamore Street, Rose Hill, NC 28458; 800-774-9634; www.duplinwinery.com.

MADEIRA

THE PORTUGUESE ISLAND OF MADEIRA, 500 MILES into the Atlantic from Morocco, would seem to have little in common with Charleston, South Carolina, except for azaleas and crepe myrtles. In fact, the luscious fortified wine the Madeirans have been making for the past 400 years was the most popular wine in Charleston in the eighteenth and nineteenth centuries. Lowcountry wine cellars were filled with Madeiras, which, along with sherries, were the only wines that could survive the long, hot ocean passage from Europe, thanks to their fortification with brandy and a bit of beneficial oxidation. (The other popular beverage in Charleston at that time was West Indian rum.) Social clubs provided men with the most socially acceptable way to indulge their obsession with the stuff, and the Madeira party—essentially an all-male wine-tasting—became a regular phenomenon.

So what was the big deal? Thanks to its fortuitous chemistry, Madeira will keep without spoiling for decades, even hundreds of years, and during this time it matures and concentrates in beautiful ways as water slowly evaporates through its cask. The result is some of the most unique and evocative flavors you can sip through a straw: elegantly toffeelike and sweet, but also nutty, spicy, and volatile. Madeira is a wine for deep contemplation after dinner, but it can be lovely as an aperitif, since it has such a bold acidity—a tart, tangy kiss that can make even a hundred-year-old wine taste fresh and lively.

We've sampled Madeiras from the 1940s that tasted like oranges, golden raisins, cherries, licorice, mint, and maple sugar. We've sampled ones from the 1850s that tasted like curry, sun-baked apricots, and toasted oats. Madeiras from the 1700s can still be had, for a price, from the Rare Wine Company (www.rarewineco.com), whose owner, Mannie Berk, may be America's foremost expert on Madeiras.

Fortunately, Madeira is experiencing a bit of a renaissance, and more and more sommeliers and wine stores are waking up to its appeal. Avoid the generic Madeiras sold at grocery and package stores, made from poor grapes that are cooked and sold immediately. Look for five- and ten-year-old blends, which use a small amount of terrific vintage Madeiras and represent great value for the money.

It would be a stretch to say that Madeiras play a significant role in southern cuisine today. The Civil War, Prohibition, and the world wars devastated the Madeira market, and the wineries are still trying to recover. But a few restaurants in Charleston, like Anson and Charleston Grill, make an effort to keep a few distinctive bottles on hand, and if you find yourself with such an opportunity, try a glass. Madeira is a spectacular match for rich fish dishes like 83 East Bay Street Shrimp and Grits (page 370) or Bobo-Style Oyster Pie (page 379).

✻ JOHNS ISLAND ICED TEA ✻

SPEND A RUSH HOUR IDLING IN LONG ISLAND EXPRESS-
WAY TRAFFIC AND YOU'LL KNOW WHY LONG ISLAND ICED TEA—THE
fabled concoction of vodka, tequila, gin, Triple Sec, cola, and whiskey sour mix—is so potent.
You'd want to be obliterated, too, if you had to experience that stress and smog every day.

River Road on Johns Island, a barrier island south of Charleston, is a narrow two-lane road
lined with oaks dripping with Spanish moss. Their gnarled limbs arc out over the road, creating a
tunnel through the semitropical forest. The only traffic you encounter is an occasional backup
behind a tractor or a sluggish tomato truck. Accordingly, our take on the island's iced tea is a
smoother, more laid-back concoction, inspired by the scuppernong grapes our friends the Hutch-
esons grow at their farm on the island, near Legareville ("la-GREE-ville").

Scuppernongs are the preferred southern grape variety (see page 132, Scuppernong Preserves). Every year Tom Hutcheson makes a big five-gallon glass carboy of wine from them, and
almost every year he apologizes for how bad it is. We will grant that some vintages are better than
others, but in an off year, adding a fifth of brandy to the carboy smooths out any rough edges.

Although Johns Island Iced Tea is not nearly as potent as Long Island iced tea, we strongly
discourage trying to navigate River Road after a couple of these.

If you can't wait to find scuppernong wine, an inexpensive five-year-old blended Madeira
makes a fine substitute in this drink for the raisiny, slightly oxidized flavor of the country wine.

Makes 1½ quarts; enough for eight 6-ounce cocktails

TIME: 5 minutes

½ cup (4 ounces) bourbon

2½ cups (20 ounces) scuppernong wine or a
5-year-old blended Madeira

1 cup (8 ounces) lemon juice (juice of about 6
lemons)

2 cups (16 ounces) seltzer water or club soda

8 scuppernong or other muscadine grapes, for
garnish (optional)

In a 2-quart pitcher, mix all the ingredients except the seltzer and grapes and stir thoroughly with a long-handled spoon. Fill eight 9-ounce rocks glasses with ice cubes and pour four ounces of the Johns Island Iced Tea into each glass until about 1 inch from the rim of the glass. Top up each drink with about 2 ounces of seltzer and garnish with a scuppernong or muscadine when in season.

A purple martin tree stands sentry in a Johns Island vineyard. Purple martins prefer nesting in hollowed-out gourds, making them one of the few animal species dependent on humans.

❋ SAZERAC ❋

NEW ORLEANS IS INDELIBLY ASSOCIATED WITH THIS ANISE- AND WHISKEY-SCENTED COCKTAIL, WHICH IS ALMOST LIKE candy in its appeal and is always served neat. Among the first cocktails, the Sazerac was invented by a French-born New Orleans pharmacist, Antoine Amedee Peychaud, to show off the bitters recipe that he had formulated and brought with him from Santo Domingo. And indeed, sipping a Sazerac has a cooling, palliative effect on the most malarial, humid days of the year.

To give the drink some Charleston elegance and complexity, we actually tone down the sweet Pernod or Herbsaint (used today instead of the original ingredient, absinthe) and bring back a whiff—just a teaspoon—of brandy, which was the backbone of the cocktail (Peychaud used the Sazerac brand of cognac; hence the name) before people switched in the late nineteenth century to the more common and affordable rye whiskey. Two ounces of rye is nevertheless our preferred ingredient for the Sazerac, but any bourbon or American whiskey will work nearly as well. Good rye, made predominantly from rye grain, has a lovely dry finish, whereas corn-based bourbon has a sweeter, more caramel-like character. Old Overholt is the most widely available brand of rye.

Though Peychaud's lollipop-red, anise-flavored bitters are mandatory for this cocktail in New Orleans, we secretly prefer to use dark Angostura bitters from the West Indies in ours, because they give the drink a spicy, woodsy note that extends the season of this great cocktail through the holidays.

Makes one 4-ounce cocktail

½ cup crushed ice

½ teaspoon Herbsaint, Pernod, Ricard, or
    other anise-flavored liqueur

2 shakes Angostura or Peychaud's bitters

4 tablespoons rye, bourbon, or American
    whiskey

1 teaspoon Simple Syrup (page 24) or
    ½ teaspoon confectioners' sugar

1 teaspoon brandy

One 2-inch-long slice lemon peel, a ¼ inch
    thick ribbon

1. Shake the ice, Pernod, bitters, rye, and simple syrup in a cocktail shaker, with extra vigor for at least 15 full seconds. Pour the brandy in an old-fashioned glass, martini, or short cocktail glass, and swirl. Add the cocktail from the shaker, holding back the ice with a strainer. If you've shaken it well, the drink should slink out of the shaker with a thin robe of froth on its surface.

2. Twist the lemon peel over the glass to release the oil. Then hang the peel on the rim of the glass or toss it into the drink.

❈ SOUR ORANGE MOJITO ❈

IN OUR SOUR ORANGE PIE (PAGE 444), WE SWAP SOUR ORANGES FOR THE EPONYMOUS KEY LIMES. LIKEWISE, OUR RIFF ON the Cuban mojito—a Caribbean cousin to the mint julep, made with mint, lime juice, and sugar — substitutes sour orange juice for the lime juice. Sour orange juice packs a bold and surprisingly nuanced, floral orange flavor, but it's got the pucker of lemon or lime. To us, it's a knockout.

Makes 1 quart; enough for 6–8 cocktails

½ cup finely chopped fresh mint, plus more
  for garnish
½ cup sugar
1¾ cups fresh sour orange juice, or substitute
  three equal parts fresh grapefruit,
  orange, and lemon juice

1¼ cups cold water
1 cup (8 ounces) dark rum, such as Mount
  Gay or Barbancourt
Seltzer water (optional)
1 sour orange, cut into wedges, for garnish

1.   In a mortar and pestle, smear and mash the mint with the sugar until it becomes a damp paste. If you don't have a mortar and pestle, use a tall narrow glass or spice bottle to muddle the mint and sugar in the bottom of a short, fat glass.

2.   In a pitcher, combine the mint paste with the juice, water, and rum. Pour the mojitos into rocks glasses filled with ice and top up with seltzer, if desired. Garnish with a sprig of mint, a wedge of lime, or both.

❋ LEE BROS. TANNENBAUM TIPPLE ❋

WHILE MATT WAS AN OFFICER OF HARVARD'S SIGNET SOCIETY, AN ARTS-AND-LETTERS CLUB (T. S. ELIOT, BENAZIR BHUTTO, and Conan O'Brien are past members), he was in charge of the holiday loving cup, a festive but often tasteless punch that is traditionally served at the black-tie holiday dinner. After the salad course, the punch is sent around the room in an immense silver vessel, for communal swigging straight from the bowl. The loving cup moves slowly from person to person, disarming guests and dispelling a little of the stuffiness in the proceedings. Typically, a tipsy college senior prepares the punch at the last minute, using a couple bottles of cheap bubbly and a packet of Kool-Aid.

One year Matt was determined to blend a punch worth drinking, so he concocted this version, which has a sprightly ale and sherry base, a discreet amount of spice (in keeping with the season), and green tea—which commonly appears in Lowcountry punch recipes and which gives this one an appetizing tannic bitterness.

With a few refinements, this punch has become a fun centerpiece for any large holiday party that needs a jolt of excitement without compromising great flavor. We recommend serving Tannenbaum Tipple in a punch bowl, slightly cool but not cold. Unless you're looking to lighten up a particularly rigid party, individual cups are recommended. Serve with Cheese Straws (page 67) and Spiced Pecans (page 85).

Makes 6 quarts; enough for about 30 drinks

TIME: 15 minutes

3 small oranges

20 whole cloves

Two 750 ml. bottles amontillado (medium-dry) sherry

Six 12-ounce bottles cold ale (preferably a hoppy American ale like Sam Adams Boston Ale or Charleston's Palmetto Pale Ale)

1 quart gunpowder tea or other green tea, brewed strong and sweetened with ½ cup sugar, at room temperature

1 cup brandy

4 cinnamon sticks

2 whole nutmegs

1 heaping tablespoon ground ginger

1. Stud 1 orange with cloves by pressing the sharp ends straight into the peel. Slice the second orange into 8 thin disks. Remove the zest from the third with a zester or a sharp knife, squeeze the juice into a small bowl, then add the zest to the juice.

2. Pour the sherry into the punch bowl, then add the ale (pour slowly to preserve the effervescence), tea, brandy, orange juice, and zest. Grate the cinnamon sticks over the brew until fatigue sets in, then toss in the remaining sticks. Grate the nutmegs into the punch until your fingers are in danger and discard the remaining nutmegs. Add the ginger and whisk to incorporate.

3. Float the studded orange and the orange slices in the bowl. Feel free to experiment with the balance of spices to suit your taste. You can turn up the spice level by adding ground allspice, ground mace, and juniper berries.

4. Ladle the tipple into punch glasses or teacups and serve.

BLENHEIM: ACQUIRING A TASTE FOR BLENHEIM'S PEP-pery ginger ale is a rite of passage in South Carolina. Blenheim is owned by the same folks who run the tourist trap South of the Border, a huge store on Interstate 95 at the North Carolina–South Carolina border, and we never pass by without picking up a case. If you're not near South Carolina, you can order it by mail from Pop the Soda Shop: 877-POP-SODA; www.popsoda.com.

ALE-8-ONE: BOTTLED IN WINCHESTER, KENTUCKY, since 1926, Ale-8-One is milder than Blenheim and has a fruity character. On our first trip to Kentucky, we fell for it. It's perfect in Jack and Gingers. To order, call 859-744-3484 or visit www.ale-8-one.com.

❉ JACK AND GINGER ❉

FRESHLY GRATED GINGER SHAKEN WITH WHISKEY FIRES
UP THIS COUNTRY CLASSIC—IMAGINE DOLLY PARTON AND COURT-
ney Love singing a duet of Neil Young's "Old Man."

Makes one 8-ounce cocktail

½ cup crushed ice

1 teaspoon grated peeled fresh ginger (about
    one 1-inch-long piece)

4 tablespoons (¼ cup) Jack Daniel's Tennessee
    Whiskey

¾ cup (about ½ bottle or can) ginger ale (see
    "Southern Ginger Ales," opposite)

One 2-inch-long slice lemon peel, ⅛ inch
    thick

Fill a cocktail shaker with the ice, ginger, and whiskey and shake vigorously. Strain into a 14-ounce glass filled two-thirds of the way to the rim with ice cubes. Pour the ginger ale into the glass and agitate with a spoon or stirrer. Twist the peel over the surface of the drink to release the oil and garnish with the peel.

❊ GARDEN AND GUN COCKTAIL ❊

CHARLESTON ONCE HAD ITS OWN VERSION OF STUDIO 54, CALLED THE KING STREET GARDEN AND GUN CLUB, FOUNDED BY Richard Robison. A producer at the Spoleto Festival USA, the performing arts festival that takes over the town each year in late May and early June, Robison opened the Garden and Gun (which was all anyone ever called it) primarily as a place for the baritones and ballerinas from out of town to unwind after their shows, but the nightspot attracted a large local following, too. Although the Garden and Gun lasted only from 1976 (the founding of the Spoleto Festival) until 1981, the bar was deeply influential, and even today many Charlestonians claim it was the first bar in the city where people of all races and sexual orientations felt comfortable dancing together. We still hear people of a certain age waxing nostalgic about the dance scene at the Garden and Gun. There was never anything like it before, they tell us, and there hasn't been anything quite like it since.

We were far from drinking age during the Garden and Gun's heyday, but the phrase always captivated us for the way it effortlessly welds together two concepts that seem so at odds, the twee domesticity of "garden" and the frightening brawn of "gun." It was only as we grew older that we realized it captures one aspect of Charleston's soul: a little bit courtly and a little bit country. It's a quality perhaps best articulated by one of Ted's contemporaries at a debutante party. "Don't you just love deb season?" said the young rake, taking a long slug of a gin and tonic. "Just change out of your camo [camouflage], and into your tuxedo."

In this cocktail, the bourbon is the gun; the watermelon rind preserves, which is basically a simple syrup infused with lemon, ginger, and the cucumber-y freshness of watermelon rind, is the garden.

Makes one 6-ounce cocktail

1 tablespoon Watermelon Rind Preserves (page 136)

4 tablespoons (¼ cup) bourbon

2 tablespoons (1 ounce) club soda or seltzer water

2 watermelon balls (optional)

Spoon the preserves into a cocktail shaker. If they seem very stiff, add a few drops of warm water and stir with a spoon to loosen. Put 4 ice cubes in the shaker along with the bourbon and shake vigorously. Pour the contents of the shaker into a glass filled with ice cubes, add the club soda, and stir with a swizzle stick. If you like, garnish with the watermelon balls (scoop the melon with a teaspoon-sized measuring spoon) skewered on the swizzle stick.

❊ PEACH SAKE ❊

WE KNOW WHAT YOU'RE THINKING: WHAT IS AN ANCIENT JAPANESE BEVERAGE DOING IN A BOOK ABOUT SOUTHERN FOOD? Although we've never found a recipe for rice wine infused with fresh fruit in a southern cookbook, rice wine was, in fact, a noted beverage in the Lowcountry in the nineteenth century, and a recipe for it appears in the classic cookbook *Charleston Receipts*. It's not such a stretch when you consider that the Lowcountry was the center of rice cultivation in North America (see page 165) from the early 1700s until the Civil War.

We do not go so far as to brew our own rice wine for this beverage, since there are so many inexpensive, delicious sakes on the market these days. Besides, true sake is not simply fermented rice but a more complicated elixir that requires specially polished rice grains, enzymatic action, and a whole host of other factors beyond even the most sophisticated home brewer. Sakes are brewed in varying degrees of sweetness; seek out a decent ($15 to $25) bottle at your local liquor store and ask the clerk to help identify the medium-dry kind.

Cold sake, served in a clear shot glass or a tiny ceramic cup, is a great way to start a meal, particularly one with fish. Sake is a classic pairing with sushi, of course, but it also works well with warm, mild fish dishes like Roasted Whole Yellowtail Snapper with Sweet Potatoes and Scallions (page 401).

It takes just a few minutes to prepare simple infusions like these and barely a day to cure them. Rice wines steeped with peaches, watermelon, or grapes are refreshing to drink—with their pale, icy pinks and reds, they are refreshing simply to look at—and they rely entirely on the fruit for their extra sweetness. If your infused sake is too dry for your taste, just add a few drops of Simple Syrup (page 24) or begin with a sweeter sake.

54

Makes 1 quart; enough for 10 drinks

TIME: 10 minutes to prepare, 24 hours to steep

2 ripe clingstone peaches
One 750 ml. bottle dry or medium-dry sake, chilled

1. Cut the peaches in half and remove the pits but not the skins. Slice them thin, reserving any juice that oozes out, and place the fruit and juice in a large glass pitcher. Pour the sake over the peaches, cover, and refrigerate for 24 hours.

2. Strain the sake through a fine-mesh strainer or cheesecloth into a clean decanter, pressing the peaches lightly into the mesh to squeeze a little extra flavor from them.

3. Serve immediately, with a marinated peach sliver in each glass, or refrigerate the sake in the decanter. Discard the peaches. Infused sake will keep for 7 days in the refrigerator.

WATERMELON SAKE: SUBSTITUTE 2 CUPS WATERMELON CUT INTO 1-INCH CUBES (FROM A 2-POUND WEDGE OF WATERMELON) FOR THE PEACHES.

SCUPPERNONG SAKE: SUBSTITUTE 1 POUND SCUPPERNONGS (OR OTHER MUSCADINES, OR MUSKY NORTHERN GRAPES LIKE CONCORD OR NIAGARA), WASHED AND HALVED, FOR THE PEACHES.

Fields Farm watermelons from Johns Island for sale at the Mt. Pleasant farmers' market.

✳ BOILED PEANUTS, GRAZES, AND HORS D'OEUVRES ✳

GRAZING IS A STATE OF BEING IN THE SOUTH. IN FACT, MANY OF OUR COMMUNITY

cookbooks from the twentieth century are front-heavy, with so many more hors d'oeuvre and finger-food recipes than main courses (or even desserts) that it makes you wonder why we even bother with the rest of the meal. It's actually plain good sense: as any southerner knows, a dizzying array of nibbles in view when your guests arrive is the utmost gesture of hospitality. And for our grandmother Elizabeth and her coevals, who seemed to go to a different cocktail party every night, the endless platters of pimento cheese sandwiches (page 89), Pickled Shrimp (page 81), and Country Ham Biscuits (page 71) were a primary form of sustenance! Oyster shooters (page 75) are a recent invention and probably don't appear at the parties our grandmother frequents, but they just might start turning up in the near future, once she gives them a try. Nothing adds more fun and color with so little effort.

BOILED PEANUTS

There are hors d'oeuvres and there are snacks. Boiled peanuts don't fit either definition. They are most often purchased by the side of the road, they are almost never served in a restaurant, and they can be carried along through the rest of the afternoon or the week, however long they last. They seem to occupy a space between snack food and a habit, like chewing tobacco. As any diehard boiled-peanut fan can attest, the salty, wet little beans inspire your mind to take a lazy walk while your hand shuttles between bag and mouth and your teeth do the chewing. People eating boiled peanuts are usually engaged in other tasks, like driving, talking, fishing, or watching television.

Peanuts (*Arachis hypogaea*) are not nuts. They are legumes, from the family Leguminosae, which includes lima beans, fava beans, soybeans, and most any bean you've ever eaten. A peanut freshly dug from the ground is as damp as a potato and has the aroma of freshly mown hay. Shell it and eat the seed kernels and you'll find a starchy, slightly sweet, grassy flavor like that of a raw lima bean or sweet pea. It's a taste of high summer, when the peanuts are harvested, and to us it seems logical—and not unusual—that you might want to boil them or steam them, the way most beans are boiled or steamed before they are eaten. (If instead you dry the peanuts and roast them in an oven, you will change their flavor, bringing out a nutty, buttery character that the legume doesn't have in its raw state. You'd then have what most Americans recognize as peanuts—roasted peanuts.)

It's not just southerners who boil peanuts. We don't know exactly how ancient Peruvians prepared peanuts, but we do know that they ate them, since archeologists have found figurines of peanut vendors in the graves of the Moche people (200 B.C. to A.D. 700). The peanut plant eventually made its way from ancient Peru to Brazil, and from there the Portuguese took them to Europe, to Africa, and beyond, to Asia, in the fifteenth and sixteenth centuries. They came to North America from Africa relatively recently, during the slave trade in the eighteenth and early nineteenth centuries. Anecdotal evidence holds that peanuts were more often boiled than roasted in the South until the soldiers of the Union Army took them north in the years following the Civil War.

We love boiled peanuts because they are an addictive snack that is fun to eat and that catches people off guard, challenging them to think about a familiar food in a new way. And they do so without adding anything. The miraculous transformation is accomplished by taking the peanut back a step, toward its natural state. Not all people fall in love with boiled peanuts' distinctive beanlike flavor, but they're undeniably interesting and full of personality.

Boiled peanuts couldn't be easier to prepare—anyone who can boil water can boil peanuts. They're a great activity for a lazy Saturday or Sunday morning; all that is required is for you to get up from the newspaper occasionally to add a little water to the pot. The peanuts are incredibly tolerant, in the sense that they're almost impossible to overcook, which allows plenty of leeway for correcting the salt level in the brine.

Eating the fragrant peanuts hot out of the pot is a wonderful way to experience them, but gobbling them at room temperature is the quintessential experience, since most peanuts are purchased by the side of the road, in soggy brown kraft paper bags. The briny peanuts seem to gain something from sitting in the fridge for a few days, too, so feel free to eat them cold; we often do. In fact, they're great in Boiled Peanut and Sorghum Swirl Ice Cream (page 429)!

❁ BOILED PEANUTS (STOVETOP METHOD) ❁

Makes 4 pounds; enough snacking for 12 people
TIME: 8 hours to soak, 5–8 hours to boil

1½ cups salt, plus more to taste
4 gallons water, plus more as needed
2 pounds raw peanuts in the shell (see "Raw Peanuts," p. 64)

1. In a 3-gallon stockpot, dissolve ½ cup of the salt in 2 gallons of water and add the peanuts (the peanuts will float, but you can keep most of them submerged by using a dinner plate as a cap). Allow the peanuts to soak for 8 hours or overnight (see note below).

2. Discard the soaking water and fill the pot with 2 gallons of fresh water and the remaining 1 cup salt. Bring to a boil, lower the heat to medium-low, and cook at a low boil, covered, for 5 to 8 hours. Keep the water in the pot at roughly the same level with hourly additions of 2 cups water until the peanuts are soft (South Carolina–style peanuts are very soft, but some cooks prefer them al dente).

3. When the peanuts have boiled for 3 hours, sample them to check for texture and saltiness. Allow a peanut to cool, then crack open the shell to get at the kernels inside. If you find them too salty, remove some brine with a ladle or small pot and replace it with an equal amount of fresh water. If the peanuts are not salty enough, add salt in ¼ cup increments, turn off the heat, and let them soak for an hour to absorb the salt. If the peanuts are too crunchy for your taste, boil on. It can take as long as 12 hours if you prefer them mushroom-soft. Sample them every hour.

4.   When the peanuts are cooked to your satisfaction, turn off the heat and cool for 1 hour. When cool enough to handle, drain and eat immediately or store (in the shell) in a sealed container in the refrigerator or freezer. Boiled peanuts will keep for 7 days in the refrigerator, several months in the freezer.

Note: If you are pressed for time, the soaking step is not essential, but it reduces the cooking time by a couple of hours and helps ensure that the peanuts cook more thoroughly and uniformly. The salt in the soaking liquid keeps yeasts and molds from developing overnight.

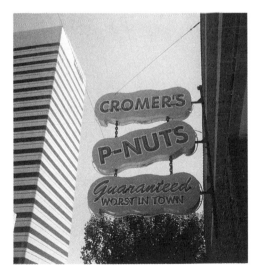

Self-effacement and a take-'em-or-leave-'em attitude
is part of the spirit of boiled peanuts. Cromers, in
Columbia, South Carolina, is famous for their "worst
in town" claim.

❊ BOILED PEANUTS (SLOW-COOKER METHOD) ❊

Makes 4 pounds; enough snacking for 12 people

TIME: 8–10 hours

⅓ cup salt, plus more to taste

3 quarts water, plus more as needed

2 pounds raw peanuts in the shell (see "Raw Peanuts," p. 64)

1. Dissolve the salt in the water in a 4-quart slow cooker. Add the peanuts, set the cooker to high, cover, and cook for 8 to 12 hours, adding fresh water occasionally, if necessary, to keep the peanuts moist. The water should be no more than 1 inch below the top of the peanuts.

2. After about 5 hours, sample the peanuts to check their saltiness. Allow a peanut to cool, then crack open the shell to get at the kernels inside. Add more salt, if needed, by teaspoonfuls. To reduce the salt, add 2 cups water and cook for 1 hour, then remove 1½ cups of (now salty) water from the slow cooker and replenish with fresh water.

3. Simmer until the kernels are as soft as a roasted chestnut, or to taste.

4. When the peanuts are cooked to your satisfaction, turn off the heat and cool for 1 hour. When cool enough to handle, drain and eat immediately or store (in the shell) in a sealed container in the refrigerator or freezer. Boiled peanuts will keep for 7 days in the refrigerator, several months in the freezer.

HOW TO SEASON BOILED PEANUTS: SEASONING BOILED PEANUTS WITH ANYTHING MORE THAN SALT SEEMS TO US A LITTLE BIT LIKE FLAVORING COFFEE—MESSING WITH A GOOD THING. BUT CAJUN BOILED PEANUTS AND HAM-FLAVORED BOILED PEANUTS ARE VERY POPULAR AT ROADSIDE STANDS, AND WE'LL READILY ADMIT THAT THE FLAVOR OF BOILED PEANUTS IS A GREAT MATCH FOR SMOKE AND SPICE. TO MAKE THE FORMER, ADD 2 TABLESPOONS LEE BROS. SHRIMP BOIL (PAGE 553) OR ANOTHER CAYENNE-BASED SPICE MIXTURE TO THE WATER AT THE START OF COOKING. FOR THE LATTER, ADD 1 SMOKED HAM HOCK, 1 SMOKED JOWL, OR A 1/4-POUND HUNK OF COUNTRY HAM. WE LIKED THE STAR ANISE BOILED PEANUTS WE'VE MADE BY ADDING 2 WHOLE STARS TO THE BOILING WATER, INSPIRED BY A SUGGESTION FROM THE ARTIST JASPER JOHNS, A SOUTH CAROLINA NATIVE. WE THOUGHT THEY WERE JOHNS'S INVENTION UNTIL WE TRAVELED TO HAWAII AND DISCOVERED THAT A CHINESE RECIPE FOR BOILED PEANUTS MADE ITS WAY TO THE ISLANDS AT THE BEGINNING OF THE TWENTIETH CEN-TURY, WHEN MANY FARMERS LEFT CHINA TO WORK ON HAWAIIAN SUGAR PLANTATIONS. EVEN TODAY FOOD MARKETS IN HAWAII OFTEN DISPLAY BAGS OF RAW PEANUTS NEXT TO BAGS OF STAR ANISE.

An early marketing image, snapped on the fire-escape of the tenement apartment on Ludlow Street, when our business plan was to sell boiled peanuts to bars and southern restaurants in New York City.

RAW PEANUTS

RAW PEANUTS ARE UNROASTED PEANUTS. MOST RAW peanuts are sun-dried in the shell to remove enough moisture to make them shelf-stable. But midsummer is high peanut season, and in markets throughout the Southeast you may be lucky enough to find "green" peanuts, which are raw peanuts freshly plucked from the ground. Their high moisture content gives them a hint more fresh-pea flavor (and cuts the cooking time in half), but it also makes them extremely perishable. If you do find them, keep them refrigerated and boil them as soon as possible.

❋ BOILED SOYBEANS (EDAMAME) ❋

IN 1996, AN ACQUAINTANCE OFFERED US WHAT HE SAID WAS "A MILLION-DOLLAR IDEA": WE SHOULD MARKET OUR BOILED peanuts as "redneck edamame," he said, referring to the boiled soybeans served in Japanese restaurants—a snack very much in vogue that year. It was a terrible idea—boiled peanuts appeal to southerners across race, class, and gender lines—but he was right about one thing: there is a kinship between soybeans and peanuts in that they both taste delicious when boiled in salty water, and they are both grown in the Southeast.

Our friend Mary Jo Wannamaker is the president of Wannamaker Seeds, a business her grandfather founded 85 miles northeast of Charleston in the tidy village of St. Matthews, South Carolina. Alongside the canal that runs through town is a barn with a large sign that reads, WANNAMAKER SEEDS. The Wannamakers have sold cotton seeds to local farmers for more than a hundred years, and they've been selling soybeans since the 1960s, primarily to customers in Japan, where arable land is scarce and the demand for soybeans is sky-high. Over the years we've encouraged Mary Jo to grow edible soybeans for the U.S. market, and in 2003 she set up a side business to sell a few varieties that folks can grow in their own backyards (www.wannamakerseeds.com). One early-developing variety is even suitable for northern climates.

2 tablespoons salt
1 quart water
1 pound fresh or frozen soybeans in the shell

Bring the salt and water to a boil in a 2- or 3-quart pot. Add the soybeans, lower the heat, and cook at a low boil for 10 minutes. Allow to cool, then drain the soybeans and serve with a bowl for the shells and a stack of hand towels.

A pot of green peanuts boils on a propane-cooker at the Mt. Pleasant farmers' market.

❈ CHEESE STRAWS ❈

FOR A FEW YEARS WE SOLD THROUGH OUR CATALOGUE SUPERB CHEESE STRAWS BAKED BY A GENTLEMAN IN VIRGINIA. WHEN the man disappeared just before the busy holiday season one year, our cheese-straw waiting list quickly grew to 150 names. He later sent us an apology, but in the meantime we'd disappointed so many people with the wait that we decided that the least we could do was to offer them a good cheese-straw recipe for emergencies like this. We began developing the cheese straw of our dreams, and in the process found that cheese straws are among the easiest baked goods in the world. If it weren't for the blade on the food processor, a toddler could do it. You don't even need to grease the cookie sheet.

There are plenty of rote, bland recipes for cheese straws out there, and most of them call for a cookie press, which seems like just another item to have to store and wash. Furthermore, the conventional broad, scalloped cheese straw, more cookie than straw, looks like the icing on grocery store cakes. We like our cheese straws long, slender, and elegant, like . . . well, straws. Although they're fragile, they bundle together nicely on end in a stout cocktail glass or silver julep cup.

In terms of flavor, the usual cheese straw has too much flour and too little cheese. We use enough cheese to make these straws unmistakably sharp, luscious and yellow, and a judicious amount of crushed red pepper flakes to add flavor, a bit of heat, and a lively red speckling to the batter. Make two batches; these cheese straws disappear quickly.

Makes 30 straws

TIME: 30 minutes

1½ cups (about 4 ounces) grated extra-sharp cheddar cheese

4 tablespoons (½ stick) unsalted butter, softened and cut into 4 pieces

¾ cup all-purpose flour, plus more for dusting

½ teaspoon kosher salt

½ teaspoon crushed red pepper flakes

1 tablespoon half-and-half

1. Preheat the oven to 350 degrees.

2. In a food processor, combine the cheese, butter, flour, salt, and red pepper and process in five 5-second pulses until the mixture resembles coarse crumbs. Add the half-and-half and process until the dough forms a ball, about 10 seconds.

3. On a lightly floured surface, using a lightly floured rolling pin, roll the dough into an 8-×-10-inch rectangle that is ⅛ inch thick. With a sharp knife, cut the dough into long, thin strips, ¼ to ⅓ inch wide (dipping the knife in flour after every few inches ensures a clean cut). Gently transfer the strips to an ungreased cookie sheet, leaving at least ¼ inch between them. The dough will sag and may break occasionally in the transfer, but don't be concerned—just do your best. The straws can be any length, from 2 to 10 inches.

4. Bake the straws on the middle rack for 12 to 15 minutes, or until the ends are barely browned. Remove from the oven and set the cookie sheet on a rack to cool.

5. Serve at room temperature. Cheese straws will keep in the refrigerator, in a sealed container, for 2 days.

❊ A NEW CRAB DIP ❊

QUICK
KNOCKOUT

THIS LIGHT, EASY DIP IS A PLAYFUL RIFF ON THE FLAVOR
OF TARRAGON AND THE SWEETNESS OF CRAB. TART LIME JUICE
focuses the sweet flavors, and finely diced raw red onion gives the dip zing and a pleasing crunch.
We serve this dip with store-bought sesame crackers or tortilla chips for grazing, but it makes
superb tea sandwiches, too, and a spoonful is great in our Summer Corn Soup with Butterbean
Dumplings (page 293). For folks like us who've been turned off by gloppy, warm crab dips that
seem to taste more like cheese than crab, this dip will be nothing short of a revelation.

Makes 1 heaping cup of dip; enough for 6 for grazing with chips or crackers

TIME: 5 minutes

6 ounces picked crabmeat (about ½ pint; see
　　Sourcery, page 70)
3 tablespoons high-quality store-bought
　　mayonnaise such as Duke's or
　　Hellmann's
2 tablespoons lime juice

3 tablespoons finely diced red onion (about ½
　　onion)
1½ teaspoons minced fresh tarragon
¼ teaspoon kosher salt, plus more to taste
¼ teaspoon freshly ground black pepper, plus
　　more to taste

In a small bowl, mix all the ingredients together until thoroughly blended. Season to taste with
salt and black pepper, and cover tightly with plastic wrap. Store in the refrigerator, not more than
24 hours.

SOURCERY: BUYING PICKED CRABMEAT

IF YOU DON'T PICK YOUR OWN CRABS, YOU MAY HAVE already discovered that picked crabmeat is expensive. But there are a number of grades of crabmeat—at least four, according to the USDA: jumbo lump, backfin lump, flake white, and claw (or "brown") meat. (Many premium crab processors now offer as many as seven.) You should buy the best crabmeat you can afford, but we would rather buy a greater quantity of a lower grade than to try to stretch an expensive grade and risk disguising the delectable sweet flavor that makes it so expensive. We take great care in every crab recipe—Crab Cakes (page 377), She-Crab Soup (page 289), and A New Crab Dip (page 69)—to let the flavor of the meat shine through. Look for plastic containers of fresh crabmeat at the fish market or at the fish counter of the supermarket. Avoid crabmeat in cans; it has tinny, off flavors that don't appeal.

❊ COUNTRY HAM BISCUITS ❊

A TRUE COUNTRY HAM IS THE BACK LEG OF A PIG THAT HAS BEEN DRY-CURED IN SALT AND SUGAR FOR SEVERAL WEEKS, smoked for another few weeks, then aged in the smokehouse for months. It is salty, gamy ham heaven.

We've heard southerners call country ham "the South's prosciutto," and they're really not so far off. Like prosciutto, country ham is a cornerstone of regional cooking, so much so that in this book it gets its own primer treatment (see page 325). You'll encounter country ham in a number of different dishes from Virginia to Kentucky to Louisiana.

These hearty biscuits are terrific to pass around at a party before the main event, but consider yourself warned: they tend to steal the show, so plan your main event accordingly.

Makes 16 biscuits

TIME: 30 minutes

1 recipe Bird-Head Buttermilk Biscuits
    (page 505)
4 tablespoons unsalted butter, melted

One ½-pound piece cured country ham,
    uncooked
1 cup Jerusalem Artichoke Relish (page 112),
    or your favorite relish

1. Prepare the buttermilk biscuits. With a fork or a knife, split each biscuit into halves. Brush the open faces of each half with butter.

2. Slice the ham as thinly as possible into small, bite-sized pieces. Layer 2 or 3 slivers of ham on the bottom half of each biscuit and dollop 1 teaspoon relish on top. Cover each biscuit with its top half and arrange them on a serving platter.

3. Serve immediately. If you need to save the biscuits for a few hours, wrap the platter in plastic and refrigerate so they don't dry out. Country ham biscuits do not keep well, so consume within a couple hours, if possible.

❋ BUTTERBEAN PÂTÉ ❋

QUICK
KNOCKOUT

WE SPREAD THIS VERSATILE BUTTERBEAN PÂTÉ, WHICH
LACES THE FRESH FLAVOR OF THE BEANS WITH A HINT OF SWEET
mint and the tang of lemon juice, on crackers or toast points for a simple vegetarian-friendly hors
d'oeuvre. It has a glorious color, and it's wonderful to have on hand for a variety of reasons. We
spread it between slices of Sally Lunn (page 500) with thin slices of red onion and a leaf of butter lettuce to make an easy, delicious lunch, and we drop dollops into Stolen Tomato Bisque (page
291) and Summer Corn Soup with Butterbean Dumplings (page 293) to add intrigue to the richness of the soup.

We love aromatic and flavorful olive oils, but in this recipe you want to use a mild olive oil;
otherwise the softer flavors of the butterbeans, mint, and parsley get muscled out. If you have only
a brawny extra-virgin olive oil on hand, use half olive oil and half canola or peanut oil.

In July and August, when butterbeans are in season, we make a crock of this spread daily and
keep it in the fridge. But there's no reason not to make it all year long. Frozen butterbeans or limas
make a more than acceptable substitute for fresh ones, but use the baby varieties, which are tenderer and more flavorful.

Makes 1½ cups butterbean spread; enough for 12 people with crackers,
for grazing, or for 6 sandwiches

TIME: 15 minutes

2 cups water
1 tablespoon kosher salt, plus more to taste
2 cups fresh butterbeans (about 10 ounces)
¼ cup tightly packed fresh mint leaves (from
about 6 stems), washed and dried
¼ cup tightly packed fresh flat-leaf parsley
leaves (from about 6 stems), washed
and dried

2 tablespoons whole or lowfat buttermilk or
sour cream
¼ cup olive oil
¼ cup lemon juice (from 1–2 lemons)
Freshly ground black pepper to taste

1. In a small saucepan, bring the water and 2 teaspoons salt to a boil over high heat. Add the but-terbeans and let boil until just tender, about 3 minutes. Drain in a colander and rinse under cold running water for about 2 minutes to cool. Shake the colander several times to drain as much water from the beans as possible.

2. Place the beans and all the remaining ingredients in the bowl of a food processor and process to a smooth, thick puree, about three 30-second-long pulses. Between pulses, push any of the mixture that clings to the side of the processor toward the blade with a rubber spatula before puls-ing again.

3. Season the pâté to taste with salt and pepper and transfer it from the processor to a small bowl or plastic container. Cover tightly, and store in the refrigerator until ready to use, not more than 3 days.

At our house, the first thing we serve to guests is a drink, and the second, just moments after the drink, is an oyster shooter, a hot/sour/salty/sweet cocktail in a shot glass, composed around a raw oyster.

Consuming oysters this way is unusual in the Lowcountry, but they're a lot of fun at parties. Immediate gratification is half the charm. And they're terrific icebreakers: they bring everyone in a room together for a collective flavor adventure. Though we've known people to be trepidatious about eating raw oysters, we have yet to have a guest decline an oyster shooter.

We rarely make the same shooter twice, but what we've found works well with a briny oyster is to build layers of complementary flavor into the glass. We always have a sweet element, a tart ingredient, and a lick of fiery heat. And though we usually add a splash of vodka to round out these sensations, shooters don't have to be alcoholic.

The order in which you put together the ingredients is important. Begin with a pinch of salt and a vegetable, like scallion or jalapeño, because they elevate the oyster slightly and keep it from sticking to the bottom of the glass. Since heavier ingredients like horseradish sink in liquid, we add them after we add the oyster so they cascade around it.

For a party of six, we set up about twenty-four shot glasses on a baking sheet and compose them assembly-line style, and if we have time, we refrigerate them so they're cold when the guests arrive.

Here are two of our tried-and-true favorites, named for the rivers we kayak on. The first shooter is named for the Edisto River, which runs through the pristine wetlands of the former rice-growing region south of Charleston. The second is named for the Cooper, which is closer to home: it flows into Charleston Harbor right outside the window of the bedroom we grew up in. A close cousin to the bloody mary, the Cooper River Oyster Shooter is for less adventurous palates.

MOST FISHMONGERS OFFER A COUPLE VARIETIES OF oysters in the shell for shucking at home (see page 417 for instructions), and many will shuck the oysters for you for a two-dollar surcharge on the price of a dozen—a great value, in our estimation. But if the price of a dozen itself is prohibitive, most independent fish markets and the fish counters of larger grocery stores offer less expensive half-pints or pint-sized plastic tubs of shucked oysters in their liquor. Packed in Washington State, Virginia, Maryland, Louisiana, North Carolina, or Florida, these oysters are mostly used in cooked preparations, but we often use them raw for our oyster shooters, and we've never once been disappointed by their quality or freshness. Most containers are marked with a packing date and a use-by date, but as with any shellfish, if you're concerned, don't hesitate to ask your fishmonger for advice or reassurance. And always buy jars labeled "selects" if possible, because they are more uniformly sized.

One caveat: to our taste, packed oysters rarely have enough brine, because the packers almost always soak them in fresh water to plump them up and bring down the salt content. Fortunately, that can be easily remedied with several pinches of sea salt to taste (we commonly use a teaspoon per pint). At about ten bucks a pint (twenty-four to thirty-six oysters, depending on their size), they're one of America's great seafood bargains.

❋ EDISTO RIVER OYSTER SHOOTER ❋

Makes 24 shooters; enough for 6 to 12 people

TIME: 20 minutes

EQUIPMENT
24 shot glasses

⅓ cup finely chopped shallots or 2 jalapeño
    peppers, sliced paper-thin
2 tablespoons Maldon salt or kosher salt
2 cups oysters, shucked, with their liquor (if
    large, cut in half; you should have 24
    pieces)

1½ cups freshly squeezed sour orange juice, or
    substitute three equal parts fresh grape-
    fruit, orange, and lemon juice
1½ tablespoons white wine or champagne
    vinegar
1 teaspoon sugar
¾ teaspoon salt

1. Place the shot glasses on a baking sheet or large tray. Drop a pinch of the chopped shallot or 1 jalapeño slice into each glass and sprinkle it with a pinch of salt. Add an oyster to each glass, followed by ½ teaspoon oyster liquor. In a small bowl, combine the sour orange juice, vinegar, sugar, and salt and whisk to combine. Add 1 tablespoon of the sour orange juice mixture to each shot glass. Sprinkle another pinch of salt over each glass and float another pinch of the shallot or another jalapeño slice on the surface of the shooter.

2. Refrigerate until ready to serve. Oyster shooters should be consumed within 4 hours.

❋ COOPER RIVER OYSTER SHOOTER ❋

Makes 24 shooters; enough for 6 to 12 people

TIME: 20 minutes

EQUIPMENT

24 shot glasses

48 paper-thin slices green onion (from about 4 stalks green onion)

2 tablespoons Maldon salt or kosher salt

1 cup oysters, shucked, with their liquor (if large, cut in half; you should have 24 pieces)

1 cup canned tomato puree (preferably made from San Marzano tomatoes)

½ cup (4 ounces) freshly squeezed lemon juice

2 tablespoons prepared horseradish

1 tablespoon (½ ounce) Worcestershire sauce

½ cup vodka

1. Place the shot glasses on a baking sheet or large tray. Drop 1 green onion slice into each glass and sprinkle it with a pinch of salt. Add an oyster to each glass, followed by ½ teaspoon oyster liquor, 2 teaspoons tomato puree, 1 teaspoon lemon juice, ¼ teaspoon horseradish, a dash Worcestershire sauce, and 1 teaspoon vodka. Sprinkle another pinch of salt into each glass and float a green onion slice on the surface of the shooter.

2. Refrigerate until ready to serve. Oyster shooters should be consumed within 4 hours.

❋ CATFISH PÂTÉ ❋

FISH PÂTÉ IS A WILDLY POPULAR HORS D'OEUVRE IN SOME PARTS OF THE SOUTH, ESPECIALLY MISSISSIPPI AND GEORGIA, where it's most often made from the local piscine treasure, catfish. The outstanding smoked catfish pâté at the Crown Restaurant in Indianola, Mississippi, has earned the restaurant a great reputation.

In our version, we love how the earthy flavor of unsmoked catfish marries with the aromatic bay leaf, onion, capers, and cognac. If you have a fresh herb like tarragon or thyme on hand, feel free to improvise. Tabasco is a gentle, heat-inducing ingredient, but it can also be used as a garnish. Substitute Pepper Vinegar (page 518) for Tabasco if you wish.

Serve catfish pâté as an hors d'oeuvre spread on crackers or crusty bread or use it as a sandwich filling the next day.

Makes 1½ cups paté; enough grazing for 6 people

TIME: 30 minutes preparation, 1 hour refrigeration

1 cup plus 1 tablespoon dry white wine, such as Pinot Grigio

1 cup Tuesday Chicken Broth (page 534) or Sunday Chicken Broth (page 532)

2 large bay leaves

¾ pound catfish fillets (2 fillets cut from one 2½-pound fish; yields approximately 1 cup cooked and chopped catfish meat)

½ red onion, thinly sliced

1 tablespoon olive oil

8 ounces cream cheese, at room temperature

1 tablespoon capers

½ teaspoon Tabasco or other pepper sauce, plus more to taste

1 teaspoon cognac, bourbon, or dark rum

½ teaspoon freshly ground black pepper

¼ teaspoon kosher salt, plus more to taste

1. In a medium skillet, bring the white wine, broth, and bay leaves to a simmer over medium-high heat. Add the catfish and poach, uncovered, adjusting the heat to maintain a gentle simmer for 10 minutes and flipping the fillets once with a pair of tongs. The fillets will be completely opaque and cooked through.

2. Heat the oil in a small or medium skillet over medium-low heat, cook the onion, stirring regularly, until soft (but not brown), about 6 minutes.

3. When the catfish is finished poaching, remove it with tongs to a cutting board and chop coarsely. Drain the fish in a fine strainer, pressing once or twice to release liquid. Discard the poaching liquid and any juices.

4. Cut the cream cheese into several pieces, place in a large bowl, and, using a fork, blend well with the softened onions, catfish, 1 tablespoon wine, capers, Tabasco, cognac, pepper, and salt. Taste for salt and adjust if necessary. Spoon the pâté into a small bowl, cover, and refrigerate for at least 1 hour or overnight.

5. Serve with crackers or small toasts, lemon wedges, and Tabasco. Catfish pâté keeps for 2 or 3 days in the refrigerator.

❋ PICKLED SHRIMP ❋

PICKLED SHRIMP ARE A LOWCOUNTRY SPECIALTY, A COCKTAIL-HOUR FINGER FOOD PERFECT FOR PASSING AROUND— like shrimp cocktail, but without the need for a messy dipping sauce. They're more complex and alluring than boiled shrimp and no less addictive. We like to conjure up the Mediterranean origins of pickled fish by using the juice of sour oranges. When sour oranges are out of season or otherwise unavailable, a blend of equal parts fresh grapefruit juice, lemon juice, and orange juice makes a fine substitute.

At the cocktail hour, serve pickled shrimp cold on a cheese or pickle plate. We often pass them with Pickled Okra (page 118) or place three of them at the center of a simple green salad.

Makes enough for 6 to 8 people to nibble on, with drinks

TIME: 35 minutes to prepare, 4 hours to marinate

2 quarts plus ½ cup water

1 tablespoon Lee Bros. Shrimp Boil (page 553)

1 pound medium shrimp, heads off and shells on (36–40 per pound; see Sourcery, page 374)

2 large bay leaves

2 whole allspice berries

½ teaspoon whole coriander seeds, toasted in a dry skillet over medium-high flame, until the flavor blooms, about 30 seconds

½ teaspoon whole black peppercorns

½ teaspoon crushed red pepper flakes

1 teaspoon kosher salt

1 cup freshly squeezed sour orange juice, or substitute ⅓ cup freshly squeezed grapefruit juice, ⅓ cup freshly squeezed lemon juice, and ⅓ cup freshly squeezed orange juice

½ cup white wine vinegar

1 teaspoon sugar

1. Fill a 4–6-quart pot with 2 quarts water, add the shrimp boil, and bring to a boil over high heat. Turn off the heat, add the shrimp, and let cook for 1 minute until they're bright pink-orange and slightly firm. Drain and rinse with cold water to keep the shrimp from cooking further.

2. Combine the bay leaves, allspice, coriander, peppercorns, pepper flakes, and salt in a mortar or spice grinder and pound or grind into a powder.

3. Peel the shrimp, reserving the shells for another use (see Sunday Shrimp Broth, page 536), and place them in a medium glass bowl. Add the sour orange juice, vinegar, ½ cup water, sugar, and spice mixture and toss with a spoon to mix. The bowl will be a riot of orange and pink speckled with the black and green spices. Cover the bowl with plastic wrap and refrigerate 4 hours or overnight. Like pickled oysters, pickled shrimp should be consumed within 24 hours from the time they were first placed in the refrigerator.

❋ ROASTED TOMATO ASPIC ❋

MOST ASPICS ARE WIMPY AND LIMPID AS CONSOMMÉ. OURS HAS THE HEFT OF ROASTED PUREED TOMATO, ONION, AND GARLIC, and though it's easier to serve individual aspics from ramekins, we like using our ring mold to make an impressive aspic inner tube, as vividly red and opaque as Sicilian marinara. We place a small bowl filled with homemade mayonnaise in the center. It's delicious and cool, and with a slice of toast makes a terrific light summer lunch.

Makes enough for 6 people, with seconds or leftovers

TIME: 30 minutes to prepare, 4 hours to set

4 tablespoons (¼ cup) extra-virgin olive oil

1 tablespoon white wine vinegar, red wine vinegar, or sherry vinegar

1½ teaspoons kosher salt, plus more to taste

¾ teaspoon freshly ground black pepper, plus more to taste

2 pounds vine-ripened tomatoes (about 3 medium), cored

1 small yellow onion, peeled and quartered

2 cloves garlic, unpeeled

4½ teaspoons (two ¼-ounce packets) unflavored gelatin

¼ cup cold water

¾ cup canned crushed tomatoes

1 teaspoon sugar

3 tablespoons lemon juice (from 2 lemons)

8 cups loosely packed salad greens (about 2 ounces), washed and dried

¼ cup plus 2 tablespoons mayonnaise, preferably Lemony Mayonnaise (page 524)

¼ cup finely chopped fresh dill, washed and dried

1. Heat oven to broil. In a small bowl, whisk together 1 tablespoon olive oil, 1 teaspoon of the vinegar, ½ teaspoon salt, and ¼ teaspoon of the pepper.

2. Place the fresh tomatoes, onion, and garlic in an ovenproof medium roasting pan or skillet. Drizzle with the oil and vinegar mixture, and shake the pan or toss with your hands. Broil until the tops of the tomatoes have blackened and blistered all over, about 6 minutes. Using tongs, turn the tomatoes upside down and broil for 6 minutes more (the onions will have developed some char on them). Remove and cool in the pan. When the tomatoes are cool enough to handle, remove their skins and peel the garlic. Puree the tomatoes, onions, and garlic in a food processor until smooth, about 2 minutes.

3. In a small bowl, dissolve the gelatin in the cold water.

4. In a 2-quart saucepan, combine the tomato puree with the crushed tomatoes, the remaining 2 teaspoons vinegar, the remaining ½ teaspoon each salt and pepper, and the sugar and bring to a simmer over medium-high heat. Turn the heat to low and add the gelatin, whisking thoroughly for a minute to dissolve. Add 2 tablespoons lemon juice, stirring to mix thoroughly, and pour the aspic into eight 4-ounce ramekins or a 4½-cup ring mold.

5. Refrigerate for 4 hours, or until the aspic jiggles stiffly when the mold is gently shaken. To unmold, run the tip of a knife about ¼ inch deep around the outer edge of the aspic (or around the outer and inner edges if using a ring mold). Fill a bowl with hot water from the tap and dip each ramekin or the ring mold into the water for 15 seconds. Hold a large plate or serving platter face down on top of the mold and invert it with a single swift motion. If the aspic doesn't immediately release, dab the mold with a clean dish towel soaked in hot water and tap it with your fingers until the aspic slides out.

6. Place the salad greens in a medium bowl. Whisk the remaining 3 tablespoons olive oil with the remaining 1 tablespoon lemon juice, pour over the salad greens, and toss to coat. Add salt and pepper to taste.

7. Place a bed of greens on each of 6 plates and top with individual aspics or slices of the aspic mold. Dollop a spoonful of mayonnaise on top of the aspic and shower about 2 teaspoons of fresh dill over each plate.

⁂ SPICED PECANS ⁂

IT'S UNCLEAR WHERE SPICED PECANS ORIGINATED, BUT IN THE SOUTH AND MIDWEST THROUGH TO TEXAS, WHERE PECAN trees are legion, a round tin of cinnamon-scented roasted pecans is a popular homemade gift in November and December. The best spiced pecans we've tasted combine the classic Christmas spices with a faint peppery afterburn. They're often seasoned to be both salty and sweet, and the wonderful butterscotch flavor of the nuts does a nice job of binding together all the different spices. It's fun to personalize each batch of spiced pecans with a slightly different formula. Whatever blend of spices you use, there should always be a mysterious note, one spice that's a little hard to place; in our recipe, it's the ground cumin. If you're averse to spicy heat, then omit the cayenne and use 2 teaspoons sweet paprika.

Makes 3 cups; enough for snacking for 8 to 10 people
TIME: 1 hour

1 teaspoon sweet paprika

1 teaspoon ground cayenne

1 teaspoon ground cinnamon

½ teaspoon ground mace or nutmeg

½ teaspoon ground ginger

½ teaspoon ground cumin

1 teaspoon kosher salt

1 tablespoon sugar

4 tablespoons unsalted butter

1 tablespoon honey, sorghum (see Sourcery, page 447), or cane syrup

3 cups shelled raw pecan halves (about ¾ pound)

1. Preheat the oven to 250 degrees.

2. Combine the spices, salt, and sugar in a small bowl and whisk to blend. Set aside 1 teaspoon of the blended mixture.

3. Melt the butter slowly over low heat in a small saucepan. After the foam subsides, turn off the heat and skim the white milk solids from the butter. Whisk the spice mixture into the butter in a slow stream. Whisk the honey into the spiced butter in a slow stream.

4. Put the pecans in a medium mixing bowl and pour the warm spiced syrup mixture over them. Toss the mixture with a spatula or wooden spoon.

5. Spread the pecans evenly on an ungreased cookie sheet and bake on the top rack for 45 minutes. The syrup should look dry (it will still be slightly sticky) and the pecans will have darkened to the color of mahogany. Remove the sheet from the oven and sprinkle the reserved 1 teaspoon spice mixture over the pecans.

6. Serve the nuts as soon as they have cooled, or store them. Stored in an airtight container, roasted pecans will keep 2 weeks.

✺ DEVILED EGGS ✺

DEVILED EGGS, THE BANE OF OUR EXISTENCE WHEN WE WERE CHILDREN, ARE MUCH MORE FUN AND A WHOLE LOT TASTIER now that we're in control. We don't do much to alter the classic mustard- and mayonnaise-based egg-yolk filling (though we do make our own mayonnaise if we're showing off), but we add plenty of flavor and texture with large quantities of great garnishes. Once we've filled the eggs and assembled them on a serving platter, we scatter on finely diced bits of crisp smoked bacon or green onion sliced razor-thin. Their crunchy and yet totally different textures make a nice contrast to the soft filling.

Generous pinches of spicy smoked red paprika and freshly ground black pepper showered over the eggs—and on to the platter—make a pretty presentation. We've also been known to toss a confetti of minced fresh tarragon or flat-leaf parsley over the entire platter. Don't be afraid to engage in a little child's play.

12 large eggs

¼ cup plus 2 tablespoons mayonnaise,
      preferably Lemony Mayonnaise
      (page 524)

2 teaspoons Pepper Vinegar (page 518) or hot
      sauce

2 teaspoons Dijon mustard

½ teaspoon curry powder

For garnish, as desired: thick-cut bacon bits,
      thinly sliced scallions, minced tarragon,
      minced flat-leaf parsley, smoked
      paprika, freshly ground black pepper

1. Pour water to a depth of 2 inches in a pan 10 inches wide or larger. (You want the eggs to cook in one layer.) Bring to a boil over high heat, then turn the heat to very low and gently lower the eggs, one by one, into the water with a spoon or ladle. Maintain as gentle a simmer as possible to avoid cracking, for exactly 14 minutes. Using a slotted spoon, transfer the eggs to a strainer and run cold water over them for a few minutes. Let cool, about 20 minutes.

2. Crack and peel each hard-boiled egg. With a sharp knife, cut the eggs in half lengthwise. Scoop out the yolks into a medium bowl and reserve the empty egg-white halves on a large serving platter. When all the eggs have been yolked, transfer the platter to the refrigerator until they are ready to fill.

3. Add the mayonnaise, pepper vinegar, mustard, and curry powder to the bowl of yolks and mix thoroughly with a fork or a whisk until smooth.

4. Fill each egg white with 1 teaspoon of the yolk mixture, shaping it with the inside of a spoon.

5. To serve, garnish the eggs with bacon, scallions, tarragon, parsley, or smoked paprika, or simply shower them with a few grindings of black pepper.

PIMENTO CHEESE

There was a time when you could eat pimento cheese sandwiches at lunch counters throughout the South, but these days you're more likely to find this lively orange spread of sharp cheddar and mild pepper served in someone's home, on crackers, at the cocktail hour. But wherever you encounter it, you'll probably find it intriguing.

Conventional pimento cheese recipes call for canned pimentos, but we broil a fresh red bell pepper, skin it, and cut it into small dice before mixing it with the cheese. Sure it makes some eyes roll in Charleston, but we think this is a simple route to a more vibrant and sophisticated (and less chemical-tasting) pepper flavor. If that seems like too much work, substitute 3½ ounces of top quality roasted red peppers, piquillo peppers, or pimentos, but dice them finely so they get distributed throughout the spread.

Another pimento cheese note: rainy-day lunches seem to demand Grilled Pimento Cheese Sandwiches (page 92). But when you heat up a typical pimento cheese, the mayonnaise breaks down and the whole spread curdles into an unsightly mess. So you'll find two recipes below, one for a spreadable pimento cheese that's great for all cold applications, and one with a higher proportion of cheese, which is perfect for grilled dishes.

✻ PIMENTO CHEESE FOR SPREADING ✻

Makes 2 cups, about ¾ of a pound; enough for 12 people for grazing, with crackers,
or for 4 large sandwiches

TIME: 20 minutes

1 red bell pepper
8 ounces (about 3 cups) finely grated extra-
    sharp cheddar cheese
2 ounces (about ¼ cup) softened cream
    cheese, cut into pieces

3 tablespoons mayonnaise, preferably Lemony
    Mayonnaise (page 524)
1 teaspoon crushed red pepper flakes
Salt and freshly ground black pepper to taste

1.   Turn on the broiler. Place the pepper on its side in a dry skillet and slide it under the broiler until the skin blackens on the side facing up, about 3 minutes. With tongs, turn the pepper so that an unblackened side faces up, and repeat until the skin is blackened on all sides. Place the pepper in a small bowl, cover it, and let it steam for 5 minutes as it cools down.

2.   Uncover the bowl. When the pepper is cool enough to handle, transfer it to a cutting board, reserving any liquid in the bowl. Remove the blackened skin with your fingers and discard. Using a paring knife, cut open the pepper, remove and discard the stem and seeds, and chop the pepper into ¼-inch dice. You should have a scant ½ cup.

3.　Place the grated cheddar in a medium bowl and add the cream cheese pieces, the mayonnaise, the diced red pepper and its liquid, and the red pepper flakes, distributing them evenly over the cheese. With a rubber spatula or wooden spoon, blend the ingredients together until the spread is thoroughly mixed, about 2 minutes. Season to taste with salt and black pepper.

4.　Transfer the pimento cheese to a plastic container or bowl, cover tightly, and store in the refrigerator. Pimento cheese keeps in the refrigerator for 1 week.

❋ PIMENTO CHEESE FOR GRILLING ❋

GRILLED PIMENTO CHEESE SANDWICHES AND PIMENTO CHEESEBURGERS ARE IN YOUR FUTURE! THIS CHEESE IS STIFFER than the spread, so before we refrigerate it, we compress it into a block that's sliceable.

Makes twelve ⅓-inch-thick slices; enough for 4 sandwiches or 6 cheeseburgers

TIME: 40 minutes preparation, 20 minutes refrigeration

Follow the recipe above, omitting the mayonnaise and creaming the diced red pepper with the cheddar and cream cheese. When the red peppers are thoroughly distributed throughout the cheese mixture, turn the blended cheese out onto a cutting board and use a spatula to gather it into a rectangular block about 5 inches long and 3 inches wide, and 2 inches high. Wrap the cheese tightly in plastic wrap and refrigerate for 1 hour, or until ready to use. Slice and serve. Grillable pimento cheese keeps for 2 weeks in the refrigerator.

FOR EACH GRILLED PIMENTO CHEESE SANDWICH

Two ⅓-inch-thick slices Sally Lunn (page 500) or other white bread
Three ⅓-inch-thick slices Pimento Cheese for Grilling
1 tablespoon unsalted butter

1. Lightly toast the bread in a toaster or under the broiler. Place the cheese between the slices of toast.

2. In a small skillet, melt the butter over medium heat. As soon as the butter is frothy, place the sandwich in the skillet. Pan-fry the sandwich for 6 minutes. Flip it with a spatula, cover the skillet, and cook for 3 minutes more.

3. Transfer to a cutting board, slice the sandwich diagonally with a serrated knife into two portable pieces, and serve with Pickled Jerusalem Artichokes (page 126) or Pickled Okra (page 118).

FOR EACH PIMENTO CHEESEBURGER

1 teaspoon canola oil
6 ounces ground beef (chuck, round, or sirloin, whichever you prefer)
Two ⅓-inch-thick slices Pimento Cheese for Grilling
1 hamburger bun, lightly toasted

1. Pour the oil into a small cast-iron skillet or grill pan and heat over high heat until the oil shimmers and just begins to smoke.

2. Form the ground beef gently into a ball and flatten it into a patty ¾ inch thick. Reduce the heat to medium and cook the burger for 3 minutes on one side. Flip the burger with a spatula, cook for 3 minutes more, and reduce the heat to medium. Flip the burger again, cook for 1½ minutes, and repeat once for medium-rare, 3 times for medium-well, and 5 times for well done. Add the slice of cheese, cover the skillet, and cook for 1 minute more.

3. Set the bottom half of the hamburger bun on a plate and transfer the burger to the bun. Let rest for 2 minutes before dressing with condiments or garnishes. We prefer a slice of tomato and a thin ring of red onion.

❊ HAM RELISH ❊

A FULL 90 PERCENT OF SOUTHERN TEA SANDWICHES ARE MADE WITH EITHER PIMENTO CHEESE, GREEN OLIVE SPREAD, EGG salad, chicken salad, or ham relish. Of these, ham relish is the rarest, perhaps because it's overshadowed by the country ham biscuit. In any case, it's too delicious to be forgotten. You can use any standard baked or boiled ham for this recipe, but add a couple tablespoons of country ham to the mix to really crank up the flavor. Tart, spicy relish and sweet raisins combine beautifully with the salty ham.

Spread a thin layer of pale pink ham relish on white bread—crusts off, of course—and see if the stack of sandwiches doesn't leap off the plate. A cup of jasmine tea, hot or iced, or a glass of fino sherry (the driest style) is a good match for ham relish sandwiches, and a bowl of cashews or roasted almonds rounds out this tea perfectly.

Makes 1½ cups relish; enough for 10 small tea sandwiches

TIME: 25 minutes

⅓ cup plus 1 tablespoon golden raisins

½ pound baked ham, a solid chunk cut into 1-inch cubes or into ¼-inch-thick slices

2 tablespoons softened cream cheese

2 tablespoons mayonnaise, preferably Lemony Mayonnaise (page 524)

1 teaspoon olive oil

1 teaspoon white wine vinegar

3 tablespoons Chowchow (page 108), finely chopped, or another sweet-and-tart relish

¼ teaspoon curry powder

1. Soak the raisins in warm water for 10 minutes and then chop medium-fine in a food processor, until no raisins are left whole. You should have a rough golden puree. Add the ham and continue processing for about 1 minute, until the mixture is smooth and no ham pieces are left whole. Alternatively, put the raisins and ham separately through a meat grinder and combine.

2. Place the ham and raisin mixture in a mixing bowl, add the remaining ingredients, and blend well with a wooden spoon or spatula. Use immediately or cover and refrigerate. Ham relish will keep refrigerated for 3 days.

❊ PICKLED OYSTERS ❊

PICKLED OYSTERS ARE A DELICIOUS HORS D'OEUVRE SERVED WITH ONLY TOOTHPICKS OR ON BUTTERED TOAST POINTS. A classic nineteenth-century southern delicacy, they seem a whole lot more contemporary when you note their similarity to seviche, the citrus-marinated raw fish and shellfish dishes of Spain that have become all the rage in North America in the past decade. A wide range of spices complement these oysters, though some traditional ones, such as nutmeg and clove, overwhelm the oyster's delicate flavor. We use crushed red pepper, bay leaf, allspice, coriander seeds, and black pepper for a lively but respectful brew.

We like to serve pickled oysters in a martini glass with toothpicks and rice crackers on the side, or to place a single oyster on each rib of Bibb lettuce or endive arranged around a platter. A few pickled oysters on a bed of greens and diced fresh tomato make a nice appetizer salad, and they are so flavorful that virtually no dressing is required, just a drizzle of extra-virgin olive oil for the lettuce.

1½ pounds shucked oysters with their liquor
(about 3 cups oysters and liquor, or
36–48 oysters, depending on size; see
Sourcery, page 76)

2 teaspoons kosher salt, plus more to taste

1 teaspoon whole coriander seeds, toasted in a
dry skillet over medium-high flame
until the flavor blooms, about 30
seconds

1 teaspoon whole black peppercorns

1 teaspoon crushed red pepper flakes

3 whole allspice berries

3 large bay leaves

1½ cups dry white wine

¾ cup water

1½ cups white wine vinegar

3 tablespoons lemon juice

1½ teaspoons sugar

¼ cup plus 3 tablespoons fruity extra-virgin
olive oil

3 tablespoons chopped fresh flat-leaf parsley

3 tablespoons minced red onion

1. Taste the oyster liquor, and if it is not salty, sprinkle the oysters with 1–2 teaspoons salt. Place the oysters and the liquor in a 3-quart saucepan and cook over medium heat for about 4 minutes, so the oysters begin to give up some liquid. Turn off the heat, remove the oysters with a slotted spoon, and reserve. Scatter a couple pinches of salt over them. Reserve the oyster liquor in the saucepan.

2. Using a mortar and pestle or spice grinder, combine and pound the coriander seeds, peppercorns, red pepper flakes, allspice berries, and bay leaves until the peppercorns are reduced to a medium-fine powder.

3. Add the white wine, water, vinegar, lemon juice, sugar, and the spice mixture to the oyster liquor in the saucepan. Bring to a boil over medium heat, stirring to combine and to dissolve the sugar. When the brine boils, reduce the heat to medium low and simmer for 8 minutes. Add the reserved oysters and any liquor that has drained from them to the spiced brine, and simmer for 2 minutes, until their edges curl. Transfer the oysters to a medium nonreactive bowl with a slotted spoon.

4.   Simmer the liquid for 5 minutes more, allow to cool 5 minutes, then strain it through a coffee filter or a strainer lined with cheesecloth into the bowl with the oysters. Cover the bowl with plastic wrap and return to the refrigerator for at least 4 hours or overnight.

5.   To serve, drain the oysters, reserving the brine, and place them in a medium bowl. Add the olive oil and 1 tablespoon (or more, to taste) of the brine and toss gently. Garnish with the parsley and onion. Pickled oysters should be refrigerated and consumed within 24 hours from the time they were first placed in the refrigerator.

❊ FIELD CAVIAR: ❊
A SOUTHERN PEA SALAD FOR DIPPING

THIS IS NOT CAVIAR IN THE TRUE SENSE OF THE WORD (THOUGH THERE WAS A TIME WHEN SOUTH CAROLINA HAD ITS OWN, see "Georgetown Caviar," page 101), but rather an appetizer for dipping modeled on "Texas caviar," the pickled black-eyed peas that were invented in the fifties, either by Helen Corbitt, the chef at Dallas's Zodiac Room, or by the east Texas cannery Home Folks to sell in Neiman-Marcus (as usual, culinarians disagree on its origins). We think it's a shame that most folks use black-eyed peas in the dish since there are so many glorious varieties of East Texas shell peas—Lady Cream Peas, White Acre Peas, Crowder Peas—that come up in early summer and don't quit until early fall.

Fortunately, those same peas grow like gangbusters throughout the southeast, and at the Mt. Pleasant, South Carolina, farmers' market, you can get many of them. Varieties of peas—and we'll talk about them more later in the vegetables chapter—are confounding (and they actually are not peas, but legumes). The Crowder Peas we use for this recipe are a buff-brown color, and have an earthy, dusky flavor a lot like a chickpea.

This salad benefits from at least a few hours' refrigeration, and we toss the salad every half-hour or so just to make sure every pea gets coated. But sometimes it's tough to resist eating immediately, and we encourage that too. It's a great side dish for fried fish.

Makes about 2½ cups; enough for 8 for dipping or 4 as a side dish

TIME: 15 minutes preparation, 3 hours refrigeration (optional)

4 cups water

2 teaspoons kosher salt, plus more to taste

2¾ cups Crowder Peas, or other variety shell peas, preferably fresh (about 1 pound)

3 tablespoons red wine vinegar

2 tablespoons extra-virgin olive oil

2 tablespoons mild-tasting olive oil, or canola, peanut, or grapeseed oil

½ teaspoon sugar

1 teaspoon Dijon mustard

½ teaspoon freshly ground black pepper, plus more to taste

¾ cup finely chopped red onion (about 1 medium red onion)

1 cup tightly packed flat-leaf parsley (about ½ ounce, or leaves from about ½ bunch), washed and dried, coarsely chopped

1. Bring the water and 1 teaspoon of the salt to a boil over high heat. Add the peas, and when the water returns to a boil, turn the heat down to medium and continue to cook the peas at a lively simmer—spooning away any froth that may rise to the surface—until they are tender, but still toothsome (about 6 to 10 minutes, depending on the variety). Drain the peas and rinse them in a colander under cold tap water. Let cool completely, and shake off any excess water.

2. In a medium bowl, whisk the vinegar with the oils, the sugar, the Dijon mustard, the remaining salt, and the black pepper until the dressing is emulsified. Add the peas to the bowl and toss to coat evenly. Add the red onion and the flat-leaf parsley and toss again, until they're distributed evenly throughout the salad. Season to taste with salt and black pepper, and if refrigerating, cover and place in the refrigerator. Toss every half-hour, then again before serving.

GEORGETOWN CAVIAR

PERHAPS THE MOST SEDUCTIVE FOOD LEGEND WE KNOW is the tale of Georgetown Caviar. When we were growing up, we heard hush-hush rumors of a high-quality, devilishly cheap sturgeon roe harvested near Georgetown, a South Carolina town just south of Myrtle Beach. We imagined good ol' boys and belles downing caviar burgers and bourbon chasers on beachfront porches. Intrigued, as adults we went sleuthing around Georgetown and were shocked to learn that the rumor had been true— and to discover that harvesting Georgetown caviar is now thoroughly illegal. But for many years, three fishermen in Georgetown harvested Shortnose and Atlantic sturgeon roe and did a very respectable job of salting and curing it. We interviewed several people (including South Carolina game warden Ben Moise) who threw "caviar parties" with large, oozing sandwiches followed by—alas—vodka "shooters." Another source, who insisted on anonymity, reports that cases of caviar in unlabeled, Ball jar pints (and sometimes quarts!) were sold at the Georgetown docks for $9, then $20, and finally $90 per pint when, in 1978, the state stepped in to shut down the harvest!

PICKLES, RELISHES, AND PRESERVES

THE ACT OF PRESERVING AND PICKLING TODAY SEEMS TINGED WITH THE OLD

ways: the dusty jars, boiling caldrons, dank cellars, and hardscrabble days of the era before affordable refrigeration. But "putting up" was often just the opposite—a heady time of great plenty, when the garden was overflowing with color, a time for optimism and maybe a little pride. The prospect of harnessing all the flavors of summer for dinners to come must have seemed as neat a trick as using a microwave does today.

We'd like to liberate southern pickling from its museum aura. Though fewer people are pickling and preserving than they used to, we continue to do it on a modest scale, year-round, simply for flavor's sake. We love the way southern-style pickling concentrates vegetables, fruits, and spices to create condiments with real sass and pep. Relishes and pickled fruits are perfect matches for creamy cheeses and roast meats. And the "freshness," the piquancy and briskness of these condiments makes them versatile—they can play the tart role in any number of sauces, snacks, hors d'oeuvres, pickup meals, and leftover smorgasbords. They can even be elegant. Toss a pound of fresh raw bay scallops with a cup of chowchow, let them cure in the fridge for an hour, and you've got a fantastic scallop cocktail to serve before a meal.

Most importantly, we vow to keep our condiments "live"—we sterilize the jars as best we can, but we don't truly seal them. By doing so we compel ourselves to treat what's inside the jars the way we would a fresh vegetable sauce, as a perishable food, storing them in the refrigerator and using them up steadily over the course of several weeks. These are condiments to keep at the front of the fridge. You'll find yourself dipping a spoon in occasionally just to remind yourself how good they are.

Don't be too high-and-mighty about your produce, either. Some friends of ours won't make a batch of pickled peaches if they can't get South Carolina produce, in season. While we respect and applaud their rectitude, if we can find California peaches with decent flavor in winter, you can bet we're going to take full advantage of them. Preserving so-so winter fruit boosts its flavor by concentrating its juices and spicing it up, and that remarkable transformation will shake the dust off your February blues.

⁂ PICKLED PEACHES ⁂

OBSERVING AND LISTENING TO A SKILLED HOME COOK IS ALWAYS THE QUICKEST WAY TO THE HEART OF A REGION'S FOOD-ways. When we travel to a place we've never been, the first order of business is talking our way into the kitchen of someone who's been growing and cooking in the area for years. But getting in the door can occasionally be difficult. Most times we cultivate a friend of a friend before we leave home, but sometimes even a contact can't ease the way. In that case we rely on our quart jars of pickled peaches, which we call "door openers."

Pickled peaches (sometimes called spiced peaches) are a deliciously sweet-and-sour relish in the round, made with whole fruit. Each tangy pickled peach is broken into smaller pieces on the plate and typically combined with forkfuls of salty ham and rice.

We've found pickled peaches to be a talisman of southern food wisdom. Offering a jar to someone raised in the South immediately shows off your food mettle—you're not intimidated by the jelly-soft orbs, eerily suspended in an orange-tinted syrup. An offering of pickled peaches also shows you're not afraid to work hard to make good food. Scalding the peaches and peeling them can be laborious, particularly if the peaches don't want to give up their skin very easily.

So it was with great trepidation that we asked Gertrude Sassard, of Mt. Pleasant, South Carolina, to put up 144 quart jars of pickled peaches for us to sell to southerners resettled in places like Madison, Wisconsin, and Somerville, Massachusetts. "You have a receipt?" she asked in her clipped drawl, glaring through the tops of her bifocals. Her use of the archaic term for "recipe" seemed a jab at our commitment to the project, to say nothing of her question.

The seventy-something Mrs. Sassard, after all, holds *all* the recipe cards in this town. Her mother-in-law, the "first" Mrs. Sassard, founded her pickling and preserving business, Mrs. Sassard's Handmade, Inc., as a way to get by during the Great Depression. Gertrude has tended to her mother-in-law's recipes with such ferocious devotion that she has overshadowed the memory of the original and become *the* Mrs. Sassard.

We did have a receipt. *Charleston Receipts* includes a fine, if vague, one, contributed by Mrs. R. C. Stoney, née Della Holmes. Though we felt like we were handing Kissinger an essay on Chinese politics, we offered Mrs. Sassard a photocopy of the pickled peach recipe. She set it aside without a glance and said she thought she might have one or two others. When could she begin? we asked. "I don't know—maybe the end of July. It'll depend on when I can get the peaches." Mrs. Sassard won't use grocery store peaches, flown in year-round from California, Mexico, or Brazil. We had to wait until a peach farmer in upstate South Carolina had a good supply of her beloved Red Havens. But the delay didn't appear to bother our customers. As one from Dallas, Texas, commented, "I've waited thirty years for a jar of pickled peaches like the ones my grandmother made; another three months won't make much of a difference."

Makes 2 quarts

TIME: 1½ hours

EQUIPMENT

2 quart-sized, wide-mouth Ball jars, with rims and lids

4 pounds small, firm peaches (about 10, no larger than 2½ inches in diameter)	2 sticks cinnamon
2 pounds sugar	1 tablespoon whole cloves
2 cups cider vinegar	1 heaping tablespoon finely chopped crystallized ginger

1. Assess whether the peaches need to be cut in half by loading them into the quart jars. Ideally, pickled peaches should be left whole, but unless they are extremely small, at most 3 or 4 whole ones will fit in a quart jar. It is perfectly acceptable to cut a few of the peaches, or even all of them, in half so that more fit in each jar, but wait until step 5 to do so.

2. Fill a large bowl or pot (or a sanitized kitchen sink) with ice water and immerse the peaches in it.

106

3. Fill a 6-quart pot three quarters full of water and bring to a boil over high heat. Using tongs, carefully lay the jars on their sides, along with their lids and a slotted metal spoon, in the boiling water to sterilize. Boil for 15 minutes, then remove from the water carefully with a pair of tongs or a jar lifter and set aside.

4. Using tongs or a long fork, plunge the peaches one by one into the boiling water. Hold each peach under the surface for 1 minute and then quickly move it back into the icewater. Peel the skin from each peach immediately, reserve, then go on to the next. (If the peaches are extremely under-ripe and hard, you can peel them using a vegetable peeler.)

5. This is the point at which you should cut the peaches in half if necessary. Cut a few of the peaches, or even all of them, in half through the stem so that more will fit in each jar. If you are halving the peaches, remove the stones. Reserve any juice that drains from the cut peaches.

6. Drain the pot, wash and dry it, and return it to the stovetop. Combine the sugar, vinegar, cinnamon, cloves, ginger, and any drained peach juice in the pot and bring to a boil over medium-high heat, stirring to dissolve the sugar. Turn the heat down to medium-low and maintain a low boil for 20 minutes to concentrate and slightly thicken the syrup. The cider vinegar gives it a slight caramel tint, but the syrup will remain clear throughout the boiling process.

7. Add half the peaches, turn the heat to medium-high, and poach the peaches for 8 minutes, stirring and carefully rolling them occasionally with a wooden spoon so they soften evenly on all sides. They may darken slightly, and cut edges may become slightly feathery.

8. With the sterilized slotted spoon, remove the peaches one by one to the sterilized jars. Repeat with the second batch of peaches. Carefully ladle or pour the hot syrup into the jars until it is ½ inch below the rim. Jiggle the jars to help release any trapped air bubbles, place the lids on them, and seal.

9. Allow the jars to cool and then serve the peaches or refrigerate. Pickled peaches will keep for 4 weeks in the refrigerator.

❋ CHOWCHOW ❋

CHOWCHOW IS A TART, MODERATELY SWEET RELISH MADE
WITH CABBAGE, ONION, AND WHATEVER YOU'VE GOT LEFT IN YOUR
vegetable drawer. We've seen chowchows with bell peppers and carrots minced extra-fine and
served as a sort of sauce for a salty country ham. We've also enjoyed chunky ones made with cut
corn, green beans, and cauliflower, drained of their vinegary brine and served as a vegetable on a
cold plate alongside roast turkey.

This is a simple recipe: vegetables soaked in brine, cooked in a spice-infused vinegar, and bottled. Don't be put off by the length of the ingredient list; the last nine ingredients make up the
spice blend we prefer for its balance of heat and aromatics, which stands up well to the pepper and
spice of the vegetables. You should feel free to simplify it, or refine it to your own taste with your
favorite (and freshest) spices from the cabinet. This chowchow is a terrific relish to use in Lee
Bros. Tartar Sauce (page 526) or in a dressing for Coleslaw (page 195).

Makes 2 pints

TIME: 1 hour to prepare, 4 hours to steep

EQUIPMENT

2 pint-sized, wide-mouth Ball jars, with rims and lids

3 tablespoons kosher salt

1 quart plus ⅓ cup water

1 cup chopped green bell pepper (about ½ large pepper)

3 cups chopped red bell pepper (about 1½ peppers)

2½ cups chopped green cabbage (a little over ¼ large cabbage)

¾ cup chopped onion (about 1 medium onion)

⅔ cup chopped green tomato or tomatillo (about ½ large green tomato or 1 large tomatillo)

2 cups distilled vinegar

½ cup light brown sugar

2 whole allspice berries, smashed

½ teaspoon celery seeds

½ cinnamon stick

½ teaspoon ground cinnamon

½ teaspoon coriander seeds, toasted and smashed

1 teaspoon grated fresh ginger

½ teaspoon ground turmeric

½ teaspoon freshly ground black pepper

½ teaspoon crushed red pepper flakes

1. In a 3-quart pot, dissolve the salt in 1 quart water. Add the green and red peppers, cabbage, onion, and green tomato (or tomatillo) and stir once or twice to distribute. Cover and let soak for at least 4 hours or overnight in the refrigerator.

2. Fill another 3-quart pot three-quarters full of water and bring to a boil over high heat. Using tongs, carefully lay the jars on their sides, along with their lids and a slotted metal spoon, in the boiling water to sterilize. Allow to boil for 15 minutes, then remove from the water carefully with a pair of tongs or a jar lifter and set aside.

3. Drain the brined vegetables and reserve them in a large bowl. Discard the brine.

4. Clean and dry one of the pots. Add the vinegar, ⅓ cup water, and brown sugar and bring to a gentle simmer over low heat, stirring to dissolve the sugar. Stir in all the spices and simmer for 10 minutes to infuse the vinegar with their flavors. Pour the vinegar "tea" into a bowl through a fine-mesh strainer to catch the seeds and woody fragments of spices, then return it to the pot.

5. Add the reserved vegetables and return to a simmer. Continue to simmer, uncovered, for 10 minutes, stirring often, until the vegetables just begin to soften and the color in the peppers begins to fade.

6. Using the sterilized slotted spoon, fill the jars with the chowchow. Carefully pour the liquid into each jar until it is ½ inch below the rim. Place the lids on the jars and seal. Allow to cool and refrigerate. Chowchow will keep in the refrigerator for 4 weeks.

JERUSALEM ARTICHOKES (*HELIANTHUS TUBEROSUS*), sometimes called sunchokes, are the crunchy root of a native North American sunflower, used as a food by Native Americans for centuries before the colonists discovered them. ("Jerusalem" is a corruption of *girasole,* Italian for sunflower.) In the South and up through New York State, the tubers are dug in late fall to early winter. A good, fresh Jerusalem artichoke is as firm as a crisp apple and has a taut, thin skin that should be buff-colored to reddish brown (depending on the variety) and unblemished by darkened scars, scratches, or bruises. A fresh artichoke has an inflated or puffed-up appearance; avoid those that appear to be shriveling. Since the tubers grow below ground in irregular, branching lobes, the harvesters usually divide them into clusters, which can range from a single chestnut-sized lobe to a branching trunk the size of a catcher's mitt. The natural sweetness of the tubers has made them a source of commercial fructose.

❋ JERUSALEM ARTICHOKE RELISH ❋

PERCHED ON THE EAST BANK OF THE COOPER RIVER, CLOSER TO THE SEA THAN CHARLESTON, IS THE OLD FISHING VILlage of Mt. Pleasant, which escaped the rush of development that followed the building of the Grace Memorial Bridge in 1929. The village's tiny, one-block main street is host to a doctor's office, a barbershop, an art gallery, and the Pitt Street Pharmacy, also known to those under the age of eighteen as Miss Linda's. Miss Linda is not the druggist but the person who presides over the soda fountain, doling out candy and whipping up malted milkshakes. This is perhaps the only place in the world where you can order a hot dog garnished with Jerusalem artichoke relish—and charge it to a house account.

The relish dog is a fixture thanks to our friends the Sassards, whose home and workshop, where the relish is made, is just a few doors up from the pharmacy, on Church Street. Gertrude Sassard doesn't let us in on any of her secrets, and we wouldn't dare ask her. But the hallmarks of her relish—the most sought-after relish she makes—are its vivid, turmeric-tinted yellow color, the even balance of sweet and sour tastes, and the triumph of the nutty, naturally sweet Jerusalem artichoke flavor over the potentially domineering apple cider vinegar. The crunch of the artichokes is preserved even though the lobes are finely chopped.

Our version is as close as possible to Mrs. Sassard's, but we take a gentler approach to the vinegar, diluting it with water and white wine vinegar, and we use just a smidgen less sugar. This relish is marvelous on a hot dog, of course, but it's also a natural condiment for sandwiches of all sorts. And like chowchow, artichoke relish makes a terrific tartar sauce and dip when it's blended in equal quantities with mayonnaise.

Makes 2 pints

TIME: 30 minutes to prepare, 4 hours to marinate, 1¼ hours to cook

EQUIPMENT

2 pint-sized, wide-mouth Ball jars, with rims and lids

1 tablespoon plus 2 teaspoons salt

1 quart plus ½ cup water

4 cups peeled and finely chopped Jerusalem artichokes (about 1¼ pounds)

1 cup finely chopped green cabbage (about ⅓ pound)

2 cups finely chopped yellow onion (about 2 medium onions)

1 cup finely chopped green or red bell pepper (about 1 large pepper)

2 cups cider vinegar

1 cup white wine vinegar

1 teaspoon mustard seeds, smashed

2 teaspoons grated peeled fresh ginger

½ teaspoon ground turmeric

½ teaspoon ground white pepper

¼ teaspoon ground mace

3 tablespoons sugar

1. In a 3-quart nonreactive bowl, dissolve 1 teaspoon of the salt in 1 quart cool water. Add the artichokes, cabbage, onion, and green pepper and stir once or twice to distribute. Cover and let soak in the brine for at least 4 hours or overnight in the refrigerator.

2. Fill a 3-quart pot three-quarters full of water and bring to a boil over high heat. Using tongs, carefully set the jars on their sides, along with their lids and a metal spoon, into the boiling water to sterilize. Boil for 15 minutes, then remove carefully from the boiling water with a pair of tongs or a jar lifter and set aside.

3. Drain the brined vegetables and reserve them in a large bowl. Discard the brine.

4. Clean and dry the pot. Add the vinegars and ½ cup water and bring to a boil over high heat. Stir in the spices, sugar, and remaining teaspoon of salt, lower the heat to medium-low, and simmer, uncovered, for 10 minutes.

5. Add the vegetables, and when the mixture returns to a simmer, continue gently simmering, uncovered, for 40 minutes, stirring occasionally, until the mixture appears to thicken and soften slightly.

6. When the relish is chunky and thick but still liquid (the consistency of a thin chutney), spoon it into the sterilized jars with the sterilized spoon. Place the lids on the jars and seal. When the relish has cooled, store in the refrigerator. Artichoke relish will keep about 4 weeks in the refrigerator.

The Sassards' factory goes through hundreds of cases of canning jars every year.

❋ HOT PEPPER JELLY ❋

HOT PEPPER JELLY SERVED ALONGSIDE A BLOCK OF CREAM CHEESE FOR SPREADING ON CRACKERS IS AMONG THE MOST POPU-lar hors d'oeuvres in the South. We love it; it's easy to make, and the flavor of sweet peppers against a mild, creamy white cheese like ricotta, Philadelphia cream cheese, or goat cheese is a timeless pairing, like tomato and basil or lamb and rosemary.

Our jelly does away with the green or red food coloring that's ubiquitous in southern pepper jellies and gets its color instead from the peppers themselves—fine bits of red and green bell pepper and fresh jalapeño pulp. Another unconventional tweak is the reconstituted dried chile—a pasilla, guajillo, or ancho—we use to give the jelly a jolt of deep, earthy pepper flavor. You may not even notice it; the raisiny Mexican chile crouches just beneath the fresh, sweet bell pepper and jalapeño flavors, offering a third peg, a bit of complexity, to the blend.

In terms of spicy heat, this jelly is quite moderate, but it's easy to turn it up: just increase the proportion of jalapeños to bell peppers while keeping the total volume of pepper pulp constant.

Makes 2 pints

TIME: 45 minutes to prepare, 15 minutes to cook, 2 weeks to set

EQUIPMENT

2 pint-sized, wide-mouth Ball jars, with rims and lids

1 dried hot chile (ancho, pasilla, guajillo, or mulato), split open with scissors, seeds and stem removed

2 cups chopped red bell pepper (about 1 large pepper)

2 cups chopped green bell pepper (about 1 large pepper)

1 cup chopped jalapeño pepper (about 4 peppers)

¾ cup distilled vinegar

⅔ cup sugar

2 teaspoons kosher salt

1 box (1¾ ounces) Sure-Jell or other brand fruit pectin

1. Fill a 3-quart pot three-quarters full of water and bring to a boil over high heat. Using tongs, carefully set the jars and lids, along with a slotted metal spoon, in the boiling water to sterilize. Boil for 10 minutes, then remove from the water carefully with a pair of tongs or a jar lifter and set aside.

2. Put the dried chile in a small bowl and pour very hot water over it to cover. Let stand for 10 minutes. The chile will become more fleshy and pliable and will tint the water slightly. Remove the chile and shake off the excess water, but do not dry it.

3. Pulse the fresh peppers and the reconstituted chile in a food processor with 2 tablespoons of the vinegar for 6 seconds (3 pulses of 2 seconds each), until the peppers are finely shredded but with the red and green shreds still distinct in an inky red slurry. Do not liquefy.

4. Transfer the peppers to a 3-quart pot, add the remaining vinegar, the sugar, and the salt, and bring to a vigorous boil over high heat. Lower the heat to medium and simmer for 3 minutes. Stir in the pectin, return to a boil, and continue to boil for 1 minute. The mixture will remain a deeply colored red-and-green slurry and will still be quite thin in consistency. It will thicken later, in the refrigerator.

5. Carefully pour the hot jelly mixture into the sterilized jars. Place the lids on the jars, seal, and allow to cool. The jelly will keep in the refrigerator for at least 2 months.

SOURCERY: FRUIT PECTIN

AS EASY AS HOT PEPPER JELLY IS TO MAKE, FINDING fruit pectin can be vexingly difficult, especially in big cities. Few grocery stores stock it, so we order the Sure-Jell brand online from the Kraft website, www.kraft.com.

❁ PICKLED OKRA ❁

OKRA IS AS IMPORTANT TO SOUTHERN COOKS AS SQUASH IS TO NORTHERN ONES. ITS MEATY TEXTURE AND BRAMBLY FLAVOR, somewhat like eggplant crossed with asparagus, add nice variety to late summer's tidal wave of zucchini and tomatoes. We eat okra sliced and fried (page 217), crisply pickled, and cut and tossed raw into salads. We sauté it with tomatoes as a side dish, and reduce it to utter silkiness in stews and gumbos (pages 259 and 267).

The delicious okra pod is the unripe fruit of a shrub (*Hibiscus esculentus*) that's closely related to hibiscus. Native to the Nile region of northeastern Africa, okra is thought to have first arrived in the Americas with French settlers in Louisiana. Slaves probably brought the plant from western Africa as a subsistence vegetable, too, along with black-eyed peas, sesame seeds, and rice. Okra has since become an important ingredient in South Asian and Latin American kitchens, and travelers and horticulturists have distributed it so widely that nowadays the sun-loving plant is farmed on every continent save Antarctica.

One reason okra hasn't become a popular ingredient in more North American households may be its reputation for having a slimy consistency. Blame the cooks, not the vegetable. When heated slowly, okra releases complex sugars and moisture that give okra a slippery, ropy consistency, making it useful as a thickener for lusty stews and Creole gumbos, but hard to love when served all on its own. As any southern chef will tell you, there are plenty of tricks for avoiding slick okra. The simplest is to sear it quickly over high heat in a hot, nearly dry skillet or grill it over glowing barbecue coals, which adds an alluring smokiness. Another excellent way to keep the ooze under control is to cook the pods whole instead of slicing them.

Freshness, too, is crucial to crisp okra. Choose pods that are firm and brightly hued, with few, if any, black spots on them. An okra pod becomes tougher the longer it grows, and once it reaches about 5 inches it becomes dramatically more fibrous and woody. Two to three-inch pods are best.

Our all-time favorite way to experience okra is pickled—a quick, easy method that preserves its crunch and at the same time allows us to embroider its flavor with judicious doses of fresh garlic and dill and hot chiles. One of our favorite surprises for okra-shy guests is to serve spears of pickled okra as an hors d'oeuvre, with cocktails. We love to watch their eyes light up as they discover a crisp, addictive snack. A spear or two of pickled okra is also a perfect companion to a Harlem Meat Loaf (page 362) sandwich or any other meaty sandwich.

Makes 2 quart jars

TIME: 2 hours to soak, 30 minutes to prepare

EQUIPMENT:

2 quart-sized, wide-mouth Ball jars, with rims and lids

1½ pounds okra	4 large cloves garlic, peeled and smashed
1 quart plus 1½ cups water	4 cups distilled white vinegar
1 tablespoon plus 2 teaspoons kosher salt	2 teaspoons sugar
2 dried hot chiles (preferably Thai)	½ teaspoon whole black peppercorns
4 sprigs fresh dill	

1.　Fill a 3-quart pot three-quarters full of water and bring to a boil over high heat. Using tongs, carefully set the jars on their sides, along with their lids, in the water to sterilize. Boil for 15 minutes, then remove from the water with tongs or a jar lifter and set aside.

2.　Trim off any woody millimeters of stem from the pods with a sharp knife. In a bowl, combine the okra with 1 quart of the water and 1 tablespoon salt and stir to dissolve the salt. Cover with plastic wrap and set on a cool countertop (out of direct sunlight) or in the refrigerator to soak for 2 hours.

119

ALTHOUGH MOST GREENGROCERS SELL FRESH OKRA in season, we enjoy growing our own at our weekend house in upstate New York. The plant is easy to start from seed, and if started early enough will produce bumper crops of pods by the end of the summer. The most productive and to our palates the best-tasting cultivar for the garden is 'Clemson Spineless,' developed in South Carolina, which puts out beautiful yellow-white blooms followed by smooth pea-green pods. Another variety with excellent, honeysuckle-like flavor is the heirloom 'Burgundy,' available through many garden catalogues; its stunning maroon-colored pods make it an exotic conversation piece in the garden. In either case, the mature okra plants will bloom continuously for weeks—a nuisance for the commercial farmer, who must harvest daily throughout the season instead of in one fell swoop, but a wonderfully constant source of pale yellow flowers and food for those of us who have planted it in a sunny corner of the kitchen garden. Picking daily not only ensures freshness but maximizes plant productivity.

3. When the okra has finished soaking, drain and rinse the okra pods, and pat them dry with paper towels or a clean dish towel. Using tongs, place 1 chile, 2 sprigs of dill, and 2 garlic cloves in each of the jars, then pack the jars with the okra.

4. In a second 3-quart pot, combine the vinegar, 1½ cups water, sugar, peppercorns, and the remaining 2 teaspoons of salt and bring to a boil over high heat. When the water boils, reduce the heat to medium-high and simmer for 4 minutes.

5. Pour the hot vinegar brine over the okra (using a funnel, if necessary) until it is ¼ inch below the rim of the jars (the okra will absorb ½ inch of brine over the next 30 minutes). Place the lids on the jars and seal, then turn the jars upside down so they are standing on the lids. Pickled okra will keep for about 4 weeks in the refrigerator.

Jars of pickled okra cool on a card table in the Sassards' working kitchen.

❋ PICKLED CORN ❋

NATURALLY SOURED CORN IS A CLASSIC APPALACHIAN PICKLE THAT WE FIRST ENCOUNTERED IN THE HOME OF BOB AND Zedia Ellis in Stoney Creek, in Eastern Tennessee (see "Sourcery: Sorghum Molasses," page 447). They packed their corn, still on the cob, into pails with a salty brine and stored it in a dark, cool attic until the acetic bacteria in the air soured the corn's sugars, which took about two months. They then cut the kernels from the cobs and sealed them in Mason jars for longer storage. The Ellises taught us the highest use of pickled corn: frying it in bacon fat and eating it as a brunch vegetable.

We enjoyed what the Ellises prepared for us so much we decided to reverse-engineer it into a "fresh" pickle or relish, so we could make it year-round from grocery-store corn. Our pickled corn gets its tartness from vinegar instead of natural souring, but it's every bit as delicious fried in smoky bacon fat. We can't resist sprinkling a little chili powder or smoked paprika on it and squirting on some lime juice to lighten it before serving. A broad spoonful of pickled corn is a great relish to accompany huevos rancheros and ties together a simple, hearty breakfast of fried eggs and black beans.

Makes 2 pints
TIME: 15 minutes to prepare, 30 minutes to cook, 24 hours to steep

EQUIPMENT

2 pint-sized, wide-mouth Ball jars, with rims and lids

4 cups fresh corn kernels, cut from the cob (about 6 ears), or 4 cups frozen sweet corn, defrosted

1 tablespoon kosher salt

2 cups distilled white vinegar

⅔ cup water

2 tablespoons plus 1 teaspoon sugar

1 teaspoon ground turmeric

¼ teaspoon ground mace

1 whole clove

1. Fill a 3-quart pot three-quarters full of water and bring to a boil over high heat. Using tongs, carefully set the jars on their sides, along with their lids and a slotted metal spoon, in the boiling water to sterilize. Boil for 15 minutes, then remove from the water carefully with a pair of tongs or a jar lifter and set aside.

2. In a large bowl, toss the corn with 1 tablespoon salt. Cover the bowl with plastic wrap and set aside.

3. In a second 3-quart pot, combine the vinegar, water, sugar, and spices. Bring to a simmer over medium heat and continue to simmer for 20 minutes, uncovered. The vinegar will be fragrant, thoroughly infused with the spices, and tinted a vivid yellow by the ground turmeric.

4. Add the corn. Bring to a low boil over medium-high heat and boil for 5 minutes. The corn will soften slightly but should still be crisp and will have absorbed some of the flavor of the tart vinegar brine.

5. With the slotted spoon, transfer the hot corn into the jars. Carefully pour the hot liquid over the corn (using a funnel, if necessary) until it is ½ inch from the rim. Place the lids on the jars and seal. Allow them to cool, then store in the refrigerator. The corn and spice flavors will meld nicely after 24 hours and will continue to steep over the course of a week. Pickled corn will keep for about 4 weeks in the refrigerator.

❊ PICKLED SCALLIONS ❊

WE STARTED PICKLING SCALLIONS ONE FALL WHEN WE RAN OUT OF OUR SUPPLY OF PICKLED RAMPS, AND YOU CAN USE either onion in this recipe. Ramps (*Allium tricoccum*) are the garlicky wild onions that shoot through the forest floor in the Appalachian Mountains in late March and early April. Eaten raw, ramp bulbs will clear your sinuses as effectively as a habanero pepper. But you can tame them easily by pickling them, and when you do, you've got an appetizing and boldly flavored onion pickle that steals the show, whether it's on an hors d'oeuvres plate, tucked into a sandwich, or dropped into a martini.

A pickled ramp or scallion has such a clean, refreshing flavor on its own that we take a minimalist approach to brining these: distilled vinegar, a bit of fresh garlic, a touch of dried chile pepper, salt, and sugar. Scallions taste somewhat more muted than ramps, but for the ten months that ramps are out of season, scallions make a fantastic substitute.

Makes 2 pints
TIME: 12 hours to brine, 20 minutes to prepare, 2 days to steep

EQUIPMENT

2 pint-sized, wide-mouth Ball jars, with rims and lids

2 pounds scallions or ramps (about 30)

¼ cup plus 2 tablespoons kosher salt

1 quart plus 1 cup water, at room temperature

4 cloves garlic, peeled

4 dried red hot chiles (Thai or chiles de arbol)

2 cups distilled vinegar

2 teaspoons sugar

1. With a small paring knife, trim the roots and any outer leaves that look tired or wilted from the scallions. Cut them crosswise 4 inches from the root end and reserve the greens for another use (Kilt Lettuce and Ramps, page 203).

2. In a 2-quart bowl, dissolve ¼ cup salt in 1 quart water. Add the scallions, garlic, and chiles, and weigh them down with a small, clean plate to keep them submerged, if necessary. Cover the bowl with plastic and store in the refrigerator overnight.

3. Fill a 3-quart pot three-quarters full of water and bring to a boil over high heat. Using tongs or a jar lifter, carefully set the jars on their sides, along with their lids, in the boiling water to sterilize. Boil for 15 minutes, then remove the jars from the water with tongs or a jar lifter and set aside.

4. Pour the vinegar and 1 cup water into a 1-quart saucepan. Add the remaining 2 tablespoons salt and the sugar and bring to a boil.

5. Drain the scallions, garlic, and chiles. Dip the tongs into the boiling vinegar brine for a few minutes, then use them to transfer the scallions, garlic, and chiles to the jars. If the bulb ends of the scallions are stout, pack half of them into each jar with their root ends facing down, and the remaining half with their root ends facing up, to maximize the space in each jar. Pour the brine into the jars and tap them to release any air bubbles. Place the lids on the jars, seal, and set aside to cool. Allow the scallions to steep in the refrigerator for 2 days before serving. Pickled scallions will keep for about 4 weeks in the refrigerator.

❋ PICKLED JERUSALEM ARTICHOKES ❋

LET'S HEAP PRAISE ON THE ANONYMOUS FOLKS RESPON-
SIBLE FOR GETTING JERUSALEM ARTICHOKES BACK INTO FARMERS'
markets and onto the menus of restaurants all across America. Everyone makes fun of food
trends—remember the truffle oil craze?—but when the trendsetters shine a light on delicious,
old-school, hard-to-find foods like fresh ramps and Jerusalem artichokes, is anyone really the
worse off for it?

Pickling Jerusalem artichokes in whole chunks shows off these tubers' crisp texture and sweet
nuttiness to great effect. And they're a sleeper: if you have only one type of pickle to serve on a
plate, you might need something else—pimento cheese and crackers, say, or hot-pepper jelly and
cream cheese. But if you add a couple lobes of artichoke to your pickle plate, it's all the hors
d'oeuvre you really need. Adjust the sugar in this pickle brine to your taste.

Makes 2 pints
TIME: 4 hours soaking, 45 minutes preparation

EQUIPMENT

2 pint-sized, wide-mouth Ball jars, with rims and lids

1¾ pounds Jerusalem artichokes, washed and patted dry
1 quart water
2 tablespoons kosher salt
3 cups cider vinegar
1 cup water
1 tablespoon plus 2 teaspoons sugar

½ teaspoon whole black peppercorns
¼ teaspoon coriander seed
3 whole allspice berries
½ teaspoon whole red peppercorns (optional)
¼ teaspoon ground turmeric
2 dried red hot chiles (Thai or chiles de arbol)

1. Bring a 3-quart pot, three quarters full of water, to a boil. Carefully set the jars on their sides, along with their lids and a slotted metal spoon, in the boiling water to sterilize. Allow to boil for 15 minutes, then remove from the water carefully with a pair of tongs or a jar lifter and set aside.

2. Peel and trim the artichokes, separating them into smaller lobes. Cut them further down into chunks that are sized about halfway between a chestnut and a grape (you should end up with about 4 cups of artichoke chunks).

3. In a bowl, combine the artichokes with the quart of water and one tablespoon of the salt, stir to dissolve, and soak for 4 hours on a shady countertop or overnight in the refrigerator. Then drain and rinse the artichokes and pat them dry with paper towels or a clean dishcloth.

4. Bring the vinegar and the cup of water to a boil in a 3-quart stockpot with the remaining salt, the sugar, and all the spices except the red chiles, and boil for 4 minutes. The steaming-hot vinegar brine will become fragrant as it steeps the spices, but its viscosity will still be quite thin.

5. Using the slotted spoon, place one pepper in each of the jars, then carefully pack the jars with the artichokes and carefully pour the hot vinegar brine over the artichokes up to ½ inch below the neck. Divide any spices that remain in the pan between the jars. Seal the jars, allow to cool, and store in the refrigerator. Pickled artichokes will keep for about 4 weeks in the refrigerator.

⚜ FIG PRESERVES ⚜

EVERYONE WE KNOW IN CHARLESTON LOVES FIG PRE-
SERVES EXCEPT FOR OUR FRIEND JOHN ZIEGLER, A RETIRED BOOK-
store owner who happens to have one of the largest fig trees in town in his backyard on
Wentworth Street. Still, John knows how prized fig preserves are, and every year he makes ninety
jars from his harvest to give to friends at Christmastime. We make an even trade: cheese straws
for preserves.

We don't know quite what we'd do without fig preserves. Spread over buttered biscuits or a
slice of toast, their mellow, winy flavor has brightened up countless mornings. But they also make
a wonderful addition to a cheese plate; they're delicious baked into a cake (see Fig Preserve and
Black Walnut Cake, page 472); and a dollop over store-bought vanilla ice cream is a simple, decadent dessert. And we've often wondered why more sandwich makers don't get hip to fig preserves;
they dress up a simple smoked turkey, Swiss cheese, or meatloaf sandwich in a way that few other
condiments can.

Most of the local figs in Charleston, known as sugar figs, have greenish yellow skins that
darken when they're ripe. They make a lovely preserve that's the brown color of a bitter-orange
marmalade. We didn't think sugar-fig preserves could be improved upon until we used some
purple-skinned figs we found at the Asheville, North Carolina, farmers' market instead. The preserves had the same flavor as the ones we were accustomed to, but the color was a glorious bright
magenta.

Makes 2½ pints

TIME: 5 minutes to prepare, 1⅔ hours to cook, 2 days to blend

EQUIPMENT

2 pint-sized, wide-mouth Ball jars or 1 quart-sized jar
and one 10-ounce jar, with rims and lids

1½ cups sugar
1 cup water
8 cups whole ripe figs, purple-skinned if
    available, stems trimmed

3 small lemons, sliced paper-thin
One 1-inch-long piece fresh ginger, peeled and
    cut into ⅛-inch rounds

1. Fill a 3-quart pot three-quarters full of water and bring to a boil over high heat. Using tongs, carefully set the jars on their sides, along with their lids and a long-handled metal spoon, in the boiling water to sterilize. Boil for at least 15 minutes, then remove from the water with the tongs or a jar lifter and set aside.

2. In another 3-quart pot, combine the sugar and water and stir to dissolve. Add the figs, lemons, and ginger, cover, and cook over medium heat, occasionally stirring gently, until the liquid comes to a simmer, about 8 minutes.

3. Turn the heat to low and cook for 1 hour, then vent the preserves by tilting the cover slightly into the pan and cook for 30 minutes more, until the mixture is thickly syrupy and the figs are very soft.

4. Transfer the preserves to the jars with the sterilized spoon. Place the lids on the jars, seal, and set aside to cool. Refrigerate for 2 days before using. Fig preserves will keep for about 4 weeks in the refrigerator.

❋ PUMPKIN CHIP PRESERVES ❋

THESE ARE AMONG OUR FAVORITE SWEET PRESERVES, PREPARED IN THE CLASSIC LOWCOUNTRY STYLE, WHOSE HALLMARK is paper-thin slices of lemon and minced candied ginger. Actually, jack-o'-lanterns (*Cucurbita pepo*) are not typically used; the traditional "pumpkin" used by Mrs. Sassard and others is a close cousin referred to colloquially as "cow pumpkin." They often grow to the size of a small guitar and have the pear-like shape of a blue Hubbard squash (*Cucurbita maxima*) and the slightly pink buff color of a butternut squash (*Cucurbita moschata*). "Chip" refers to the way the pumpkin is chopped into flat pieces to make the preserves softer and more spreadable.

One fall weekend in New York, eager for pumpkin chip preserves we decided to try using butternut squash, since its color so closely resembles the cow pumpkin's. The test batch worked perfectly, and was nearly indistinguishable from the original, with the same soft texture, luminous deep orange color, and nutty flavor. It's hard to know what was more exciting about that discovery—knowing that we could make pumpkin chip preserves year-round or figuring out something new to do with those ubiquitous butternut squashes.

Makes 2 pints

TIME: 1½ hours to prepare, 8 hours to marinate

EQUIPMENT

2 pint-sized, wide-mouth Ball jars, with rims and lids

4 pounds butternut squash or cow pumpkin
1 cup lemon juice (from 6–8 lemons)
1 cup very warm water
2 cups sugar

1 tablespoon lemon peel (from ½ lemon)
1 tablespoon finely chopped crystallized
    ginger (about 1 large slice)

1. Peel and seed the squash, cut it into chips roughly ⅛ inch thick, ½ inch wide, and 1 inch long, and put the chips in a large bowl. (You can use a food processor to chip the squash by cutting the squash into sections and feeding them through the neck onto the slicing blade.)

2. In a small bowl, mix the lemon juice with the warm water and sugar, and stir until the sugar dissolves. Pour the liquid over the squash, cover the bowl with plastic wrap, and marinate overnight in the refrigerator.

3. The next day, fill a 3-quart pot three-quarters full of water and bring to a boil over high heat. With tongs carefully set the jars on their sides, along with their lids and a long-handled, slotted metal spoon, in the boiling water to sterilize. Boil for 15 minutes, then remove from the water with tongs or a jar lifter and set aside.

4. Pour the squash chips and the marinade into another 3-quart pot and add the lemon peel and ginger. Cook over medium-high heat until the syrup boils. Reduce the heat to medium-low and simmer until the chips have darkened and become slightly translucent, 35 to 40 minutes. Don't be alarmed if the syrup seems thin; it will thicken as it cools.

5. Transfer the chips to the jars with the sterilized spoon. Carefully pour the syrup into each jar until it is ½ inch from the rim. Slide a knife into each jar and agitate the preserves so that any air bubbles rise to the surface. Place the lids on the jars, seal, and set aside to cool. Store in the refrigerator. Pumpkin chip preserves keep for about 6 weeks in the refrigerator.

❊ SCUPPERNONG PRESERVES ❊

THE SCUPPERNONG IS ONE OF THE FEW INDIGENOUS GRAPES OF THE AMERICAN SOUTHEAST, A WILD TANGLE OF FRUIT that can be found at the edges of the forest canopy each August from North Carolina to northern Florida. Few European grape varieties will withstand the intense heat of a deep southern summer, and none of them thrive here, so today the thick-skinned, brassy green scuppernongs are cultivated in small vineyards throughout the region. Although they are beloved in the Lowcountry, like most native grape varieties, they are underappreciated elsewhere. Out-of-state grocery chains opening stores here for the first time have to be begged and practically picketed to stock them. And for no good reason, since their flavor is huge: a burst of nectar with hints of honeysuckle, orange flower, and jasmine, with a spike of acidity and lingering accents of cola and ripe melon. Next to a scuppernong, a grocery-store table grape has all the charm of warm sugar water.

To our palates, the scuppernong is the most floral of the southern native grape varieties, the muscadines (*Vitis rotundifolia*). Other muscadines have a lovely banana or cinnamon-and-coconut character, and some varieties have deep burgundy skins. The labrusca or fox grapes (*Vitis labrusca*) found up north, like Concords and Niagaras, are floral and musky—cola-like—too, but their flavor is slightly less loud, maybe an eight to a scuppernong's eleven. What is common to all American grape varieties is their deeply individual character.

Which makes it all the more puzzling why we've yet to find commercially produced scuppernong preserves that actually preserve the grapes' amazing flavor. Even among small-batch local brands, we've found few that tasted any different from standard-issue grape jelly, whose flavor is flattened by dilution, overcooking, cheap grapes, and commercial-grade sugars.

Making scuppernong preserves takes a lot of willpower, since the grapes are so delicious and addictive eaten out of hand. But the flavor of native grapes is the essence of a hot summer's end, and when you come across a jar of scuppernong preserves in the pantry in deep October, you may scream with joy. Scuppernongs aren't easy to come by outside the South (see "Sourcery: Muscadine Grapes," page 135), but you can substitute the much more widely available labruscas, which are grown from New York to Wisconsin to Washington State.

The color of pure scuppernong preserves is as one grape grower put it, "ucky, like dirty dishwater." Our trick is to use a small proportion of red-hulled muscadines (or any other red grape) to impart a lovely violet color.

Makes 2 pints

TIME: 30 minutes to prepare, 45 minutes to cook, 2 days to blend

EQUIPMENT

2 pint-sized, wide-mouth Ball jars, with rims and lids

3 pounds scuppernong or other muscadine grapes or labrusca grapes, such as Concords or Niagaras (about two quarts)

¼ cup lemon juice (from 2–3 lemons)
1 cup sugar
Two 2-inch-long strips lemon peel

1.   Fill a 3-quart pot three-quarters full of water and bring to a boil over high heat. Using tongs or a jar lifter, carefully set the jars on their sides, along with their lids and a long-handled metal spoon, in the boiling water to sterilize. Boil for 15 minutes, then remove from the water with the tongs or a jar lifter and and set aside.

2.   Set 2 large bowls, one for the skins, and one for the pulps and juice, on the kitchen counter. Separate the grape pulps from their skin by pointing each grape's stem scar toward one bowl and pinching the opposite side of the grape. The pulp should fall into the bowl, along with some grape juice. Press the skin between your thumb and forefinger, using a rubbing motion to extract any further juice that clings to the inside of the skin. Place the empty skins in the second bowl.

3.   Strain the juice from the bowl of pulps and set aside (you should have about 2 cups). Transfer the pulps to a 2-quart sauté pan and add any remaining juice or, if there is none, ½ cup water. Cover and cook over medium heat until the pulps collapse and begin to give up their seeds, about 15 minutes. Underripe grapes will take longer; you may need to add a few tablespoons water to prevent scorching.

4.   While the pulps cook, chop the grape skins coarsely until you have 1½ cups, tightly packed. Place the skins in a medium saucepan with ½ cup of the reserved grape juice and the lemon juice. Cover and cook over medium heat for 15 minutes, until the skins have softened and become slightly paler. Remove from the heat and reserve.

5.   When the pulps have collapsed, pour them into a medium-fine strainer or colander set over a large bowl and press them through with the back of a wooden spoon, leaving the seeds behind. (Don't use a food mill: the blades break the seeds into a sandy substance that makes the preserves bitter.) You should have about 1¾ cups of seeded pulp.

6.   Add the pulp and the remaining 1½ cups reserved grape juice to the skins, then add the sugar and lemon peel. Bring to a boil over medium-low heat and simmer, uncovered, for 15 minutes, until the volume is reduced by a fifth. Don't be alarmed if the syrup seems thin; it will thicken as it cools.

7.   Transfer the preserves to the jars with the sterilized spoon. Tap the jars so that any air bubbles rise to the surface. Place the lids on the jars, seal, and set aside to cool. Refrigerate for 2 days before using. Scuppernong preserves will keep for 4 weeks in the refrigerator.

Vineyards throughout the southeast grow native American grape varieties, such as these bronze-colored scuppernongs from Three Star Vineyard in Aiken, South Carolina.

IN U.S. CITIES OUTSIDE THE SOUTH, MUSCADINES CAN be found at greengrocers that specialize in southern produce. Young Spring Farm Fruit and Vegetables, in Harlem (62 West 125th Street, New York, NY 10027; 212-348-3481), is one such market. If you can't find muscadines or a suitable substitute, the Texas grower Ceres Specialty Fruit has both green and purple ones available by mail-order (Ceres Specialty Fruit, P.O. Box 1106, Orange, TX 77630; 409-381-0239; www.ceresfruit.com).

❋ WATERMELON RIND PRESERVES ❋

WATERMELON RIND PRESERVES ON BUTTERED BISCUITS OR TOAST IS ONE OF OUR FAVORITE BREAKFASTS, AND THESE DAYS watermelons are available virtually all year long. Until recently, the labor-intensive recipe for watermelon rind preserves kept us from making them at all. The typical recipe involves one (if not two, even three) overnight soakings in lime and/or salty brine; scraping down the watermelon flesh until it's snow-white; and making sure the rind is the right thickness (it varies widely from melon to melon). We took the traditional recipe back to the drawing board and came up with quicker, easier, and more delicious watermelon rind preserves than any we've made before.

Another thing: don't spend precious kitchen time scooping off the pink flesh until the rind is bone-white. A few millimeters of pale pink watermelon clinging to the rind makes the preserves absolutely gorgeous, like rose-tinted quartz. A 6¼-pound slice of a larger, whole melon with a medium-thick rind should yield 8 cups of peeled rind and make 2 pints of preserves.

We're usually left with more gingery, lemony syrup than we need. We bottle that, too, and use it to glaze a Baked Country Ham (page 327). We also substitute the syrup in drink recipes that call for simple syrup; it gives a glass of Lee Bros. Sweet Tea (page 23) an otherworldly sweetness, and it was the inspiration for our Garden and Gun Cocktail (page 52).

EQUIPMENT

2 pint-sized, wide-mouth Ball jars, with rims and lids

One 6–7-pound piece watermelon
1 cup lemon juice (from 6–8 lemons)
1 cup water
2 cups sugar

One 1-inch-long piece fresh ginger, peeled and
    sliced into ¼-inch-thick rounds
Six 4-inch-long strips lemon peel (from
    ½ lemon)

1. Fill a 3-quart pot three-quarters full of water and bring to a boil. Using tongs, carefully set the jars on their sides, along with their lids and a long-handled, slotted metal spoon, in the boiling water to sterilize. Boil for 15 minutes, then remove from the water with tongs or a jar lifter and set aside.

2. Scoop the flesh from the watermelon and reserve for another use. With a vegetable peeler or a knife, peel the thick green skin from the watermelon rind and discard. Cut the rind roughly into ½-inch dice. You should have about 8 cups.

3. Place the diced rind in a 3-quart pot and add the lemon juice, water, sugar, ginger, and lemon peel. Cover and bring to a boil over high heat, stirring a few times to distribute the ingredients evenly and help dissolve the sugar. Reduce the heat to low and simmer, covered, over medium low heat for 40 minutes, or until the watermelon rind is translucent.

4. With the slotted spoon, transfer the pieces of rind to the jars, and leave the syrup to simmer and thicken for 10 minutes more. Carefully pour the syrup into the jars (using a funnel, if necessary) until it is ½ inch from the rim. Place the lids on the jars, seal, and set aside to cool. Refrigerate for 2 days before using. The preserves will keep for about 4 weeks in the refrigerator.

☀ PEAR CHUTNEY ☀

IN EASTERN INDIA, WHERE THEY ORIGINATED, CHUTNEYS
ARE CULINARY EXCLAMATION POINTS, A DAB OF CONCENTRATED
sweet, salty, spicy, or sour (and often all four at once) on the plate. These savory fruit jams, typically based on firm fruits like mango, lime, and lemon and spiced with ginger, chile peppers, and
cumin (among many other Asian spices), contrast nicely with cool yogurt and with any dish that
seems one-dimensional, like creamed spinach. Each household has a slightly different, personal-
ized, chutney blend.

Charlestonians caught on to the joys of tangy chutneys early in the eighteenth century. The
bustling port, for a time second only to New York in volume and importance, exposed residents
to a wide array of exotic goods from around the world. Chutneys have had a role in Lowcountry
cuisine and in southern recipe books ever since. Most recipes nowadays are based on pear and
onion, though mango and fig chutneys are common, too. All of them taste delicious and offer
plenty of latitude for you to add your personal touch.

This recipe nicely balances sweet and tart with simmered pear and lemon and is seasoned
with fresh garlic and ginger, mustard seeds, chiles, and a little curry powder. Raisins and onion
contribute plenty of sweetness even if the pears aren't at their ripest. In fact, firm, underripe pears
work the best in this recipe, because their texture remains pleasantly toothsome even when they
are fully cooked.

A spoonful of piquant pear chutney should be on every plate that includes salty ham, leftover
baked chicken, or any other meat that can use more flavor, zip, or moisture.

Makes 2 pints

TIME: 20 minutes to prepare, 1 hour to cook, 1 week to blend

EQUIPMENT

2 pint-sized, wide-mouth Ball jars, with rims and lids

1 cup cider vinegar

½ cup water

1½ cups light brown sugar

3½ cups coarsely chopped Bosc pears, unpeeled but cored (about 2 pears)

1½ cups chopped yellow onion (about 1 large onion)

1 tablespoon finely chopped lemon peel (from ½ lemon)

1 tablespoon lemon juice

5 tablespoons finely chopped garlic (about 6 large cloves)

½ cup dark raisins

¼ cup finely chopped fresh ginger (one 2-inch piece)

1 tablespoon Worcestershire sauce

2 teaspoons crushed red pepper flakes

1 tablespoon mustard seeds, smashed

1 teaspoon curry powder

1 teaspoon freshly ground black pepper

1 teaspoon kosher salt

2 whole cloves

1. Fill a 3-quart pot three-quarters full of water and bring to a boil over high heat. Using tongs, carefully set the jars on their sides, along with their lids and a slotted metal spoon, in the boiling water to sterilize. Boil for 15 minutes, then remove from the water with tongs or a jar lifter and set aside.

2. Put the vinegar and water in another 3-quart pot and bring to a boil over high heat. Add the brown sugar and stir to dissolve. Add the remaining ingredients and bring to a boil, then lower the heat to medium-low and simmer vigorously for 1 hour, stirring occasionally, until the chutney is thick, syrupy, and dark brown.

3. Carefully transfer the chutney to the jars with the sterilized spoon. Place the lids on the jars, seal, and set aside to cool. Refrigerate for 1 week before using. Pear chutney will keep for up to 6 weeks in the refrigerator.

139

GRITS AND RICE

A Grits Guide

Like "scrapple," or "Vegemite," the word "grits" doesn't *sound* tasty. And for that reason alone, grits run a close second to lard as the longest-running joke about southern food, perceived by the uninitiated to be a curiosity rather than what they are: a pillar of southern cooking. In fact, you could say that rice is the grits of China.

Grits begin as hard, dried corn kernels, which are then stripped from the cob, shattered in a grain mill, and sifted to separate the powdery cornmeal from the larger fragments, called grits. At this stage they should be no more of a conceptual challenge than starches like rice, pasta, or couscous. All are prepared by simmering in a hot liquid (water or broth), which softens them and subtly gives flavor. They also take flavor from ingredients you might stir into them—in the case of grits, cheeses of all kinds, meats, herbs, or mushrooms are favored admixtures. You name it, grits will go with it, and we would wager that in the South, corn is consumed more often as grits than it is either fresh or frozen. We eat a soft mound of grits with eggs and bacon, with greens, with duck, and even with fish for a hearty breakfast (a custom in the fishcentric Carolina Lowcountry). Like mashed potatoes, grits love gravies and juices, so they form a fantastic base on the plate beneath a variety of savory fish or meat dishes.

Grits can be white or yellow, depending on the color of the corn they're made from, and their flavor can vary slightly because of the variety of corn and environmental factors like soil composition and weather. But the single most important factor in making great-tasting grits is the way they are ground. Grits ground between cool stones, as opposed to those processed with warmer steel rollers in a high-speed commercial mill, are superior, more intense and fuller-bodied in both flavor and texture, because they retain all of the heat-sensitive corn oils contained in the corn kernel. Commercial mills deliberately remove the oil-rich heart of the corn kernel so the grits won't turn rancid on the grocery store shelf. Like many whole-grain meals and flours, stone-ground grits are truly perishable. They're at their peak the moment they're ground and will slowly fade at room temperature over the course of the next three to six weeks, so we strongly advise you to buy them from the mill if possible (see "Sourcery: Old Mill of Guilford," page 145), and store them in a sealed bag or container in the refrigerator or freezer. Fortunately, when you turn to grits as easily as you turn to rice, a two-pound bag will disappear before the weekend is over.

When the commercial millers remove the fragile corn oils, they take out much of the robust corn flavor in the process. That's one reason that grocery store grits are as bland and smooth as glue; the uniform fineness of the typical commercial grind is another. If you've only tasted this kind of grits—truck-stop or diner grits, we call them—you've got a wonderful revelation in store when you take your first forkful of fluffy, robust, real corn grits. It's as dramatic as tasting freshly ground coffee for the first time if all you've known is instant.

We keep a steady supply of our favorite stone-ground grits, from the Guilford Mill in Oak Ridge, North Carolina, but to find a source in your area, you might not even have to pick up a phone. We've visited mills all over the United States, and chances are if the stones are still spinning, grits are being ground, whether the mill happens to be in upstate New York, Iowa, or Rhode Island. The Society for the Preservation of Old Mills (www.spoom .org) can help you find an operating mill in your area.

We recently went one step further and ordered from the Lehman's Non-Electric Catalogue a five-pound jug of dried organic corn kernels and an inexpensive, hand-operated, cast-iron mill that enables us to grind our grits just seconds before they go into the pot.

But leave extreme grits zealotry to us. If you can't find stone-ground grits at stores in your area and you don't have the patience to order them by mail, use the highest-quality grits that commercial millers make, which are always labeled "old-fashioned." They will take slightly less time to cook than stone-ground, and we recommend adding a teaspoon of white refined sugar for every cup of dry grits to enhance their flavor. The only grits we absolutely discourage using in any of our recipes are the ones labeled "instant."

Another hallmark of grits is their endless adaptability; you can adjust their richness to suit your taste as you cook: the amount of liquid required to "bring up" a pot of grits is a little bit more than four times the quantity of the dry grits. Most often we use a fifty-fifty mixture of whole milk and water, and if we're feeling particularly decadent, we'll substitute half-and-half for the whole milk, or we'll use only milk and no water. But you should taste as you cook—you can always enrich the grits just before they're done with milk, butter, cheese, or any combination thereof.

Here you'll find our recipe for Simple Grits and several ideas for enhancements once you take them off the heat. Southerners tend to roll their eyes at the mention of doctored grits, and there's certainly a purity to the flavor of grits with just a pat of melting butter on top and nothing else. But we remember how exciting it was back in 1986 when grits with Clemson blue cheese—a deliciously funky blue made in the northwest corner of South Carolina with milk from Clemson University's dairy herd—appeared on the menu at Carolina's, a restaurant just a couple blocks from our house. It seemed to us as modern as the first Coke float must have back in the Roosevelt era (Teddy, that is).

We encourage you to do to grits whatever you care to do, so long as it creates a dish delicious enough to return to again and again. And don't forget the sweet applications, like breakfast grits garnished with a pat of butter and drizzled with sorghum syrup or honey. We once ate a fantastic chocolate soufflé made with grits by the chef Eberhard Mueller back when he was at the helm of the fabled French restaurant Lutèce in New York. His soufflé was the inspiration for our Chocolate Grits Ice Cream (page 438).

When Are Grits Not Hominy?

In some parts of the South—especially in Charleston—grits are referred to as "hominy grits," which some people shorten simply to "hominy." This creates confusion, because "hominy" in the rest of the country refers to corn kernels that have been soaked in an alkaline solution to remove the corn kernel's hulls and to subtly transform the flavor of the corn in the process (see Squash and Mushroom Hominy, page 219). For simplicity's sake, we always call grits "grits" and hominy "hominy."

SOURCERY: OLD MILL OF GUILFORD

YOU DON'T HAVE TO BE A NATIVE SOUTHERNER TO devote your life to grits. Charlie Parnell, a Welsh retiree, is living proof. He is the blue-coverall-wearing custodian of the Old Mill of Guilford, a fully functioning mill established in 1753, which he and his wife, Heidi, own in Oak Ridge, North Carolina. The mill's water wheel now powers a generator, creating electricity that drives the belts that turn the millstones and the sifters, but otherwise everything runs much as it has over the past two centuries, thanks to daily tweaking from Parnell, a former ship's engineer. His training in boat machinery, it turns out, was perfect preparation for the job of tending this three-story wood-framed mill, whose roaring gears, belts, and chutes seem to tug and strain at the structure when the mill is running at full tilt. When the hard kernels of organic corn, which Parnell buys from nearby farms in the North Carolina Piedmont, cascade through the chutes they make a sound like rushing water. Old Mill of Guilford, located at 130 NC 68 North; mailing address: Box 623 Rt. 1, Oak Ridge, NC 27310; 336-643-4783; www.oldmillofguilford.com.

❈ SIMPLE GRITS ❈

Makes 3 cups; enough for 4 people

TIME: 50 minutes

2 cups whole milk

2 cups water

1 cup stone-ground grits

¾ teaspoon kosher salt, plus more to taste

½ teaspoon freshly ground black pepper, plus
more to taste

1 tablespoon unsalted butter

1.   Pour the milk and water into a 2-quart saucepan, cover, and turn the heat to medium-high. When the milk mixture boils (about 5 minutes), uncover the pot, add the grits and salt, and reduce the heat to medium. Stir constantly until the grits are the consistency of thick soup and release a fragrant sweet-corn perfume, about 8 minutes. Reduce the heat to low and simmer, stirring every 2 to 3 minutes, for about 20 minutes, until the grits thicken and fall lazily from the end of the spoon. Cook about 15 minutes more, stirring constantly to prevent the grits from sticking to the bottom of the pan.

2.   When the grits are creamy and fluffy and soft, turn off the heat, add the pepper and butter, and stir to incorporate. Season to taste with salt and pepper, if desired, and serve immediately.

BOILED PEANUTS, PAGE 60

SHELLED BOILED PEANUTS, PAGE 60, ready to eat

From left to right: SCUPPERNONG PRESERVES, PAGE 132; SORGHUM SYRUP, PAGE 447; PICKLED SCALLIONS, PAGE 124; PICKLED JERUSALEM ARTICHOKES, PAGE 126

DERBY DAY GRAZES, *from left to right:* CHEESE STRAWS, PAGE 67; CATFISH PÂTÉ, PAGE 79, BENNE WAFERS *(foreground)* PAGE 485; PICKLED SHRIMP, PAGE 81; COUNTRY HAM, PAGE 329, ON BIRD-HEAD BUTTERMILK BISCUITS, PAGE 71, WITH JERUSALEM ARTICHOKE RELISH, PAGE 112; DEVILED EGGS, PAGE 87; AND A PITCHER OF MINT JULEPS, PAGE 27

SLAB BACON AND CHEDDAR CHEESE BROILED GRITS, PAGE 158

NEW YEAR'S DAY DINNER (*top to bottom*): GRAN'S MIMOSA, PAGE 34; CRISPY
CORN BREAD, PAGE 497; SUNDAY COLLARDS, PAGE 205;
SAIGON HOPPIN' JOHN, PAGE 170

A NEW AMBROSIA, PAGE 190

THE SIMPLE GRITS RECIPE STANDS UP TO MULTIPLICA-tion very well. But the larger your saucepan is, the more likely it is that the grits will become scorched during cooking, because the burner's heat is concentrated on the bottom. Stirring the grits with a whisk or an electric beater will prevent that and ensure a more consistent texture (and the latter will save your wrist from fatigue!).

❈ SUMMER-HERBED GRITS ❈

MILD "SUMMER" HERBS LIKE BASIL, MINT, PARSLEY, LOVAGE, AND EVEN CILANTRO ADD A GENTLE, AROMATIC SWEET-ness to grits just as they do to fresh corn. Feel free to create your own herb blend, but limit the total quantity to ½ cup.

Makes 3 cups; enough for 4 people

TIME: 50 minutes

1 recipe Simple Grits (page 146)
½ cup coarsely chopped fresh basil, other fresh "summer" herb, or a mixture
1 heaping teaspoon finely chopped green onion

After the butter and pepper have been added to the grits, stir in the basil and the green onion, mixing thoroughly until the basil wilts and turns bright green. Then season with salt and pepper to taste.

VARIATION—WINTER-HERBED GRITS: "WINTER" HERBS SUCH AS ROSEMARY AND SAGE WORK EQUALLY WELL WITH GRITS' CORN TASTE, BUT THEIR ASSERTIVE FLAVOR CALLS FOR A MORE JUDICIOUS HAND. STIR JUST 1 TABLESPOON COARSELY CHOPPED FRESH ROSEMARY OR SAGE INTO THE GRITS ONCE THE FLAME UNDER THE POT HAS BEEN TURNED OFF, AND BEFORE THE FINAL SEASONING WITH SALT AND PEPPER.

❈ SLAB BACON GRITS ❈

WE BUY SLAB BACON—WHICH IS SIMPLY UNSLICED BACON—WHENEVER POSSIBLE, BECAUSE IT ALLOWS US TO DECIDE how thick we want to cut it. Thicker bacon doesn't shrivel and shrink as much as thin supermarket bacon does, and in a recipe such as this one, with its simple pairing of creamy sweet corn and salty, smoky bacon, we prefer to dice thick bacon, like the lardoons the French scatter over frisée salads. Any good neighborhood butcher will offer unsliced bacon, but a great source for it is Early's Authentic Southern Foods in Tennessee (see "Sourcery: Slab Bacon," page 202). If you're in a pinch, you can always use the bacon labeled "thick-cut" that is offered by large commercial processors.

For 4 people
TIME: 50 minutes

1 recipe Simple Grits (page 146), minus the 1 tablespoon butter
¼ pound slab bacon or 4 slices thick-cut bacon, diced

1. While the grits are cooking, scatter the diced bacon in a small, dry skillet over medium-high heat. With a wooden spoon, move the pieces around until the bacon is firm and barely crisp, about 4 minutes. Remove with a slotted spoon and drain on paper towels. Reserve the bacon fat.

2. When the grits have finished cooking but before the final seasoning with salt and pepper, stir the diced bacon and the reserved fat into them. Then season to taste and serve.

MEATY GRITS VARIATIONS: GRITS WITH DICED COUNTRY HAM, HAM, OR BACON MAKES A HEARTY, DELICIOUS DISH. SIMILARLY, THE MEDITERRANEAN DRY-CURED PORK PRODUCTS PANCETTA AND SPECK WORK WELL IN THIS RECIPE. BECAUSE THE SALTINESS OF THE DIFFERENT MEATS VARIES GREATLY, BEGIN BY ADDING 1/4 CUP OF DICED MEAT AFTER THE BUTTER AND BLACK PEPPER HAVE BEEN ADDED. THEN ADD MORE MEAT TO TASTE, BEFORE SEASONING WITH SALT AND PEPPER TO TASTE.

Allen Bros. Milling in downtown Columbia, South Carolina, is famed for their "Adluh" brand cornmeal.

❋ CLEMSON BLUE CHEESE GRITS ❋

CLEMSON BLUE CHEESE IS A DELECTABLE BLUE MADE FROM THE MILK OF CLEMSON UNIVERSITY'S DAIRY HERD AND AGED for six months. As teenagers, we were captivated by a tale that the cheese was aged in a half-completed nineteenth-century railroad tunnel through a mountain, one that just happened to have the perfect conditions for making blue mold. In 1999 we paid a visit to the university's creamery and cheese-making operation and were nearly heartbroken to find the cheese curing in a spotless modern refrigerator. But we confirmed that the tunnel beneath Stumphouse Mountain was indeed used to cure the cheese from 1940 until 1958. Today, Stumphouse Tunnel Park, in Mountain Rest, South Carolina, is owned by Clemson University but maintained by the state, and is a favorite destination of hikers.

We're not big hikers, but we'd trek a ways for the promise of these blue cheese grits. They're a clarion wake-up call on a lazy bacon-and-eggs morning.

For 4 people
TIME: 50 minutes

1 recipe Simple Grits (page 146)
¼ cup crumbled Clemson blue cheese or other creamy blue cheese, such as Maytag

When the grits have finished cooking, add the cheese and stir thoroughly. Then season with salt and pepper, if desired.

CHEESE GRITS VARIATIONS: ALMOST ANY CHEESE IS AN APPEALING MATCH FOR GRITS' WARM CORN FLAVOR. CHEDDAR, FETA, PARMIGIANO-REGGIANO, PECORINO ROMANO, RICOTTA, GOAT'S MILK CHEESES, AND SHEEP'S MILK CHEESE ALL MELT BEAUTIFULLY INTO HOT GRITS. BEGIN BY ADDING 1/4 CUP. THEN ADD MORE TO TASTE, BEFORE A FINAL SEASONING WITH SALT AND PEPPER.

❊ LEMON GRITS ❊

THESE LEMON-LACED GRITS ARE THE PERFECT SIDE DISH
FOR FLOUNDER WITH GRANNY SMITH APPLE AND GREEN TOMATO
Pan Gravy (page 396) Grilled Mahimahi with Fresh Peach Relish (page 384), or any simply pre-
pared whole fish.

For 4 people

TIME: 50 minutes

1 recipe Simple Grits (page 146)
1 teaspoon finely minced lemon zest

After the butter and pepper have been added to the cooked grits, stir in the lemon zest. Then season with salt and pepper to taste.

VARIATION: LIME IS AN ESPECIALLY APPEALING MATCH FOR SHELLFISH, SO WHEN WE WANT A SIMPLE
ACCOMPANIMENT TO PAN-SEARED SCALLOPS OR A FRIED SOFT-SHELL CRAB, WE SUBSTITUTE LIME ZEST
FOR LEMON ZEST.

GRITS CAKES

When grits cool, they gel into a firm medium that can be cut into cakes and fried. Grits cakes have almost as many uses as George Washington Carver's peanuts. You can make grits cakes using any of our grits recipes, and in our kitchen, we give many main dishes the Downtown Touch simply by adding an herbed grits cake to the plate. Since leftover grits are prime for the grits cake treatment—the cooking is already done!—we make grits cakes the foundation for countless simple lunches and brunches; a favorite is slender asparagus arranged over a grits cake and drizzled with Buttermilk-Lime Dressing (page 519).

Grits cakes can be either deep-fried or pan-fried. Pan-frying is easier, but we have to admit we prefer the former; there's something irresistible about the crispy crust that forms around the creamy, hot grits, when you deep-fry a grits cake.

Grits croutons, which are simply grits cakes that have been cut into crouton size before being deep-fried, may well make you a convert. The fact that we've only encountered grits croutons in restaurants that have a deep-fryer running around the clock seems logical. What home cook, after all, would fire up a skillet and oil for a mere salad topping? We would when we're feeling decadent. Grits croutons take a salad of sturdy lettuces such as butter, Boston, Bibb, and frisée to a textural height.

☀ DEEP-FRIED GRITS CAKES ☀

For 4 grits cakes

TIME: 55 minutes to prepare, 4 hours to chill, 20 minutes to cook

1 recipe Simple Grits (page 146), Summer-Herbed Grits (page 148),
    Slab Bacon Grits (page 149), Clemson Blue Cheese Grits (page 151),
    or Lemon Grits (page 153)
1½–2 cups peanut oil

1. Prepare the grits, and when they have been seasoned to taste, and are still hot, pour them into 4 lightly oiled 8-ounce ramekins or a lightly oiled plastic container or baking pan, to a depth of ½ inch. Press plastic wrap onto the surface of the grits cakes, and refrigerate until the grits are firm, about 4 hours or overnight.

2. Preheat the oven to 250 degrees.

3. Pour the oil into a large cast-iron skillet or sauté pan to a depth of ⅓ inch. Heat over high heat until it reaches 350 degrees on a candy thermometer. Turn the grits out of their containers onto a cutting board. If not using ramekins, cut the grits into 4 equal cakes. With a spatula, transfer 2 of the cakes to the oil and fry until golden brown on each side, about 3 minutes per side. Transfer to a plate lined with a paper towel and keep warm in the oven. Repeat with the remaining 2 cakes.

4. Serve the cakes immediately.

✳ PAN-FRIED GRITS CAKES ✳

Makes 4

TIME: 55 minutes to prepare, 4 hours to chill, 20 minutes to cook

1 recipe Simple Grits (page 146), Summer-Herbed Grits (page 148),
    Slab Bacon Grits (page 149), Clemson Blue Cheese Grits (page 151),
    or Lemon Grits (page 153)
1 tablespoon peanut or canola oil

1.   Prepare the grits, and when they have been seasoned to taste, and are still hot, pour them into 4 lightly oiled 8-ounce ramekins or a lightly oiled plastic container or baking pan, to a depth of ½ inch. Press plastic wrap onto the surface of the grits, and refrigerate until the grits are firm, about 4 hours or overnight.

2.   Preheat the oven to 250 degrees.

3.   Turn the grits out of their containers onto a cutting board. If not using ramekins, cut the grits into 4 equal cakes. In a large skillet over high heat, heat the oil until it shimmers. With a spatula, gently transfer 2 of the cakes to the skillet and sauté them over medium-high heat, until the edges brown slightly, about 4 minutes. Turn them and cook on the other side, about 4 minutes. Transfer them to a plate lined with a paper towel and keep warm in the oven. Repeat with the remaining 2 cakes.

4. Serve the cakes immediately.

KILLER LEFTOVER—GRITS CAKES AND GRITS CROUTONS: AT THE END OF A MEAL, IF THERE ARE ANY GRITS LEFT IN THE PAN, ADD ABOUT A QUARTER AS MUCH WATER AS THERE ARE GRITS AND PLACE THE PAN OVER MEDIUM-LOW HEAT. WHISK TO LOOSEN THE GRITS, AND CONTINUE TO WHISK VIGOROUSLY AS THE WATER WARMS AND THE GRITS GRADUALLY BECOME LOOSE AGAIN, ABOUT 4 MINUTES. SPREAD THE GRITS INTO LIGHTLY OILED RAMEKINS OR A LIGHTLY OILED PLASTIC CONTAINER OR SMALL BAKING PAN TO A DEPTH OF 1/2 INCH. PRESS PLASTIC WRAP ONTO THE SURFACE AND REFRIGERATE 4 HOURS OR OVERNIGHT. PREPARE THE GRITS AS DESCRIBED IN THE GRITS CAKES RECIPES ABOVE.

❈ SLAB BACON AND CHEDDAR CHEESE ❈ BROILED GRITS

BREAKFAST'S HERO. WE SERVE THESE GRITS WITH SCRAMBLED EGGS, BUT THEY ARE SO RICH THAT ON SOME MORN-ings a Gran's Mimosa (page 34) is the only accompaniment required.

For 4 people
TIME: 1 hour

1 recipe Simple Grits (page 146), minus the 1 tablespoon butter
¼ pound slab bacon or 4 slices thick-cut bacon, diced
1¾ cups coarsely grated extra-sharp cheddar cheese (about ¼ pound)

1.   While the grits are cooking, scatter the diced bacon in a dry skillet. Cook over medium-high heat, moving the pieces around with a wooden spoon, until the bacon is firm and barely crisp, about 4 minutes. Remove with a slotted spoon and drain on paper towels. Reserve the bacon fat.

2.   When the grits are cooked, stir in 1¼ cups of the cheese, the diced bacon, and the bacon fat. Stir until the cheese melts. Transfer the grits to a small baking dish or cast-iron skillet or divide among four 6-ounce ramekins. Scatter the remaining cheese over the surface.

3.   Broil the grits (in the skillet) about 2 inches beneath the flame or heating element until the cheese is nicely browned, about 3 minutes. Serve immediately, with scrambled eggs and a mimosa.

CHEESE-GRITS CHILES RELLENOS
WITH ROASTED TOMATO GRAVY

CANTINA LOS GUANAJUATO OPENED IN 1993 IN A DEFUNCT CINDER-BLOCK GAS STATION ON JOHNS ISLAND, IN THE MIDST OF the most fertile farmland of the Charleston area. The restaurant catered almost exclusively to the migrant workers of Mexican descent who picked tomatoes at the nearby farms. The gas station had played host to restaurants and bars before—a different one every summer, it seemed—and sure enough, by the following season, Cantina los Guanajuato had been replaced by another establishment.

But we owe that restaurant a great debt, not only for introducing us to the wonder that is chiles rellenos—roasted fresh poblano peppers stuffed with cheese and deep-fried until gooey and delicious—but also for showing us that southern cuisine and Mexican cuisine have many common elements, namely a preference for deeply flavored pork shoulders, a taste for dried chiles (which South Carolinians call simply "hot peppers"), and a love of corn in all its myriad forms, especially cornmeal and hominy. Consider this Mexican-southern interpretation, which stuffs poblanos with cheese grits and slathers them with a "gravy" of charred onion, tomato, and garlic, a partial repayment. It is fairly rich for a side dish, so we often serve it as a main course for vegetarians, with plenty of crisp, bitter lettuces such as arugula and dandelion greens as a salad.

Once Mexico-born farmworkers passed through Charleston as they followed summer harvests up the coast, but the community on Johns Island has become less seasonal and more permanent. Although the old gas station now has no tenant, a number of full-service Mexican restaurants have established themselves in the community to fulfill the need the cantina once served. On Johns Island—and in rural towns all across the Southeast—we now find *tiendas mexicanas*, or

Mexican groceries, which are terrific sources for authentic corn tortillas and canned hominy, a wealth of dried chile varieties, and fresh produce like the poblano peppers that are essential to this recipe.

For 6 people

TIME: 1 hour

1 large tomato or 4 plum tomatoes (about ¾ pound)
6 medium fresh poblano peppers (1¼–1½ pounds)
1 medium yellow onion, peeled and quartered
2 large cloves garlic, unpeeled
1 tablespoon extra-virgin olive oil

½ teaspoon salt, plus more to taste
3 cups cooked Cheddar Cheese Grits (page 152)
Freshly ground black pepper to taste
½ cup coarsely grated extra-sharp cheddar cheese

1. Core the tomato with a sharp paring knife. Arrange the tomato, peppers, onion, and garlic in a 9-×-13-inch roasting pan, with the peppers gathered at one end. Brush all the vegetables with the olive oil and sprinkle them with the salt. Slide the pan under the broiler about 3 inches from the flame or heating element, with the peppers nearest you; you'll be turning them frequently as they roast. Turn the peppers every 3 minutes until their skins are blistered and blackened all over, about 9 minutes total. The onion, garlic, and tomato will be nicely charred as well. Transfer the peppers to a large bowl, transfer the tomato, onion, and garlic to a medium bowl, and let them cool. Set aside the roasting pan.

2. Preheat the oven to 400 degrees.

3. When the peppers are cool enough to handle, gently massage their skins to remove them and discard. Cut a 3-inch slit down the side of each pepper and gently spoon out the seeds and any whitish, fibrous veins. Fill each pepper with ½ cup cheese grits and place in the roasting pan.

4.   When the tomato, onion, and garlic have cooled, remove the skins from the tomato and garlic and discard. Process the tomato, onion, and garlic to a chunky puree in a blender or food processor, about 30 seconds. Season to taste with salt and pepper. Pour the sauce over the peppers.

5.   Bake the peppers on the middle rack until the tomato sauce bubbles gently, about 15 minutes. Scatter the cheese on top and place the pan under the broiler about 2 inches from the flame or heating element until the cheese has browned.

6.   Serve immediately.

❋ ROASTED GARLIC AND ROSEMARY ❋ GRITS SOUFFLÉ

A GRITS SOUFFLÉ IS SIMILAR TO A SPOONBREAD, BECAUSE GRITS ARE BASICALLY A VERY COARSELY GROUND CORN-meal. But it is also a little bit miraculous, because while the coarse grind of the grits makes its texture sandy and variegated, the soufflé is as light as air, a fine counterpoint to robust, meaty entrées like Texas Red-Braised Beef Short Ribs (page 320) and Conley's Braised Stuffed Quail (page 313).

This dish harmonizes the mellow corn flavor of creamy grits with the piney aromatics of rosemary and the funkiness of roasted garlic. It is great fun to make. We encircle each ramekin with a 4- to 6-inch-wide strip of parchment tied with butcher's twine to contain the soufflé as it rises above the level of the ramekin. You can use six 4-ounce ramekins for a more formal occasion, but sometimes we use three 8-ounce ones for six people, because—as enjoyable as this dish is to make—it is just as fun to watch people enjoy it, and there's something about two diners sharing the job of ripping open the parchment and dipping into the soufflé that's really festive.

For 6 people

TIME: 1¼ hours

EQUIPMENT

Six 4-ounce ramekins
Six 4- to 6-inch-wide strips parchment paper
Butcher's twine

½ cup stone-ground grits

½ cup half-and-half

3 cups water

1½ teaspoons kosher salt

6 cloves garlic, unpeeled

1 teaspoon extra-virgin olive oil

2 egg yolks

1 teaspoon finely minced fresh rosemary

½ teaspoon freshly ground black pepper

6 egg whites

3 tablespoons finely grated pecorino Romano

1. Place the grits in a small bowl and fill the bowl with water. Stir the grits gently. When they settle, pour off any chaff floating on the surface and drain the grits.

2. Put the half-and-half, water, and 1 teaspoon salt into a 2-quart saucepan, cover, and bring to a boil over medium-high heat. Add the grits and reduce the heat to medium. Stir constantly for 8 minutes, then reduce the heat to low. Simmer the grits for about 25 minutes, stirring them every 2 to 3 minutes, until they are creamy, soft, and just slightly soupy (they should fall easily from a spoon).

3. Meanwhile, place the garlic cloves in a small ovenproof dish and brush them with the olive oil. Broil the garlic about 2 inches beneath the flame or heating element until the skins blacken and the cloves have softened, about 6 minutes. Remove and cool. Cut the skin off and discard. Sprinkle the remaining ½ teaspoon salt over the garlic and mash to a puree with the flat side of a chef's knife. Set aside.

4. Preheat the oven to 350 degrees.

5. In a medium bowl, beat the egg yolks until creamy yellow in color. Slowly pour 1 cup of grits into the yolks, whisking constantly. When the mixture is smooth and a sunny pale yellow, add it to the pan with the remaining grits and whisk thoroughly. Add the garlic puree, rosemary, and pepper and whisk to distribute evenly.

6. Using an electric mixer or a whisk, beat the egg whites in a large bowl to stiff peaks. Using a large serving spoon, fold them gently into the grits by spoonfuls, just until they are combined.

7. Pour the mixture into the ramekins. Tie a paper strip around each ramekin with twine so it extends 3 inches above the rim. Sprinkle each soufflé with 1½ teaspoons cheese. Bake on the middle rack for 35 minutes, or until the soufflés have risen into their paper collars and are barely browned on top.

8. Remove from the oven and serve immediately, letting the guests unwrap the parchment.

RICE LAND

Like the kitchen houses found behind grander homes in downtown Charleston or the oyster-shell mounds left by Native Americans along the coast, the food history of the South is often inscribed in its landscape.

In South Carolina, this is nowhere more apparent than in the ACE Basin, the pristine, well-preserved area south of Charleston named for the Ashepoo, Combahee, and Edisto Rivers, which run through the 400,000-acre estuary. Every Friday after Thanksgiving, we kayak the waters of the ACE Basin, which we've taken to calling simply "Rice Land," after a roadside sign in the region. We're always amazed to come across the topographical vestiges of rice cultivation here: two-hundred-year-old canals that slaves cut as straight as plumb lines through the marsh grasses; rice "trunks"—simple valves made of wood through which planters controlled the rise and fall of water in their rice fields; and here and there a few spindly stalks of wild rice spiking high out of the marsh grass.

Rice was imported from Africa and Asia as early as the seventeenth century, along with African slaves, upon whose labor and knowledge of rice cultivation the industry was entirely dependent. The swampy, brackish, and still tidal marshes of the southeastern coastal plain were ideally suited to the cultivation of rice, and the Lowcountry remained prime rice-producing territory until Emancipation, finally dying for good early in this century when the hurricane of 1911 wiped out what rice production remained. By that time new growing regions on firmer ground in Texas, Arkansas, and Louisiana had already begun to surpass the South Carolina rice plantations, thanks to the development of high-capacity water pumps.

Though cultivation of rice all but disappeared in the Southeast in the early twentieth century, the taste for rice never has. Grits certainly has wider name recognition, but the rice dish pilau, or purloo, as many southerners call it, may be the definitive southern dish: it's one-pot cooking in which rice absorbs the broth of the protein it's cooked with. This method, whose roots culinary historians trace to thirteenth-century Baghdad, saves dishwashing, but more importantly, it achieves a fullness of flavor that may be the quiet hallmark of southern cooking.

CAROLINA GOLD IS THE NAME GIVEN TO A PARTICU-larly aromatic, nutty variety of rice, a bushel of which was brought from Madagascar to Charles Town (as the city was then called) in the late 1600s by a ship's captain named John Thurbur. Thurbur gave the rice to a local surgeon, Dr. Henry Woodward, and the rest, as they say, is history. It may be named for the burnished color the rice takes on when it matures in the field (the husked grains are snow-white), but we suspect the name also has something to do with the extent to which the crop filled the pockets of plantation owners.

These days, the former rice-growing region south of Charleston is prime hunting land, and some landowners grow rice to attract migratory waterfowl. One such grower, Dr. Richard Schulze, an ophthalmologist, tracked down a few remaining grains of Carolina Gold in a USDA seed bank in Texas back in the 1970s, when the grain was thought to be extinct. He propagated it on his Jasper County plantation through the mid-1980s and turned his burgeoning acres of Carolina Gold into a premium rice hobby. Dr. Schulze mills the rice in a restored 1899 mill and donates the crop to the Church of the Holy Trinity in Ridgeland, South Carolina. The church bags the rice and sells it to defray its operating expenses.

Until recently, because the supply of Carolina Gold was very limited and because the church relied on parishioners to bag the rice in their spare time, there was often a long waiting list of individuals and restaurants who wanted to buy it. One year we were able to jump to the top of that list by offering to drive down to the parish hall, don hairnets and food-service gloves, and bag the rice ourselves. These days, though, we purchase our Carolina Gold from a broker who arranged to have the seed grown on a commercial scale in Arkansas. Supplies are still limited, but the rice is becoming more plentiful with every passing year. As chefs in the Southeast become aware of it, they're stoking demand by including it on the menus of finer restaurants, where the steep price (over $9 retail for a 1½ pound bag!) is less of a concern.

✻ HOPPIN' JOHN ✻

HOPPIN' JOHN ENTHUSIASM BUBBLES OVER AROUND THE
FIRST OF JANUARY, BECAUSE THE DISH IS BELIEVED TO BRING GOOD
luck in the New Year. We get excited about hoppin' John all year long. In fact, during times of
stress, or on mornings after a late party, we seem to crave it. Nutritionists tell us that's because
peas and rice mixed together contain all fourteen amino acids our bodies need to form a complete
protein.

There are a number of theories about how hoppin' John got its name. One historian claims it
is a derived from *bhat kachang*, a thirteenth-century Iraqi name for a similar dish of peas and rice.
Others claim it's a mispronunciation of *pois de pigeon*, French for the pigeon peas used in a very
similar dish common in the French West Indies. We can hear academics stretching their muscles
in both these theories, and are thrilled that we don't need to know how the dish got its name to
love the way the flavors come together in it: smoked pork, earthy-sweet field peas, tart tomato. We
give the whole thing heft by using pork broth to bring up the rice.

For 6 people

TIME: 4 hours to soak peas, 1½ hours to cook

1 cup dried black-eyed peas or field peas
2 tablespoons olive oil
1 smoked hog jowl (or ¼ pound slab bacon or
    4 slices thick-cut bacon)
1 medium yellow onion, coarsely chopped
6 cups Rich Pork Broth (page 548)

½ teaspoon freshly ground black pepper
1 teaspoon crushed red pepper flakes
1 teaspoon salt
One 14-ounce can crushed Italian tomatoes
1½ cups long-grain rice

1. Wash the peas in a strainer, place them in a medium bowl, and soak for 4 hours in fresh water to cover.

2. Heat the olive oil in a 4-quart pot over medium-high heat and brown the hog jowl on both sides, about 5 minutes. (If using bacon, omit the olive oil and simply render the fat in the pot for 5 minutes.) Add the onion and cook until softened, about 5 minutes. Add the broth, black pepper, red pepper, and salt and bring to a boil.

3. Let the broth boil vigorously for 10 minutes, then add the drained peas. Boil gently over medium-high heat, uncovered, until the peas are tender but still have some bite, about 25 minutes for black-eyed peas, 30 minutes for field peas. Add the tomatoes and the rice to the pot, cover, reduce the heat to low, and simmer vigorously for 20 minutes, until most of the broth has been absorbed but the rice and peas are still very moist.

4. Remove the pot from the heat and allow the hoppin' John to steam, covered, until all the liquid has been absorbed, about 5 minutes. Remove the hog jowl and pull off any meat.

5. Fluff the hoppin' John with a fork. Transfer to a serving dish, sprinkle the shredded hog jowl over the top, and serve.

☀ SAIGON HOPPIN' JOHN ☀

HOPPIN' JOHN, LIKE BOILED PEANUTS, IS NOT AN EXCLU-
SIVELY SOUTHERN DELICACY. RICE AND BEANS HAVE TRAVELED
throughout the world, so it stands to reason that someone somewhere might also have combined
the two. A friend's daughter, in fact, spied a slightly soupy version of rice and black-eyed peas
offered for sale by a street vendor in Saigon. The only hint that it wasn't going to taste the same as
a Charleston hoppin' John was a spear of lemongrass sticking out of it. Excited by her sighting,
we took the liberty of creating a zingy lemongrass- and ginger-inflected dish that turns the typically meaty character of a Lowcountry hoppin' John into an aromatic vegetarian porridge.

For 6 people

TIME: 4 hours to soak peas, 1 hour to cook

1 cup dried black-eyed peas
6 cups Sunday Vegetable Broth (page 539)
1 cup uncooked long-grain rice
1 teaspoon ground ginger
Two 4-inch stalks fresh lemongrass, 1 bruised
    and cut into 4 sections, 1 for garnish

1 cup unsweetened coconut milk
½ teaspoon salt, plus more to taste
½ teaspoon sugar
¼ cup finely chopped cilantro
Freshly ground black pepper to taste

1.　Place the peas in a strainer and wash for 1 minute under cold running water, gently tossing them with your hand or a wooden spoon. Place in a large bowl, cover with fresh water, and soak for at least 4 hours.

2.　Bring the broth to a boil in a 4-quart pot. Add the drained peas, reduce the heat to medium-high, and boil gently until the peas are just tender but still have some bite, about 25 minutes. Add the rice, ginger, bruised lemongrass, coconut milk, salt, and sugar and return to a boil. Reduce the heat to low, cover, and simmer gently until the rice and peas are tender and the dish has the soupy character of a porridge, about 20 minutes. Stir in the cilantro with a spoon and add salt and pepper to taste.

3.　Cut the remaining stalk of lemongrass into 6 sections. Serve the hoppin' John in bowls, steaming hot, with a piece of fresh lemongrass in each.

☀ RED RICE ☀

FOUND ON MOST SOUTHERN BUFFETS BETWEEN THE BOWL OF COLESLAW AND THE VAT OF SWEET TEA, THIS DISH GETS ITS "red" from a troika of tomatoes, crushed red pepper flakes, and paprika. Most recipes for red rice add precooked white rice to a skillet with tomato paste or ketchup and bacon and then bake it for an hour. We cook ours up pilau-style, with tomatoes, spices, and chicken broth, so the rice gets infused with flavor as it cooks.

We're not timid about heating up red rice spicewise, with crushed red pepper and smoked paprika. In Spain, paprika chiles are smoked before they are dried to make the spice, so the *pimentón*, as it's called there, has a powerful smoky flavor. Smoked paprika is available in the United States at specialty food stores and from a number of mail-order sources (see "Sourcery: Buying Dried Chiles," page 284). If you can't wait, use Hungarian paprika, made from peppers that are dried but not smoked. Make certain it is fresh—there's nothing sadder than spent paprika, which is just red dust. The aroma of freshly ground paprika is like roasted fruit and raisins and as invigorating as the smell of freshly ground coffee.

Serve Red Rice with Fried Shrimp (page 391), Fried Oysters (page 388), or Fried Whiting (page 386).

Makes 5 cups; enough for 4 people

TIME: 1 hour

3 ounces slab bacon or 2 slices thick-cut
    bacon cut into small dice
1½ cups diced yellow onion (about 1 large
    onion)
3 cloves garlic, crushed
1½ cups long-grain rice
2–2½ cups Sunday Chicken Broth (page 532)

One 28-ounce can whole Italian tomatoes,
    drained
1 teaspoon crushed red pepper flakes
1 teaspoon Spanish smoked paprika
    (*pimentón*)
1 teaspoon salt
½ teaspoon freshly ground pepper

1. Preheat the oven to 425 degrees.

2. In a 12-inch ovenproof skillet over medium-high heat, fry the bacon until firm and barely crisp, about 4 minutes. Using a slotted spoon, transfer to a small bowl and reserve. Sauté the onion and garlic in the bacon fat over medium heat until softened, about 5 minutes. Add the rice and cook, stirring occasionally, for 1 to 2 minutes, until fragrant and slightly translucent. Add 2 cups broth and turn off the heat.

3. In a food processor or food mill, puree the tomatoes. Stir in the crushed red pepper flakes, smoked paprika, salt, and pepper and pour the puree into the skillet. Stir to combine the ingredients.

4. Bring the mixture to a boil over high heat, then reduce the heat to medium-low, cover, and simmer vigorously until the rice is tender but soupy, about 20 minutes. Add more broth 1 tablespoon at a time if the rice is not soupy.

5. Transfer the skillet to the oven and bake on the middle rack for 25 minutes, or until all the liquid has been absorbed.

6. Serve the rice in a bowl, garnished with the reserved bacon.

VARIATION—DIRTY RED RICE WITH SAUSAGE AND JALAPEÑO: THIS SPINS A CLASSIC SIDE DISH IN THE ENTRÉE DIRECTION. BEFORE ADDING THE GARLIC AND ONION TO THE SKILLET IN STEP 2, CUT 6 HOT ITALIAN SAUSAGES ON THE BIAS INTO 2-INCH-THICK PIECES, SEAR THEM IN THE BACON FAT FOR SEVERAL MINUTES, AND RESERVE. THEN ADD THE GARLIC AND ONION TO THE SKILLET, ALONG WITH 2 FRESH JALAPEÑOS THAT HAVE BEEN STEMMED, SEEDED, AND ROUGHLY CHOPPED. FOLLOW THE RECIPE THEREAFTER, AND NESTLE THE PIECES OF RESERVED SAUSAGE INTO THE RICE JUST BEFORE THE SKILLET GOES INTO THE OVEN.

KLO

KILLER LEFTOVER—RED RICE OMELETTE: CHEF ROBERT STEHLING, OF CHARLESTON'S HOMINY GRILL, HAS MORE SOUTHERN-FOOD STROKES OF GENIUS TO HIS NAME THAN ANYONE WE KNOW, LIKE CREAMED COLLARDS, DEEP-FRIED CORN BREAD (TRUST US!), AND SHAD ROE CASSEROLE. BUT HIS RED RICE OMELETTE JUST MIGHT BE OUR FAVORITE. WARM ANY LEFTOVER RED RICE IN THE MICROWAVE, THE OVEN, OR WITH 1 TABLESPOON WATER IN A SKILLET, THEN FOLD IT INTO YOUR FAVORITE OMELETTE. USE 1 CUP RICE FOR A 3-EGG OMELETTE, 1/2 CUP FOR A 2-EGG OMELETTE.

❋ OYSTER PURLOO ❋

OYSTER PURLOO IS AMONG THE MOST COMFORTING OF
COMFORT FOODS AND A NICE MARRIAGE OF A MARSH-DWELLING
creature with a marsh-dwelling plant. The pluff mud (as the chocolate pudding–like marsh mud
is called) banks of the Lowcountry tidal creeks often are ridged with clusters of sharp oyster
shells. Above them wild rice grows among the spartina grass that predominates in the estuaries of
North Carolina, South Carolina, and Georgia.

The Rustic Touch in this dish comes from chicken gizzards browned in the skillet, which rein-
force the fleshy, mineral flavor of the oysters. You could add a tonic pinch of fresh marjoram or a
spicy dash of red pepper flakes at the end, but we prefer to let the rice stand alone, plumped up
with the brininess of oyster liquor and the wisp of bacon smoke. Pair it with a crisp salad.

For 6 people

TIME: 45 minutes

1 pint shucked oysters and their liquor (see Sourcery, page 76)

1 teaspoon kosher salt (optional), plus more to taste

¼ pound slab bacon or 4 slices thick-cut bacon, diced

4 chicken gizzards (optional)

1 tablespoon olive oil

3 tablespoons minced shallots or finely diced yellow onion (about 1 large shallot or 1 small yellow onion)

2 cups long-grain rice

3½ cups Sunday Chicken Broth (page 532)

Freshly ground black pepper to taste

1. Taste the oyster liquor. If it lacks a salty, seawater tang, scatter a light dusting (about 1 teaspoon) of salt over the oysters and toss to combine.

2. Scatter the diced bacon in a 12-inch skillet or 2-quart saucepan over medium-high heat and fry, rendering the fat until the bacon is firm and barely crisp, about 3 minutes. Using a slotted spoon, transfer to a small bowl and reserve. Sauté the gizzards, if using, in the bacon fat over medium heat, turning once or twice to ensure even browning, about 4 minutes total. Reserve the gizzards on a small plate.

3. Using a small fine-mesh strainer, strain the oysters over a small bowl, reserving their liquor. Add the olive oil to the skillet and turn the heat to high. When the oil and fat begin to pop, add the oysters all at once and sauté until their edges curl and they release some liquid, about 20 seconds. Using a slotted spoon, transfer the oysters to another small bowl and dust them lightly with salt.

4. Add the shallots to the skillet and sauté until translucent, about 3 minutes. Add the rice, and gizzards, if using, and stir with a wooden spoon to coat the grains with oil. Allow the oils to "bake" into the rice for 1 minute, stirring occasionally.

5. If the reserved oysters have released more liquid, strain them again, adding to the reserved liquor. Measure the amount of liquor and add it to the skillet, along with enough chicken broth to make 4 cups. Bring the liquid to a simmer over medium-high heat, then turn the heat to low and cover. Simmer vigorously until the rice is just tender but still wet, about 15 minutes.

6. Add the reserved oysters, folding with a large spoon to incorporate (don't be afraid to break them up), and a few grinds of fresh black pepper over the top. Cover and continue cooking over low heat until the rice has fully absorbed all the liquid in the pan, about 5 minutes. Turn off the heat.

7. Scatter the reserved bacon over the top of the dish, and allow the rice to steam, covered, in the skillet for a few minutes before serving.

❋ SQUAB PURLOO ❋

RICE SEEMS TO HAVE A SPECIAL AFFINITY FOR POULTRY, AND THE RICHER, THE BETTER. SQUAB IS THE IDEAL PARTNER, AS ruddy and fine-grained as a tenderloin of venison or beef. We grew up with a taste for squab because Charleston isn't far from the Palmetto Pigeon Plant in Pelion, South Carolina, the preeminent squab ranch in the country, and the source for most East Coast-American restaurants.

But if you can't find squab, quail or game hens make excellent substitutes in this recipe. It is similar in principle to our Oyster Purloo (page 175), but where we let the subtle ocean flavor of the oysters shine through in that recipe, here we bounce the deep poultry flavor off the sweeter, sprightlier taste of tomatoes and carrots.

For 4 people
TIME: 1 hour

¼ pound slab bacon or 4 slices thick-cut bacon, diced

3 tablespoons olive oil

2 squabs, split in half, wingtips trimmed and necks, gizzards, livers, hearts, and any trimmed fat reserved (if included; if not, substitute 4 chicken gizzards)

3 cups Sunday Chicken Broth (page 532)

½ cup finely diced carrots (about 1 large carrot)

½ cup chopped yellow onion (about 1 medium onion)

2 cups long-grain rice

1 cup canned crushed Italian tomatoes

1 teaspoon tomato paste

1. In a 12-inch cast-iron skillet or sauté pan, fry the bacon over medium-high heat until it is firm and barely crisp, about 3 minutes. Using a slotted spoon, transfer to a small bowl and reserve. Add 1 tablespoon olive oil to the bacon fat in the pan, and brown the squab necks, gizzards, livers, hearts, and trimmed fat for 1 to 2 minutes to render flavor and fat. Remove these trimmings with the slotted spoon and discard. In the same fat, sauté the squabs on all sides until they are a rich nut-brown, about 3 minutes per side; transfer to a plate and reserve. Add 2 tablespoons of the chicken broth, and using a wooden spoon, scrape up the flavor-laden brown bits from the bottom of the skillet. Add the carrots and sauté about 2 minutes. Add the onion and sauté until it just begins to turn translucent, about 2 minutes.

2. Pour the remaining 2 tablespoons olive oil into the skillet and add the rice, stirring to coat. Cook over medium-high heat for about 2 minutes. Add the remaining broth, tomatoes, and tomato paste and bring to a boil. Reduce the heat to medium-low, cover, and simmer vigorously for 5 minutes.

3. Uncover the skillet and bed the squab halves in the soupy rice, adding any juices that may have drained from the birds. Cover and continue to simmer vigorously until all the liquid has been absorbed, 20 to 25 minutes.

4. Turn off the heat and let the purloo rest for 5 minutes before serving. Ladle a bed of rice onto each plate, place half a squab on top, and scatter reserved bacon over the plate. Provide many napkins, because nibbling on the carcass is obligatory.

VARIATIONS—MOUNTAIN COUNTRY, FRENCH, OR MIDDLE EASTERN SQUAB PURLOO: A HEAPING TABLE-SPOON OF COUNTRY HAM BITS, A SPRIG OF THYME AND A BAY LEAF, OR A COUPLE STEMS OF FRESH MINT ADDED WITH THE TOMATOES COMPLEMENT THIS DISH. THE COUNTRY HAM MAKES IT MORE SOUTHERN, THE THYME AND BAY LEAF MAKE IT MORE FRENCH, AND THE MINT HONORS THE MIDDLE EASTERN ORIGINS OF THE PURLOO TECHNIQUE.

❊ COLD RICE SALAD WITH COUNTRY HAM, ❊ ENGLISH PEAS, AND MINT

QUICK
KNOCKOUT

IF SQUAB PURLOO (PAGE 178) TELLS US IT'S FALL, THIS COLD RICE SALAD, A LIVELY MEDLEY OF SWEET, TART, AND SALTY flavors, is a harbinger of summer—perfect for packing in Mason jars and taking to the beach or the park for a picnic.

For 4 people
TIME: 30 minutes

⅓ cup plus 1 tablespoon extra-virgin olive oil

1 cup long-grain rice

3 cups water

1 teaspoon salt, plus more to taste

1½ cups fresh English peas, shelled

2 tablespoons white wine vinegar

1 tablespoon lime juice

2 teaspoons Dijon mustard

¼ pound country ham (see "A Country Ham Primer," page 325), finely diced

½ cup coarsely chopped fresh mint (from about 8–10 stems)

Freshly ground black pepper to taste

1. Pour 1 tablespoon of the oil into a 1-quart saucepan over medium-high heat. When it shimmers, add the rice and sauté, stirring, until it releases some of its fragrance, about 1 minute. Add 2 cups of the water and 1 teaspoon salt and give it a gentle stir to distribute the rice evenly. When the water boils, reduce the heat to low, cover, and simmer vigorously until all the liquid is absorbed and the rice is tender, about 20 minutes. Spread the hot rice in a 9-×-13-inch roasting pan and place it in the freezer until chilled but not frozen, about 10 minutes.

2.   While the rice cooks, bring the remaining 1 cup water to a boil in a small saucepan over high heat. Add the peas and blanch until they are al dente, about 3 minutes. Strain the peas and run them under ice-cold water to stop the cooking.

3.   In a small bowl, whisk the remaining ⅓ cup oil with the vinegar, lime juice, and mustard until well blended, about 2 minutes.

4.   In a large bowl, combine the rice with the peas, ham, and mint. If the dressing has begun to separate, whisk again to emulsify. Pour the dressing evenly over the salad and toss gently to combine. Season to taste with salt and pepper.

✸ JAMBALAYA ✸

THE CREOLE DISHES OF LOUISIANA HAVE AN EVERY-
THING-BUT-THE-KITCHEN-SINK REPUTATION THAT SEEMS TO BE
reinforced by their very names—gumbo, étouffée, jambalaya. In reality, jambalaya is a complex,
carefully textured purloo of chicken, shrimp, and sausage that should be accorded the stature
Spain gives its much-heralded paella. A well-composed jambalaya provides nearly all the drama
and nutrition of a multicourse meal and needs only a bucket of cold beer or perhaps a simple green
salad to make it a small supper-party solution.

For 6 people

TIME: 1¼ hours

1 pound headless medium shrimp (41–50 per
      pound; see Sourcery, page 374), shells on
3½ cups Sunday Chicken Broth (page 352)
1 tablespoon Lee Bros. Shrimp Boil (page 553)
1 tablespoon canola oil, plus more if necessary
10 ounces smoked andouille sausage or
      chorizo, cut on the bias ¾ inch thick
6 chicken thighs, skinned (about 2 pounds)
About 2 teaspoons salt

About 2 teaspoons freshly ground black
      pepper
1 cup chopped yellow onion (about 1 large
      onion)
5 large garlic cloves, chopped
One 28-ounce can whole Italian tomatoes,
      drained, juice reserved
1 cup long-grain rice
Six 3–4-inch-long fresh thyme stems

1. Peel the shrimp and place in a bowl, reserving the shells separately. In a medium saucepan, bring the chicken broth to a boil over medium-high heat. Add the shrimp shells and the shrimp boil, turn the heat to low, and simmer for 30 minutes. Remove the shells and discard. Turn off the heat.

2. In a broad-bottomed 4-quart pot, heat the oil over medium-high heat until it shimmers. Add the sausage, turning the pieces with tongs until the outer surface of the sausage pieces are browned all over, about 6 minutes total. Remove to a plate and reserve the sausage.

3. Brown the chicken: Add the chicken thighs to the sausage fat in the pot—in batches, if necessary; don't crowd the pan—and sprinkle them with pinches of salt and pepper. Sauté them on one side until they are a rich golden brown, about 4 minutes, agitating them every so often and adding drops of oil, if necessary, to keep them from sticking. Turn the thighs, sprinkle them again with pinches of salt and pepper, and sauté until the other side is nicely browned. Remove to a plate and reserve.

4. **Add** the onion, garlic, and ¼ cup reserved tomato juice to the pot and sauté, stirring and scraping up any brown bits from the bottom, until the vegetables are softened and fragrant, about 3 minutes. Add the tomatoes, crushing them as you add them. Turn the heat to medium-low and simmer until the ingredients are thoroughly mixed and thickly soupy, 4 to 6 minutes. Add the chicken, nestling the thighs in the stew. Then add the sausage and any juices that may have drained from the chicken and the sausage.

5. Strain the broth into a measuring cup and add enough of the remaining tomato juice to make 3 cups of liquid. Add the liquid to the pot and then add the rice. Cover and cook over low heat for 25 minutes, or until the rice is tender and has absorbed most of the liquid. Turn off the heat and add the shrimp, stirring to distribute.

6. Let the jambalaya rest for 10 minutes before serving. The rice should be plump and very moist but not soupy. Serve in bowls, and garnish with the thyme.

❋ GREENS, PEAS, CORN, OKRA, CABBAGE, ❋
MUSHROOMS, AND SQUASH

WHERE DID THE SOUTH GET ITS REPUTATION FOR BEING HOSTILE TO VEGETARI-

ans? We don't know the answer, but we have a hunch that the brawnier side of southern food—the all-night vigil with a whole hog over a log fire, the catfish caught with bare hands and dunked in a fryer—is what southerners tend to show off (and people outside the South like to imagine). Growing heirloom beans, hunting for chanterelles, or pinching off tender, asparagus-like shoots of chainey briar that grow among the sand dunes just doesn't have quite the same ring.

Bill Best's stand at the farmers' market in Lexington, Kentucky, is a lesson in how deeply people in the South care about their vegetables and how fast they hold to their preferences. Best and his son Michael grow only heirloom tomatoes and beans, and they sell out their stock most every Saturday. Their plywood market tables flex beneath the weight of vibrantly colored tomatoes—the persimmon-orange Carolina Gold variety and the deep burgundy Cherokee Purples—and hillocks of several bean varieties, as different from one another in color and flavor as the tomatoes.

On a trip to the Lexington market, we eavesdropped on a man bagging handfuls of greasy beans (so called for their waxy appearance), who dared to say aloud, "You just can't beat these long greasies for flavor." Within seconds, a woman hefting tomatoes shot back, "I've always been a half-runner girl myself."

When we visited the Best Family Farm outside Berea, Kentucky, we had a revelation about the place of vegetables in southern cooking. Bill, a stocky seventy-something, with sprays of white hair shooting out from beneath his trucker's cap, taught English and physical education at Berea College until his retirement in 2002. But his passion has always been farming, particularly the varieties of beans and tomatoes he ate growing up in Haywood, North Carolina. In 1999 he founded the Sustainable Mountain Agricultural Center, a seed bank dedicated to preserving the bean and tomato heritage of the mountain South.

The Bests grow about twenty different beans (they keep hundreds more in the bank), and we struggled to keep up with Bill as he marched up and down his bean rows, rattling off the names of his varieties like a tobacco auctioneer: "Robe Mountain pole bean! Lazy-wife greasy bean! Striped-Hull greasy cut-short bean! Tennessee cornfield bean!" He split open pods to show us the speckled color of one bean, the milky-white complexion of another. Some pods had beans crowded up against each other so their ends appeared squared off; in other pods, there was a pinkie-width's space between beans.

As we walked, Best picked some beans and tossed them in a basket. Coming upon a row of heirloom tomato plants, he plucked a Cherokee Red and a Yellow German, the latter as big as a softball, colored deep lemon-yellow with red stripes. From a patch of dirt closer to the house, he dug up an onion. And then—hallelujah!—he invited us in for a simple supper of (you guessed it) salted and simmered beans, slices of raw onion and tomato, and corn bread.

Later that evening, we realized that in three days of traveling in eastern Kentucky, we had eaten no meat. Growing up in Charleston, we rarely ate meals without some sort of fish or shellfish, pork, beef, or game. A friend of ours, Ronni Lundy, who grew up in Corbin, not far from Berea, explained that in eastern Kentucky, vegetable pride and hardship often meant that dinners composed of full-flavored vegetables were the norm.

Okra, sweet potatoes, and collards get most of the attention as southern vegetable icons, but the truth is that southerners tease flavor out of all sorts of vegetables, including squash, corn, and particularly fresh shell peas (*Vigna unguiculata*, in the legume family, like common beans *Phaseolus vulgaris*), of which there is a dizzying array in late summer: crowder peas, field peas, cow peas, lady cream peas, and purple-hull peas, just to name a few. Most often, southerners give their vegetables the gift of understatement, cooking freshly picked vegetables unadorned or with a little salty seasoning meat such as smoked hog jowl. But southern cooks have developed colorful dishes like squash casserole, corn pudding, and field-pea salads that build on the vegetables' flavors and often transform them from side players into stunning centerpieces.

❋ BEST FAMILY FARM CORN-BREAD SALAD ❋

THIS SALAD IS A TRIBUTE TO THE MEAL BILL AND BERTIE BEST SHARED WITH US IN BEREA, KENTUCKY, WHICH INCLUDED sweet raw onions, terrific corn bread, and the best (no pun intended) tomatoes we've ever tasted. Theirs were old varieties, ridged orbs in radiant colors: orange, purple, yellow, citronella green, and a deep red. They were juicy and had the acidity, sweetness, and fernlike aroma you expect from a tomato at the height of summer.

You don't have to use the rarest heirloom tomato varieties for this recipe, but try to find the freshest, ripest ones you can. They make all the difference in this salad, a close cousin to the Italian panzanella (a salad enriched with cubes of bread). The dish is an excellent lunch on its own or a terrific vegetable plate with Matt's Honey-Glazed Field Peas (page 226) and Sneaky Collards (page 210).

We peel our tomatoes because our mother did, and they may taste better that way. If we're pressed for time, we'll take a small bite out of a tomato and decide whether the skin is tender enough to chew. If it is, we'll gladly skip the peeling step, and you can, too.

For 8 people

TIME: 30 minutes

1 recipe Crispy Corn Bread (page 497), cut
    into 1-inch squares
2 cups water
1½ pounds ripe tomatoes (4–6 medium
    tomatoes)
6 cups roughly torn sturdy fresh lettuce, such
    as Bibb, butter, or Boston lettuce

2 cups bitter greens, such as arugula or
    dandelion greens
1 large Vidalia onion, trimmed, peeled, sliced
    crosswise as thinly as possible, and
    separated into rings
1 recipe Buttermilk-Lime Dressing (page 519)

1. Preheat the oven to 250 degrees.

2. Scatter the corn bread in a single layer on a half-sheet pan, and bake until the pieces are lightly toasted, about 7 minutes.

3. While the corn bread toasts, peel the tomatoes. Pour the water into a small saucepan and bring to a boil over high heat. Drive a dinner fork into the stem end of one tomato and plunge it into the boiling water for 30 seconds. Remove and run the tomato under a vigorous stream of cold water for 30 seconds. The skin should begin to break around the fork's tines. Lift the skin away, with the help of a paring knife if necessary. Repeat with the remaining tomatoes.

4. Cut each tomato in half crosswise. Using your index finger, tease out the seed clusters and their juice into a small bowl and reserve. Chop the tomatoes and reserve them in a large salad bowl. Hold a wire-mesh strainer above the bowl of tomatoes and dump the reserved seed clusters and juice into it. Tap the strainer quickly and forcefully against your palm for about 1 minute to extract as much juice as possible from the seeds. You should be left with only seeds in the bottom of the strainer. Discard them.

5. Add the lettuce, greens, 3 cups of the toasted corn bread (reserve any excess cornbread for another use), and onion to the bowl of tomatoes and toss to combine. Drizzle the buttermilk dressing over the salad, toss again, and serve immediately.

✳ A NEW AMBROSIA ✳

AMBROSIA IS THE NAME OF A COLD, SWEET, CHUNKY
SALAD FOUND IN MOST SOUTHERN CAFETERIAS. WE'VE REINVENTED
it from top to bottom.

The original ambrosia calls for canned tangerine segments, canned pineapple chunks, mini-marshmallows, shredded coconut, and mayonnaise. It is bracingly sweet, but we often find it served, bizarrely enough, as a side dish with the main course, which seems out of whack—a salad created for someone who'd rather eat dessert first. But the idea of "a food for the gods"—a cool, creamy salad that isn't coleslaw—appeals greatly to us, so we fiddled with the elements and came up with something new.

Here we substitute fresh grapefruit and orange for the canned tangerines and crisp cucumber and celery for the pineapple. Chopped avocado provides the soft creaminess of the marshmallows in the original. There is no mayo here, but instead a brisk dressing of buttermilk, lime juice, tarragon, and garlic, with the gentle sweetness of shredded coconut (a direct carryover from the original). It's a salad with beautiful contrasting textures, pretty colors, and bright flavors. This ambrosia is as crunchy and cool as coleslaw but with herbal notes instead of vinegary ones. Like coleslaw, it's brilliant paired with anything fried or spicy. Sometimes we serve a scoop of New Ambrosia over a small bed of arugula as the salad course in a larger meal.

For 4 people

FOR THE SALAD

1 large grapefruit, supremed (see Technique, page 192)

1 large navel orange, supremed

¾ cup chopped celery (about 2 stalks)

1¼ cups finely diced Haas avocado (about 1 avocado)

1½ cups seeded and chopped cucumber (about 1 large cucumber)

¼ cup coarsely chopped fresh basil

1 fresh jalapeño pepper, seeded and minced

FOR THE DRESSING

⅔ cup buttermilk

2 tablespoons lime juice

1 tablespoon extra-virgin olive oil

1 garlic clove, mashed to a puree

1 tablespoon plus 1 teaspoon finely chopped fresh tarragon

2 tablespoons unsweetened shredded coconut (if unsweetened is unavailable, use 1 tablespoon plus 1 teaspoon sweetened shredded coconut)

1 teaspoon kosher salt

½ teaspoon freshly ground black pepper

1. In a large bowl, combine all the salad ingredients.

2. In a medium bowl, whisk the buttermilk, lime juice, and olive oil until blended. Whisk in the garlic puree, tarragon, coconut, salt, and pepper. Pour the dressing over the salad and toss.

3. If you wish, cover with plastic wrap and refrigerate for up to 1 hour to cool the salad and allow the flavors to meld. Toss again before serving, and serve with a slotted spoon.

191

{ GREENS, PEAS, CORN, OKRA, CABBAGE, MUSHROOMS, AND SQUASH }

SUPREMES ARE SEGMENTS OF GRAPEFRUIT AND ORANGE that contain only pulp—no peel, no pith, not even the thin membrane that articulates sections of the fruit. The unadulterated, pure pulp of citrus supremes is perfect in salads, and it's easy to create. Start by trimming off the bottom and top of the fruit (about a 3-inch round for a grapefruit, a 2-inch round for a navel orange). Now you have a flat surface on which to balance the fruit, and at the stem end you have a cross-section that reveals where the pulp meets the pith. Begin peeling the fruit by placing the tip of a sharp knife just inside the border where pith meets the pulp and slicing down with a firm, clean stroke, following the curvature of the fruit. Repeat until the entire fruit has been peeled. Gently cut out the segments of pulp with a sharp paring knife by cutting toward the core, as close as possible to the membrane that separates the segments.

☀ SUCCOTASH SALAD ☀

THIS EASY AND REFRESHING SALAD IS THE QUINTES-
SENCE OF SUMMER, AND PERFECT FOR PICNICKING. OUR GRANDMA
Lee made a similar salad with ingredients from the garden she tended ferociously in upstate New
York, but it reminds us of long summer days surfing at Isle of Palms, just north of Charleston.
We'd put it in Mason jars, pack it in a cooler, and take it to the beach. It tastes every bit as good on
a dinner plate.

For 6 people
TIME: 20 minutes

2 quarts water
4 ears fresh sweet corn, husks removed
2 cups fresh or frozen shelled beans, such as
    butterbeans, baby limas, or lady cream
    peas (about 1½ pounds unshelled)
3 ripe medium tomatoes, skinned, seeded, and
    roughly chopped

½ cup coarsely chopped fresh basil
3 tablespoons lime juice
¼ cup extra-virgin olive oil
1 teaspoon Dijon mustard
Kosher salt to taste
Freshly ground black pepper to taste

1. In a large stockpot over high heat, bring the water to a rolling boil. Add the corn, return to a boil, and boil vigorously for 2 minutes. Using tongs, transfer the corn to a colander. Place it beneath a stream of cold water to halt the cooking. Reserve.

2. Add the beans to the corn cooking water, return to a boil, and boil vigorously until the beans are soft, 13 to 18 minutes. Strain the beans in a colander and place them beneath a stream of cold water for 1 minute to halt the cooking. Reserve.

3. Cut the corn from the cobs, making sure to scrape the cobs up and down with the edge of a spoon to remove the juicy bits still adhering to them. Place the corn kernels and corn juice in a large bowl and add the beans, tomatoes, and basil. Stir gently to combine.

4. Whisk together the lime juice, olive oil, and mustard until emulsified. Season to taste with salt and pepper. Pour the dressing over the salad and toss.

5. Cover the salad with plastic wrap and refrigerate until ready to serve, up to 4 hours. Toss every 30 minutes to make certain the flavors meld evenly, and toss once again before serving.

Heirloom beans aglow in the waning summer sun, on the Best Family Farm outside Berea, Kentucky.

❄ COLESLAW ❄

QUICK
KNOCKOUT

FRIED FOOD SEEMS TO DEMAND THE COOL CRUNCH OF COLESLAW. PROMISE US THAT YOU'LL MAKE THIS SLAW WHENEVER you make Sunday Fried Chicken (page 335), Tuesday Fried Chicken (page 333), Fried Oysters (page 388), Fried Green Tomatoes (page 214), Crispy Fried Okra (page 217), or Chicken-Fried Steak with Vidalia Cream Gravy (page 364). But this recipe's also a knockout with Easy North Carolina–Style Half Picnic Shoulder (page 355) and Oven BBQed Picnic Shoulder (page 349). Come to think of it, this may be the most get-along recipe in the book; it will flatter virtually any dish it's served with.

Two secrets to great coleslaw: a delicious dressing, and cutting the cabbage as thinly as possible, so that it looks more like spaghetti than coleslaw. Trust us. If your slaw is light and thin, you don't have to blanch the cabbage at all.

For 8 people

TIME: 15 minutes

One 3-pound napa or green cabbage
½ cup mayonnaise, preferably Lemony
   Mayonnaise (page 524)
½ cup Chowchow (page 108), Jerusalem
   Artichoke Relish (page 112), or your
   favorite store-bought, not-too-sweet
   pickle relish

1 tablespoon Dijon mustard
2 tablespoons lemon juice (from 1 lemon)
Kosher salt to taste
Freshly ground black pepper to taste

195

1.   Cut the cabbage in half with a sharp knife and cut out the dense wedge of core. Slice each half into quarters and slice each quarter into very thin ribbons, about ⅛ inch thick, with a knife or a mandoline. You should have about 10 cups.

2.   Whisk together the mayonnaise, relish, mustard, and lemon juice.

3.   Place the cabbage in a large bowl, pour the dressing over it, and toss to coat evenly. Season to taste with salt and pepper and toss again.

4.   Cover the coleslaw with plastic wrap and refrigerate until ready to serve, up to 4 hours. Toss it every 30 minutes to make certain the flavors meld evenly, and toss once again before serving.

✺ BLACKENED POTATO SALAD ✺

REMEMBER BLACKENED REDFISH, A FILLET COATED WITH CREOLE SPICES AND SEARED? IT TOOK NORTH AMERICAN RESTAU-rant menus by storm in the late eighties. When our uncle John Maxwell opened Allen's, his Toronto restaurant, in 1986, he invented this salad, an addictive marriage of "blackened" tech-nique with our favorite picnic side dish.

When John gave us this recipe, he warned us that it creates an alarming amount of smoke. He's right: it's better suited to a power-vented restaurant kitchen than a home kitchen, but the results are so good that we had to include it. We've learned that if you keep your windows open and you have tolerant neighbors, you'll be richly rewarded.

For 8 people

TIME: 1½ hours

¼ cup plus 2 teaspoons kosher salt

5 pounds red potatoes, peeled and cut into
   quarters

½ cup Hungarian paprika

½ cup stone-ground cornmeal

¼ cup dried oregano

2½ tablespoons ground cayenne pepper

1½ tablespoons freshly ground black pepper

2 teaspoons garlic powder

2 teaspoons dehydrated onion

2 tablespoons dried thyme

1 tablespoon peanut oil, canola oil, or
   grapeseed oil

4 tablespoons (½ stick) unsalted butter

1½ cups top-quality store-bought mayonnaise, such as Duke's or Hellmann's

1 cup plain yogurt

½ cup finely chopped green onion

½ cup chopped cilantro (optional)

1. Fill an 8-quart stockpot with water, add ¼ cup salt, and bring to a boil over high heat. Add the potatoes and cook until just fork-tender, about 9 minutes.

2. Mix the paprika, cornmeal, oregano, cayenne pepper, black pepper, the remaining 2 teaspoons salt, garlic powder, dehydrated onion, and thyme thoroughly together in a large bowl.

3. Drain the potatoes and let cool completely. Toss half the potatoes in the bowl until they are coated evenly and well with the spice mixture. Transfer to a coarse-gauged strainer or colander, and shake off any excess spice mixture. Place in a second large bowl. Repeat with the remaining potatoes and reserve. Discard any excess spice mixture and wipe the first bowl clean.

4. Turn the ventilation fan to high and open all windows. Pour 1½ teaspoons oil into a 12-inch cast-iron skillet or large sauté pan over high heat and tilt the pan to coat the bottom thinly and evenly. When the oil begins to smoke, add half the potatoes and cook, shaking the pan frequently, about 3 minutes. Add 2 tablespoons butter and cook for 4 minutes more, continuing to shake the pan, until the potatoes are blackened. Transfer to the clean bowl. With a metal spatula, scrape up any bits of char and blackened spice that cling to the pan and discard. Add the remaining 1½ teaspoons oil and tilt the pan to coat the bottom evenly. Add the remaining potatoes and repeat until blackened, then transfer to the bowl.

5. Add the mayonnaise, yogurt, green onion, and cilantro, if desired, to the blackened potatoes and toss until the potatoes are evenly coated, about 1 minute.

6. Serve immediately, with grilled hamburgers and hot dogs, or refrigerate for up to two days. When serving leftovers that have been refrigerated, bring to room temperature before serving.

❧ HOT SLAW À LA GREYHOUND GRILL ❧

QUICK
KNOCKOUT

THE GREYHOUND GRILL, IN ERLANGER, KENTUCKY, HAS SOME OF THE FINEST FRIED CHICKEN WE'VE EVER TASTED, AND perhaps more important, it introduced us to hot slaw—cabbage cooked in spicy vinegar and studded with smoky, hand-cut bacon. This dish is now such a regular on our table that we can't believe we ever lived without it.

The bacon is key here. Greyhound uses a deeply smoked bacon, real bacon, the kind most midwesterners take as a birthright and other folks can go a lifetime without ever tasting. We find slab bacon—which is simply unsliced bacon—at a butcher shop and dice it chunkily to get that Midwest effect. You can also mail-order it (see "Sourcery: Slab Bacon," page 202), but if you can't find great bacon and can't wait for it, use the thickest, smokiest bacon you can (most supermarkets now stock at least one decent bacon, considered a premium product and often labeled "thick-cut").

The Greyhound uses green cabbage, but we prefer red, or a mix of the two. The color will appear to leach out as it blanches, the leaves turning a pallid grayish purple. Not to worry. Once you toss it in the hot vinegar in the skillet, the color will return, an electric, vibrant magenta that's a dazzling contrast to the golden crust of a Sunday Fried Chicken leg (page 335).

For 6 people

TIME: 15 minutes

One 3-pound red cabbage, cored and coarsely shredded, or a mix of red and green cabbages (10–12 cups)

¼ pound slab bacon or 4 slices thick-cut bacon, diced

½ cup white vinegar, cider vinegar, or white wine vinegar

½ teaspoon celery seeds

¼ teaspoon crushed red pepper flakes

2 teaspoons salt

1 teaspoon freshly ground black pepper

Pepper Vinegar (page 518) to taste

1. In an 8-quart stockpot, bring 4 quarts water to a boil over high heat. Blanch the cabbage by submerging it in the boiling water just until it turns a dull grayish purple, about 5 minutes. Drain in a colander, shake the colander for a minute or so to remove excess water, and reserve.

2. Scatter the bacon in a 12-inch dry skillet over medium-high heat. With a wooden spoon, move the pieces around until the bacon is firm and barely crisp, about 4 minutes. Remove with a slotted spoon and reserve.

3. Pour the vinegar into the skillet. It will hiss and pop at first but will soon subside. Swirl the vinegar around with the spoon, stirring up any browned bits of bacon. Add the celery seeds and red pepper flakes and stir.

4. Add the cabbage to the skillet and toss to coat it with the vinegar. Add the salt, pepper, and reserved bacon, and continue to sauté, stirring the cabbage around the pan until all its bright magenta glory has returned, about 4 minutes.

5. Place the slaw in a bowl and shake pepper vinegar over it to taste. Pass the cruet at the table for those who wish to fire it up further.

SOURCERY: SLAB BACON

WE DICE SMOKED SLAB BACON OFTEN IN THIS BOOK for the simple reason that frying several ounces as you begin a recipe yields two excellent ingredients: a cooking oil that, used judiciously, adds an indescribable savoriness and smokiness to the finished dish; and a garnish of crisp lardoons that pack terrific flavor and provide an appealing textural counterpoint. We simply adore slab bacon, but if it doesn't fit into your cooking style, substitute olive oil, canola oil, or peanut oil, or blend the vegetable oil half-and-half with the bacon grease if you prefer.

Most butchers and even supermarket delicatessens offer slab bacon, but if you can't find it locally, one great source is Early's smokehouse in Spring Hill, Tennessee, which has been smoking sausages and bacon since 1925. They sell half-slabs (4 to 5 pounds for $28.95 plus shipping) with the rind cut off; most places do. But if you can only get slab bacon with the rind on, simply trim it off with a sharp chef's knife. Early's also makes a big deal about how lean its hickory-smoked bacon is, but we find it renders plenty of fat for our recipes that call for bacon fat. Early's Authentic Southern Foods and Gifts, P.O. Box 908, Spring Hill, TN 37174; 1-800-523-2015; www.earlysgifts.com.

⚛ KILT LETTUCE AND RAMPS ⚛

"KILT LETTUCE," OR "KILLED LETTUCE," IS USED BY MOUNTAIN FOLK THROUGHOUT THE APPALACHIANS TO REFER TO any lettuce that has been partly wilted with hot salad dressing. It's a subtle dish and a fresh, warm alternative to a chilly salad or a soggy mound of steamed spinach. Kilt lettuce works best with smooth, tender greens like Bibb and butter lettuce. We like to "kill" ours in combination with an unsubtle allium, like chives, scallion tops, or ramps, the pungent wild onions whose dark green bladelike leaves emerge from the forest floor in springtime throughout the mountain range that runs from upstate New York to eastern Georgia. Ramps are appearing more and more frequently at farmers' markets these days, but when we can't find them, the tops of any grocery-store bunch of green onions (called scallions in the Northeast and spring onions in Britain) work perfectly in this dish.

Since ramps are collected by hand and are typically quite expensive to buy at market, one way to stretch their flavor is to mince the bulbs and incorporate them in the salad dressing. We discovered this when we cooked an Appalachian feast at a museum event in western Massachusetts. We flew in by FedEx all the ramps we could get—five pounds collected by the Facemires, in West Virginia. Admittedly, ramps pack a terrific punch. So after washing the floppy greens and peeling the outer layer off the pink bulbs (which are wonderful pickled, see page 124), we chopped the bulbs finely and sautéed them in the smoky bacon fat we used in the salad dressing. The bracing, garlicky flavor of the ramps permeated the entire batch, over a hundred heads of Boston lettuce (and over 250 heads of Massachusetts folk!).

6 cups tightly packed hand-torn Bibb or
    butter lettuce

1⅓ cups coarsely chopped ramp greens or
    scallion greens, bulbs reserved and
    finely chopped

¼ pound slab bacon or 4 slices thick-cut
    bacon, diced

2 tablespoons extra-virgin olive oil

½ cup red wine vinegar

2 teaspoons Dijon mustard

½ teaspoon sugar

Kosher salt to taste

Freshly ground black pepper to taste

1. Toss the lettuce and ramp greens together in a large salad bowl.

2. Scatter the bacon in a 12-inch cast-iron skillet or sauté pan over medium-high heat. Move the pieces around until the bacon is firm and barely crisp, about 4 minutes. Remove with a slotted spoon and reserve.

3. Reduce the heat to medium and pour the oil into the skillet. Add the chopped ramp bulbs and sauté until very fragrant and just beginning to lose their opacity, about 2 minutes.

4. In a small bowl, whisk the vinegar with the mustard and sugar, and pour the vinegar into the skillet. It will hiss and pop at first but will soon subside. Swirl the liquid around with the spoon, stirring up any browned bits of bacon. Add half the greens to the skillet and turn them until the lettuce begins to wilt, about 15–30 seconds. Add the remaining greens and continue to turn until most of the greens have wilted about 30 more seconds.

5. Transfer the contents of the skillet into the salad bowl, dressing and all, and toss a few times to incorporate the dressing. Scatter the reserved bacon over the kilt greens and toss again. Season to taste with the salt and black pepper and serve immediately.

VARIATION—KILT COBB SALAD: JUST TWO CHANGES TO THIS RECIPE MAKE IT A SNEAKY AND DELI-CIOUS SOUTHERN TAKE ON A TIRED NORTHERN CLASSIC. SUBSTITUTE FRESH SPINACH FOR THE LET-TUCE, AND TOSS 4 SLICED HARD-BOILED EGGS INTO THE KILT LETTUCE AT THE SAME TIME YOU ADD THE CRISPED BACON.

❋ SUNDAY COLLARDS ❋

NOT EVEN BLUEBERRIES HAVE MORE ANTIOXIDANTS—
THOSE MYSTERIOUS ANTI-AGING ENZYMES—THAN CRUCIFEROUS
greens like collards. And it's a good thing, too, because no one eats many blueberries in the winter months, when the sturdy greens are abundant in markets north and south. In fact, New Jersey,
one of the preeminent blueberry-growing states in the East, is also among the biggest producers
of collard greens. Makes you wonder what's in the water there!

Braised greens often get a bad rap for being one-dimensional and overcooked, and while this
is too often the case, overcooking isn't the only culprit. It's usually clumsy seasoning that makes
them pallid. The key to getting depth of flavor in a minerally green is a low simmer and a richly
seasoned pot likker. For more information about buying and preparing collards, see "Sizing a
Bunch of Collards," page 212, and "Washing and Cutting Collards," page 213.

We like to freeze this pot likker to use as stock when we make soup. But more often, the likker
doesn't linger beyond the afternoon after we've served the collards. A few wedges of Crispy Corn
Bread (page 497) crumbled into a hot bowl of it makes a delicious lunch, garnished with minced
onion and a shot of Pepper Vinegar (page 518) or Tabasco.

For 6 people

TIME: 2 hours

1 tablespoon extra-virgin olive oil, peanut oil,
    or canola oil
1 smoked ham hock or smoked hog jowl or
    ¼ pound slab bacon, diced
8 cups water
3 dried chile peppers or 1 tablespoon crushed
    red pepper flakes

1 tablespoon kosher salt
3¾ pounds collard greens (about 72 leaves, or
    3 bunches), ribbed, washed, and cut
    into 1-inch-wide strips

1.   Pour the oil into an 8-quart stockpot over medium-high heat and swirl it around so it covers the bottom. Score the ham hock with a small sharp knife, and when the oil begins to shimmer, set it in the pot. Sear the hock all over as best you can and allow it to render some fat, about 6 minutes (since a hock's shape is so oblique, it will become spottily browned, but that is fine).

2.   Pour the water into the pot; it will hiss and pop for a few seconds. Add the chiles and salt and bring to a boil over high heat. Reduce the heat to medium-low and simmer for 30 minutes, until the stock is deeply flavored with smoke and spiciness.

3.   Add a few handfuls of the collards to the pot. The greens will float on the surface, so stir them frequently, submerging them with the spoon, until they have turned a bright kelly green (3 to 5 minutes) and become floppier and more compact, so you can add more handfuls. Continue adding handfuls of collards, stirring and submerging them, until all the greens are in the pot (6 to 10 minutes). Turn the heat to low and simmer very gently for 1 hour. The greens will be a very dark matte green and completely tender.

4.   Place on plates with a slotted spoon, and pass a cruet of Pepper Vinegar at the table.

KILLER LEFTOVER—COLLARD GREENS EGG-DROP SOUP: WE SAVE LEFTOVER COLLARD GREENS IN THEIR LIQUOR IN THE REFRIGERATOR, BECAUSE WITH STRATEGIC ADDITIONS OF CANNED TOMATOES, BEANS, ONIONS, OR POTATOES, THEY BECOME THE FOUNDATION FOR TERRIFIC SOUPS. OUR HANDS-DOWN FAVORITE IS COLLARD GREENS EGG-DROP SOUP, WHICH WE MAKE BY REHEATING LEFTOVER GREENS AND LIQUOR IN A LARGE SAUCEPAN OVER MEDIUM-HIGH HEAT AND GENTLY CRACKING INTO THEM 2 EGGS FOR EVERY 2 CUPS OF LEFTOVER GREENS AND LIQUOR (ONE LARGE SERVING WILL BE EXACTLY THAT SIZE). WE SIMMER THE SOUP UNTIL THE EGGS ARE JUST POACHED, ABOUT 8 MINUTES. IF YOU PREFER YOUR YOLKS HARDER, YOU CAN CONTINUE COOKING THE SOUP UNTIL THE EGGS ARE DONE TO YOUR LIKING, ABOUT 3 MINUTES FOR A YOLK WITH A HARD EXTERIOR AND A SOFT CENTER AND 5 MINUTES FOR A YOLK THAT IS COMPLETELY HARD-COOKED.

❧ TUESDAY COLLARDS ❧

WHEN IT COMES TO COLLARDS, THERE'S A DIVIDE BETWEEN THE ANCIENTS, WHO BELIEVE THAT COLLARDS HAVE TO be simmered for many hours in water to be digestible, and the Moderns, who claim to have invented braising collards lightly in a skillet. The Ancients, the Moderns say, are wasting time, and cooking the life—and the nutrition—from their greens.

Both claims are specious. There are numerous ways to cook collards, and each method coaxes different flavors and personalities out of these wondrous greens. Sometimes we crave the dense, murky, turniplike flavor of our slow-simmered Sunday Collards (page 205), but we also love these vibrant, skillet-cooked Tuesday Collards, which take half as long to prepare. We slice the greens thinner, so they cook more quickly, and they come out only slightly less tender than slow-simmered collards. And we don't take the time to remove the ribs from the leaves; since we're cutting the collards so thin, we just trim the toughest stems from the bunch with a single stroke of the knife. The flavor of collard greens (a bit like broccoli, and virtually irresistible when you're washing them) plays off the smoky heat of chiles and bacon. They're a welcome pick-me-up at the end of a long day's work.

For more information about buying and preparing collards, see "Sizing a Bunch of Collards," page 212, and "Washing and Cutting Collards," page 213.

For 4 people

TIME: 30 minutes

¼ pound slab bacon or 4 slices thick-cut bacon, diced

2 pounds collard greens (about 48 leaves, or 2 large bunches), stemmed, washed, and cut into ¼-inch-wide strips

1 cup Tuesday Chicken Broth (page 534) or Tuesday Vegetable Broth (page 540)

¼ teaspoon crushed red pepper flakes (optional)

2 tablespoons white wine vinegar or cider vinegar

½ teaspoon sugar

Kosher salt to taste

Freshly ground black pepper to taste

1. Scatter the bacon in a 12-inch skillet or sauté pan over medium-high heat and cook until just firm, about 3 minutes.

2. Turn the heat to medium and add 2 handfuls of collards to the skillet. Using a slotted spoon, turn them in the bacon fat for a couple of minutes until they wilt; just steam them in the small amount of water that clings to them, but don't let them brown. Add more collards, 2 handfuls at a time, and turn them until they wilt, until all the collards are wilted in the pan.

3. Add the chicken broth and the red pepper flakes, if using. Turn the heat to medium-high and cook until the broth comes to a simmer. Reduce the heat to low, cover, and cook until the greens have turned dark, about 5 minutes.

4. Add the vinegar and sugar to the greens, toss to distribute, and cook, uncovered, about 5 minutes more to let the cooking liquid reduce and concentrate.

5. Season with salt and pepper and serve hot, with Tuesday Fried Chicken (page 333) or Pork Loin Chops with Pear and Vidalia Pan Gravy (page 316).

❋ SNEAKY COLLARDS ❋

VEGETARIANS SHOULDN'T HAVE TO GO WITHOUT LUSTY, SMOKY GREENS, SO WE DEVISED THIS RECIPE, WHICH WE CALL "sneaky" because these collards might fool you into believing they're made with bacon.

For more information about buying and preparing collards, see "Sizing a Bunch of Collards," page 212, and "Washing and Cutting Collards," page 213.

For 6 people

TIME: 70 minutes

8 cups water

3 dried chiles or 1 tablespoon crushed red pepper flakes

1 tablespoon plus 1 teaspoon kosher salt, plus more to taste

3¾ pounds collard greens (about 72 leaves or 3 bunches), ribbed, washed, and cut into 1-inch wide strips

1 large onion, trimmed, peeled, and quartered

1 large tomato, cored and quartered

2 tablespoons extra-virgin olive oil

1 tablespoon balsamic vinegar, sherry vinegar, or red wine vinegar

1 teaspoon Spanish smoked paprika (*pimentón*) or Hungarian paprika

3 cloves garlic

1 teaspoon freshly ground black pepper

1. In an 8-quart stockpot, bring the water to a boil over high heat. Add the chiles and 1 tablespoon salt, reduce the heat to medium-low, and simmer until the stock has a nice salty spiciness, about 10 minutes.

2. Add a few handfuls of greens to the pot. They will float on the surface, so stir them frequently, submerging with the spoon, until they have turned a bright kelly green, 3 to 5 minutes. They will become floppy and more compact, so you can add more handfuls of greens. Continue adding greens, stirring and submerging them until all the collards are in the pot (6 to 10 minutes). Turn the heat down to the gentlest simmer, and note your time at this point.

3. While the greens simmer, place the onion and tomato in a small bowl. Drizzle the olive oil and vinegar over them, add 1 teaspoon salt, the paprika, and the pepper, and toss to coat. Transfer the vegetables to a medium cast-iron skillet and add the garlic. Place the skillet under a hot broiler, about 3 inches from the flame or heating element, until the vegetables are nicely charred, 6 to 8 minutes. Set them on the stovetop to cool.

4. When the garlic is cool enough to touch, peel the cloves and return them to the skillet, discarding the charred skins. Transfer the broiled onion, tomato, and garlic to a blender or food processor and blend at high speed until the mixture is completely smooth, about 3 minutes. You should have close to 1½ cups of puree.

5. With a ladle, remove 6 cups of stock from the collards pot and discard or save for soup. Add the puree and continue to simmer the greens, for a total of 1 hour from the point at which you noted the time. The greens will be a very dark matte green and completely tender, bathed in pale red gravy.

6. Transfer servings to plates with a slotted spoon, and pass a cruet of Pepper Vinegar (page 518) at the table.

AT OUR LOCAL MARKET, WHICH CHARGES BY THE bunch, not by the pound, a bunch can weigh anything from 1½ to 3 pounds. A bunch might have one plant with 28 leaves or three plants with only 18 leaves among them. So we did some not-so-scientific research and found that if you budget 12 Romaine-lettuce-sized leaves per serving, everyone gets a generous portion. In our recipes, you'll always find a weight, a leaf count, and an approximate bunch count.

TECHNIQUE: WASHING AND CUTTING COLLARDS

ON EACH PLANT—WHICH IS TO SAY, EACH GROUPING of leaves that rise from a central trunk—chop off the stems where they meet the leaf and discard them. If the collards look clean, you might get away with simply soaking them in a large stockpot. But we recommend washing each leaf by rubbing it briefly between your hands under a stream of cold water.

We find collards to be more manageable to cook, and to cook more evenly, if you cut the ribs—the tough extension of the stem that rises up the center of the leaf—from the leaves and discard them. So when we have the time, we slice the rib from each leaf on a cutting board with a small paring knife, which leaves us with two half-leaves, roughly mirror images of each other. As we remove the ribs, we stack these halves on top of one another into piles a few inches high. We roll the stack into a tight cigar, then we take a large chef's knife and cut the cigar crosswise, on the bias, into strips about ½ to 1 inch wide (¼ inch for Tuesday Collards, page 208).

If that sounds compulsive, just tear the leaves from the ribs with your hands as you wash them. But be sure to tear each leaf into strips. The larger the pieces, the more unwieldy they are when it comes time to transfer them to the pot.

❋ FRIED GREEN TOMATOES ❋

GREEN TOMATOES, WHICH ARE SIMPLY UNRIPE TOMA-
TOES, HAVE A TART, BRISK FLAVOR AND APPLE-LIKE CRUNCH THAT
brightens up salsas and makes a marvelous jam. But they are especially delectable sliced and deep-
fried; their tangy flesh is a perfect foil for a rich, toasty crust. We amp up the tartness by serving
them with ramekins of Buttermilk-Lime Dressing (page 519) for dipping. If it's a more ambitious
affair, we'll lay a few tomato slices on small beds of fresh spinach and arugula and drizzle each
plate with the dressing.

If we can't find green tomatoes (see "Sourcery: Green Tomatoes," page 216), we use supermarket red tomatoes, which most months of the year are so firm they might as well be green. Since
such tomatoes are rarely as sour and flavorful as green ones, we sprinkle a pinch of salt and a
squirt of lemon juice on each slice before dredging it to coax out more tomato flavor.

For 6 people

TIME: 30 minutes

3 pounds green tomatoes (about 6–8 medium
tomatoes)
3 large eggs, beaten
¾ cup whole milk
3 cups peanut oil

3 batches Lee Bros. All-Purpose Fry Dredge
(page 552)
Kosher salt, if needed
Lemon juice, if needed

1. Cut out the stem ends from the tomatoes and slice them ¼-inch-thick with a serrated tomato or bread knife; reserve. Whisk the eggs and milk together in a broad, shallow bowl.

2. Pour the oil into a 12-inch skillet and heat over medium-high heat until the temperature on a candy thermometer reads 365 degrees. (If using a different size skillet or pan, fill with oil to a depth of ⅓ inch.)

3. Heat the oven to 225 degrees. Set a baker's rack on a cookie sheet on the top rack.

4. Spread the dredge on a large plate or pie pan or in a small, shallow baking pan. Taste the tomatoes. They should have a bright tartness like citrus fruit. If they don't, sprinkle the slices with salt and lemon juice. Then press 1 tomato slice into the dredge, once on each side, shaking any excess loose. Dunk in the egg mixture, then dredge the slice on both sides again. Shake off any excess and place the slice on a clean plate. Repeat with more slices until you've dredged enough for a batch (3 or 4 slices). With a spatula, transfer the first batch of slices to the oil.

5. As the first batch cooks, dredge the second batch of tomatoes, but keep a watchful eye on the first. Once the slices have fried to a rich golden brown on one side, about 2 minutes, flip them carefully and fry for 2 minutes more, or until golden brown. Transfer the fried tomatoes to a plate lined with a double thickness of paper towels and leave them to drain for 1 minute.

6. Transfer the slices to the baker's rack in the oven, arranging them in a single layer, so they remain warm and crisp. Repeat with the remaining slices until all the green tomatoes have been fried. Serve right away with Buttermilk-Lime Dressing (page 519).

GREEN TOMATOES RARELY MAKE IT TO MARKET, SO TRY to find a farm or farmstand you can request them from. Since the season for green tomatoes is longer than that of ripe tomatoes—because they're available from the moment the fruit appears on the vine until the first frost—just talk to a local tomato grower. We've never met one who hasn't been delighted to turn his or her green tomatoes into greenbacks.

❊ CRISPY FRIED OKRA ❊

QUICK
KNOCKOUT

FRIED OKRA IS A DYNAMITE SIDE DISH FOR ALL SORTS OF ENTRÉES, OUR FAVORITE MATCHES BEING CITY HAM STEAK WITH Red-Eye Gravy (page 346), Grilled Mahimahi with Fresh Peach Relish (page 384), and Shrimp Burgers (page 382). But it's as addictive as popcorn, so we often pass it during cocktail hour as a snack. Keep the fried okra warm in the oven in an uncovered earthenware dish. When the first guests arrive, fill a few butcher-paper or newspaper cones with the okra, shake some chile flakes and sea salt over them, and pass the cones around while the guests are tucking into their cocktails.

Makes 2 pounds; enough for 6 to 8 as a side dish, and 12 for snacking

TIME: 30 minutes

4 cups peanut or canola oil

2 large eggs, beaten

¾ cup whole milk

2 cups stone-ground cornmeal

3 tablespoons all-purpose flour

1½ teaspoons salt

1½ teaspoons freshly ground black pepper

2 pounds fresh okra, sliced into ½-inch-thick rounds (about 7 cups)

Crushed red pepper flakes to taste (optional)

Sea salt to taste (optional)

217

1. Preheat the oven to 225 degrees.

2. Heat the oil in a 12-inch cast-iron skillet or a 3-quart enameled cast-iron casserole until the temperature on a candy thermometer reads 375 degrees.

3. In a large bowl, whisk together the eggs and milk until they are well combined, about 1 minute. In a medium bowl, sift the cornmeal, flour, salt, and pepper together twice. Add the okra to the egg mixture and toss until it is evenly coated. Scatter half the dredge over the okra and toss to coat. Scatter the remaining dredge over the okra and toss again.

4. Transfer about one-third of the okra to the oil with a slotted spoon and fry in batches, turning as necessary with the spoon, until the slices are golden brown all over, about 2 minutes per batch.

5. Using the slotted spoon, transfer the okra to a plate lined with a double thickness of paper towels. When it has drained, transfer to a ceramic serving dish that holds heat well and place in the oven until ready to serve.

6. Dust the okra with red pepper flakes and sea salt, if desired, and pass a cruet of Pepper Vinegar (page 518) around the table when you serve.

❋ SQUASH AND MUSHROOM HOMINY ❋

HOMINY IS SEVERELY UNDERAPPRECIATED NORTH OF HOUSTON. IT IS SIMPLY CORN THAT'S BEEN PREPARED IN THE MANner of the early Mesoamericans, who soaked the whole kernels in an alkaline solution (of wood ashes mixed with water; processors today use slaked lime) to remove the tough outer hull. The corn becomes more nutritious, as the niacin in it is made more absorbable, which also alters the flavor slightly. This almost chalky skew of corn's flavor is arguably one hallmark of Mexican cooking. Hominy is still a staple throughout Central America, so the surest way to find it is at a grocery with a large Latin foods section.

Hominy is fairly common in the American Southeast, where it is served as a starchy side dish, boiled in broth and often served alongside pork. We combine it with other ancient American foodstuffs—squash and mushrooms—to yield some beautifully harmonious, earthy flavors. The hominy forms the backbone of a dish that seems to capture the spirit of the harvest season. We garnish it with top notes of parsley and lemon zest. The dish has become a Thanksgiving tradition in our family, but it gets plenty of exposure the rest of the year, since the ingredients are nearly seasonless. Try to find intensely flavored mushrooms like portobellos, hens-of-the-woods, or creminis—but don't use shiitakes, which overwhelm the balance of flavors in this recipe.

Note: The word "hominy" is used colloquially in the Lowcountry to refer to grits (see page 144), which are made by grinding dried but untreated corn kernels. You can be sure that the double meaning of the word causes plenty of confusion, but as far as we know, no lives have been lost to it.

For 6 people

TIME: 35 minutes

¼ pound slab bacon or 4 strips thick-cut bacon, diced

1 tablespoon extra-virgin olive oil

1 cup chopped yellow onion (about 1 large onion)

3 cups hominy, drained (one 30-ounce can)

1 cup Sunday Chicken Broth (page 532)

1 pound mixed richly flavored fresh mushrooms, such as Portobello, cremini, or hen-of-the-woods, roughly chopped (about 4 cups)

½ teaspoon freshly ground black pepper

3 small yellow crookneck or straightneck squash, sliced lengthwise and cut into ¼-inch-thick half-moons (about 3 cups)

2 tablespoons lemon juice (from ½ lemon)

½ cup chopped fresh flat-leaf parsley

1 teaspoon lemon zest

1. Scatter the bacon in a small dry skillet over medium-high heat. With a wooden spoon, move the pieces around until the bacon is firm and barely crisp, about 4 minutes. Remove with a slotted spoon and reserve.

2. Pour the fat from the skillet into a small ceramic bowl and rest the skillet on a cool burner or trivet. Using a measuring spoon, measure the amount of fat in the bowl. Place 2 tablespoons back in the skillet. Add the oil and return the skillet to the lit burner. Reduce the heat to medium and add the onion. Sauté the onion until it begins to be translucent, about 2 minutes. Add the hominy and sauté, stirring occasionally to keep it from sticking, until it has absorbed most of the moisture in the skillet, about 5 minutes. Add the broth and stir several times. Add the mushrooms and pepper and stir again. Turn the heat to medium-low and cover.

3. Simmer until the mushrooms have darkened significantly, about 5 minutes. Add the squash, cover, and continue to simmer vigorously, stirring once or twice, until the white flesh of the squash has given up most of its pigment, about 5 minutes. Remove the cover, add the lemon juice, and continue to simmer with the cover off until the liquid has become a thick gravy, about 5 more minutes. Toss in the parsley, lemon zest, and reserved bacon (if desired) just before serving.

4. Serve immediately, making sure to pool some of the gravy around the vegetables.

❋ CREAMED CORN ❋

FEW DISHES YIELD SO MANY ACCOLADES FOR SO LITTLE WORK. HONESTLY, MAKING CREAMED CORN AT HOME IS ALMOST easier than finding a can of the horrible stuff that used to be served in school cafeterias nationwide. When we serve the real McCoy to southerners weaned on the canned version, we get the kind of praise usually reserved for the main course.

Creamed corn has a wonderful affinity for freshly crushed peppercorns, either black or white. You can calibrate the richness to suit your taste by varying the dairy product you use, from superseductive heavy cream to skinny skim. We use half-and-half for a rich, velvety body that doesn't weigh down the dish. Don't make this dish only in summer, when the corn is sublime; starchy out-of-season corn can easily be ameliorated with a teaspoon of sugar!

For 6 people
TIME: 15 minutes

8 ears fresh corn
6 tablespoons unsalted butter
1 cup plus 2 tablespoons half-and-half, whole
    milk, skim milk, or heavy cream

1½ teaspoons kosher salt
1 teaspoon freshly ground black pepper or
    white pepper, to taste
1 teaspoon sugar (optional)

Cut the corn from the cobs and scrape the cobs with the edge of a spoon to extract as much juice and material as possible. You should have 5¼ cups of corn. In a 12-inch skillet, melt the butter over medium-high heat until it is frothy. Add the corn and stir constantly for 1 minute. Pour in the half-and-half and add the salt and pepper. Reduce the heat to low and simmer, stirring vigilantly until the liquid has thickened to a dense, yellowish sauce, about 12 minutes. Turn off the heat, cover, and let steam for 2 minutes. Serve immediately, making sure to pool some sauce around each serving.

❊ CORN MACQUE CHOUX ❊

QUICK
KNOCKOUT

LEGEND HAS IT THAT NATIVE AMERICANS LIVING IN SOUTHERN LOUISIANA INTRODUCED MACQUE CHOUX, A SUCCO-tash variant, to French settlers in the 1700s.

Compared to other Cajun and Creole dishes, such as Sunday Gumbo (page 262) and Jambalaya (page 182), corn macque choux takes so little time to prepare that it's a wonderful shortcut to the flavor of southern Louisiana. These days Louisiana chefs dress up their macques choux with alligator, crawfish tails, or mirliton, the sturdy tropical squash also called chayote and alligator pear. In our own macque choux, we pare the dish down to its essence: fresh tomato cooked in butter, corn, and bell peppers.

For 6 people

TIME: 15 minutes

6 ears fresh corn

2 cups plus 2 tablespoons water

2 ripe medium tomatoes

4 tablespoons butter

1 cup finely diced red bell pepper (about
    1 large pepper)

1 cup finely diced green bell pepper (about
    1 large pepper)

¾ cup finely diced yellow onion (about
    1 medium onion)

½ teaspoon sugar

¾ teaspoon kosher salt

½ teaspoon freshly ground black pepper

1. Cut the corn from the cobs and scrape the cobs with the edge of a spoon to extract as much juice and material as possible. You should have about 4 cups of corn.

2. Pour 2 cups water into a small saucepan and bring to a boil over high heat. Drive a dinner fork into the stem end of one tomato and plunge it into the boiling water for 30 seconds, turning the handle of the fork so the tomato spins in the water. Remove the tomato and spin it beneath a vigorous stream of cold water for 30 seconds. The skin should begin to break around the fork's tines. Lift the skin away with a paring knife. Repeat with the second tomato.

3. Cut each tomato in half crosswise, and with the tip of your index finger, tease out the seed clusters and their juice into a small bowl. Chop the tomatoes and place them in another small bowl. Hold a wire-mesh strainer above the bowl of chopped tomatoes and dump the reserved seed clusters and their juice into it. Tap the strainer quickly and forcefully against your palm for about 1 minute to extract as much juice as possible from the seeds. You should be left with only seeds in the bottom of the strainer. Discard them.

4. In a 12-inch cast-iron skillet, melt the butter over medium-high heat just until frothy. Add the corn, tomatoes, and the remaining 2 tablespoons water and cook until the tomatoes begin to lose their shape, about 3 minutes. Add the remaining ingredients to the skillet and sauté, stirring frequently, until the onion has become translucent and the peppers have slightly lightened in color,

224

about 12 minutes. During the first half of the sautéing, the tomatoes collapse entirely and blend with the liquid released from the vegetables to create a saffron-colored sauce that will simmer vigorously; during the latter half of the cooking, the sauce will reduce, concentrating to become more of a coating for the vegetables than a sauce.

5.   Serve immediately with Pork Loin Chops with Pear and Vidalia Pan Gravy (page 316) or City-Ham Steak with Red-Eye Gravy (page 346).

Fields Farm tomatoes from Johns Island at the Mt. Pleasant farmers' market. The sandy soils of Johns Island have been used in the last century primarily for "truck farming," the growing of mass-market tomatoes, watermelons, onions, and other vegetables that are sturdy enough to ship by truck.

❊ MATT'S HONEY-GLAZED FIELD PEAS ❊

MATT HAS DEVELOPED WHAT COULD FAIRLY BE CALLED AN OBSESSION WITH FIELD PEAS, FOR THEIR RICH FLAVOR BUT ALSO for their mysterious behavior.

Field peas (sometimes called cow peas) are a lentil-sized legume (*Vigna unguiculata*) that seems to chase corn around the South. Plant a stand of corn on Johns Island, Wadmalaw Island, Yonge's Island, or pretty much any of the Sea Islands of the southeastern United States and you're guaranteed to find a few pea vines snaking their way up the stalks by July. The symbiosis is chemically logical, the agricultural scientists tell us, even if it doesn't make a whole lot of sense aboveground. To us, the phenomenon reflects just how wildly popular this pea was to southerners—the soil is positively littered with dropped, discarded, dormant peas just waiting for the corn to come along.

There's a good reason for the field pea's former popularity: like lentils, the little mahogany-colored pea has a beguiling earthy flavor all its own, distinct from that of other beans and black-eyed peas (a different cultivar of *Vigna unguiculata*). Little red field peas, not black-eyed peas, are the traditional bean in the rice-and-bean mixture hoppin' John, at least as it was practiced in the Lowcountry in the last two centuries. There's no explanation for field peas' lowly status now. Our best guess is that southerners who love them take them for granted, assuming that when they visit Reykjavík, Iceland, they'll be able to pick up a couple bags of field peas and a jar of Duke's Mayonnaise at the grocery store. Perhaps it's because southerners don't obsess about them enough that others haven't caught on to them.

We all got a wake-up call a few years ago, though, when the Harris-Teeter grocery store dropped field peas from its inventory. The store's manager may never forget that week after Christmas, when the low-level whine of discontent became a roar of mass indignation as Charlestonians planning their New Year's dinners realized what had happened. By the 29th of December, the manager had close to a thousand pounds of field peas stacked up in one of those watermelon corrals in the prime retail space at the end of an aisle.

Fortunately, we've found that dried field peas are available in plastic sacks alongside pinto and great northern beans in grocery stores that cater to Central and South American customers. Wherever the Goya brand is sold, bags of field peas, labeled "cow peas," are likely to be nearby.

This recipe makes a hearty lunch-on-the-go or a surprisingly elegant side dish. We flavor the peas with nuggets of country ham—the cured ham that is the South's prosciutto (see "A Country Ham Primer," page 325)—and white pepper, which we find grinds more finely than black pepper and spreads a soothing, tame heat throughout the dish. The bouquet of fresh thyme and an aromatic honey enhance the field pea flavor and temper the salty kick of the country ham. Feel free to substitute another cured ham and black pepper for the country ham and white pepper.

For 6 people

TIME: 1 hour

2⅓ cups dried field peas (1 pound), picked over and rinsed

8 cups water

¾ cup aromatic honey, such as palmetto, tupelo, or cotton

¾ cup dry sherry

6 ounces country ham cut into ½-inch dice

1 large yellow onion, trimmed, peeled, and coarsely chopped

3 large garlic cloves, minced

1 tablespoon extra-virgin olive oil

1 teaspoon kosher salt

1 teaspoon freshly ground white pepper

1. Place the field peas and the water in a large saucepan and bring to a boil over high heat. Cover tightly (with aluminum foil if the pan doesn't have its own lid), reduce the heat to low, and simmer gently until the peas are just tender, about 35 minutes. Drain, reserving the cooking liquid.

2. Preheat the oven to 325 degrees.

3.   In a 3-quart enameled cast-iron pot or casserole, combine the peas, ½ cup honey, and the sherry, ham, onion, garlic, olive oil, salt, and pepper. Stir in 2½ cups of the reserved pea-cooking liquid. Cover and bake for 1½ hours, or until the peas are tender and most of the liquid has been absorbed. Uncover, drizzle the remaining ¼ cup honey on top, and bake until all the liquid has been absorbed and the peas are glazed, about 45 minutes.

4.   Serve hot.

Polyporus sulphureus, the sulphur shelf mushroom, grows on oak trees along River Road on Johns Island, South Carolina.

❊ CREAMED MUSHROOMS ❊
ON CORNMEAL WAFFLES

ONE LEGENDARY CHARLESTON WOMAN WAS SO DEVOTED TO THE FLAVOR OF THE SULFUR SHELF MUSHROOM (*POLYPORUS sulphureus*), which grows wild in the Lowcountry, that she became known as "Mushroom." Mushroom Jervey had an understanding with the line repairmen of the local telephone company that they would deliver to her any chicken mushrooms, as they're known locally, they happened to find on the job. She paid cash, although often the mushrooms were a gift, a tribute to her obsession.

We met with Mushroom Jervey's grandaughter, Langhorne Howard, to find out whether the decades-old tale was true. Ms. Howard wasn't aware of that particular deal, but she told us an even more remarkable story about her great-grandmother, Mushroom's mother, Ida Jervey, a self-taught mycologist, wild foods expert, and watercolorist in Arden, North Carolina, around the turn of the century.

Ida Jervey's husband died young, leaving her to care for their four children. Because money was tight, gathering food from the wild was critical, so Ida Jervey instilled her knowledge of wild foods in her children by way of flashcards she made herself. When we met with Ms. Howard, she pulled from the bottom drawer of an empire chest those very cards, rimmed in gold leaf, with her great-grandmother's softly rendered watercolor of a mushroom on one face, and on the back the mushroom's Linnaean classification and a list of its identifying features written in a nineteenth-century script. It was through these flashcards that Ida Jervey's passion for mushrooms was passed down to Mushroom, to Mushroom's five children, including Langhorne Howard's mother, Arden, and finally to Langhorne.

Ms. Howard also put us in touch with her mother's sister, Dodie Condon, who lives in

Charleston and is also steeped in mycology. When we visited Mrs. Condon to talk mushrooms, she proudly showed us her freezer, stocked with chopped chicken mushrooms she'd harvested from a park downtown (she wouldn't divulge which one; no serious hunter would). They were in zipped plastic bags and suspended in a luminous orange broth made from the woodier stems and cap edges, which she trims off before freezing them (see Wild Mushroom Broth, page 550). She was saving them for New Year's Day brunch, she said, when she would serve creamed mushrooms over waffles.

Fresh sulfur shelf mushrooms are a shocking fluorescent orange color and they can grow as large as a basketball. They grow throughout North America and Europe and in parts of Africa, New Zealand, and Australia, from late summer to early fall. Their impressive appearance belies their flavor, which is mild, slightly sweet, and milky (probably the source of their nickname, chicken mushroom).

Creamed mushrooms on toast or waffles is a fantastic, simple-to-make brunch dish, as wonderfully rich as eggs Benedict but more savory and somehow more serious. In fact, it makes a nice dinner, too. In this recipe, any flavorful, woodsy mushroom, whether cultivated or wild, will work marvelously. We like to use a combination of shiitake and portobello mushrooms.

For 4 people

TIME: 35 minutes

FOR THE CREAMED MUSHROOMS

2 tablespoons unsalted butter

1½ tablespoons all-purpose flour

1 small yellow onion, finely chopped

2 tablespoons extra-virgin olive oil

6 ounces shiitake mushrooms, trimmed and roughly chopped (about 2 cups)

6 ounces portobello mushrooms, trimmed and roughly chopped (about 2 cups)

1 teaspoon chopped fresh thyme or tarragon

2 tablespoons Madeira or dry sherry (optional)

1 teaspoon salt, plus more to taste

1 cup heavy cream

FOR THE CORNMEAL WAFFLES

1 cup stone-ground cornmeal

½ cup all-purpose flour

½ teaspoon kosher salt

½ teaspoon baking soda

1 teaspoon baking powder

1 teaspoon sugar

1¾ cups whole or low-fat buttermilk
     (preferably whole)

4 tablespoons unsalted butter, melted

2 large eggs

1. Start by preparing the mushrooms. In a 12-inch skillet or sauté pan, melt the butter over medium heat until frothy, about 1 minute. Add the flour, whisking to break down any lumps, and when the flour is well incorporated, add the onion. Cook the onion until soft and translucent but not yet browning, about 5 minutes. Add the olive oil, mushrooms, thyme, Madeira, and salt and cook until the mushrooms have darkened and released some of their liquid, about 3 minutes. Add the cream and stir to distribute it throughout the pan. Once the cream begins to simmer gently, cook until it takes on some of the mushrooms' color—a rich beige hue—about 3 minutes. Remove from the heat.

2. While the mushrooms are cooking, preheat the oven to 225 degrees. Place a rack in the middle.

3. Sift the dry waffle ingredients together into a bowl. In a separate bowl, whisk the wet waffle ingredients together. Add them to the dry ingredients and whisk until thoroughly blended.

4. Ladle the batter onto a hot buttered waffle iron (a 4-×-4-inch iron will require ½ cup batter) and cook 8 minutes, or until the outside is crisp and golden brown. As the waffles come off the iron, place them in a single layer on the oven rack so they stay warm and crisp.

5. When creamed mushrooms are cooked and the waffles are ready, ladle the mushrooms over the waffles and serve immediately.

❧ GREEN TOMATO AND APPLE TART ❧

AS OUR COLLEGE FRIENDS BEGAN TO HAVE BABIES, WE BEGAN TO SEE LESS AND LESS OF THEM. IT DIDN'T SEEM FAIR, SO we started a tradition of hosting brunches on weekends for all our friends with children (and a few without, to mix things up).

This dish was developed for such parties. It's easy to eat, and it plays with sweet and savory the way great brunch dishes do. Toddlers love it, because it has two things they're intimately familiar with, apples and cheese.

Served with a glass of Sercial or Bual Madeira, slices of this tart make a suave dessert or cheese course.

For 6 people
TIME: 1 hour

FOR THE TART CRUST

1¼ cups cold, sifted all-purpose flour
¼ teaspoon salt
4 tablespoons cold butter, cut into small
    pieces

4 tablespoons cold lard, cut into small pieces
3 tablespoons cold water

1 tablespoon canola oil

1 pound green tomatoes (about 2 large tomatoes), sliced ¼ inch thick

2 tablespoons unsalted butter

2 Granny Smith apples, cored and sliced into ¼-inch-thick rounds

1 medium onion, chopped (about ¾ cup)

¾ cup half-and-half

2 cups coarsely grated Gruyère cheese (6 ounces)

2 large eggs

2 teaspoons chopped fresh thyme

Kosher salt to taste

Freshly ground black pepper to taste

1. First, make the crust. Preheat the oven to 350 degrees.

2. In a large mixing bowl or a food processor, combine the flour and salt and toss with a fork or pulse twice to mix thoroughly. Add the butter and lard and cut them into the flour with a pastry blender, 2 knives, or your fingers or pulse (about three 10-second pulses) until the mixture resembles coarse crumbs. Add the water and toss with a fork or process until the dough just comes together.

3. Pat the dough into a round about 6 inches in diameter and ½ inch thick. With a floured rolling pin, roll the dough on a floured board to a ¼-inch-thick round about 13 inches in diameter. Transfer to an 11-inch tart pan and gently press the dough into the pan. Fold any excess dough on top of the edge of the tart. Prick the bottom with a fork and place the crust in the freezer for 15 minutes.

4. Remove the crust from the freezer, place a sheet of parchment paper over it, and fill it with pie weights or dried beans. Bake for 15 minutes. Remove the weights and paper, return the crust to the oven, and bake for 10 minutes more, until the rim is gently brown and the bottom no longer appears moist. Remove and let rest on a cooling rack until ready to fill. Leave the oven on.

5. Now prepare the filling. In a 12-inch skillet, heat the oil over high heat. When it begins to shimmer, add half the tomato slices and sauté until they just begin to brown, about 2 minutes per side. Transfer to a plate and repeat with the remaining tomato slices until they are all gently browned. Add 1 tablespoon butter to the skillet and sauté the apple rounds in 2 batches until they are gently browned, about 2 minutes per side. Transfer to a bowl and reserve.

6. Reduce the heat to medium, add the remaining 1 tablespoon butter and the onion, and sauté over medium heat until the onion is gently browned and completely soft, about 12 minutes. Remove from the heat and reserve.

7. Heat the half-and-half in a small saucepan over medium-high heat until it just begins to simmer, about 6 minutes. Add the cheese and turn off the heat. Stir the mixture until the cheese melts, about 1 minute.

8. In a medium bowl, beat the eggs thoroughly. Pour the milk and cheese mixture into the eggs slowly in a thin stream, whisking constantly. Stir in the onion and thyme and season to taste with salt and pepper.

9. To assemble the tart, layer the tomato slices and the apple rounds in the crust, arranging them in a fan pattern, and pour the cheese custard in and around them. The tart should look rustic, with tomatoes and apples piercing the surface of the custard in places.

10. Bake the tart until the custard sets and a toothpick inserted in the center comes out clean, about 25 minutes. Let cool slightly, slice into wedges, and serve warm.

⁑ MACARONI AND CHEESE ⁑

IN A CHAPTER ON VEGETABLE DISHES? OF COURSE! AT PUBLIC SCHOOLS THROUGHOUT THE SOUTH AND IN MEAT-AND-threes we frequent (cafeterias built around meals that offer a choice of meats and three side dishes), mac 'n' cheese is *always* considered a vegetable. In our house it is, too.

How to make a great macaroni and cheese? One, high-quality cheese, and two, lots of it. In this recipe, we drench the macaroni in a cheese sauce made with extra-sharp cheddar and bay leaf. Then we layer the sauced macaroni with more extra-sharp cheddar and slices of Swiss cheese for good, gooey measure.

If you have access to an aged Gruyère, substitute it for the Swiss, because it adds an appealingly funky character. But there's plenty of charisma already in this macaroni and cheese, so feel free to incorporate any of the brands of Swiss cheese you find at the supermarket, such as Cracker Barrel or Boar's Head. Either way, you won't be disappointed.

For 12 people

TIME: 1 hour

1 tablespoon plus 1 teaspoon kosher salt, plus
more to taste
1 pound elbow macaroni
3 tablespoons unsalted butter
3 tablespoons all-purpose flour
3 cups whole milk
3 bay leaves

6 cups coarsely grated extra-sharp cheddar
cheese (about 1 pound)
½ teaspoon freshly ground black pepper, plus
more to taste
1 pound Gruyère or Swiss cheese, cut into
¼-inch-thick slices

1. Preheat the oven to 350 degrees.

2. Pour 2 quarts water into a large stockpot. Add 1 tablespoon salt and bring to a boil over high heat. Add the macaroni, reduce the heat to medium-high, and cook, stirring occasionally, 7 minutes, or until al dente. Drain, and reserve in a large bowl.

3. In a medium saucepan, melt the butter over low heat until frothy. Add the flour and cook, stirring continuously, for 3 minutes. Add the milk, bay leaves, and 1 teaspoon salt, increase the heat to medium, and bring to a simmer. Simmer gently, stirring frequently, until the sauce has thickened enough to coat the back of a spoon, about 10 minutes. Add half of the cheddar cheese and stir until it is completely melted. Turn off the heat. Season to taste with salt and pepper.

4. Pour the cheese sauce over the macaroni and stir gently but thoroughly so that it is evenly distributed. Season to taste with salt and pepper. Spread half the macaroni and cheese (about 4½ cups) in the bottom of a 3-quart casserole and flatten into an even layer with a spatula or wooden spoon. Sprinkle half the remaining grated cheddar cheese over it, then place half the slices of Swiss cheese on top. Spread the remaining macaroni and cheese in the casserole, scatter the remaining cheddar cheese over it, and top with the remaining slices of Swiss cheese. Bake on middle rack of oven until bubbly, about 30 minutes. If desired, transfer to top rack for last five minutes to gently brown the top.

5. Serve immediately, and—as you would with greens, with okra, or any other southern vegetable, really—pass a cruet of Pepper Vinegar (page 518) at the table.

✺ CORN AND OKRA PUDDING ✺

A POD OF YOUNG OKRA PLUCKED STRAIGHT FROM THE PLANT AND POPPED IN YOUR MOUTH HAS A FLAVOR LIKE HONEY-suckle nectar. Okra's gentle sweetness goes well with corn, so we created this pudding. It's an extraordinary vegetable side dish, or a terrific brunch entrée when served with salad greens coated with a bright, tart dressing.

We begin by cooking the okra in a dry skillet, which serves two functions: it cooks out most of its "rope," and it gently caramelizes the okra, giving it an appealing toasty flavor.

For 6 people
TIME: 1 hour

2½ tablespoons unsalted butter
¾ pound fresh okra, sliced into rounds ½ inch thick (about 2 cups)
1½ cups half-and-half
1 teaspoon kosher salt

1 teaspoon sugar
2 large eggs
1½ cups fresh corn, cut from the cob (from about 4 ears)

1. Preheat the oven to 350 degrees. Grease a 1-quart ovenproof baking dish with ½ tablespoon of the butter.

2. Scatter the okra in a single layer in a dry 12-inch skillet or large sauté pan. Cook over medium-high heat, moving the pieces around the pan frequently, until the okra is just browning around the edges, about 8 minutes. Remove from the heat and reserve.

3. Cut the remaining 2 tablespoons butter into pieces. In a small saucepan, heat the butter, half-and-half, salt, and sugar over medium heat until the butter melts and the half-and-half just begins to simmer.

4. In a large bowl, beat the eggs with a whisk until they are lemon-yellow. Pour the hot half-and-half mixture slowly into the eggs in a thin stream, whisking constantly.

5. Place the okra and the corn evenly in the baking dish and pour the milk and egg mixture over them. Bake for 40 minutes, or until a toothpick inserted in the center comes out clean.

6. Cut the pudding into 6 equal servings with a spatula and serve immediately.

❋ SUMMER SQUASH CASSEROLE ❋

THIS CHURCH-SUPPER STAPLE, WITH MASHED YELLOW SQUASH AND BREAD CRUMBS, USED TO BORE US. IT ALWAYS SEEMED soggy and bland. But we love soft summer squash like yellow crooknecks and yellow straightnecks, so we reengineered it, creating a layered casserole that heightens the subtle flavor of the squash with basil and presents a range of textures: squash slices cooked just past snappy, sautéed onions and red bell peppers, and melted cheddar cheese. Here the bread crumbs get toasted in butter. We know you'll love the result.

For 6 people
TIME: 1 hour

2 tablespoons unsalted butter, plus more for greasing the pan

3 red bell peppers, cored, seeded, and cut into ½-inch-thick strips

4 small yellow onions, trimmed, peeled, and thinly sliced (about 1 pound)

5 medium yellow crookneck or yellow straightneck squash, trimmed and sliced into ¼-inch-thick rounds (about 2½ pounds)

4 large eggs

¼ cup whole milk

1 teaspoon kosher salt

½ teaspoon freshly ground black pepper

¼ cup coarse bread crumbs, preferably homemade

2 cups grated extra-sharp cheddar cheese

½ cup roughly chopped fresh basil

1. Preheat the oven to 375 degrees. Lightly butter a 2-quart casserole.

2. Melt 2 tablespoons butter in a 12-inch skillet over medium-high heat until frothy, but not yet brown. Add the peppers and onions and sauté for 12 minutes, stirring frequently, until the onions are translucent and the peppers are flexible. Remove from the heat and reserve.

3. Meanwhile, pour 2 inches of water into a steamer fitted with a steamer basket and place it over high heat. When the water boils, add the squash and cook until it begins to turn translucent, about 6 minutes. Remove the steamer basket and reserve the squash in it.

4. In a large bowl, whisk the eggs with the milk, salt, and pepper until thoroughly blended.

5. In a small skillet, toast the bread crumbs over medium-high heat, stirring them continuously until they are a deep, golden brown, about 3 minutes.

6. Dust the bottom of the casserole with 1 tablespoon bread crumbs. Divide the onions and peppers, the squash, the cheese, and the basil into 3 equal amounts and layer them in the pan as you would a lasagne. Begin with the squash, place the onions and peppers on top, followed by the cheese, and finally by the basil. Sprinkle 1 tablespoon bread crumbs over the top and repeat, making 2 more layers. Pour the egg mixture over the top of the casserole and shake the pan gently from side to side to distribute the liquid evenly.

7. Bake until the bread crumbs on the surface of the casserole are a dark chocolate-brown, 35 to 45 minutes. Divide into portions with a spatula or pie lifter and serve piping hot.

❋ WINTER SQUASH CASSEROLE ❋

WE SUSPECT THAT THE WOODY ACORN, BLUE HUBBARD, BUTTERNUT, AND CYMLING SQUASHES OF LATE SUMMER AND FALL are an underutilized resource for most home cooks, since they can be so ornery to peel. A few easy tips for peeling and a simple, fail-safe recipe or two can transform these nutty, nutritious squashes, making them as welcome in your grocery cart as a summer tomato.

Every variety of winter squash has its own personality. Butternuts are plentiful in markets and perfect in this recipe, but if we can find kabocha—a sweet, green-skinned, orange-fleshed Japanese native now being planted throughout the South and becoming increasingly available nationwide—we use it. It has a hint of sweetness that makes this casserole soar.

For 8 to 10 people
TIME: 1¼ hours

3½ pounds winter squash, such as butternut, kabocha, or acorn, peeled and cut in ¼-inch-thick slices (about 6 cups)

5 tablespoons unsalted butter, plus more for the pan

1 tablespoon extra-virgin olive oil

2 large yellow onions, trimmed, peeled, and chopped (about 3 cups)

1 cup whole or low-fat buttermilk

2 large eggs, beaten

2½ teaspoons minced fresh thyme

½ cup bread crumbs, preferably homemade, toasted

¾ teaspoon kosher salt

½ teaspoon freshly ground black pepper

¼ cup pumpkin seeds or pecans, toasted

2 cups coarsely grated cheddar cheese (about 6 ounces)

1. Preheat the oven to 375 degrees. Butter a 9-×-13-inch baking dish or a 4-quart casserole.

2. Place 3 quarts water in a large stockpot and bring to a boil over high heat. Add the squash to the water, return to a boil, and cook for 6 minutes. The squash will turn a deeper orange. Drain it and set it aside.

3. Melt the butter in the stockpot and add the oil. Add the onions and sauté over medium-low heat until translucent and limp, about 8 minutes, stirring to prevent browning. Add the warm squash and the buttermilk, eggs, thyme, bread crumbs, salt, pepper, ⅛ cup pumpkin seeds, and 1⅓ cups cheese. Blend with a wooden spoon or spatula until the ingredients are well combined.

4. Spread the mixture evenly in the baking dish. Bake for 45 minutes. Remove from the oven and sprinkle the remaining ⅛ cup pumpkin seeds and ⅔ cup cheese over the casserole. Bake for 15 minutes more, or until the pumpkin seeds have turned chestnut brown and the cheese is bubbling and gently browning.

5. Remove from the oven and serve immediately.

VARIATION—BEN'S SAUSAGE SQUASH CASSEROLE: WE'VE ALWAYS THOUGHT OF SQUASH CASSEROLE AS A SIDE DISH. OUR FRIEND BEN WIZNER, WHO WAS MATT'S ROOMMATE AT HARVARD AND LATER SHARED AN APARTMENT WITH US FOR THREE YEARS ON RIVINGTON STREET, IN NEW YORK CITY, THINKS OTHERWISE. HE TOOK OUR SQUASH CASSEROLE RECIPE AND FELT COMPELLED TO TURN IT INTO AN ENTRÉE, TORQUING UP THE RICHNESS AND PIQUANCY WITH HOT PEPPER–LACED SAUSAGE— THE KIND YOU FIND AT THE FABLED PIZZA PARLORS SALLY'S AND PEPE'S, IN NEW HAVEN, WHERE BEN GREW UP. WE EXPERIMENTED WITH THAT IDEA AND FOUND WE LOVED IT, TOO. FOLLOW THE RECIPE ABOVE, BUT USE 2 1/2 POUNDS WINTER SQUASH AND 1 POUND HOT ITALIAN SAUSAGE, CUT ON THE BIAS INTO 1/2-INCH-THICK PIECES AND SEARED IN A 12-INCH SKILLET OVER HIGH HEAT UNTIL GOLDEN BROWN ALL OVER. ADD THE SAUSAGE TO THE SQUASH MIXTURE IN STEP 3 AND COMPLETE THE RECIPE AS ABOVE.

FRIED GREEN TOMATOES, PAGE 214,
WITH BUTTERMILK-LIME DRESSING, PAGE 519

PEPPERPOT, PAGE 270

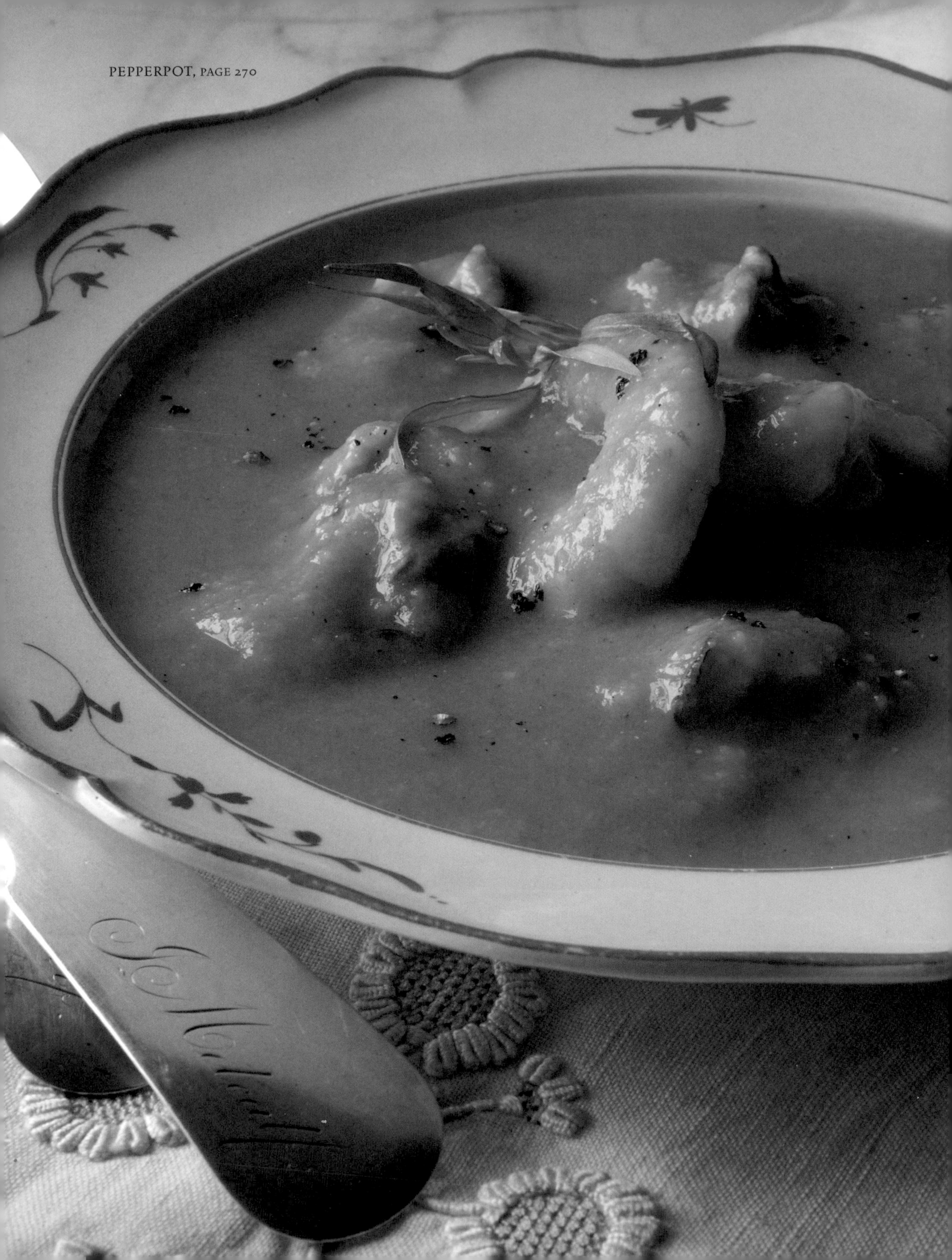

SQUAB PURLOO, PAGE 178

BEST FAMILY FARM CORN-BREAD SALAD PAGE 188

TUESDAY FRIED CHICKEN, PAGE 333, WITH
SUCCOTASH SALAD, PAGE 193

FRANCISCO'S TRACTOR-DISK WOK VENISON, PAGE 360

JAMBALAYA, PAGE 182

CRISPY FRIED OKRA, PAGE 217

THE TRICK TO EFFICIENT, SAFE, AND STRESS-FREE PEEL-ing is to separate the squash into flat-bottomed pieces that flare outward, so that you can place the piece on the cutting board and safely slice downward and slightly away from you. Here's how:

Butternut squash: Begin by separating the cylindrical end of the squash from the bulbous end, slicing clean through where they join. Stand the cylindrical end up on a cutting surface. Holding it firmly upright with your left hand (or your right hand, if you are left-handed), peel the skin with downward strokes of a large, sharp knife. Slice the bulb end in half at its widest point, parallel to the original slice. Lay each half flat on the cutting surface, largest face down, and slice the skin off, cutting down and away from you.

Cymling: Lay the squash flat in front of you and line up one of the crevices at twelve o'clock. Cut the squash in half from twelve o'clock to six o'clock. Stand each half on its cut and separate the squash into heart-shaped wedges by cutting through every other crevice. Stand each heart on its side and peel with downward knife strokes.

Acorn, kabocha, Hubbard: Cut the squash crosswise into two hemispheres. Lay each hemisphere on the cutting board, cut side up, and slice downward. Don't try to salvage the flesh in the ridges unless you're a neurosurgeon.

❋ STEWS AND SOUPS ❋

STEWS

We may owe our appreciation of stews to Matt's brief career as an auto mechanic. The summers he worked at Import Auto Service ("The Best Damn Garage in Town"), he was introduced to a Cadillac-driving retiree whose name nobody seemed to know but whom all the other mechanics, car detailers, and panel beaters in the Belgrade Avenue auto-repair district referred to as "the fish stew man." From the trunk of his immaculate Caddy, Fish Stew Man sold quart-sized Mason jars of a tomato-based fish stew he prepared at home. A classic Lowcountry red fish stew, it was stunning—almost as white as it was red—thick with waxy slices of potato and meaty flakes of a mystery fish. Ketchup, onion, and bay leaf seemed to be its only seasonings. A dash of milk may have smoothed out the acidity of the tomatoes, as did the sweetness of ketchup (and perhaps even a pinch or two of sugar). The stew was a textbook lesson in how to build nuanced flavor and texture from a hodgepodge of everyday ingredients, and it encouraged us to reappraise all the stews we'd made as teenagers, which had always seemed less than the sum of their parts.

Red fish stew, which goes by the name muddle along the North Carolina coast, is just one in a pantheon of southern stews bristling with textural subtleties and articulated by true highlights from tart or particularly aromatic ingredients like lemon juice, chiles, black pepper, bay leaves, wine, and fresh herbs. The bass notes are typically contributed by meats. Layered in the middle are the different vegetal components of flavor—the carrots and garlic, the potatoes and beans.

Kentucky's got burgoo. Brunswick County, Virginia, and the town of Brunswick, Georgia, both lay claim to the origins of the namesake stew, a tomato-based chicken recipe. South Carolina has Frogmore stew, pork hash, and chicken bog. Louisiana's got gumbo, and Texas has its chili. Each is a distinct expression of terroir: burgoo contains the lamb common in Kentucky barbecue; the crab- and shrimp-laden Frogmore stew tastes like it came straight from the salt marshes around the town of Frogmore, South Carolina.

Like most southern icons, stews tend to arouse people's passions. We don't usually add beans to our chili, but we don't see why Texans get so huffy when someone proposes doing so, or why Virginians get upset up when Charlestonians add onions and potatoes to their Brunswick stew. "You put *what* in your gumbo?" was a phrase we heard often at one gumbo cookoff.

246

That a food as nourishing and soul-warming as stew might be a source of one-upsmanship to us seems a bit unsporting. True, there are stews that are heavenly and stews that are merely delicious, but we believe the key to creating the former has less to do with checking off ingredients on a list than with what you do to your ingredients. A stew that really soars has the full flavor of a concentrated broth, and to achieve this, we take a page from braising technique—a series of easy steps we perform at the beginning of each stew we make. These steps aren't often used in southern stew recipes, but we think they can help build superior depth of flavor and nuance, whether it's Brunswick or burgoo.

We begin by searing the stew meat in batches in a large Dutch oven (we often use bacon fat rendered from diced slab bacon, but you can use extra-virgin olive oil, peanut oil, canola oil, or unsalted butter). The aroma of sizzling meat fills the kitchen and gets the whole process off to a promising start. After all the meat is nicely browned, we reserve it in a bowl. Then we add dried chiles that have been stemmed, slit down their sides, seeded, and flattened and "toast" them briefly in the Dutch oven to coax out their fruity, smoky dimensions (see "Sourcery: Buying Dried Chiles," page 284). Once all the meat and toasted chiles have been set aside, we add some wine or a little broth to the hot pan and stir it vigorously with a wooden spoon to pick up the caramelized seared bits from the bottom and reduce the liquid slightly to concentrate the flavors. And then we're ready to add the rest of the broth, the reserved meat and chiles, and the remaining ingredients.

These first steps to building a rich stew are a tad unconventional in the South—traditional stew recipes call for simply simmering and seasoning water and adding the raw meat to it. But we find that browning helps to boost the underlying flavor and adds shape to the tastes of the stew.

Another thing to remember is that stew truly does taste better a day after it's made, when it has "cured" in the refrigerator. We rarely have the foresight to plan ahead, but the leftovers—if there are leftovers—are a just reward for the chef at lunch the day after.

Stews are the ultimate congregational food—they bring people together. The recipes in this chapter are great for feeding crowds and can be doubled, or even tripled, quite easily, as long as you have the patience (and large-enough stew pots).

Besides introducing us to one of the world's great fish stews, Matt's summers in the auto shop taught us the importance of stew to the social commerce of life in the South. Sam VanNorte, the proprietor and head mechanic (who, like Fish Stew Man, had his own handle: the Wizard), would buy five or six Mason jars of red fish stew at a time. He'd keep a couple in the shop's refrigerator to take home for himself and his wife, Jan; a couple he'd distribute to friends on the drive back to his home on Edisto Island, and he'd give two jars to Matt to deliver to elderly friends and customers downtown whom he hadn't seen in a while. These weren't gifts for occasions, like a funeral casserole or a get-well soup, and there was never any duty implicit in them, the way there is with those pass-it-on starter doughs (the culinary equivalent of a chain letter, in our estimation). Sam's generous gifts of stew were the simplest expression of how delicious food and good friends share the same emotional real estate.

❋ FISH STEW MAN'S RED FISH STEW ❋

FROM OUR MEMORY OF FISH STEW MAN'S HANDIWORK,
WE CONJURED UP OUR OWN FISH MUDDLE. WE TONE DOWN THE
sweetness a shade, and add the smoke and fire of bacon and toasted chiles and the nuance of
white wine. To our minds, it's one of the finest warm-weather stews around, truly the king of the
muddles.

Any sweet, flaky white fish works well in this recipe. We prefer to use fish caught locally and
commonly found in Charleston markets, such as spottail bass (a river fish called red drum in the
lowcountry), the creek-dwelling sheepshead, or the Atlantic wreckfish (a grouperlike fish that
lives near the ocean floor and was long thought to have little commercial value). Wreckfish is currently in vogue in South Carolina among supporters of sustainable aquaculture, because deep-sea
fishermen found plentiful stocks living near the Charleston Bump, a cliff formation on the bottom of the sea 100 miles offshore from Charleston Harbor.

Red fish stew keeps for a couple days in the refrigerator, but it rarely remains there that long.

❋

WHAT TO DRINK   *A white with some lusciousness, such as a dry Riesling or a Chardonnay with a
modest amount of oak, would underscore the sweet edge of the tomatoes in this stew.*

¼ pound slab bacon, cut into small dice, or 4 strips thick-cut bacon, cut into small dice

2 serrano, Thai, or other dried red chiles, stems trimmed, slit down their sides, seeded, and flattened

1½ pounds Yukon Gold or other waxy potatoes, peeled and sliced into ¼-inch-thick half-moons

2 cups chopped yellow onion (about 2 large onions)

1½ cups Rich Fish Broth (page 546) or Sunday Shrimp Broth (page 536)

1 cup full-bodied white wine, such as Chardonnay, Riesling, or Viognier

3 bay leaves

One 28-ounce can whole peeled tomatoes, with their juice

1 teaspoon kosher salt, plus more to taste

½ teaspoon freshly ground black pepper, plus more to taste

2 teaspoons mustard seeds, pounded with a mortar and pestle to a fine powder

2 teaspoons whole coriander seeds, toasted and pounded with a mortar and pestle to a fine powder

1 tablespoon brown sugar

2 teaspoons Worcestershire sauce, plus more to taste

2 tablespoons ketchup

1½ pounds flaky white fish such as spottail bass, sheepshead, wreckfish, hake, catfish, cod, or whiting, cut into 1½-inch chunks

½ cup half-and-half

1 cup fresh corn kernels, cut from the cob (about 2 ears)

1. Scatter the diced bacon in a 6-quart stockpot or Dutch oven over medium-high heat. With a slotted spoon, move the pieces around until the bacon is firm and just golden brown, about 3 minutes. Transfer the bacon to a small bowl with the slotted spoon. Pour off all but 2 tablespoons of the bacon fat. Add the chiles and gently toast until they discolor and release some of their fragrance, about 30 seconds per side. Remove with the spoon and reserve in the bowl with the bacon.

2. Add the potatoes and sauté in the bacon fat for about 5 minutes, stirring occasionally to keep them from sticking. Add the onion and sauté, stirring frequently, until fragrant and beginning to soften, about 3 minutes. Add the broth, wine, and bay leaves and bring to a simmer. Continue to simmer vigorously until the liquid is reduced by one quarter, about 6 minutes. Add the tomatoes one by one, lightly crushing each as you add it, followed by the tomato juice. When the stew returns to a simmer, reduce the heat to low, cover, and simmer vigorously for 20 minutes, or until the potatoes are not quite tender.

3. Add the salt, pepper, mustard, coriander, brown sugar, Worcestershire sauce, and ketchup and simmer for 10 minutes more, covered, until the potatoes are completely tender when pierced with a fork.

4. Add the fish to the pot. Return to a simmer and continue to simmer gently for 5 minutes, stirring occasionally to break the fish into flakes. Add the half-and-half and the corn and simmer very gently for 5 minutes more, until the corn has softened slightly but still has some bite. Season to taste with salt, pepper, and Worcestershire sauce.

5. Serve over hot white rice or with wedges of Crispy Corn Bread (page 497), garnished with the reserved bacon.

✺ BRUNSWICK STEW ✺

ACCORDING TO A HISTORICAL MARKER ON HIGHWAY 46 IN BRUNSWICK, VIRGINIA, THE TOWN'S NAMESAKE STEW WAS invented by Jimmy Matthews, an African-American chef who in 1828 stirred up the first batch of the tomato-based chicken stew for a hunting party hosted by his employer, Dr. Creed Haskins.

Four hundred and eighty miles south of Brunswick, Virginia, is the Golden Isles Welcome Center, a rest stop on Interstate 95. There, a bronzed stew pot with a plaque claims the invention of Brunswick stew for the town of Brunswick, Georgia. An annual Brunswick Stew cookoff that pits Virginia "stewmasters" against their counterparts in Georgia takes place every October.

The rivalry of the two Brunswicks is an indication of the stew's strong popularity; in the twentieth century, it quickly became a pan-southern classic. Early recipes called for squirrel meat, and although these nut-loving rodents rarely make it into pots today, we like to honor the small-game tradition by using rabbit. Rabbit and chicken work beautifully together to keep the stew milk-mild and subtle. Some southern cooks grind the meat to give their Brunswick stew a completely smooth finish, but we prefer to let the silky stewed shreds of chicken and rabbit float free. Potato, cooked to the point of almost dissolving, serves to thicken this stew, and diced carrots and butterbeans add color, textural interest, and a certain sweetness. If rabbit is difficult to find in markets in your area, substitute 1½ pounds of boneless pork shoulder cut into 1-inch dice.

We should note that the current Brunswick Stew world champion, Henry Hicks, a tobacco farmer from Alberta, Virginia, claims tutelage from Theo Matthews, the great-grandson of Jimmy Matthews. With all due respect to Georgia stewmasters, we think the Virginians tell a more convincing tale.

WHAT TO DRINK   *The mellow chicken flavor of this dish lends itself to wines with real nuance; a Pinot Noir with notes of cherry and leather, or a white Bordeaux.*

For 12 people

TIME: 3 hours

¼ pound slab bacon, cut into two or three ¼-inch-thick strips, or 4 strips thick-cut bacon

2 serrano, Thai, or other dried red chiles, stems trimmed, slit down their sides, seeded, and flattened

One 2-pound rabbit, quartered and skinned

One 4–5-pound chicken, quartered and skinned

1 tablespoon kosher salt for seasoning rabbit and chicken, plus more to taste

1 tablespoon freshly ground black pepper, plus more to taste

2½ quarts (10 cups) Sunday Chicken Broth (page 532)

2 bay leaves

2 large celery stalks

2 pounds Yukon Gold or other waxy potatoes, peeled and diced (4½ cups)

1½ cups diced carrots (about 5 small carrots)

3½ cups chopped yellow onion (4 medium onions)

2 cups fresh corn kernels, cut from the cob (about 4 ears)

3 cups butterbeans, preferably fresh (1¼ pounds), or defrosted frozen butterbeans

One 35-ounce can whole peeled tomatoes, drained

¼ cup red wine vinegar

Juice of 2 lemons

Pepper Vinegar (page 518) or Tabasco sauce to taste

1.   In a 10- to 12-quart stockpot or Dutch oven, fry the bacon over medium-high heat until barely crisp and just golden brown, about 3 minutes per side. Transfer to a large bowl with tongs and reserve. Pour off and reserve all but 2 tablespoons fat and return the pot to the burner. Add the chiles and gently toast until they discolor and release some of their fragrance, about 30 seconds per side. Remove with tongs and reserve in the bowl with the bacon.

2.   Season the rabbit and chicken pieces liberally with about 1 tablespoon each of salt and pepper. Add the rabbit pieces to the pot and sear them over medium-high heat, turning them with tongs, until they are golden brown all over, about 4 minutes per side. (Don't crowd the pieces; if your stockpot has a narrow bottom, brown the pieces in batches, 2 at a time.) Remove with tongs and reserve in the same bowl as the bacon and chiles. Add the chicken pieces to the pot and sear them, adding reserved bacon fat (or extra-virgin olive oil, peanut oil, or canola oil if you prefer) by teaspoons if the bottom of the pot becomes dry. Turn with tongs until the chicken is golden brown all over, about 4 minutes per side. Transfer to the bowl with the rabbit, bacon, and chiles.

3.   Add 2 cups chicken broth to the pot. Using a wooden spoon, stir in tight circles, scraping up the caramelized bits from the bottom. Bring the broth to a boil and boil until it is reduced by one quarter, about 6 minutes. Add the remaining 8 cups broth, the bay leaf, celery, and potatoes, and the contents of the reserving bowl, including any juices that may have gathered in the bottom. Bring the stew to a simmer over medium-high heat. Reduce the heat to low, cover, and simmer gently for 1½ hours, stirring every 15 minutes to meld the flavors. At this point the broth will have become a milky yellow and stray bits of chicken and rabbit may float on the surface; the celery and the chiles will be nearly as limp as the bacon. Taste the broth: it should taste like the best chicken soup you've ever had.

4.   With tongs, remove the bay leaf, celery, bacon, and chiles and discard. Transfer the chicken and rabbit pieces to a cutting board with a drain and allow to cool enough to handle. Pick all the meat off the bones, leaving the stew to simmer gently as you work (about 35 minutes). Return the picked rabbit and chicken to the pot and discard the bones. Add the carrots and simmer gently, uncovered, for another 25 minutes, until the stew has concentrated and the carrots have softened and paled a bit.

5.   Add the onion, corn, butterbeans, and tomatoes, crushing the tomatoes as you add them. Simmer gently for another 30 minutes, uncovered, until the stew has further reduced and concentrated and the onion, corn, and butterbeans are tender. Turn off the heat. Add the vinegar and lemon juice and stir to distribute. Season to taste with salt, pepper, and pepper vinegar.

6.   Refrigerate for 24 hours for optimal flavor. Serve hot, in bowls, with wedges of Crispy Corn Bread (page 497) and Coleslaw (page 195), or over steaming white rice with any braised greens (see the collard greens recipes, pages 205–210).

❋ FROGMORE STEW ❋

FROGMORE, SOUTH CAROLINA, IS A TOWN OF ABOUT
10,000 PEOPLE IN THE LOW-LYING WETLANDS BETWEEN BEAUFORT
and St. Helena Island. Its namesake stew quite literally (and not surprisingly) seems to have
emerged from the marshes: it puts shrimp and crab front and center, and it's often served by out-
doorsy characters at hunting stations, fish shacks, and boatyards. More than any other stew, Frogmore (which is also sometimes referred to as Lowcountry boil) lives up to the spirit of one-pot
dining, with whole, shell-on shrimp, split crabs, corn on the cob, and sausages bobbing around in
a richly concentrated shellfish broth. Sucking the cooked shrimp before peeling them is encouraged; picking the crabs, whose primary function is to lend their rich flavor to the broth, is also
highly sanctioned. And eating this stew over sheets of newspaper is practically required!

Frogmore stew is meant to be consumed outdoors, where its messiness seems less onerous,
but the dish gets people in an upbeat, fun-loving mood the way a good soundtrack does, and for
that reason, we often serve it indoors, over a layer of newspaper, with clean dish towels for napkins and plenty of wasters (empty bowls) for the shrimp shells, crab shells, and spent corncobs.

Frogmore stew is so rustic that applying the Downtown Touch merits its own variation,
which follows the recipe below. Of course, a quick short-cut to downtown aspirations would be to
serve the dish in all its shell-on rusticity and simply supply finger bowls.

❋

WHAT TO DRINK   *A tart white like an Albariño or even a Muscadet would be the right match for this
stew's marriage of shellfish and smoky sausage.*

For 6 people

TIME: 1¼ hours

1 tablespoon extra-virgin olive oil, peanut oil, or canola oil

1½ pounds smoked pork sausage, Cajun andouille, or kielbasa (see Sourcery, page 258), cut on the bias into 1¼-inch-thick pieces

2 serrano, Thai, or other dried red chiles, trimmed, slit down their sides, seeded, and flattened

1 cup chopped celery (about 2 stalks)

2 cups chopped yellow onion (about 2 large onions)

2 quarts (8 cups) Sunday Shrimp Broth (page 536)

1 teaspoon Lee Bros. Shrimp Boil (page 553)

1 teaspoon kosher salt

3 bay leaves

6 live blue crabs or ½ pound lump crabmeat (see Sourcery, page 70)

1½ pounds peeled Yukon Gold or other waxy potatoes (about 3 large potatoes), cut into 1-inch dice

3 ears fresh corn, cut into 6 pieces

6 whole canned plum tomatoes, drained and crushed

2 pounds large headless shrimp (26–30 per pound; see Sourcery, page 374), shells on

1 medium lemon, thinly sliced, for garnish

1. Heat the oil in an 8-quart stockpot or Dutch oven over medium-high heat until it shimmers. Add the sausage. (Don't overcrowd the pot; if you have a narrow-bottomed stockpot, cook the sausage in batches.) Sear until golden brown along the sides, then turn and brown on another side, about 6 minutes total. Remove with tongs and reserve in a medium bowl. Add the chiles and gently toast in the oil and sausage fat until they discolor and release some of their fragrance, about 30 seconds on each side. Add the celery and onion and cook until softened, about 6 minutes.

2. Add 2 cups broth to the pot. Using a wooden spoon, stir in tight circles, scraping up any caramelized brown bits from the bottom. Bring the broth to a boil and boil until reduced by one quarter, about 6 minutes. Pour the remaining 6 cups broth into the pot, add the shrimp boil, salt, and bay leaves, and cover. When the broth simmers, turn the heat to medium-low, uncover, and simmer vigorously while you clean the crabs.

3. Using tongs, drop 2 live crabs at a time into the simmering broth and cook until their shells turn bright orange, about 2 minutes. Transfer the crabs to a colander set in the sink and run cold water over them. Add the next 2 live crabs to the pot and repeat until all the crabs have been cooked. As each cooked crab becomes cool enough to handle, remove the face (the strip on the front that encompasses the eyes and the mouth) with kitchen scissors. Then slip your thumb in the gap created between the top and bottom shells and pull off the top shell, exposing the feathery gills. Discard the top shell and the gills. Turn the crab over and slide the tip of a knife beneath where the cape of shell tapers to a point; lift the bottom shell off and discard. (If you find any orange crab roe, add it to the pot.) With a cleaver (or with your hands), split each crab down the middle and drop both halves in the stew. Repeat until all the crabs have been returned to the pot.

4. Add the potatoes and continue to cook until they have softened a bit but are not yet fork-tender, about 10 minutes. Add the corn, tomatoes, and reserved sausage, along with any juices it may have released, cover, and increase the heat to medium-high. When the stew comes to a vigorous simmer, reduce the heat to low, uncover, and continue to simmer gently for 10 minutes, or until the tine of a fork easily pierces the potatoes. Add the crabmeat, if using, and the shrimp, stir to distribute them throughout the stew, and simmer about 3 minutes more, or until the shrimp are pink and cooked through.

5. For optimal flavor, refrigerate for 24 hours, then reheat the stew gradually, over medium-low heat, stirring frequently to prevent scorching. Serve in large bowls, garnished with the lemon slices.

DOWNTOWN FROGMORE STEW: MAKE A FEW SIMPLE CHANGES TO THE RECIPE ABOVE: 1) PEEL AND DEVEIN THE SHRIMP WHILE THE POTATOES ARE PARBOILING IN STEP 4 (YOU CAN TIE UP THE SHRIMP SHELLS IN CHEESECLOTH AND ADD THEM TO THE POT IF YOU WISH, FOR FLAVOR). 2) IN STEP 4, CUT THE CORN FROM THE COB BEFORE YOU PUT IT IN THE POT. 3) ADD 1 POUND LUMP CRABMEAT ALONG WITH THE SHRIMP IN STEP 4, AND DISCARD THE SPLIT CRABS (AND REMOVE THE CHEESECLOTH WITH THE SHRIMP SHELLS, IF USED) BEFORE SERVING.

SOURCERY: SMOKED PORK SAUSAGE

WE LOVE SAUSAGE THAT'S BEEN SMOKED THE REAL way, over hickory, apple, pecan, alder, or other hardwood fires (instead of the lazy way, which is to season the mixture of pork and pork fat with "smoke-flavored" additives). Such sausage is increasingly difficult to find. We get ours from Marvin's Meats in Hollywood, South Carolina, which is about a half-hour's drive from Charleston, but is it ever worth it! You'll probably be able to find a source near your own home, but if you can't, wonderful artisanally smoked sausages are available by mail-order. One of our favorite sources is Bradley's Country Store just outside Tallahassee, Florida (Bradley's Country Store, 10655 Centerville Road, Tallahassee, FL 32308; 805-893-1647; www.bradleyscountrystore.com). Or try Early's Authentic Southern Foods in Tennessee (see page 202). In a pinch, use the best supermarket brand of smoked pork sausage, commonly labeled "kielbasa."

❋ KENTUCKY BURGOO ❋

THE ORIGINS OF KENTUCKY BURGOO ARE EVEN MURKIER THAN THOSE OF BRUNSWICK STEW. ACCORDING TO LEGEND, THE town of Bergoo (*sic*), West Virginia, played host to a large hunting party, and at the end of a successful week of hunting bear, deer, and squirrel, the participants dined on a stew that included everything they'd shot. That tale doesn't go a long way toward explaining why burgoo became the state dish of Kentucky, 220 miles southwest of Bergoo, nor why the spelling changed when it crossed the state line. Others claim that the word "burgoo" was a common term for the oatmeal-like gruel cooked as sailors' rations in the eighteenth century, and that it was adapted by some witty Kentuckian to describe a very different dish, an everything-but-the-kitchen-sink affair that includes lamb, beef, chicken, okra, corn, tomatoes, and beans.

These days burgoo is often cooked at community events, to celebrate times of plenty. You'd expect such a come-hither stew to lack focus, but burgoo's got a distinctly gamy, beefy flavor we call "deep holler." The dried beans absorb the meaty broth and give the stew a lustiness that plays nicely off the summery flavors of the vegetables. Cook the chicken on the bone (until it falls *off* the bone) to give the stew the stockiest flavor you can. And while you can make some effort to remove the bones, don't go overboard. We cooked burgoo for 250 people at an event in Massachusetts, and not a single person complained about the bones.

WHAT TO DRINK   *The rich foundation of seared meats in a burgoo demands an uncomplicated,*
plummy red like a young Merlot or Syrah.

For 12 people

TIME: 1½ hours

2 pounds beef round or shank, flank steak, or
  skirt steak, cut into 1-inch dice
1 pound lamb shank, shoulder, or flank, cut
  into 1-inch dice
One 4½–5-pound chicken, quartered and
  skinned
2 tablespoons kosher salt, plus more to taste
1 tablespoon plus 1 teaspoon freshly ground
  black pepper, plus more to taste
¼ pound slab bacon or 4 slices thick-cut
  bacon, diced
6 serrano, Thai, or other dried red chiles,
  stems trimmed, slit down their sides,
  seeded, and flattened
2 cups full-bodied red wine, such as Merlot,
  Cabernet, or Syrah
6 cups Sunday Beef Broth (page 542) or
  Sunday Chicken Broth (page 532)
4 cups cold water
½ pound dried great northern beans, small
  lima beans, or butterbeans
1¾ pounds Yukon Gold or other waxy potatoes (about 4 medium potatoes) peeled
  and cut into 1-inch dice

2½ cups chopped yellow onions (about
  4 medium onions)
1 cup finely diced carrots (about 2 large
  carrots)
1½ cups fresh corn kernels, cut from the cob
  (about 3 ears)
10 ounces fresh okra, sliced into ½-inch-thick
  rounds (2 cups), or one 10-ounce package defrosted frozen sliced okra
3 cups chopped red bell pepper
  (about 3 peppers)
3½ cups chopped green bell pepper
  (about 3 peppers)
3 cups chopped fresh tomatoes (about 3 large
  tomatoes)
2½ cups canned crushed tomatoes and juice
1½ cups chopped fresh flat-leaf parsley
1 small lemon, thinly sliced
5 cloves fresh garlic, peeled and crushed

1. Season the beef, lamb, and chicken all over with 1 tablespoon salt and 2 teaspoons black pepper. Scatter the diced bacon in an 8-quart stockpot or Dutch oven over medium heat. With a slotted spoon, move the pieces around until the bacon is firm and just golden brown, about 3 minutes. Transfer to a large bowl with the slotted spoon. Pour off and reserve all but 2 tablespoons of fat from the pot and return it to the burner. Add the chiles and gently toast until they release some of their fragrance, about 30 seconds on each side. With tongs, remove and reserve in the bowl with the bacon.

2. Add the beef to the pot in batches, taking care not to crowd the pan, and sear, turning the pieces with tongs as each side becomes golden brown (about 2½ minutes per side), until all the beef has browned. Add reserved bacon fat (or extra-virgin olive oil, peanut oil, or canola oil, if you prefer) by teaspoons if the bottom of the pot becomes dry. Transfer the beef to the bowl with the bacon and chiles. Using the same technique, brown the lamb and then the chicken, transferring both to the same large bowl when they are browned.

3. Add the wine to the pot. With a wooden spoon, stir in tight circles, scraping up the flavorful browned bits from the bottom. Bring the wine to a boil and boil until it has reduced by one quarter, about 6 minutes. Add the broth, water, beans, and reserved beef, lamb, chicken, bacon, and chiles to the pot and cover. Bring to a simmer, then turn the heat to low, cover, and simmer vigorously for 1½ hours, until the beans are just tender and the stew base is a meaty, concentrated stock.

4. Add the potatoes, onions, carrots, corn, okra, bell peppers, tomatoes, and the remaining 1 tablespoon salt and 2 teaspoons black pepper. Return to a simmer. Turn the heat to low, uncover, and simmer gently, stirring occasionally to meld the flavors, for 30 minutes, or until the potatoes can be easily pierced with a fork. Turn off the heat. Stir in the parsley, lemon, and garlic and season to taste with salt and black pepper.

5. Serve in deep bowls, with a side plate of Kilt Lettuce and Ramps (page 203).

❈ SUNDAY GUMBO ❈

GUMBO IS SIMPLE: AN AROMATIC, SPICY STEW OF MEATS, SHELLFISH, AND VEGETABLES, THICKENED WITH OKRA, ROUX, AND filé (pronounced "fee-LAY," the ground dried leaves of a sassafras tree), or any combination thereof. Greener, spicier flavors take the middle ground. But by the way some armchair epicures talk, you'd think gumbo was a blood sport, like politics. They make the partisanship of gumbo styles into a kind of affiliation test which brooks no compromise.

Needless to say, we were once too intimidated to cook gumbo. Then we called Leah Chase, the reknowned New Orleans restaurateur, who cooks and serves gumbo daily. Her honeyed voice and refreshing good humor served as a motivating call back to the kitchen. "You can do whatever you like to gumbo, sweetheart," she said. In fact, she'd just made a gumbo with quail for a group of hunters who'd shot the birds and offered them to her.

We realized that honing in on the most "authentic" gumbo recipe was like trying to find the most traditional preparation of meat loaf—your time's better spent in the kitchen, cooking it and cooking it well. The Smithsonian will not be auditing your culinary performance this evening.

Our Sunday Gumbo might be termed a New Orleans–style gumbo, distinguished by its use of both meats and shellfish—a rich trio of smoked sausage, beef, and chicken gizzards as well as shrimp and oysters—and by its use of both roux and filé powder as thickeners. It qualifies as a Sunday dish because the crabs take a bit of time to clean, there are several meats to sear, and it involves a handmade roux. But the process is fun and rewarding. Chase told us that filé powder has long been thought to have voodoo powers, and while we can't confirm that, we can tell you that cooking this stew gives you the feeling of being a sorcerer.

WHAT TO DRINK *The riot of spicy, salty, meaty and aromatic flavors in this gumbo calls for a gutsy Rioja with cedar and spice, or a full-flavored white like a California Chardonnay.*

For 12 people

TIME: 1¾ hours to cook, 24 hours to "cure"

1 pound headless large fresh shrimp (26–30 per pound; see Sourcery, page 374), shells on

½ cup canola oil, peanut oil, lard, or unsalted butter

½ cup all-purpose flour

1 teaspoon kosher salt, plus more to taste

1½ cups chopped yellow onion (about 1 large onion)

1 cup chopped celery (about 1 large stalk)

1 cup diced carrots (about 2 large carrots)

1 tablespoon extra-virgin olive oil, plus more if necessary

4 serrano, Thai, or other dried red chiles, stems trimmed, slit down their sides, seeded, and flattened

1½ pounds smoked pork sausage, Cajun andouille, or kielbasa (see Sourcery, page 258), cut on the bias into 1¼-inch-thick pieces

1 pound beef round or shank, flank steak, or skirt steak, cut into 1-inch dice

½ pound chicken gizzards, cut into small dice (optional)

1 cup full-bodied white wine, such as Chardonnay, Riesling, or Viognier

3 quarts (12 cups) Sunday Shrimp Broth (page 536) or 3 quarts water mixed with 1 tablespoon Lee Bros. Shrimp Boil (page 553), 3 bay leaves, and 1 stalk celery cut into 2-inch-long pieces

6 live blue crabs

24 shucked oysters, with liquor (see Sourcery, page 76)

1 tablespoon filé powder (optional)

Freshly ground black pepper to taste

¼ cup chopped fresh flat-leaf parsley, for garnish

¼ cup thinly sliced green onion, for garnish

1.   Peel the shrimp (and devein them if you prefer). If using shrimp broth, discard the shells or reserve them for making more broth. If you're not using shrimp broth, reserve the shells for step 5.

2.   Pour the canola oil into a large cast-iron skillet, add the flour, and whisk over medium-low heat until the roux is a café-au-lait brown, about 20 minutes. Add the salt, onion, celery, and carrots and sauté, stirring until the onion and celery have softened and the carrots have paled slightly, about 10 minutes. Turn off the heat. Transfer the roux and vegetables to a medium bowl.

3.   In a 6-quart stockpot or Dutch oven, heat the olive oil over medium-high heat until it shimmers. Add the chiles and gently toast until they discolor and release some of their fragrance, about 30 seconds per side. With tongs, transfer to a large bowl. Add the sausage pieces to the pot, taking care not to crowd them (add them in batches, if necessary). Sear until golden brown along the sides, then turn and brown on another side, about 6 minutes total. Transfer to the bowl with the chiles.

4.   Add the beef to the pot in batches, taking care not to crowd the pan, and sear, turning with tongs as each side becomes golden brown (about 2½ minutes per side), until all the beef has browned. Add more olive oil (or peanut oil, canola oil, or lard, if you prefer) by teaspoons if the bottom of the pot becomes dry. Transfer the beef to the bowl with the chiles and sausage. Add the gizzards to the pot (if using) and sauté, stirring them with a wooden spoon, until they are golden brown all over, about 6 minutes. Transfer to the bowl of chiles, sausage, and beef.

5.   If using shrimp broth, add the wine and 1 cup broth to the pot. Bring to a boil, stirring with a wooden spoon in tight circles, scraping up the flavorful browned bits from the bottom. Boil until the stock is reduced by one quarter, about 6 minutes. Add the remaining 11 cups broth and bring to a boil. Reduce the heat to low and simmer vigorously, uncovered, as you clean the crabs.

   If not using shrimp broth, add the wine to the pot and bring to a boil over high heat. Continue to boil until the wine is reduced by one quarter, about 3 minutes. Add the water and shrimp boil, cover, and bring to a simmer. Tie the shrimp shells, bay leaves, and celery in a tight cheesecloth bundle and submerge it in the boiling water. Reduce the heat to medium-low and simmer vigorously, uncovered, as you clean the crabs.

6. Using tongs, drop 2 live crabs into the simmering broth and cook until their shells turn bright orange, about 2 minutes. Transfer the crabs to a colander set in the sink and run cold water over them. Add the next 2 live crabs to the pot and repeat until all the crabs have been cooked. As each cooked crab becomes cool enough to handle, remove the face (the strip on the front that encompasses the eyes and the mouth) with kitchen scissors. Then slip your thumb in the gap created between the top and bottom shells and pull off the top shell, exposing the feathery gills. Discard the top shell and the gills. Turn the crab over and slide the tip of a knife beneath where the cape of shell tapers to a point; lift the bottom shell off and discard. (If you find any orange crab roe, add it to the pot). Cleaning the crabs will take about 15 minutes. With a cleaver (or with your hands), split each crab down the middle and place the halves in the bowl with the meats and chiles.

7. Add the roux and vegetable mixture and the reserved meats, chiles, and crabs to the broth and simmer gently for 20 minutes, until the flavors have melded. Remove the cheesecloth sack from the broth (if using) and press it against the side of the pot to extract as much liquid as possible. Add the peeled shrimp and the oysters and turn off the heat. Stir in the filé powder, if using, and pepper to taste.

8. We strongly advise letting this gumbo cure for 24 hours in the refrigerator for optimal flavor. Reheat over medium-low heat until the gumbo is piping hot, and serve in wide bowls over rice, garnished with the parsley and green onion.

ROUX

ROUX IS A MIXTURE OF EQUAL PARTS FLOUR AND FAT, cooked over low heat until the flour darkens in color. It thickens any soup or stew you add it to, but it also imparts an alluringly nutty flavor, depending on how long you cook it. Roux becomes darker and its flavor more robust the longer you cook it, but the darker the roux, the less effective its thickening capacity, so it's a tradeoff; a blond-colored roux is a superb thickener but has a somewhat flat, floury flavor. We like to make our roux the color of milk chocolate—brown enough to give flavor but light enough to be an effective thickener.

Making roux is easy. You simply mix the flour and fat over low heat in a skillet, whisking constantly, until the roux becomes the color you desire. You need only elbow grease and some vigilance, because you want to avoid scorching the roux (you'll be able to tell, because scorched flour turns black).

You can use virtually any fat—canola oil, peanut oil, lard, and butter are the most common—but we don't recommend using extra-virgin olive oil. Since it has a lower smoking point than most fats, it's easier to scorch. The idea is to thicken with a nutty flavor, not a burned one.

Roux adds its own flavor to a stew, but you can also use it as a shortcut to enhanced flavor by adding ingredients at the beginning of the browning process. Don't have any smoked sausage? Throw ¼ cup diced slab bacon into your roux to give it smoky flavor. Don't want to clean those crabs but want some crab flavor in the gumbo? Throw a few crab claws into your roux.

❧ TUESDAY GUMBO ❧

OUR TUESDAY GUMBO MIGHT BE SAID TO BE LOWCOUN-
TRY-STYLE, FOR ITS BOUNTY OF SHELLFISH (AND ITS LACK OF MEAT)
and for its use of tomatoes and okra. There are a number of words to describe okra's texture; the
one we like most is one our friend Leah Chase uses: "ropey." It's so simple and descriptive without invoking swamp monsters or other unpleasantries. You can cook out the ropiness by heating
fresh okra in a dry skillet over medium heat for about 10 minutes—news that may delight those
who don't like okra's texture. But the longer you cook it, the more you compromise its thickening
capacity, so keep some filé powder on hand. If your gumbo is too soupy for your taste, add a couple teaspoons of powder once the heat is off.

❧

WHAT TO DRINK   *The interplay of shellfish and okra here requires a white that is equally playful,*
like a Sauvignon Blanc with fruity pineapple and floral honeysuckle notes.

For 12 people

TIME: 1 hour

1 pound headless large fresh shrimp (26–30 per pound; see Sourcery, page 374), peeled

3 quarts (12 cups) Sunday Shrimp Broth (page 536) or 3 quarts water mixed with 1 tablespoon Lee Bros. Shrimp Boil (page 553), 3 bay leaves, and 1 stalk celery cut into 2-inch pieces

3 cups sliced fresh okra (1½ pounds)

2 tablespoons canola oil, peanut oil, lard, or unsalted butter

3 cloves garlic, crushed

1 cup diced yellow onion (1 large onion)

1½ cups diced red or green bell pepper (about 1 large pepper)

¾ cup chopped celery (about 1 large stalk)

1 teaspoon kosher salt, plus more to taste

½ teaspoon freshly ground black pepper, plus more to taste

½ teaspoon cayenne pepper, plus more to taste

One 28-ounce can chopped tomatoes, with juice

1 tablespoon finely minced fresh thyme

1 pound lump or backfin crabmeat (see Sourcery, page 70)

24 shucked oysters, with their liquor (see Sourcery, page 76)

Up to 1 tablespoon filé powder (optional)

1. Peel the shrimp (and devein if you prefer) and reserve in a small bowl. If using shrimp broth, discard the shells or reserve for making more broth. If you're not using shrimp broth, place the shells in a 6-quart stockpot or Dutch oven, add the water, shrimp boil, bay leaves, and celery, and simmer over medium heat for 30 minutes.

2. In a large dry skillet, cook the okra over medium-high heat, stirring occasionally, for about 10 minutes. The okra will lose its liquid, which will caramelize on the bottom of the pan; the okra may become gently browned around the edges, but turn off the heat before it becomes completely browned.

3. In another large skillet, heat the oil over medium-high heat. When it shimmers, add the garlic, onion, bell pepper, celery, salt, black pepper, and cayenne pepper. Sauté until the vegetables have softened, about 6 minutes, then add the tomatoes and their liquid. Stir to incorporate and cook 2 minutes to meld the flavors.

4.   If using shrimp broth, place it in a 6-quart stockpot. If making broth, strain it and return it to the stockpot. Add the vegetable mixture and the thyme. Bring to a vigorous simmer over medium-high heat, reduce the heat to low, and simmer gently for 10 minutes. Turn off the heat. Add the peeled shrimp, the crabmeat, and the oysters and their liquor.

5.   For optimal flavor, let the gumbo "cure" for 24 hours in the refrigerator, but if you do so, add the oysters after the gumbo has been reheated; when stored beyond a few hours, the acid in the tomatoes makes the oysters bitter. Add the filé powder, if desired, and season to taste with salt, black pepper, and cayenne pepper. Serve the gumbo in wide bowls over hot white rice.

❊ PEPPERPOT ❊

THE SOUTHERN FOODWAYS SYMPOSIUM TAKES PLACE IN
OXFORD, MISSISSIPPI, EVERY OCTOBER, AND IT'S ONE OF THE HIGH-
lights of our calendar. Every symposium has a theme—"Barbecue" was the theme one year, "The
Appalachian Larder" another—and there are panel discussions where academics and cultural
studies enthusiasts speak alongside farmers and the CEOs of food companies. We watch the slide
presentations, listen to folks bicker about whether gumbo is African or European in origin, and
occasionally throw in our own two cents. But for us, the real thrill of the symposium is the food
served there.

Some of the culinary events we've been lucky enough to catch are a pimento cheese contest, a
barbecue feed cooked by the late, legendary Memphis pitmaster J. C. Hardaway, and a country ham
summit at which four top producers of the South's version of prosciutto convened beneath an
enormous circus tent, slicing sliver after salty sliver of our cured national treasure. But perhaps
the most revelatory event we attended was the gumbo cookoff that pitted the nation's most
esteemed Creole chef, Leah Chase, against Fritz Blank, the rotund, flamboyant chef of the
Philadelphia French restaurant Deux Cheminées.

At that contest we ate pepperpot, a dish that we had read about in *The Carolina Rice Cook Book*
(1901) by Louisa C. S. Stoney, a treasure among the early cookbooks published in the Lowcountry. The pepperpot on page 43 seems like a gumbo, with shrimp, oysters, and hot peppers (two different types), but it gets its body from pureed sweet potato.

Blank's pepperpot was a distinctly highbrow affair, with chunks of lobster bobbing in a
habanero-spiked butternut puree. The chef explained that the dish was brought to Philadelphia

by West Indian slaves and was one of the most popular foods in the city in the late nineteenth century. The one we developed also gets its luminescent orange color from butternuts, but we give it a Charleston spin with shrimp and oysters, and the fresh habanero and ginger give this velvety stew a distinct Caribbean fire.

※

WHAT TO DRINK   *The tropical-fruit notes of a voluptuous white like a Viognier would complement the heat of Pepperpot's habaneros. Alternately, a spicy, medium-bodied red such as a Cabernet Franc.*

For 8 people

TIME: 1 hour

8 tablespoons unsalted butter, cut into 8 pieces

1 teaspoon kosher salt, plus more to taste

1½ pounds yellow onions (about 4 medium onions), peeled and chopped (about 3 cups)

2 quarts (8 cups) Sunday Chicken Broth (page 532) or Sunday Shrimp Broth (page 536)

1 bottle (750 ml) dry, full-flavored white wine, such as steel-aged Chardonnay or Sancerre

3½ pounds butternut squash (about 2 large squash), peeled, seeded, and cut into ½-inch dice (about 5 cups)

1 cup long-grain rice

3 tablespoons grated fresh ginger

¼ cup fresh tarragon leaves (stripped from twelve 5-inch-long stems) or 1 tablespoon dried tarragon

2 fresh habanero or Scotch bonnet chiles, seeded and minced (about 1 tablespoon)

2 cloves garlic, minced (about 1 tablespoon)

One 14-ounce can chopped tomatoes, drained

1 teaspoon freshly grated nutmeg

1 teaspoon freshly ground black pepper

1 cup half-and-half

1½ pounds headless large fresh shrimp (26–30 per pound; see Sourcery, page 374), peeled

2 pints shucked oysters (see Sourcery, page 76), optional; if not using oysters double the quantity of shrimp above

1.   In a 6-quart stockpot or Dutch oven, melt the butter over medium-high heat until frothy, about 3 minutes. Add the salt and onions and sauté, stirring with a wooden spoon, until the onions are softened and translucent, about 6 minutes.

271

2.   Add the broth, wine, squash, rice, ginger, tarragon, chiles, garlic, tomatoes, nutmeg, and black pepper and cover. Bring to a vigorous simmer, then reduce the heat to low and simmer gently for 25 minutes, or until the squash can be easily pierced with a fork, and the rice is completely cooked.

3.   With a ladle, transfer a batch of broth and solids to a food processor or blender, filling one third of the bowl or blender. Puree until smooth, then set aside in a large bowl. Repeat until all the soup has been pureed. Return the pureed soup to the pot, stir in the half-and-half, and bring to a gentle simmer over low heat. Turn off the heat. Add the shrimp and any liquid and the oysters and their liquor, if desired.

4.   For optimal flavor, let the pepperpot "cure" for 24 hours in the refrigerator, but if you do, add the oysters after the gumbo has been reheated; when stored beyond a few hours, the acid in the tomatoes makes the oysters bitter. After reheating, allow the pepperpot to rest for 5 minutes. Season to taste with salt and pepper and serve in wide bowls, ladled over hot white rice.

❄ CAROLINA PORK HASH ❄

MOST EVERYWHERE IN NORTH AMERICA, A HASH IS A SAVORY SIDE DISH MADE WITH SEASONED MEAT AND POTATOES, but the chunky potato/corned beef/onion medley that gives heft to a plate of fried eggs in Chicago and Manhattan bears little resemblance to the hashes of the Carolinas, which are velvety-smooth stews of finely ground pork, always served over warm white rice. At most barbecue restaurants and at meat-and-threes in the Carolinas, you'll find two hashes: one made from pork shoulder and another made with a proportion of hog livers. The darker liver hash has a surprisingly mellow liver flavor. They are both delicious, but we find the former—imagine a smoky, pulled pork barbecue stew—to be the better crowd-pleaser.

Our Carolina pork hash bucks tradition in a few ways. We sear the pork shoulder before slowly stewing it in the oven, and we add wine to the braising liquid. To lend it a smoky, fiery top note, we add chipotles (smoked jalapeño chiles) to the small amount of barbecue sauce that traditionally gets mixed in. We serve this hash over deep bowls of white rice, with a heaping side of Coleslaw (page 195).

❧

WHAT TO DRINK   *A hoppy American pale ale would flatter the pulled-pork barbecue flavors in this hash as equally as a peppery Malbec.*

For 8 people

TIME: 4 hours

3½ pounds fresh, bone-in pork shoulder (half-picnic or Boston butt)

3 teaspoons kosher salt, plus more to taste

1½ teaspoons freshly ground black pepper, plus more to taste

2 tablespoons extra-virgin olive oil, canola oil, peanut oil, or lard

1 cup full-bodied white wine, such as Chardonnay, Riesling, or Viognier

5 cups Rich Pork Broth (page 548), Sunday Chicken Broth (page 532), or Sunday Beef Broth (page 542)

2 bay leaves

1 teaspoon whole mustard seeds, pounded with a mortar and pestle to a fine powder

2 tablespoons finely minced chipotles in adobo (see Sourcery, page 284) or 2 teaspoons Spanish smoked paprika (*pimentón*)

¾ cup canned crushed tomatoes, with juice

¼ cup ketchup

2 tablespoons Dijon mustard

1 teaspoon sugar

1½ cups chopped yellow onion (about 1 large onion)

2 cups peeled diced Yukon Gold or other waxy potatoes (about 2 large potatoes)

1. Preheat the oven to 400 degrees.

2. With a sharp knife, trim the broad cape of fat from the pork shoulder and discard or reserve for another use. Season the pork all over with 1 teaspoon salt and ½ teaspoon pepper. Pour the oil into a 4-quart enameled cast-iron stockpot or Dutch oven and heat over high heat. When it shimmers, sear the pork, turning it with sturdy tongs as each side becomes golden brown, about 4 minutes per side. Remove and reserve in a large bowl.

3. Add the wine to the pot and bring to a boil over high heat, stirring in tight circles to scrape up the browned bits from the bottom. Boil the wine until it is reduced by one quarter, about 4 minutes. Add the broth, bay leaves, and mustard seeds and bring to a vigorous simmer. Turn off the heat. Return the pork to the pot, cover, and bake for 30 minutes. Reduce the heat to 300 degrees (you don't need to wait for the temperature to come down), turn the pork in the pot, and cook until the meat falls from the bone, about 2½ hours, turning the pork every hour.

4. While the pork cooks, make the barbecue sauce. Mix 2 teaspoons salt, the remaining pepper, and the chipotles, tomatoes, ketchup, Dijon mustard, and sugar in a small bowl and reserve.

5. When the pork has finished cooking, return the pot to the stovetop and transfer the pork to a bowl or a cutting board with a drain to cool. Add the onion and potatoes to the pot, cover and cook until the potatoes can be pierced easily with a fork, about 25 minutes.

6. When the pork has cooled, pull it from the bone. Drain the potatoes and onion, reserving the broth (you should have about 6 cups). Add the vegetables to the bowl with the pork and let cool.

7. Return the broth to the pot, add ½ cup of the barbecue sauce, and simmer gently over low heat. When the potatoes, onion, and pork have cooled, pass them through a meat grinder fitted with a medium blade and return the mixture to the broth. Stir to incorporate and simmer gently for 15 minutes more, until the flavors have melded and the broth has reduced by a fifth. Add the remaining barbecue sauce ¼ cup at a time, to taste.

8. Season with salt and pepper to taste and serve in wide bowls over hot white rice.

SOURCERY: CHIPOTLE PEPPERS

CHIPOTLE PEPPERS ARE SMOKED JALAPEÑO CHILES, and they're most commonly packed in small cans in a sauce called adobo (at supermarkets, they are often on the shelves of the Mexican food aisle). If you can't find them, look for Buffalo brand chipotle puree in a tall, slender bottle, and substitute chipotle puree one-to-one for the minced chipotles in Carolina Pork Hash. If you have dried chipotle peppers, trim the stems when you're ready to use them, cut a slit down their sides and seed them, and soak them in 1 cup very hot water for 10 minutes to reconstitute. For Carolina Pork Hash, mince 2 reconstituted dried chipotles to substitute for the 2 tablespoons chipotles in adobo.

❧ CHICKEN BOG ❧

THE SECOND CHICKEN BOG WE TASTED WAS THE CHARM, THE ONE THAT GOT US SPRINTING TO THE KITCHEN. WHATEVER covered-dish supper occasioned our first chicken bog was long lost to memory, and if not for an extra-long coffee break, we might never have gotten our second chance.

It was late afternoon on a weekday in October, and we'd checked out of work early to follow our friend the late Ted Phillips back to his house on Church Street, around the corner from our offices, in the old French quarter. His eighteenth-century row house was in a block that had once harbored pirates on the lam, and was adjacent to St. Philip's Church Cemetery, where John C. Calhoun is buried.

Ted was writing a history of Magnolia Cemetery, where more than 30,000 Charlestonians are buried. His library/living room was a place where the morbid and salacious secrets of Charleston met their keeper—Ted just happened to be among the best storytellers and social historians of our time. In his extensive collection were first editions of books that their living authors hoped to forget, forgotten books with remarkable prints or inscriptions in them, histories (partly) suppressed, cemetery maps, rare watercolors—every item (including the framed finger-paintings by his two daughters, Alice and Sarah) a launching pad for a story of great fascination and even greater utility at your next cocktail party.

Ted, a lawyer by trade and a former president of the Harvard Lampoon, had nearly given up his practice to pursue his historical sleuthing. About halfway into a typically hilarious story of dirty dealings in the upper branches of a distinguished family tree, Janet Hopkins, Ted's wife, set a casserole of chicken bog down on the table for supper. We fell in love with the dish, a deeply flavored mass of chicken and rice, with a concentrated chicken taste that can come only from long cooking, to the point where the chicken begins to dissolve into luscious threads.

The "bog" in chicken bog refers to its thick casserole quality, and the dish would appear, but for a few details, to be a close cousin to the classic Lowcountry pilau. Its origins aren't well known, but the first use of the name was during the World War II era. The dish was probably invented as a use for leftover chicken. Chicken bog gets its velvety texture from concentrating the chicken; the natural gelatin in the bones gives it body, and the starches released by the rice further thicken it.

Our own bog starts with a fresh chicken and brings out its dark-meat flavor by adding minced giblets and chicken livers. We prefer to simmer the brew to near-thickness by itself and serve it over fluffy, hot white rice. The leftover chicken bog is thus longer-lived.

⊰⊱

WHAT TO DRINK   *A gutsy Sangiovese or Tempranillo blend with spice and rich red fruit can stand up to the liver-tinged chicken-funk of the bog.*

For 6 people

TIME: 1¾ hours

1 tablespoon extra-virgin olive oil, canola oil, peanut oil, or lard

2 serrano, Thai, or other dried red chiles, stems trimmed, slit down their sides, seeded, and flattened

One 4½–5-pound chicken, quartered and skinned, giblets finely chopped

½ pound sweet Italian sausage (about 4 links), cut from casing

1 cup full-bodied red wine, such as Merlot, Cabernet, or Syrah

3 tablespoons unsalted butter

2 tablespoons all-purpose flour

2 cups chopped yellow onion (about 2 large onions)

1¾ cups chopped celery (about 6 stalks)

2 cups chopped red or green bell peppers (about 3 peppers)

2 cloves garlic, minced

One 28-ounce can chopped tomatoes

2 tablespoons minced fresh thyme

2 cups Sunday Chicken Broth (page 532)

Kosher salt to taste

Freshly ground black pepper to taste

½ cup chopped fresh flat-leaf parsley

½ cup chopped green onions

1. Place the oil in an 8-quart stockpot or Dutch oven and heat over medium-high heat. When the oil shimmers, gently toast the chiles until they discolor and release some of their fragrance, about 30 seconds per side. Remove with tongs and reserve in a large bowl.

2. Add the chicken pieces to the pot (don't crowd them; brown in batches, 2 at a time, if necessary) and sear until golden brown on both sides, about 4 minutes per side. Remove and reserve in the bowl with the chiles. Add the sausage and the chicken giblets to the pot and stir, breaking up the sausage with a wooden spoon. Cook until completely browned, about 6 minutes. Remove and reserve in the bowl with the chicken and chiles.

3. Add the wine to the pot and bring to a boil over high heat, stirring with a wooden spoon to scrape up any browned bits on the bottom. Boil until the wine is reduced by one quarter, about 4 minutes. Pour the reduced wine over the reserved meats and chiles.

4. Turn the heat down to medium-high and add the butter. When it has melted, stir in the flour. Stir constantly for 2 minutes until smooth, then add the onion, celery, peppers, and garlic and sauté, stirring constantly, until the onions begin to turn translucent, the peppers begin to pale, and the flour has turned a pale tan, about 6 minutes. Add the tomatoes, the contents of the reserving bowl, the thyme, and the broth, cover, and bring to a vigorous simmer over medium-high heat. Turn the heat to low, uncover, and simmer gently for 25 minutes, or until the broth has reduced by about one quarter. Turn off the heat.

5. With tongs, transfer the chicken pieces to a bowl or a cutting board with a drain. When they are cool enough to handle, pick the meat from the bones and discard the bones. Return the picked chicken to the pot, turn the heat to medium, and simmer for 15 minutes, breaking the chicken into threads as you stir. Turn off the heat and season to taste with salt and pepper.

6. Let rest for 5 minutes before serving in deep bowls. (For optimal flavor, "cure" in the refrigerator for 24 hours; if you wish, spoon the fat from the surface before reheating.) Serve over hot white rice, garnished with the parsley and green onions.

❋ RUSSWOOD CIRCLE CHILI CON CARNE ❋

WHEN WE WERE IN COLLEGE IN MASSACHUSETTS, OUR
MOTHER APPLIED FOR HER DREAM JOB, AS HEADMISTRESS OF THE
Hockaday School, a girls' school in Dallas, and she got it. So our parents sold 83 East Bay Street
and moved into a low, sprawling ranch house in North Dallas.

Our parents were ready for a new adventure and immediately loved "Big D" and their new
jobs. We weren't thrilled with the change, but we didn't have much say in the matter; we had
already left home. So we just moved what belongings were left in the house on East Bay Street into
our grandmother's carriage house a few blocks away, on Meeting Street. And we worked out a deal
with our parents: we would gather in Charleston for Thanksgiving and in Dallas for Christmas.

The one-story ranch on Russwood Circle was very different from 83 East Bay. None of the
windows in the Texas house opened; it had been built in a brash, pre-oil-crisis 1960s, when
builders imagined people living in sealed, expertly climatized boxes. Gone were the sounds of the
harbor—the lapping water, the pilot boats' thrum, the cargo ships' horns. In their place was a
creepy oceanic sound that seeped into the house through the skylights, caused by thousands
of rubber tires whooshing at 60 miles per hour up and down the eight lanes of the Dallas North
Tollway.

But we soon warmed to Dallas's charms, particularly its cuisine. We were introduced to the
wondrous Tortilla Soup (page 307), a different way to make chicken and dumplings, and the pleasures of Texas barbecue (Russwood Circle is only a few minutes' drive from Sonny Bryan's, a
deservedly fabled spot for ribs and beef brisket). And the chiles! We'd never encountered nor
imagined the wide selection of dried chiles that was considered commonplace in Dallas markets.

To be sure, Charlestonians are no strangers to chiles, but Lowcountry recipes that feature "hot pepper" usually call for red pepper flakes, a useful kitchen staple, or for a long, thin variety of red chile that carries more heat than flavor. In Dallas we found chiles we'd never seen before: tiny orange ones the size of pine nuts, large black anchos as wide as a human palm, and slender, raisiny-tasting pasillas (which means "small grape"). Each chile's fire was surprisingly unique, but even more exciting were their flavors. Some tasted fruit-forward, with flavors like dried cherries, plums, or grapes. Others had smokier profiles and tasted of chocolate, roasted nuts, or tea. (See "Sourcery: Buying Dried Chilies," page 284).

We also learned that you can amplify these flavors by "toasting" chiles—frying the seeded, trimmed, torn chiles very briefly in a small amount of fat in a skillet—and that once you've toasted them, you can soak them in water or broth to reconstitute and soften them, then whir them up in a blender to make a sauce that is the essence of the chiles themselves. Hotheads can reserve the seeds to add more heat later, if the sauce isn't fiery enough for their palates.

Chiles are inexpensive; buy them and experiment with them often. Find out which ones you prefer and combine them in different ways to personalize recipes. When we developed this chili con carne, we made a number of different single varietal chile purees, then blended them in various quantities, in much the same way a winemaker blends the juice of different grapes. Eventually we arrived at a combination we think gives just the right amount of smoky, nutty, and fruity flavor to play off the beef, charred onions, and tomatoes.

Serve this chili in deep bowls, with wedges of Crispy Corn Bread (page 497) or Sally Lunn (page 500), slices of fresh avocado, and sour cream. Or ladle it over grilled or boiled hot dogs to make the chili dogs we serve when we host a Legareville Oyster Roast (page 414).

※

WHAT TO DRINK   *A jammy, unsubtle young Beaujolais would be the right match for this chili's beefy, smoky flavors; a white with a hint of effervescence would temper its heat.*

For 12 people

TIME: 1¼ hours

5 pounds ground beef (chuck or round)

1½ teaspoons salt, plus more to taste

¾ teaspoon freshly ground black pepper, plus more to taste

¼ pound slab bacon or 4 slices thick-cut bacon, diced

6 whole dried guajillo chiles, stems trimmed, seeded (seeds reserved, if desired), and torn into flat pieces

4 ancho chiles, stems trimmed, seeded (seeds reserved, if desired), and torn into flat pieces

1 cup Sunday Beef Broth (page 542)

2½ pounds yellow onions, peeled

12 cloves garlic, husks removed

2 teaspoons extra-virgin olive oil

Two 28-ounce cans chopped tomatoes (preferably "fire-roasted"), with juice

¼ cup semisweet chocolate chips (optional)

¼ cup chopped green onion

1.   Place the ground beef in a large bowl and season with 1 teaspoon salt and ½ teaspoon black pepper (you do not need to mix the seasonings into the meat).

2.   Scatter the diced bacon in a 6-quart stockpot or Dutch oven over medium heat. With a wooden spoon, move the pieces around until the bacon is firm and barely crisp, about 4 minutes. Remove with a slotted spoon and reserve in a small bowl. Add the torn chile pieces to the bacon fat in batches and gently toast until they discolor and release some of their fragrance, about 30 seconds. Remove and reserve in the bowl with the bacon.

3.   Working with 1¼-pound batches, add the ground beef to the pot and cook, stirring to break it up, until the beef is cooked through and has begun to brown, about 8 minutes. Remove and reserve in the large bowl. Repeat until all the beef has been cooked.

4.   Add the beef broth to the pot, and using a wooden spoon, stir in tight circles, scraping up any browned bits from the bottom. When the broth boils, pour it over the bowl of chiles and bacon. Submerge the chiles and let stand for 10 minutes.

5.   Turn off the heat beneath the stockpot and return the reserved beef to it. Place the yellow onions and garlic in a 9-×-13-inch roasting pan and drizzle the olive oil over them. Shower them with ½ teaspoon salt and ¼ teaspoon black pepper and turn them with a serving spoon until they are evenly coated with the oil. Place the pan under a broiler, 3 to 4 inches from the flame or heating element, and broil until the onions are nicely charred, about 8 minutes. Peel the garlic cloves by squeezing them at the stem end with tongs (or let cool and peel by hand). Transfer half the garlic and half the onions to a food processor, add 1 can tomatoes and their juice, and process to a smooth puree, about 1 minute. Pour the puree into the pot with the beef, then process the remaining garlic and onions with the remaining tomatoes and add to the pot.

6.   Place the reserved bacon, chiles, and beef broth in the processor bowl (you do not need to wash it) and process to a smooth puree, about 1 minute. Add half of the chile puree to the pot and stir with a wooden spoon until the ingredients are thoroughly mixed.

7.   Turn the heat to medium and heat the chili. When the surface begins to bubble, reduce the heat to low, partially cover, and simmer gently, stirring every 15 minutes to ensure even cooking, until the chili has thickened and darkened to a chocolate brown, about 1 hour. Add the chocolate chips, if using, and stir to distribute them. When they have melted completely, taste the chili and adjust the seasoning to taste with salt, black pepper, and more chile puree. Simmer gently for 1 hour more, partially covered, stirring every 15 minutes, until the chili is very thick. Taste again and add salt and pepper, if desired. If the chili isn't hot enough for your palate, add reserved chile seeds by ½ teaspoonfuls, stirring them into the chili thoroughly and letting it simmer gently for 5 minutes before testing again.

8.   For optimal flavor, let the chili "cure" in the refrigerator for 24 hours, then reheat over low heat, stirring the chile every 10 minutes, until ready to serve. Garnish with chopped green onion.

IF YOU ARE SENSITIVE TO THE HEAT OF CHILES, BY ALL means don't write them off, because there are plenty that have great flavor without a lot of heat. Chile heat is rated in one of two ways and often marked as such on a package. The not-so-accurate way is the hotness scale of 1 to 10, with 10 being the hottest and 1 being the mildest. The more scientific way is the Scoville index of heat, which rates chiles in "Scoville units," with mild, fruity chiles such as ancho, pasilla, and Anaheim earning 1,000–1,500 SUs and hotter chiles such as Thai, Scotch bonnet, and habanero earning 50,000–150,000 SUs.

When buying chiles, avoid flashy packaging designed for people who don't speak Spanish. At the market near our Harlem roost, there's a section with chiles simply packaged for people familiar with Mexican cooking, and then there are the chiles packaged for non-Spanish-speakers. The latter cost more than twice as much as the former, and their quality is about the same.

The mail-order source we prefer for dried chiles is Pendery's, for its breadth of varieties, the quality of the chiles, and its customer service. The online catalogue can be downloaded. Pendery's, 1211 Manufacturing St., Dallas, TX 75207; 800-533-1780; www.penderys.com.

❄ CHICKEN AND ❄
SWEET POTATO–ORANGE DUMPLINGS

IT'S A CLICHÉ TO SAY THAT CHICKEN AND DUMPLINGS ARE THE SOUTH'S CHICKEN NOODLE SOUP, BUT THEY ARE. THIS dish uses soft white wheat flour dumplings to grab hold of the concentrated chicken broth flavor that has such a comforting, elemental, firm grip on the medulla. In southern homes, we've found two types of dumplings in soups: pillowy "drop" dumplings, which puff up when you cook them, and flat, noodlelike "rolled" dumplings. Both are terrific, but here we use rolled dumplings, and we whip sweet potato and orange zest into the dumpling dough for an extra layer of great flavor.

❄

WHAT TO DRINK   *Slow-cooked comfort foods like this beg for a wine that's easy to love. A mature (four years or older) Cabernet Franc or Cabernet Sauvignon with low acidity would be our pick.*

For 4 people

TIME: 1¼ hours

FOR THE SOUP

2 teaspoons kosher salt, plus more to taste

1 teaspoon freshly ground black pepper, plus more to taste

One 4–5-pound chicken, cut into serving pieces

1 tablespoon canola oil

½ cup crisp white wine, such as Pinot Grigio or Sauvignon Blanc

8 cups Sunday Chicken Broth (page 532) or Sunday Vegetable Broth (page 539)

12 whole black peppercorns

2 bay leaves

½ teaspoon crushed red pepper

1 cup roughly chopped onion (about 1 large onion)

⅔ cup chopped carrot (about 1 large carrot)

⅓ cup chopped celery (about 1 stalk)

½ cup chopped fresh flat-leaf parsley, for garnish

1 lemon, thinly sliced, for garnish

FOR THE DUMPLINGS

8 ounces sweet potato, peeled and cut into small dice

4 ounces (1 cup) sifted all-purpose flour, plus more for dusting

1 large egg, beaten

1 teaspoon fruity olive oil

1 tablespoon plus 1 teaspoon orange zest (from about 2 large Valencia oranges)

1 teaspoon kosher salt

¼ teaspoon freshly ground black pepper

1. To make the soup, mix the salt and pepper in a small bowl and season the chicken pieces generously with the mixture. Pour the oil into a 4- to 6-quart wide, heavy-bottomed stockpot or Dutch oven and place it over medium-high heat. When the oil shimmers, brown the chicken pieces in batches, taking care not to crowd them in the pot, until they are golden brown, 3 to 5 minutes per side. Remove to a plate and reserve.

2. Pour the wine into the pot and stir up any browned bits on the bottom. When the wine has reduced by one half, add the broth, peppercorns, bay leaves, red pepper, onion, carrot, celery, and the reserved chicken. Cover and bring to a vigorous simmer. Uncover, turn the heat to low, and simmer gently until the meat nearly falls from the bone, 35 to 40 minutes.

3. While the soup cooks, make the dough for the dumplings. Pour an inch of water into a stockpot fitted with a strainer basket and bring to a boil over high heat. Add the sweet potato and steam until very soft, 15 to 20 minutes. Transfer to a large bowl and mash to a puree with a whisk or wooden spoon. Let cool.

4. Add the remaining dumpling ingredients to the sweet potato puree and mix thoroughly with a spoon or rubber spatula until the dough comes together in a ball. Divide the dough in half. Using a lightly floured rolling pin, roll each ball on a floured board until it is ⅛ inch thick (if the pin sticks to the dough, scatter flour by ½ teaspoonfuls on the dough). Cut into strips about ¾ inch wide and 2 inches long. Each half makes about 32 dumplings.

5. When the soup has cooked, transfer the chicken to a cutting board and let cool. Strain the broth, return it to the pot, and simmer vigorously over medium heat. When the chicken is cool enough to handle (about 15 minutes), strip the meat from the bones, pulling it into bite-sized pieces; discard the bones and any skin.

6. Return the chicken to the pot, reduce the heat to low, and add the dumplings, only as many as achieves your desired ratio of soup to dumplings. Freeze any extra dumplings between sheets of waxed paper in an airtight container to use in another soup. Simmer until the dumplings are cooked through, 5 to 8 minutes.

7. Serve in large bowls, garnished with the parsley and lemon slices.

Soups

Rustic, hearty stews speak to our souls, but silky, understated soups definitely have a cherished place in our lives, too. We serve soups when we want a dish that's elegant and uncomplicated, something lively to launch a successful meal. Liquids frame savory flavors in an electric way, coating the palate immediately. We've found that in our own hurried lives, soup is often a meal in itself, with a slice of corn bread or Sally Lunn (page 500). As a result, we've developed many of these soups as quick knockouts (QKOs), easy to prepare but with enough interest to knock an unsuspecting family member's socks off on a sleepy weeknight.

We take more than a few liberties with southern soup conventions. We've morphed shrimp bisque into a chowder, and we serve our she-crab soup out-of-season, substituting a plentiful lookalike, taste-alike roe for the crab roe. Heck, we've even turned our beloved roadside staple, the humble boiled peanut, into an exotic, delicious soup.

❊ SHE-CRAB SOUP ❊

QUICK KNOCKOUT

DRIVERS OF THE HORSE-AND-CARRIAGE TOURS THAT AMBLE ALONG CHARLESTON STREETS AROUSE PLENTY OF IRE FROM locals, for telling the tourists tall tales about our hometown. One falsehood in particular always sticks in our craw: when the carriage drivers pass a certain restaurant near our office, they never fail to say that it has "the best she-crab soup in Charleston." We've tried that soup, and the kindest thing we can say is that the carriage drivers must not dine out much.

In fact, many restaurants serve she-crab soup worth raving about. As much a culinary icon of Charleston as shrimp and grits or benne wafers, the creamy, sherry-spiked soup gets its pinkish orange tint and salty, seaweedy tang from a dollop of crab roe dissolved in it. During the winter and spring, when crab roe is scarce, we substitute any fine-grained pink, orange, or golden fish roe, such as trout, carp, capelin, or tobiko, the flying fish roe that is plentiful in Asian markets.

We like to serve she-crab soup as a late light supper, with a green salad and a couple slices of buttered Sally Lunn (page 500) speckled with flakes of Maldon salt.

❊

WHAT TO DRINK   *The driest of Rieslings or a Sauvignon Blanc with herbal, green-pepper tones would pair nicely with this creamy soup.*

For 6 people

TIME: 30 minutes

2 tablespoons unsalted butter

2 finely minced shallots

½ teaspoon kosher salt, plus more to taste

1 tablespoon all-purpose flour

4 cups half-and-half

2 cups Sunday Shrimp Broth (page 536) or
    Rich Fish Broth (page 546)

4 tablespoons crab roe or any fine-grained
    orange or pink fish eggs, such as trout
    roe, carp roe, capelin roe, or tobiko

5 tablespoons sherry

1½ cups picked lump or backfin crabmeat
    (8 ounces; see Sourcery, page 70)

Freshly ground black pepper to taste

1. Heat the butter in a 3-quart saucepan over medium-high heat until frothy. Add the shallots and salt and sauté, stirring, until the shallots are just soft but not browned, about 4 minutes. Sprinkle the flour over the shallots and whisk around the pan, until it is completely incorporated into the butter and shallots, about 1 minute.

2. Add the half-and-half, broth, 2 tablespoons roe, and 1 tablespoon sherry and whisk until the roux is incorporated. Cover. When the soup comes to a simmer, turn the heat to low, uncover, and simmer gently, stirring occasionally, until the soup has reduced by one sixth, about 12 to 15 minutes. Strain the soup through a fine-mesh strainer and return it to the pan.

3. Add the crabmeat and cook for 2 minutes over low heat, stirring to combine. Season the soup with salt and pepper.

4. To serve, place 1 teaspoon roe in the bottom of each of 6 bowls and ladle the soup on top of it. Drizzle 2 teaspoons sherry into each bowl before serving.

DOWNTOWN TOUCH—SHE-CRAB ARTICHOKE SOUP: THE DOWNTOWN TOUCH IS TO ADD PUREED JERUSALEM ARTICHOKES, WHICH GIVE THE SOUP A MORE VELVETY BODY AND A MILKY, NUTTY SWEETNESS THAT'S PERFECTLY SUITED TO THE FLAVOR OF THE CRAB. PEEL AND DICE 3/4 POUND JERUSALEM ARTICHOKES AND STEAM IN A POT FITTED WITH A STRAINER BASKET UNTIL TENDER, 8 TO 12 MINUTES. DRAIN. PUREE THE COOKED ARTICHOKES IN A FOOD PROCESSOR OR BLENDER UNTIL SMOOTH, ABOUT 2 MINUTES. ADD THE PUREE TO THE SOUP IN STEP 3 AND FINISH ACCORDING TO THE INSTRUCTIONS ABOVE.

❊ STOLEN TOMATO BISQUE ❊

THOUGH WE SHARE NO BLOOD RELATIVES WITH OWEN LEE, ON OCCASION WE CLAIM KINSHIP. FOR TWENTY YEARS OWEN lived on Edisto Island, a fertile barrier island south of Charleston with a large farming community, and taught art to two generations of students there. As a result, she knows just about everybody on the island, and their parents and children, grands and great-grands. If we come up a few dollars short at the Piggly-Wiggly or if we've had a few too many beers at the beachfront bar the Pelican, we just say we're related to Owen Lee and everything seems to turn out fine.

We'll never forget the August day we were in Owen's old Volvo, speeding toward Edisto Beach on Highway 164, the main thoroughfare on the island, when she shouted, "Stolen tomatoes!" and pulled the car to a halt. Stretching out from the roadside was a scraggly tomato field that had been stripped bare by the harvesters the previous week. Owen claimed that any ripe tomatoes left on the vines that late in the summer were free to the community—which didn't explain why she called them "stolen," or why she hustled in and out of the field.

You don't have to steal tomatoes to make Stolen Tomato Bisque, a soup we love for, among other things, its versatility. When it's warm out, we serve it cold, garnished with a few cooked shrimp, which add a shade of sweetness and evoke the saltwater creeks that wind through the Edisto marshes. When it's cold out, we serve this bisque hot, with warmed cheese grits croutons. Either way it's the perfect start to a meal, or a delicious lunch with a wedge of Crispy Corn Bread (page 497) or a hank of dressed greens.

WHAT TO DRINK   *The velvety tannins of a Chianti or a Brunello highlight the aromatics of the onion and tarragon in this tomato bisque.*

For 8 people
TIME: 1 hour

8 cups chopped fresh ripe tomatoes (about 3 pounds) or three 28-ounce cans chopped tomatoes

1½ cups Sunday Chicken Broth (page 532)

1 cup crisp, tart white wine, such as Pinot Grigio or Sauvignon Blanc

¼ cup freshly grated red onion (about ½ medium onion)

2 teaspoons salt, plus more to taste

1 teaspoon freshly ground black pepper, plus more to taste

4 stems fresh tarragon or 1 teaspoon dried tarragon

½ cup half-and-half

16 peeled, steamed large fresh shrimp (26–30 per pound; see Sourcery, page 374), sliced in half lengthwise, for garnish (optional), or 1 recipe warm Cheese Grits Croutons (page 157; optional)

1.   Puree the tomatoes in a food processor or in batches in a blender until smooth, about 1 minute, and pour into a 6-quart stockpot. Add the broth, wine, onion, salt, pepper, and half the tarragon. Bring to a vigorous simmer over medium-high heat, about 6 minutes. Partially cover and turn the heat to low.

2.   Simmer gently for 45 minutes, stirring occasionally. The tarragon will darken and the puree will thicken considerably. With tongs, remove the tarragon sprigs, or, if using fresh tomatoes, pass the soup through a fine-mesh strainer to remove the tarragon and bits of skin; press the skins to squeeze out all liquid. Return the soup to the pot, add the remaining tarragon, and stir in the half-and-half in a slow stream until thoroughly incorporated.

3.   If you plan to serve the soup cold, refrigerate for 4 hours or overnight and garnish each bowl with 4 pieces of shrimp. If you plan to serve it warm, ladle it into bowls and gently place 3 or 4 croutons on the surface of each.

❊ SUMMER CORN SOUP ❊
WITH BUTTERBEAN DUMPLINGS

THERE ARE TWO ESTABLISHED FARMERS' MARKETS IN CHARLESTON: THE TUESDAY EVENING MARKET IN MT. PLEASANT, just four miles across the Cooper River from downtown, and the city market, which takes place on Marion Square, a park and former parade ground at the major crossroads in the city, every Saturday morning.

This simple corn soup combines two of our absolute favorite things about visiting the markets in late summer: hand-shelled fresh butterbeans and the local sweet corn varieties, like Sweetie and Silver Queen, that the Fields family grows. The Fieldses, like many local farmers, sell their produce regularly at both markets.

We let the essence of corn sing in this soup, modifying it only slightly with shallot and a touch of fresh jalapeño pepper. The butterbean dumplings are not true dumplings at all, but rather dollops of Butterbean Pâté (page 73). The pâté's lemony, minty flavor plays the right contrasting note to the soup's creamy sweetness, but in the same summery key.

❋

WHAT TO DRINK   *A rosé with red-berry flavors and a brisk acidity would be right for this soup, whose sweetness has a tart citrus edge.*

6 ears fresh corn

2 tablespoons unsalted butter

½ cup chopped shallots

1 small fresh jalapeño chile, stem trimmed, seeded, and finely diced

1 teaspoon salt, plus more to taste

½ teaspoon finely ground white pepper, plus more to taste

1 quart Sunday Vegetable Broth (page 539)

½ cup heavy cream

1 recipe Butterbean Pâté (page 73)

6 large mint leaves

1.   On a cutting board with a drain, cut the corn kernels from the cobs. Scrape the cobs up and down with the edge of a spoon to extract as much juice and material as possible. You should have 4 cups.

2.   Melt the butter in a 4-quart stockpot or Dutch oven over medium heat until frothy. Add the shallots, jalapeño, and salt and sauté, stirring occasionally, until the shallots are translucent and softened but not yet browning, about 3 minutes. Add the white pepper and 3 cups corn kernels and their liquid to the pot and sauté, stirring, until nearly all the liquid has evaporated, about 8 minutes. Add the broth and bring to a simmer over medium-high heat. Simmer vigorously until the corn has softened, about 3 minutes.

3.   Transfer the soup to a food processor (or in batches to a blender) and puree until smooth, about 3 minutes. Pass the soup through a fine-mesh strainer into a large bowl, pressing the solids to extract as much liquid as possible. Discard the solids.

4.   Add the remaining corn kernels and the cream to the soup, stir to distribute, and ladle the soup into 6 bowls. Form the dumplings with a teaspoon, using the bowl of the spoon to roll a small amount of butterbean pâté into small zeppelins. Float 3 dumplings on the surface of each bowl of soup, about 2 inches apart, and float a single mint leaf between them.

❊ SHRIMP CHOWDER ❊

SHRIMP SEASON IN SOUTH CAROLINA RUNS FROM MID-
MAY TO OCTOBER. THE LEGAL HARVEST DATES ARE SET FIRMLY EACH
year by the South Carolina Department of Natural Resources. But in towns along the coast with
sizable shrimping fleets, such as Georgetown, McClellanville, and Beaufort, shrimp season begins
when a man or woman of the cloth blesses a gathering of the town's shrimp boats with prayers for
safe passage and large hauls. The ceremony, called "the Blessing of the Shrimp Fleet," often pre-
cedes a townwide festival celebrating the geographical good fortune of its coastal location.

We developed this recipe at the opening of a recent shrimping season. We wanted to create a
soup as elegant as a bisque but with texture, smoke, and fire. We ended up turning the recipe in
the direction of chowder, with cream, bacon, and potatoes.

Dunk a thick slice of Sally Lunn (page 500) in this, put a glass of white wine on the table, and
call it a meal.

❊

WHAT TO DRINK   *The forward citrus notes of an unoaked Chardonnay—or the even more nuanced
ones of a Rousanne—would match nicely with the bacon and cream in this chowder.*

For 6 people

TIME: 45 minutes

1 pound headless large fresh shrimp (26–30 per pound; see Sourcery, page 374), shells on

6 cups Sunday Shrimp Broth (page 536) or 6 cups Sunday Chicken Broth (page 532) plus 1 tablespoon unsalted butter

1 pound Yukon Gold or other waxy potatoes, peeled and finely diced (2 cups)

¼ pound slab bacon or 4 slices thick-cut bacon, diced

2 serrano, Thai, or other dried red chiles, stems trimmed, slit down their sides, seeded, and flattened

1 cup chopped yellow onion (about 1 large onion)

⅔ cup chopped celery (about 2 large stalks)

1 teaspoon minced fresh thyme

1 bay leaf

1 cup dry, full-flavored white wine, such as steel-aged Chardonnay or Sancerre

2 cups half-and-half

¼ teaspoon finely minced lemon zest

1 tablespoon plus 1 teaspoon salt

½ teaspoon freshly ground black pepper

½ cup chopped green onions or fresh flat-leaf parsley

1. Peel the shrimp (devein, if desired).

If using shrimp broth: Discard the shrimp shells or reserve for making more broth. Pour the broth into a 4- to 6-quart pot and bring to a boil over high heat. Add the potatoes, reduce the heat to low, and simmer vigorously until the stock has reduced by one third and the potatoes are just soft, 12 to 15 minutes. Strain and reserve the broth (you should have 4 cups) and potatoes separately. Rinse and dry the pot and return it to the stovetop.

If using chicken broth: Melt the butter in a 4- to 6-quart pot, and when it is frothy, add the shells. Sauté until the shells turn bright orange but have not begun to brown, about 4 minutes. Using a slotted spoon, transfer the shells to a piece of cheesecloth, tie them up in a tight bundle, and return them to the pot. Pour in the chicken broth and bring to a boil over high heat. Add the potatoes, reduce the heat to low, and simmer vigorously until the broth has reduced by one third and the potatoes are just soft, 12 to 15 minutes. Strain and reserve the broth (you should have 4 cups) and potatoes separately. Discard the bundle of shells. Rinse and dry the pot and return it to the stovetop.

2.   Scatter the diced bacon in the pot and sauté over medium-high heat until it is firm and just golden brown, about 3 minutes. With a slotted spoon, transfer it to a small bowl. Pour off and discard all but 2 tablespoons bacon fat and return the pot to the burner. Add the chiles and gently toast them until they become discolored and release some of their fragrance, about 30 seconds per side. Remove and reserve in another small bowl. Add the onion, celery, thyme, and bay leaf and sauté, stirring with a wooden spoon to scrape up any browned bits on the bottom, until the onion is slightly translucent, about 3 minutes. Add the reserved broth, the wine, and the reserved chiles and bring to a vigorous simmer. Reduce the heat to low and simmer gently for 15 minutes, or until the broth is reduced by one quarter and the celery has lost all its color. Remove the bay leaf.

3.   Add half the shrimp to the broth and simmer until they are pink and cooked through, about 2 minutes. Turn off the heat. Ladle some of the broth, vegetables, and shrimp into a food processor or blender and process to a smooth puree, about 3 minutes. Repeat, processing in batches until all the soup is pureed. Clean the pot. Pass the puree through a fine-mesh strainer into the pot.

4.   Add the reserved potatoes, the half-and-half, and the lemon zest and stir to distribute. Return to a gentle simmer over medium heat. Roughly chop the remaining shrimp, add them to the pot, and simmer until they are pink and cooked through, about 2 minutes. Turn off the heat. Season with the salt and pepper.

5.   Serve in bowls, garnished with the reserved bacon and the green onions or parsley.

❋ BUTTERBEAN SOUP ❋
WITH CURRIED BUTTERMILK

THE BUTTERBEAN SEASON IN LATE SUMMER IS A BANNER TIME FOR SOUTHERN GOURMANDS, AS THE FARMERS' MARKETS AND roadside stands quietly fill with zippered plastic bags of freshly shelled "peas" (little beans) and butterbeans (a dainty variety of lima bean). We say "quietly" because even though freshly hand-shelled butterbeans and field peas are pricey, they often sell out before a sign can be raised announcing their arrival. They exist as a kind of secret—conventional and innocuous-appearing to visitors, who are often unaware of how amazing the flavor of a humble lima can be when it's sparklingly fresh. The quintessential way to eat butterbeans is to boil them in seasoned water and top them with a pat of butter before serving. We love to concentrate their flavor by making this simple chilled soup. A drizzle of tart curried buttermilk highlights the cool green color of the soup and sets off the flavor of the precious beans.

❋

WHAT TO DRINK   *The lively acidity of a Sauvignon Blanc like Sancerre is the right match for a soup with summery green flavors and a tinge of salty ham.*

For 6 people

TIME: 35 minutes

1 tablespoon extra-virgin olive oil, canola oil, peanut oil, or lard

4 ounces country ham (see "A Country Ham Primer," page 325), cut into 2 pieces

1¼ cups chopped yellow onion (about 1 large onion)

6 cups Sunday Vegetable Broth (page 539)

2 pounds butterbeans, preferably fresh

2 cups tightly packed fresh spinach (6 ounces)

¼ cup dry white wine, such as Pinot Grigio or Sancerre

¼ cup half-and-half

½ cup whole or lowfat buttermilk

1 teaspoon curry powder

¼ teaspoon kosher salt, plus more to taste

½ teaspoon freshly ground pepper, plus more to taste

1. In a 3-quart saucepan, heat the oil over medium-high heat until it shimmers. Add the ham and sear, turning the pieces as each side becomes golden brown, until the ham is browned all over, about 6 minutes. Remove and reserve in a small bowl. Add the onion to the pan and sauté until softened and translucent, about 4 minutes.

2. Add the broth, turn the heat to high, and bring to a boil. Add the butterbeans and boil until very tender, 15 to 20 minutes. Add the spinach and cook until it is electric green, about 1 minute. Turn off the heat.

3. Transfer some of the soup to a food processor or blender and puree until smooth, about 3 minutes. Repeat, processing in batches until all the soup has been pureed. Pass the soup through a fine-mesh strainer into the pot and add the wine and half-and-half. Turn the heat to low and reheat, stirring, until the surface begins to steam, about 3 minutes.

4. While the soup heats up, whisk the buttermilk with the curry powder and salt in a small bowl. Chop the reserved ham into thin shreds. Taste the soup and season with the salt and black pepper.

5. Ladle immediately into wide bowls, drizzle a splash of curried buttermilk over each bowl, and drop a pinch of country ham threads in the center.

DOWNTOWN TOUCH—BUTTERBEAN SOUP WITH RAW PEANUT "PISTOU": GREEN PEANUTS FRESHLY DUG FROM THE GROUND ARE A TREASURE AND HAVE ROUGHLY THE SAME SEASON AS SHELLED PEAS LIKE BUTTERBEANS. THE DOWNTOWN TOUCH IN THIS DISH IS TO POUND TO A PASTE WITH A MORTAR AND PESTLE 1/4 CUP FRESH BASIL, A HANDFUL OF GREEN PEANUTS, AND 1 TEASPOON KOSHER SALT AND TO SERVE GUMBALL-SIZED DOLLOPS OF THE INTENSE, SALTY PASTE IN THE MIDDLE OF EACH BOWL OF SOUP. OMIT THE CURRIED BUTTERMILK AND COUNTRY HAM GARNISHES.

❧ BOILED PEANUT SOUP ❧

QUICK
KNOCKOUT

BOILED PEANUT LOVERS OFTEN WONDER WHY ROASTED PEANUTS HOLD SWAY IN SUCH A VARIETY OF RECIPES—NOODLE dishes, desserts, and soups—whereas boiled peanuts seemed to be pigeonholed in the snack category. We make every effort to be contrarian in this regard (see Boiled Peanut and Sorghum Swirl Ice Cream, page 429). Why not show off the bean-like flavor of peanuts, which is virtually obliterated when they get roasted?

This soup marries boiled peanuts with bacon and onion. It's elegant and soothing, like an English pea soup, and the dash of white wine vinegar livens it up and focuses its flavor. It makes a great lunch alongside half a Grilled Pimento Cheese Sandwich (page 92) and a glass of Iced Tea (page 21).

❧

WHAT TO DRINK   *An earthy, gently-oaked Rhone-style red blend would flatter both the deep bean flavor and the top note of zesty thyme in this soup.*

For 4 people

TIME: 30 minutes

¼ pound slab bacon or 4 slices thick-cut
    bacon, finely diced
1½ cups chopped yellow onion (1½ large
    onions)
3 cups Sunday Chicken Broth (page 532)
2 cups Boiled Peanuts (page 58), shelled

1 tablespoon plus 1 teaspoon fresh thyme
    (from twelve 5-inch sprigs)
1½ cups two-percent milk
2 teaspoons white wine vinegar
Kosher salt to taste
Finely ground white pepper to taste

1. Scatter the diced bacon in a 12-inch skillet and sauté over medium-high heat, moving the pieces around with a slotted spoon until the bacon is firm and just golden brown, about 3 minutes. Transfer the bacon to a small bowl. Pour off all but 2 tablespoons of the bacon fat and discard.

2. Add the onion to the skillet and sauté until softened and translucent, about 5 minutes. Add the broth, peanuts, and 2 teaspoons thyme, increase the heat to high, and bring to a boil. Reduce the heat to low and simmer vigorously, uncovered, until the peanuts have slipped their skins and the broth is reduced by one quarter, about 10 minutes.

3. Transfer some of the soup to a food processor or blender and puree until smooth, about 3 minutes. Repeat, processing in batches until all the soup is pureed. Pass the soup through a fine-mesh strainer into the pot; you should have about 3 cups. Add the milk and vinegar and season to taste with salt and pepper.

4. Ladle into bowls and garnish each bowl with pinches of the remaining thyme leaves.

THE BOILED PEANUTS VENDOR

THE BOILED PEANUTS VENDOR IS A FIGURE IN THE LIT-
erature, lore, and music of the South. President Jimmy Carter's first job, at age
six, was selling bags of boiled peanuts on the streets of Plains, Georgia. One of
the first characters to appear in Charles Frazier's Civil War novel, *Cold Mountain*,
is a boiled peanuts vendor. In "Southland in the Springtime," a paean to road-
tripping in the Southeast, the Indigo Girls celebrate the hand-warming capacity
of a bag of boiled peanuts. In Charleston, a shy, elderly boiled peanuts vendor,
one of the last of Charleston's door-to-door food vendors, sold paper bags of
boiled peanuts from an old four-wheeled baby carriage.

THE PEANUT PLANT IS DIFFERENT FROM OTHER BEANS in the Leguminosae family, because it is the only one whose fruit develops underground. Once the spindly green plant grows to a height of about 24 inches, its flowering branches develop nodes that grow back toward the ground. When a node touches the soil, it works its way beneath the soil, and the peanut develops underground, in much the same way a potato does. A field planted in peanuts is covered with rows of tangly, ground-hugging foliage, so the act of harvesting them, at least on a small scale, means taking a pitchfork and pulling the plants out of the soil, roots, peanuts, and all.

✻ GREENS-AND-ROOTS REUNION SOUP ✻

QUICK KNOCKOUT

TURNIP GREENS ARE OFTEN SOLD SEPARATELY FROM THEIR ROOTS. THIS IS A BOTANICAL NECESSITY, SINCE THE LEAVES of a root mature enough to reach market size are unpleasantly bitter; only the young, tender greens of an immature root taste so deliciously peppery. It's too bad, because turnips have a bittersweet flavor that perfectly tames the pepperiness of the greens. In this soup—based on a popular side dish, "greens and roots," found at meat-and-threes throughout the South—we reunite turnip greens with their roots. We give the soup heft by poaching eggs in the simmering broth and serving two eggs in each bowl; when the spoon pierces them, the yolk gives the broth silky body. The pepper vinegar sharpens the turnip flavor that's the soup's foundation and adds a nice hot-and-sour element to the greens, but it also serves to catalyze the poaching of the eggs.

Bowls of Greens-and-Roots Reunion Soup, with wedges of Crispy Corn Bread (page 497) and glasses of Lemonade (page 36), make the perfect lunch break from spring planting.

✻

WHAT TO DRINK   *A medium-weight Pinot Noir, with lively fruit, would soften the sharp, savory flavors in this soup.*

For 6 people

TIME: 30 minutes

¼ pound salt pork, diced

2½ pounds turnip greens, washed, ribbed, and finely chopped (about 4 cups)

1 teaspoon kosher salt, plus more to taste

1½ pounds turnips, peeled and cut into ¼-inch dice (about 2⅓ cups)

12 cups Sunday Vegetable Broth (page 539)

2 tablespoons Pepper Vinegar (page 518) or white wine vinegar, plus more to taste

12 large eggs

Freshly ground black pepper to taste

1. Scatter the diced salt pork in a 6-quart stockpot or Dutch oven and sauté over medium-high heat, moving the pieces around with a slotted spoon until the salt pork is firm and just golden brown, about 3 minutes. Transfer to a small bowl. Pour off all but 2 tablespoons of the pork fat and return the pot to the burner.

2. Add the turnip greens to the pot, shower 1 teaspoon salt over them, and sauté, turning occasionally with tongs, until the greens have lightened in color and wilted, about 4 minutes. Add the diced turnips and broth, cover, and bring to a vigorous simmer, 8 to 12 minutes. Reduce the heat to low and add the vinegar.

3. Crack the eggs one by one into the bowl of a soup ladle and lower them into the soup, submerging them gently. When all the eggs have been added, simmer gently for 9 minutes, or until the eggs are just poached. Season the soup to taste with salt, black pepper, and vinegar.

4. Serve immediately in deep bowls, and pass a cruet of pepper vinegar around the table.

⁂ RAINY DAY IN DALLAS TORTILLA SOUP ⁂

TORTILLA SOUP IS TO DALLAS WHAT SHE-CRAB SOUP IS
TO CHARLESTON: FAMILIES TREASURE THEIR RECIPES FOR IT, EVERY
other restaurant serves one, and there's fierce debate over which restaurant (or family) serves the best. It commonly mellows the fruity fire of chiles and tomatoes with the earthy, slaked-corn flavor of tortillas. We find it difficult to compare different recipes because they range so broadly, from thin chile consommés with fried tortilla strips floating on the surface to soups as dense as chili con carne, thickened with crushed fried tortillas.

Our favorite tortilla soup is this one, which begins with a brash mixture of raisiny pasilla chiles (pasilla means "small grape") and sweet-hot ancho chiles. We toast them and puree them with crushed tomatoes and fried corn tortillas. The garnishes—fresh cilantro and the runny Mexican sour cream *crema*—provide the right creamy-cool note of contrast. If you can't find *crema* in your area, mix buttermilk with an equal amount of sour cream.

This rustic soup is the right appetizer for a meal with gentle, cool flavors. It's also a delicious rainy-day lunch on its own.

⁂

WHAT TO DRINK   *The concentrated red fruits of a Cabernet Sauvignon blend can stand up to the fire of the chiles in this soup; ditto a cold Mexican beer with a squeeze of lime.*

For 6 people

TIME: 40 minutes

2 cups corn oil

4 whole dried pasilla or guajillo chiles, stems trimmed, slit down their sides, seeded, and flattened

2 whole dried chiles ancho or mulato chiles, stems trimmed, slit down their sides, seeded, flattened, and torn into two pieces

8 soft white or yellow corn tortillas (no larger than 6 inches in diameter), 4 left whole, 4 cut into ½-inch thick strips

6 cups Sunday Vegetable Broth (page 539) or Sunday Chicken Broth (page 532)

One 28-ounce can chopped tomatoes (preferably "fire-roasted"), with juice

1 cup chopped yellow onion (about 1 large onion)

6 garlic cloves, peeled and crushed

½ teaspoon kosher salt, plus more to taste

Freshly ground black pepper to taste

½ cup chopped cilantro

¾ cup Mexican *crema* or ⅓ cup low-fat or whole buttermilk and ⅓ cup sour cream

3 ripe, peeled avocados, pitted and sliced lengthwise (optional)

1. Heat ¼ cup of the oil in a 10-inch skillet over medium-high heat. When it shimmers, add the chiles in batches, taking care not to crowd the pan. Toast the chiles until they discolor slightly and release some of their fragrance, about ½ minute. Remove and reserve in a small bowl.

2. Add the remaining oil to the skillet and heat until a candy thermometer reads 350 degrees (monitor the temperature and adjust the heat to keep the oil at 350 degrees as you cook). Gently submerge one of the whole corn tortillas into the oil and fry until crisp, about 1 minute. Transfer to a half-sheet pan lined with a double thickness of paper towels to drain. Repeat with the remaining whole corn tortillas, then add the tortilla strips. Fry them until they're crisp, about 45 seconds, and transfer them with a slotted spoon to the paper towels to drain. Discard the oil or reserve for another use.

3. Pour 2 cups broth into a 4- to 6-quart stockpot or Dutch oven. Add the tomatoes, onion, garlic, and salt. Bring the soup to a boil over medium-high heat, then add the reserved chiles. Crumble the whole fried tortillas into the soup, and stir thoroughly to combine. Reduce the heat to low and simmer vigorously until the liquid has reduced by one quarter, about 10 minutes.

4. Transfer the soup in batches to a food processor or blender and process to a smooth puree, about 3 minutes per batch. Return the soup to the pot, add the remaining 3 cups broth, stir to incorporate, and bring to a vigorous simmer over medium-high heat. Season to taste with salt and black pepper. Turn off the heat.

5. Serve in deep bowls and garnish with the reserved tortilla strips, the cilantro, the *crema,* and fanned slices of avocado, if using.

❋ POULTRY, PORK, BEEF, AND GAME ❋

THE COUNTRY STORE OFTEN PLAYS
SECOND FIDDLE TO THE COUNTRY BUTCHER'S

premises as a place of fascination, food ferment, and gossip in the South: that's where you go to find out who's farming what, what hunters are shooting where, who's having a barbecue or getting married. And in an age when centralized mass butchering and refrigerated transport conspire to prevent all but the most common cuts from coming to market, this southern institution excels at offering a tempting array of treats like veal sweetbreads, kidneys, and smoked hog jowls, and of services (hunters can get their venison and ducks dressed; backyard farmers bring their fattened hogs).

Marvin's Meats in Hollywood, South Carolina, is our favorite country butcher. Frank Marvin, the owner, grew up on nearby Yonge's Island, a Sea Island once famous for its cabbage. Back in 1964, Citizens and Southern Bank denied Marvin a loan to start his business (the bank's letter is framed on the wall of the shop), but Marvin wangled the money from friends and relatives, and the place has thrived for forty years. When you pull into the crushed-lime parking lot of Marvin's Meats, free-roaming chickens and pigs scatter. Aside from steaks, pork shoulders, and cuts, there are the unadvertised specials: liver puddings, light-as-air fried pork skins, mountain oysters (testicles, both boar and bull). An air of boundless culinary possibility hovers over the store, and when we get frustrated by the dead-end displays of supermarkets downtown, we just take a trip out to Hollywood.

We once took a crew from the Food Network to meet Marvin. The show's director was thrilled by the visuals at Marvin's Meats—the butchers in their hard hats and lab coats, the sausage links hanging from the ceiling, the hand-lettered signs—as well as by Frank's distinctive Sea Island accent, which brings a Caribbean lilt to a Scotch-Irish drawl. The director's instructions to Marvin and his butchers were "Do whatever it is that you do—just be going about your business." This was not a tall order, since it was a busy Friday, with people coming in to pick up whole hogs dressed and wrapped in brown butcher's paper for the weekend's barbecues.

When the cameras began rolling, Marvin flipped a whole hog onto a table and began sawing off the head with a hacksaw. "CUUUUUUUT!" the director shouted, aghast that the task at hand was too grisly for his show.

❊ CONLEY'S BRAISED STUFFED QUAIL ❊

OUR FRIEND CONLEY ROLLINS DIDN'T EXACTLY DEVELOP THIS RECIPE, BUT IT'S AS MUCH HIS AS IT IS OURS, BECAUSE HE'S the one who shoots the birds for an annual quail dinner we host.

Quail tend to be expensive and more difficult to find than good-sized game hens, which work beautifully in this recipe. Both birds have a deliciously intense poultry flavor, which calls for a boldly flavored gravy. Our braising liquid gets its power from the aromatic triumvirate of carrot, bell pepper, and onion cooked down in a red wine gravy infused with bacon smoke.

Stuffed birds always make a festive presentation, so prepare this dish on special occasions, or invent a reason for celebration whenever you make it. Its luscious gravy is a perfect complement for Simple Grits (page 146) or Oyster Purloo (page 175).

❊

WHAT TO DRINK   *A deep, soft red (the Syrah, Merlot or Bordeaux blend being used in the dish, perhaps?) with plum or currant flavors to play off the thyme in the dish.*

2 cups water

1 tablespoon plus 2 teaspoons kosher salt, plus more to taste

2 cups red onions, diced (about 2 large onions)

1½ cups red bell pepper, diced (about 1 large pepper)

1½ cups green bell pepper, diced (about 1 large pepper)

½ cup all-purpose flour, plus more as needed

1 tablespoon freshly ground black pepper, plus more to taste

Twelve 8-ounce quail or six 1¼–1½-pound game hens

¼ pound slab bacon or 4 slices thick-cut bacon, diced

½ cup canola oil

2 cups carrots, diced (about 2 large carrots)

2 tablespoons chopped fresh thyme

3½ cups Sunday Chicken Broth (page 532)

1 cup full-bodied red wine, such as Syrah, Merlot, or a Bordeaux blend

2 slices stale bread or toast, cut into ¼-inch dice

Juice of 1 large lemon

1. Preheat the oven to 350 degrees.

2. In a small saucepan, bring 2 cups of water to a boil over medium-high heat. Add 2 teaspoons salt, half the onions, half the red bell pepper, and half the green bell pepper. Boil for 3 minutes, or until the diced vegetables have slightly lightened in color and are just tender. Drain and reserve in a medium bowl.

3. In a large bowl, mix the flour with the remaining salt and the pepper. Dredge the quail in the mixture, turning to coat thoroughly. Shake off any excess. Set the quail aside and reserve any unused dredge.

4. Scatter the bacon in a 12-inch cast-iron skillet and sauté over medium-high heat, moving the pieces around with a slotted spoon until the bacon is firm and just golden brown, about 3 minutes. Transfer to the bowl with the blanched vegetables and reserve. Pour off all but 2 tablespoons bacon fat and reserve the surplus. Add the quail to the skillet in batches, taking care not to crowd the pan, and cook until golden brown all over, 2 to 3 minutes per side (add reserved bacon fat 1 tablespoon at a time if the skillet becomes too dry). Transfer the browned quail to a 16-×-22-inch roasting pan, placing them breast side up.

5.   Reduce the heat under the skillet to medium low and add the oil. Measure the reserved dredge and add enough flour to make ¼ cup, then add to the oil, stirring constantly with a wooden spoon or a whisk to prevent it from scorching. Cook until the flour is toasty and café-au-lait in color, about 6 minutes.

6.   Raise the heat to medium-high, and add the remaining onions and red and green bell peppers, carrots, and 1 tablespoon thyme to the skillet. Cook, stirring, for 4 to 5 minutes, until the vegetables are slightly softened. Add 3 cups chicken broth and the wine and bring to a simmer. Simmer vigorously for 2 to 3 minutes to let the flavors meld.

7.   Add the remaining 1 tablespoon thyme and the bread to the bowl containing the blanched vegetables and bacon, and gently toss with a wooden spoon. Pour the remaining ½ cup stock in a thin stream evenly over the contents of the bowl, then squeeze the lemon juice over them. Toss until the ingredients are evenly moistened. Fill the cavity of each quail with the stuffing.

8.   When all the quail have been stuffed and returned to the roasting pan, pour the wine and vegetable mixture over them, cover with aluminum foil, and bake for 40 minutes (1 hour for game hens), or until the juices run clear when the skin above the thigh joint is pierced (baste at the halfway mark, or every 20 minutes for game hens). Remove the quail from the oven and let rest in the pan for 10 minutes. Season the braising liquid to taste with salt and black pepper.

9.   Serve on large plates—2 quail or 1 game hen per guest—and pour a ladleful of the braising liquid over them.

❋ PORK LOIN CHOPS ❋
WITH PEAR AND VIDALIA PAN GRAVY

QUICK
KNOCKOUT

EVERYONE NEEDS A GREAT RECIPE FOR SPUR-OF-THE-MOMENT MEALS: YOU RUN INTO FRIENDS FROM OUT OF TOWN WHOM you haven't seen in ages and invite them to dinner, or you're craving a comforting late-night supper after a movie or a performance. This hearty main dish brings together the flavors of fresh pears and sweet Vidalia onions in a gravy for pork chops (think of it as a more compelling version of pork chops and applesauce). You can whip it up in a flash, and if you add a skillet of Creamed Corn (page 221) and a leafy green salad, you've got an impressive meal.

"Vidalia" is a trade name referring to the standard Yellow Granex variety of sweet onion when it's grown in the rich, loamy soils of fourteen counties in and around Vidalia, Georgia, in the state's southeastern corner. You can grow a Yellow Granex anywhere in the world, but you can't call it Vidalia, because in 1986 the state of Georgia trademarked the name. No matter. Vidalias have become so popular that they're available in most of the nation's supermarkets and by mail-order from a number of sources (see "Sourcery: Vidalia Onions," below). But any sweet onion works perfectly in this recipe.

❋

WHAT TO DRINK   *The gentle sweetness of onion and pear in this dish encourage a pairing with a drier, less overtly fruity red wine, such as an earthy Rioja from Spain or a Tuscan Chianti.*

For 4 people

TIME: 30 minutes

1 teaspoon kosher salt, plus more to taste

1 teaspoon freshly ground black pepper, plus more to taste

1½ teaspoons all-purpose flour

1 tablespoon peanut oil

Four 1¼-inch-thick bone-in pork loin chops (8 ounces each)

1¼ cups Vidalia or other sweet onion (10–12 ounces), peeled, trimmed, and thinly sliced (about 1 jumbo onion)

1 cup Bartlett pears, peeled, cored, trimmed, and cut into ¼-inch dice (about 2 large pears)

2 tablespoons unsalted butter

¾ cup Rich Pork Broth (page 548), Sunday Chicken Broth (page 532), or Sunday Vegetable Broth (page 539)

1 tablespoon dry sherry, Madeira, or tawny port

1 teaspoon sherry vinegar

1 bunch scallions, sliced on the bias, for garnish (optional)

1. Preheat the oven to 425 degrees.

2. In a small bowl, mix the salt, pepper, and ½ teaspoon flour. Using half the mixture, sprinkle 1 side of each pork chop.

3. Place the oil in a 12-inch cast-iron skillet or ovenproof sauté pan and heat over high heat until the first wisp of smoke rises. Grasp the handle and tilt the skillet gently in a circular motion so the oil coats the bottom thinly and evenly. Place the chops, seasoned side down, in the hot skillet and sprinkle the remaining half of the seasoning mixture on the sides facing up. Sear the pork chops until they are a rich golden brown, turning when the first side is done, about 3 minutes per side.

4. Turn the chops so the first side faces down again and transfer the skillet to the oven. Bake 2 minutes for rare, 4 minutes for medium-rare, and 6 minutes for well-done. Remove the skillet from the oven and place it over an unlit burner. Transfer the chops to a large plate or platter and tent them with aluminum foil.

5. Add the onion, half the pears, and the butter to the skillet and turn the heat to medium-low. Stir with a wooden spoon, scraping any caramelized pork bits off the bottom, and sauté, stirring, until the onion softens and turns translucent, about 4 minutes.

6. Pour the broth into a small bowl and whisk the remaining 1 teaspoon flour into it until no lumps are visible. Add the broth mixture, sherry, and vinegar to the skillet and turn the heat to medium-high. When the liquid comes to a simmer, add any juices that may have collected on the plate of reserved pork chops and continue to stir and simmer vigorously until the liquid has reduced by one half, about 4 minutes. Turn off the heat, add the remaining pears, and stir until they are evenly incorporated. Season to taste with salt and pepper.

7. Place a pork chop on each of 4 plates, ladle a generous quantity of gravy over each, and garnish with sliced scallions, if desired.

The late Mike Lee operated this superlative barbecue stand out of a toolshed set up in a parking lot in Cumberland, Kentucky. His ribs were smoked on-site in a soot-black steel rig he towed behind his truck.

SOURCERY: VIDALIA ONIONS

THE SWEET JUMBO VIDALIAS GROWN AT MORRIS FARMS, in Uvalda, Georgia, are about 3 inches in diameter and cost under $20 (including shipping) for a 10-pound box. Morris Farms, 157 Georgia Highway 56 West, Uvalda, GA 30473; 800-447-9338; www.sweetonion.com.

❧ TEXAS RED-BRAISED BEEF SHORT RIBS ❧

IN TEXAS, "RED" IS ARCHAIC SLANG FOR CHILI CON CARNE, BUT EVEN NOWADAYS YOU CAN FIND "A BOWL OF RED" ON RESTAU- rant menus in Dallas and Fort Worth. In this recipe, we take our own "red" recipe (Russwood Circle Chili con Carne, page 280) and have a little fun with it. We take out the ground beef, so the chili becomes more like a Mexican mole, and then we use the meatless "red" as a braising liquid for cooking beefy, tender short ribs until they're falling from the bone.

"Red" always describes rustic cowboy food, and our reinterpretation of it may qualify as such. But this dish also has a show-stopping presentation that elevates it to Downtown Touch status. Paper plates will do. Serve these delicious ribs with wedges of Crispy Corn Bread (page 497), over steamed white rice, or with your favorite grits recipe (pages 146–162).

A note on short rib cuts and serving size: Butchers cut beef short ribs in two ways—English-style, parallel to the bones, or flanken-style, across the bone. You may use both in this recipe, but we prefer to serve flanken-style ribs because they are more consistently sized (English-cut ribs range in size). 3½ pounds of flanken-style beef short ribs is about 8 ribs. Because these ribs are richly meaty, we've found that we can budget one rib per person when serving them as the main dish of a large, multicourse meal (the two extra ribs get cut up and served to those folks who want seconds). But for a one-course supper, we'd budget 2 ribs per person; this recipe makes enough braising liquid for a larger pan of 10–12 ribs.

WHAT TO DRINK   *A refreshing lager like Shiner Bock from Austin, Texas, is a natural choice to quench the heat of this dish when served during warmer months; but the mole-like chocolate tones in the ribs also recommend a red wine, the darkest California Zinfandel or the heartiest Australian Syrah.*

For 6 people

TIME: ½ hour preparation, 2 to 2½ hours cooking

3½ pounds flanken-style beef short ribs
    (about eight 7½-inch-long ribs)
1½ tablespoons kosher salt, plus more to taste
3 large yellow onions, trimmed, peeled, and
    quartered lengthwise
8 garlic cloves, husks removed
3 tablespoons plus 2 teaspoons canola oil,
    peanut oil, or extra-virgin olive oil
1½ teaspoons freshly ground black pepper,
    plus more to taste

2 cups Sunday Beef Broth (page 542) or one
    14½-ounce can beef broth
3 ancho chiles, torn in half, stemmed, and
    seeded
3 pasilla chiles, torn in half, stemmed, and
    seeded
One 28-ounce can crushed tomatoes
¼ cup semisweet chocolate chips

1.   Up to a day in advance, season the short ribs with 2 teaspoons salt. Cover with plastic wrap and refrigerate.

2.   Place the onions and garlic in a 9-×-13-inch roasting pan. Drizzle 2 teaspoons oil over them and turn with a spatula to coat. Sprinkle 1 teaspoon salt and ½ teaspoon pepper over them and broil about 3 inches from the flame or heating element for 8 to 10 minutes, until the garlic skins have blackened and the onions have charred slightly.

3.   Preheat the oven to 325 degrees.

4.   In a small saucepan, bring the broth to a boil over high heat. Turn off the heat. Place the remaining 3 tablespoons oil in a large cast-iron skillet and heat over medium-high heat until it shimmers. Add the chiles and toast them on all sides, turning them with tongs until they are soft, fragrant, and slightly lighter in color, about 30 seconds. With tongs, transfer the chiles to the hot broth. Cover and let stand until completely soft, about 6 minutes.

5. Turn the heat under the skillet to high and heat until the oil remaining in the skillet just begins to smoke. Add several short ribs, making certain not to crowd them in the pan. Sear them, turning once their surfaces are browned, about 3 minutes, until they are richly browned on both sides. Remove with tongs and reserve. Repeat with the remaining ribs, in batches, until all the ribs are browned. Turn off the heat.

6. When the garlic has cooled, remove and discard the skins. Transfer the garlic and the onions to a food processor or blender. Add the tomatoes and process to a smooth puree, about 2 minutes. Reserve in a bowl. You should have 4 cups.

7. Add the chiles and broth to the processor or blender and puree until smooth, about 2 minutes. You should have about 2½ cups. Add as much chile puree to the vegetable puree as you wish to achieve the degree of flavor and heat you prefer (we always add it all). Stir to incorporate thoroughly, and season to taste with the remaining 1½ teaspoons salt and 1 teaspoon pepper. Add the chocolate chips and stir to incorporate (don't worry if they don't melt immediately; they will melt in the oven).

8. Place the short ribs in the roasting pan and pour the "red" sauce over them. Cover the pan with aluminum foil and bake for 2 hours, or until the ribs are tender and falling from the bone. Skim any fat floating on the surface.

9. Serve the ribs on plates with a ladleful of sauce.

❊ SCUPPERNONG GRAPE ❊ AND HOT-PEPPER—ROASTED DUCK

IN JULY 2003, THE *NEW YORK TIMES MAGAZINE* ASKED US TO TRY TO DETERMINE WHAT THE FLAVORS OF THE FUTURE MIGHT be, so we polled a nationwide sampling of chefs, growers, and the scientists (called "flavorists") who put the beef in bouillon cubes. Many of our interviewees told us that the nation's palate is getting more and more turned on to the flavors of chiles in combination with fruit.

This duck recipe uses some of the Southeast's most beloved fruits—*capsicum* pepper and scuppernong grapes—to create a tangy, spicy roast duck that just might be the dish of the (near) future. We've taken to serving it around Christmastime in Charleston, with super-festive, wintry side dishes such as Corn and Okra Pudding (page 237) and Red Rice (page 172).

❊

WHAT TO DRINK   *The chile in this recipe expresses itself forcefully, complicating a pairing with red wine, so a gutsy white with plenty of fruit, oak, and richness—think Viognier, Marsanne, and Roussanne grapes—would stand up to the assertive flavors in the duck. North Carolina, California, and South Africa produce great wine with those French grapes.*

For 4 people

TIME: 15 minutes preparation, 3 hours cooking

One 5-pound duck

1 tablespoon crushed Thai or other fiery dried chile

2 teaspoons kosher salt

1 teaspoon freshly ground black pepper

⅓ cup Scuppernong Preserves (page 132) or other top-quality grape preserves

1 teaspoon white wine vinegar

1 tablespoon sorghum molasses (see Sourcery, page 447), cane syrup, molasses, or honey

1. Preheat the oven to 275 degrees.

2. Trim the duck of any excess skin around the neck cavity. Rinse it inside and out with cold running water and dry thoroughly, inside and out, with two changes of paper towels. With a sharp paring knife, cut six ¼-inch vents in the skin of the breast and two ¼-inch vents in the skin of each leg to allow excess fat to drain during roasting. In a small bowl, mix the crushed chiles with the salt and pepper. Sprinkle the duck breast, legs, and cavity with 1 tablespoon of the mixture. Position the duck breast side down on a rack in a roasting pan and season the back with 1 teaspoon of the mixture.

3. Roast the duck on the middle rack for 1 hour, then remove it from the oven. It will have drained some fat into the pan, and the skin will have lost some of its pallor. With a sharp paring knife, cut 5 or 6 vents in the skin of the back. Turn the duck breast side up, and return it to the oven. Roast until the skin of the breast begins to take on a golden-brown hue, about 1 hour.

4. Remove the duck from the oven and increase the temperature to 375 degrees. Lift the duck (still breast side up on the rack) from the pan and place on a baking sheet. Pour off the fat from the roasting pan and return the duck (still on the rack) to the pan. Place the preserves in a small bowl and whisk in the vinegar and sorghum until blended. Baste the breast and legs generously with the preserves mixture and sprinkle the glazed skin with a few generous pinches of the chile seasoning. Return the duck to the oven and roast for 1 hour more, basting every 15 minutes with the syrup mixture and following each basting with a couple pinches of the chile mixture, until the skin has achieved a deep reddish brown, lacquered appearance.

5. Remove the roasting pan from the oven and let the duck rest 15 minutes before carving and serving.

A Country Ham Primer

A true country ham—the meat of which is mostly hip and thigh—is one that's been dry-cured in salt and sugar for several weeks, then smoked for another few weeks, then aged for months. During this curing process, which may take a year or more, depending on who's doing it, a country ham will lose as much as 25 percent of its weight from evaporating water, so the result is a super-concentrated, salty, gamy, hyper-ham, akin to Italian speck (a smoked version of prosciutto).

Road-tripping through the mountain South, you may encounter smokehouses on farmsteads, but you'd be lucky to find anyone still curing his or her own hams. Most of these smokehouses are used as toolsheds or tractor garages nowadays. Fortunately, there are a number of commercial producers of country ham, and we, of course, have our favorites (see "Sourcery: Country Ham," page 332). As you might imagine, because it takes such a long time to cure, country ham tends to be pricey, but it is worth every last dollar. Some firms sell shards by the quarter pound or larger sections shrink-wrapped in plastic. But the best way to experience a country ham is to save your pennies and buy a whole one (a good country ham may set you back $50 to $100). When you do, here are some things to know about consuming it.

The first is, *be not afraid of the mold.* Since country hams are aged in open-air smokehouses, they often grow a powdery mold on their skin. This mold is beneficial (though unlike mold on cheese, it's not good to eat), but it certainly causes confusion in people unfamiliar with the product. We once bought two country hams that had been aged for seventeen months—they were among the last cured by Colonel Newsom before he passed away in 1999—and gave one to a friend as a wedding gift, assuming that she was familiar with them. A few weeks later our friend reported that because the ham had sat in the trunk of her brother-in-law's car with the other wedding presents, it had grown mold and had to be discarded. We didn't have the heart to tell her that there was nothing that could have happened in the trunk of a hot car that hadn't already happened to that ham in the stifling hot smokehouse. Thousands of outstanding country hams are thrown away each year because people receive them as gifts, see the surface mold, and assume the meat has gone bad.

There are two ways you can serve country ham—cooked or uncooked. You can boil and then bake a whole ham for a large celebration and slice it the way you would any brined and baked fresh ham. Or you can just leave it uncooked and use it as you would use a European cured ham, like prosciutto, by trimming the skin off and slicing it paper-thin.

A whole country ham can last a year or more if kept at cool room temperature and wrapped in a breathable fabric like burlap. Once you cut into it, you'll need to wrap and refrigerate it, but it will last several months. We kept one ham that way for three years wrapped in plastic wrap, and while it certainly toughened as it dried, it remained a fabulous seasoning meat for soups and pasta salads. When the last block we cut from it was rock-hard, we grated it with a standard cheese grater and made a delicious "salt" that we sprinkled over everything.

❊ BAKED COUNTRY HAM ❊

BAKED COUNTRY HAM IS THE CENTERPIECE OF A PROPER THANKSGIVING OR CHRISTMAS MEAL IN MANY PARTS OF THE South and a culinary achievement comparable to the Chinese thousand-year-old egg. Its flavor is powerfully porky, deliciously robust, minerally and deep, perfectly complemented by the flavor of cinnamon and cloves. Though it's nowhere near as salty as uncooked, unsoaked country ham, it's still a good idea to have on hand some great relishes (pages 108, 112), Watermelon Rind or Fig Preserves (pages 136, 128), or a few Pickled Peaches (page 105) to take the edge off. A baked country ham takes some time to prepare, but it's not complicated and it's well worth the effort.

Note: Before you begin, make sure you have a boiling pot big enough to accommodate the ham. Most cooks arrange for their butcher to cut off the narrow hock end of the ham to make the ham fit better; we prefer to let the hock protrude a few inches above the surface of the water. As long as the meaty majority of the bulb-shaped ham is submerged, you're in good shape. We've found small, eight-pound hams that fit nicely, hock and all, in an 8-gallon boiling pot.

❊

WHAT TO DRINK   *A perfectly baked country ham, scented with clove and bracingly salty, is an ideal excuse for serving the South's greatest wine, made from native Scuppernong grapes (page 135). Resist the urge to drink bone-dry wines on this occasion and seek out off-dry varieties made by Duplin Winery (see Sourcery, page 40) in Rose Hill, North Carolina, and Irvin House Vineyards on Wadmalaw Island, South Carolina.*

For 6 to 10 people

TIME: 24 hours to soak, 4½ hours to cook

1 whole 8–11-pound country ham	3 cups cider vinegar
10 bay leaves	24 whole cloves
2 tablespoons mustard seeds	1 cup dark brown sugar

1.   Under warm running water, scrape any surface mold, seasonings, cobwebs, or any other matter from the ham with a stiff brush. Place the ham in an 8-gallon stockpot and fill it with water to cover the ham. Let the ham soak for 24 hours, changing the water as often as possible, ideally once every 6 hours.

2.   Change the water a final time and transfer the pot to a stovetop. Add the bay leaves, mustard seeds, and vinegar and bring to a boil over high heat. Lower the heat to medium and simmer for 2 hours, topping up, as necessary, with fresh water.

3.   Preheat the oven to 375 degrees.

4.   Remove the ham from the stockpot and turn off the heat. When the ham is cool enough to handle, shave off the skin (but not the fat) with a sharp knife. Score the fat and exposed flesh in a diagonal pattern, stud it with a single clove in the center of each scored diamond, and pat it thoroughly on all sides with the brown sugar.

5.   Place the ham on a rack in a 9-×-13-inch roasting pan and bake for 45 minutes to 1 hour, or until the fat has crisped and the sugar has melted into a nice glaze. Let rest on the rack for 15 minutes. Transfer to a cutting board and carve.

❧ UNCOOKED COUNTRY HAM ❧

WHEN YOU CHOOSE TO GO THE UNCOOKED ROUTE, YOU'LL HAVE A LOT OF TERRIFIC-TASTING HAM ON YOUR HANDS FOR A good long time (even if you eat a lot of it, like we do). All that's required is to scrub the ham clean, pat dry, and cut into it. Uncooked country ham is wonderful to keep at the ready in the refrigerator because it can serve as the foundation for so many memorable pick-up meals. Here are some things we love to do with uncooked country ham.

❧

WHAT TO DRINK   *Salt-flecked country ham sliced paper-thin reminds us of Spanish serrano ham and tapas, so a fresh, fizzy Cava (Freixenet is one example) would be our first choice. In fact any bubbly would be appropriate!*

COUNTRY HAM PÂTÉ IS A DELICIOUS SPREAD FOR CRACKERS OR TOAST POINTS. WITH A WOODEN SPOON, BLEND 1/4 CUP FINELY MINCED COUNTRY HAM WITH 2 OUNCES CREAM CHEESE AND 1 TABLESPOON OF YOUR FAVORITE RELISH. REFRIGERATE FOR AT LEAST 1 HOUR AND SERVE COLD IN A 4-OUNCE RAMEKIN. MAKES ENOUGH FOR 6 TO SNACK ON WITH CRACKERS OR TOAST POINTS AND COCKTAILS.

COUNTRY HAM OMELETTES: ADD A SCANT 1/4 CUP ROUGHLY CHOPPED COUNTRY HAM TO EACH 3-EGG OMELETTE.

COUNTRY HAM FETTUCINE CARBONARA: A PASTA DISH IN A SOUTHERN COOKBOOK? IF IT'S THIS GOOD, YES. TOSS 10 OUNCES (ABOUT 2 CUPS) COOKED BUTTERBEANS (PREFERABLY FRESH), 1/2 CUP UNCOOKED COUNTRY HAM CUT INTO SMALL DICE, 3 OUNCES GOAT CHEESE BROKEN INTO BITS, 2 TABLESPOONS BUTTERMILK, 2 TABLESPOONS OLIVE OIL, AND 1 TEASPOON FRESHLY GROUND BLACK PEPPER WITH 1 POUND FRESHLY COOKED FETTUCINE. ADD KOSHER SALT TO TASTE. SERVES 4.

COUNTRY HAM SALT: DON'T THROW OUT THE EXPOSED PIECES OF HAM TOWARD THE HOCK THAT BECOME AS HARD AS AMBER. GRATE THESE WITH A CHEESE GRATER TO MAKE A VERSATILE CONDI-MENT THAT YOU CAN USE IN THE SAME WAY YOU WOULD A FLAKY SEA SALT—SPRINKLED OVER SOUPS AND STEWS, ON BUTTERBEANS AND BROCCOLI, EVEN OVER SASHIMI.

HOW TO TRAVEL WITH
YOUR COUNTRY HAM/COUNTRY HAM SUITCASE

WE SHUTTLE FREQUENTLY BETWEEN NEW YORK AND South Carolina, and although we could have a ham in each place, sometimes you just love a ham so much you want to take it with you and share it with people.

We used to get funny looks from baggage screeners when we carried our hams wrapped in those plastic sleeves your newspaper gets delivered in on rainy days. And then we acquired a stainless steel Zero Halliburton (founded by an estranged member of the defense contractor family) suitcase, the kind that photographers and cameramen carry their equipment in, and we cut the foam padding inside to fit the contours of the ham. There's something about the professional fit and finish of that suitcase that inspires confidence in both us and baggage screeners. Now when we go through airport security, the ham barely raises an eyebrow.

COLONEL BILL NEWSOM IS NO LONGER WITH US, BUT his daughter, Nancy Mahaffey, carries on his curing tradition, notable for using no nitrites whatsoever, just salt, pepper, and smoke. The result is pure Kentucky mountain style, and, we'd wager, the sweetest, woodsiest ham you can find, with a clean finish. Colonel Bill Newsom's Aged Kentucky Country Hams, 208 E. Main St., Princeton, KY 42445; 270-365-2482; www.newsomscountryham.com. For a tamer country ham that also has great character, S. Wallace Edwards & Sons (P.O. Box 25, Surry, VA 23883; 800-222-4267) sells superior hams in steady volume. Edwards sources hams from nearby farms and favors tasty heirloom pig breeds like the Tamworth, descended from English settlers' stock.

☀ TUESDAY FRIED CHICKEN ☀

FRIED CHICKEN IS EASY TO PREPARE AND MAKES A TER-
RIFIC PICK-ME-UP AT THE END OF A LONG, BLUESY WORKDAY. THERE
are no esoteric secrets to making great fried chicken. Temperature is the deciding factor. The temperature of the oil in your skillet and the temperature of the chicken when it gets dunked into the
oil can separate great fried chicken from less-great fried chicken. Be sure your chicken is at room
temperature before frying, and use a candy thermometer, the kind that clips to the edge of the skillet, to keep the oil as close as possible to 325 degrees. It's as simple as that.

People get baroque with fried chicken, seasoning their brines with chile or honey or tamarind
paste and battering with all manner of dairy products to make it crusty. We believe fried chicken
at its most minimal, delicate, and crisp is its finest expression—like a raw oyster straight from the
marsh, or shrimp boiled up dockside. If you prefer extra-crusty, we offer a variation on page 335.

We hear people say they don't fry chicken at home because they don't want to live with the
grease, and our answer to that is this: we've fried in galley-sized kitchens with no ventilation
whatsoever, and it's rarely been a problem. If you were running a fried-chicken restaurant from
such a kitchen, there might be cause for concern, but you're not. So just open your windows wide
and fry away. You'll be glad you did.

We serve Tuesday Fried Chicken with piquant QKO sides like Coleslaw (page 195) and Hot
Slaw à la Greyhound Grill (page 200).

WHAT TO DRINK   *Light, fruity rosés are a good match for the crunch and richness of a warm plate of fried chicken, and often suit the informal mood of any fried chicken occasion. Look for outstanding rosé wines (dry to off-dry, please) being produced in Australia, Italy, Spain, and the U.S. too.*

For 4 people

TIME: 50 minutes

3 cups peanut oil, canola oil, clarified butter, or lard
1 recipe Lee Bros. All-Purpose Fry Dredge (page 552)
3 pounds chicken legs and thighs (about 6 legs and 6 bone-in thighs)

1.   Preheat the oven to 250 degrees.

2.   Pour the oil into a 12-inch skillet and heat over medium-high heat until it reaches 325 degrees on a candy thermometer. If using a different-sized skillet or pan, fill with oil (or melt enough lard and clarified butter) to a depth of ⅓ inch.

3.   Place the fry dredge in a medium bowl or a 1-gallon plastic bag. Dredge the chicken thoroughly, by dipping each piece in the bowl or shaking it in the bag. Shake off any excess dredge. Using tongs, transfer 3 legs and 3 thighs to the skillet, skin side down, and cover. Fry the chicken, checking the temperature of the oil and adjusting the heat as needed to maintain the temperature between 325 and 350 degrees, until the chicken is golden brown, about 6 minutes. Uncover the skillet, turn the chicken pieces with the tongs, and fry 6 minutes more, until the chicken is golden brown all over. Turn it and fry for 3 minutes, then turn again and fry for 3 minutes more.

4.   With tongs, transfer the chicken to a paper-towel-lined plate and place in the oven to warm. Repeat step 3 with the remaining chicken.

5.   When all the chicken is done, serve immediately, and pass a cruet of Pepper Vinegar (page 518) at the table.

❋ SUNDAY FRIED CHICKEN ❋

SUNDAY FRIED CHICKEN GETS ITS ROBUST CHICKEN FLA-
VOR FROM THE SIMPLE BRINE OF SALT AND WATER IN WHICH YOU
soak the chicken pieces before you dredge. Follow the recipe for Tuesday Fried Chicken, above, but
at least 4 hours before you begin (or the night before), pour 1 quart water into a 3-quart bowl, add
⅓ cup salt, and stir until it dissolves. Trim any excess fat from the thighs, submerge the legs and
thighs in the brine, cover the bowl, and refrigerate. Remove the bowl from the refrigerator 2 hours
before frying so the chicken can come to room temperature.

❋

WHAT TO DRINK   *An elegant, drier German Riesling (often marked "Kabinett" or "Spatlese") would*
suit a Sunday Fried Chicken supper, offering lively acidity—to complement the richness of the
crust—and a floral component that may inspire your side dishes. Be sure to purchase enough so you
can drink a glass as you cook!

VARIATION—CRUSTY TUESDAY OR SUNDAY FRIED CHICKEN: IF YOU LIKE YOUR FRIED CHICKEN WITH A
THICK CRUST, MAKE JUST A FEW ADJUSTMENTS TO THE RECIPES ABOVE. AFTER DREDGING EACH PIECE
OF CHICKEN ONCE, DIP IT INTO A BOWL OF 1 WHOLE EGG WHISKED WITH 1 CUP BUTTERMILK. LET THE
EXCESS DRIP OFF AND THEN DIP THE CHICKEN IN THE DREDGE AGAIN. FRY AT A LOWER TEMPERATURE,
275 TO 300 DEGREES, TURNING THE CHICKEN EVERY 3 MINUTES SO THE CRUST DOESN'T BURN.

☀ TED'S FIERY BBQ PORK TENDERLOIN ☀

BECOMING A CERTIFIED BARBECUE JUDGE REQUIRES A RIGOROUS THREE-HOUR COURSE OF STUDY, BUT WE STUCK WITH IT and received our diplomas from the Kansas City Barbecue Society. We needed certification because we'd been invited to judge the prestigious Jack Daniel's World Championship Invitational Barbeque and weren't about to turn down the opportunity.

The first principle of barbecue is that nothing is called barbecue (or BBQ or bar-b-que) that has not been cooked for a very long time using wood smoke or coals for heat. In other words, we may get our diplomas revoked for giving the name "BBQ" to pork tenderloin that has been seared, then roasted in a gas oven.

We'll risk it for this recipe (and one or two more in this chapter), which was inspired by the datil peppers we encountered in the Florida panhandle. The datil, a cousin of the habanero, was brought to Florida in the late 1700s by Minorcans who settled around St. Augustine. Traveling in the area today, you still find a few farmstands and kitchen "factories" turning out hot sauces and pepper jellies, sausages and pilaus, with datil peppers. Like a habanero or a Scotch bonnet, a datil is searingly hot, but it also has a soaring, aromatic flavor that most folks claim to be indescribable. Since we're in the business of pinning it down, we'd say it has hints of smoked bergamot tea and orange peel.

☀

WHAT TO DRINK   *A zesty Sancerre (made from Sauvignon Blanc grapes) from the Loire Valley, or a Sauvignon Blanc from New Zealand, with enough fruit flavor to balance the mix of spices and peppers that infuse the tenderloin.*

For 4 people

TIME: 1 hour to marinate, 35 minutes to cook

⅓ cup bourbon

⅓ cup water

1 tablespoon sherry vinegar

1 tablespoon minced fresh ginger

1 datil pepper or habanero chile, blistered over a burner or in a hot, dry skillet, then seeded and minced

1 teaspoon minced garlic

Two ¾-pound pork tenderloins

¼ cup sorghum molasses (see Sourcery, page 447) or cane syrup

¼ cup ketchup

½ teaspoon kosher salt, plus more to taste

¼ teaspoon freshly ground black pepper, plus more to taste

1 tablespoon extra-virgin olive oil, plus more for brushing

1. In a shallow bowl, combine the bourbon, water, vinegar, ginger, chile, and garlic. Add the pork tenderloins and turn to coat. Marinate at room temperature for 1 hour, turning every 15 minutes.

2. Preheat the oven to 450 degrees.

3. Remove the pork from the marinade; brush off any excess and pat dry. In a small saucepan, boil the marinade over high heat until reduced by one third, 7 to 8 minutes. Add the sorghum molasses and ketchup and cook over medium heat until thickened, about 5 minutes. Season to taste with salt and pepper.

4. Heat the oil in a large cast-iron skillet. Brush the tenderloins lightly with oil and season them with ½ teaspoon salt and ¼ teaspoon pepper. Sear the pork over high heat, turning occasionally, until browned, 3 to 4 minutes. Pour the barbecue sauce over the pork and transfer the skillet to the oven. Roast for about 12 minutes, or until cooked through, turning the meat in the sauce. Transfer the pork to a work surface, cover with aluminum foil, and let stand for at least 5 minutes.

5. To serve, thickly slice the meat across the grain and serve with any remaining sauce.

VARIATION—FIERY PORK TENDERLOIN WITH SOUR ORANGE AND HONEY GLAZE: IN PLACE OF THE BOURBON, SHERRY VINEGAR, GINGER, AND GARLIC, USE 1 CUP SOUR ORANGE SAUCE (PAGE 528) IN THE MARINADE. THEN SUBSTITUTE 1/2 CUP HONEY FOR THE 1/4 CUP SORGHUM MOLASSES AND 1/4 CUP KETCHUP.

KLO

KILLER LEFTOVER—FIERY BBQ PORK TENDERLOIN SANDWICHES: REFRIGERATE LEFTOVER BARBECUED PORK AND SAUCE. REHEAT THE FOLLOWING DAY IN A SKILLET OR A MICROWAVE OVEN AND SERVE ON A TOASTED HAMBURGER BUN.

Roadside fun in Florida on US 90, near Suwannee River State Park.

INGREDIENTS FOR FROGMORE STEW, PAGE 255 *(clockwise from top):* potatoes, blue crabs, shrimp, bay leaf, Lee Bros. Shrimp Boil, PAGE 553, garlic, corn, smoked sausage

A POT OF FROGMORE STEW, PAGE 255

SHE-CRAB SOUP, PAGE 289

SCUPPERNONG GRAPE AND HOT-PEPPER–ROASTED DUCK, PAGE 323

A COUNTRY HAM, PAGE 329, before washing and baking

BAKED COUNTRY HAM, PAGE 327, WITH
SQUASH AND MUSHROOM HOMINY, PAGE 219

HARLEM MEAT LOAF SANDWICH, page 362,
on SALLY LUNN BREAD, page 500

BILL WHARTON, A PROFESSIONAL BLUES GUITARIST from Monticello, Florida, makes a stellar datil pepper hot sauce. Half the year, he cooks and bottles sauce; the other half, he tours jazz clubs around the world as the "Sauce Boss." When he comes to your town, you won't want to miss his blues-and-gumbo show. Included in the ticket price is a bowl of the gumbo Wharton makes before the show. To order sauce and get a tour schedule, go to www.sauceboss.com. In a pinch, you could substitute a tablespoon of Liquid Summer for the fresh roasted datil or habanero pepper in the tenderloin recipe above.

❋ COUNTRY CAPTAIN ❋

COUNTRY CAPTAIN, A CHICKEN CURRY CASSEROLE, IS A MAINSTAY OF SOUTHERN JUNIOR LEAGUE COOKBOOKS FROM THE postwar period and a welcome sight at community buffets. The dish was perhaps the most famous southern dish for a brief time between the world wars, when FDR took a shine to it.

The bustling trade in plants and spices with the Orient in the eighteenth and nineteenth centuries exposed Charlestonians to the charms of curry powder, green tea, and camellias, among other Asian imports. The spices worked their way into chutneys, chowchows, and other relishes, and many of the ornamental plants and flowers have become fixtures in Charleston's gardens.

A southern curry is not a fiery thing and is often softened further by sweet raisins or currants. Since we're big fans of Southeast Asian seasonings, we couldn't resist elaborating a little bit on the spice element of the dish, adding to the typical curry powder some garam masala, the aromatic Indian spice blend that in the past few years has become available from most major spice bottlers. If we're cooking for real spiceheads, we grind our own blend and add a few dried hot peppers.

The texture of the rich casserole is set off by the crunch of toasted almonds, a traditional garnish. We go a step further, adding carrots to the other vegetables—bell peppers and onions—to give a firmer element to the dish. The yellow peppers, orange carrots, and green parsley look gorgeous, too.

An earthy Cotes du Rhone or Argentine Malbec that picks up on the smoky bacon in the Country Captain would be the right choice for a formal meal; but a good India Pale Ale (a hoppy style of ale offered by many breweries, Dogfish Head is among our favorites) would also work well with the ginger and gentle spice in this dish.

For 4 people

TIME: 1½ hours

½ cup Tuesday Chicken Broth (page 534) or Sunday Chicken Broth (page 532)

½ cup dried currants or raisins

1 tablespoon curry powder

1 tablespoon garam masala

1½ teaspoons kosher salt, plus more to taste

½ teaspoon freshly ground black pepper, plus more to taste

¼ pound slab bacon or 4 strips thick-cut bacon, diced

12 chicken thighs, skin on, trimmed of excess skin and fat

2⅓ cups carrots, peeled and sliced into

¼-inch-thick rounds (about one 1¼-pound bunch weighed with tops)

2 cups yellow bell peppers, diced (about 2 peppers)

2 cups yellow onions, diced (about 2 medium onions)

3 cloves garlic, unpeeled

One 28-ounce can crushed tomatoes, with juice

2 tablespoons grated fresh ginger

4 cups cooked white rice

⅔ cup slivered, chopped, toasted almonds

½ cup chopped fresh flat-leaf parsley

1.   Preheat the oven to 350 degrees.

2.   Pour the broth into a small saucepan and bring to a boil over high heat. Place the currants in a small bowl and pour enough broth over them to cover; let stand. In another small bowl, combine the curry powder, garam masala, salt, and black pepper and reserve.

3.   Scatter the bacon in a 3- to 4-quart enameled cast-iron pot or Dutch oven over medium-high heat. With a slotted spoon, move the pieces around occasionally until the bacon is firm and just golden brown, about 3 minutes. With the slotted spoon, transfer to a small bowl and reserve.

4. Pour off all but 2 tablespoons of fat from the pot, reserving the excess fat in a small bowl. Brown the chicken thighs in batches over medium-high heat, taking care not to crowd them in the pot, until they are golden brown, about 5 minutes per side. Add the reserved bacon fat 1 teaspoon at a time if the pot becomes too dry. Remove the chicken and reserve in a medium bowl.

5. Add the carrots, bell peppers, onions, and garlic to the pot and cook until slightly softened, about 6 minutes. Add the tomatoes, spice mixture, ginger, and currants and their broth, reduce the heat to medium-low, and simmer until the tomatoes have cooked down to a puree and the sauce has thickened around the vegetables, about 8 minutes.

6. Nest the chicken thighs gently in the vegetable sauce so that the skin side faces up and is above the surface of the gravy. Tent the pot loosely with foil and transfer to the middle rack of the oven. Bake for 20 minutes, until the country captain resembles a roiling stew around the chicken thighs, about 20 minutes. Remove the foil and bake until the sauce has thickened further and the chicken skin is just beginning to crisp, about 15 minutes more.

7. Remove from the oven, skim any excess fat from the surface, and season to taste with salt and pepper. With tongs, transfer 3 thighs to each of 4 wide, deep bowls filled with 1 cup hot white rice. Spoon the sauce over the chicken and the rice and garnish with the reserved bacon, almonds, and parsley.

KLO

KILLER LEFTOVER—COUNTRY CAPTAIN EGGS "BENEDICT": MIX ANY LEFTOVER SAUCE AND RICE TOGETHER AND REFRIGERATE. REHEAT THE FOLLOWING MORNING IN A MICROWAVE OR SMALL SAUCEPAN. MAKE A BED OF 1/2 CUP COUNTRY CAPTAIN ON A PLATE AND DRAPE 2 SOFTLY POACHED EGGS ON TOP.

❋ HOLLYWOOD LIVER PUDDING ❋

WHAT A MISFORTUNE OF NOMENCLATURE IS SOUTH CAROLINA'S BELOVED LIVER PUDDING! PAIR THE WORD "LIVER" with a word that connotes a sweet, comforting dessert and you end up with a dish plucked straight from a child's nightmare. In order to get this dish the attention it deserves, we call it "Holly-wood"—partly because Hollywood, South Carolina, is where we find our favorite butcher-made liver pudding, at Marvin's Meats, and partly because we think the California connotation might get it the star turn it deserves.

This liver pudding really is a red-carpet number—a rustic, starch-enriched, pepper-flecked liver pâté, with all the versatility of its French analogue. We've found slices of it served up as a meat option at several meat-and-threes, but it also makes a terrific hors d'oeuvre served on toast or crackers with dabs of Fig Preserves (page 128).

We use calves' liver because it's easier to procure than the traditional pig's liver, but you can use any liver you wish. Lawrence Mitchell (a.k.a. LAMI), a former operations manager for the Lee Bros. Boiled Peanuts Catalogue, makes his grandmother's liver pudding with chicken livers. More significant than what kind of liver you use is what starch you use to enrich and bind it, because that choice shows whether you're from upstate South Carolina or the coast. Upstate folks favor cornmeal, whereas downstate recipes—logically, since the low-lying coastal areas were histori-cally involved in rice production (page 165)—tend to use rice.

Southern butchers who make liver pudding often stuff large, liverwurst-style casings to make cylindrical "chubs" for easy electric slicing. When we cook liver pudding at home, we use rice because we're from the coast, and we bake our pudding in a loaf pan, like a terrine. For a richer flavor, we cook the rice with the broth we poached the liver in.

⚜

WHAT TO DRINK   A good cheap Beaujolais Villages, or a glass of fortified wine, like a dry sherry (look for "Fino") or Madeira ("Verdelho" or "Sercial"), would be nifty with any paté, but particularly with the seasonings in this liver pudding.

For 6 to 8 people as a main dish, 24 as a snack

TIME: 1 hour to cook, 4 hours to chill (if desired)

1¼ cups water

1 bay leaf

2 teaspoons kosher salt

1 pound calves' liver, cut into 1-inch cubes

½ cup long-grain rice

1 cup chopped yellow onion (about 1 large onion)

2 tablespoons Madeira or dry sherry such as fino or amontillado

1 teaspoon minced fresh thyme

1 tablespoon minced fresh sage

2 large eggs, beaten

6 ounces slab bacon, cut into slices about ¼ inch thick, or 6 slices thick-cut bacon

1 teaspoon crushed dried Thai or other fiery red chile

½ teaspoon freshly ground black pepper

1.   Preheat the oven to 350 degrees.

2.   Pour the water into a 2-quart saucepan. Add the bay leaf and 1 teaspoon salt and bring to a boil over high heat. Add the liver, reduce the heat to medium-low, and cook until the liver is firm and a dull beige, about 4 minutes. Drain, reserving the broth (you should have 1 cup) and liver separately.

3.   Return the broth and the bay leaf to the saucepan and bring to a boil over high heat. Add the rice, turn the heat to low, cover tightly, and cook for 20 minutes, or until the rice is tender, dry, and fluffy. Discard the bay leaf.

4.   While the rice cooks, mix the cooked liver and the onion in a medium bowl and pass through the fine blade of a meat grinder into a second medium bowl. Add the cooked rice, the Madeira, the remaining 1 teaspoon salt, the thyme, and 2 teaspoons sage and blend with a rubber spatula until thoroughly mixed. Add the eggs and mix again.

5.   Line the bottom and sides of an 8½-×-4½-inch (6-cup) loaf pan with the bacon strips and sprinkle the chile, black pepper, and remaining 1 teaspoon sage generously over them. Spoon the liver and rice mixture into the pan and smooth out the top with a spatula. Fold down any bacon that rises above the level of the pudding on top of it. Bake for 35 minutes. Remove from the oven and let rest 10 minutes.

6.   If serving as a spread for toast points, discard bacon, scoop pudding into a bowl and serve immediately. If serving sliced, as a main dish for brunch or supper, place in the refrigerator for 4 hours.

7.   Fill the sink or a large roasting pan with hot water to a depth of about 2 inches. Dip the loaf pan carefully into the water for about thirty seconds to melt the thin layer of fat that holds the bacon to the pan. Run a sharp paring knife around the edge of the pan beneath the layer of bacon, and gently turn the pudding out onto a cutting board. Discard the bacon. With a serrated knife, cut the pudding into ½-inch-thick slices, sear in a seasoned pan, and lay the slices gently on a bed of Simple Grits (page 146) or alongside fried eggs.

❀ CITY HAM STEAK WITH RED-EYE GRAVY ❀

QUICK
KNOCKOUT

WE CALL HAMS CURED IN BRINE "CITY" HAMS TO DISTIN-
GUISH THEM FROM COUNTRY HAMS, WHICH ARE DRY-CURED WITH
salt and sugar, smoked, and aged for months (See "A Country Ham Primer," page 325). In this
recipe, we fry ham shank steaks from a "city" ham in a skillet and use the pan drippings to make
the popular southern gravy called red-eye gravy.

Like hoppin' John and burgoo, the name red-eye gravy has inspired tall tales and folklore
aplenty. Here are the three most common: 1) the cross-cut bone of a ham steak looks like a red eye;
2) President Andrew Jackson told his hungover camp cook one morning to make a gravy as red as
the cook's eyes; 3) the gravy is made with brewed coffee, so it's a pick-me-up for red-eyed folks.
Feel free to invent your own.

It's unfortunate that most red-eye gravy recipes call for using leftover coffee, because freshly
ground, freshly brewed coffee—preferably a tasty, mild bean like Sumatra or Ethiopia—makes
quite a difference in the flavor of your gravy. And it makes sense that you'd use freshly brewed coffee, since this dish is often served at breakfast and brunch, when you've already got a pot going.

Ham and red-eye gravy makes a marvelous brunch meal with eggs and any of the recipes from
our "Grits Guide" (pages 142–164). When preparing this dish for dinner, we pair it with slightly
sweet side dishes to balance the intensely salty and smoky flavors of the ham and gravy. We
recommend Creamed Corn (page 221), Cheese Grits (page 151), Coleslaw (page 195), or Oyster
Purloo (page 175). Pass the gravy at the table.

WHAT TO DRINK   *Guinness, or any other dark stout, would be delicious with the bold flavors of this brunchy dish; on the lighter side, a sparkling white wine would be a pleasant sip.*

For 4 people

TIME: 25 minutes

1 tablespoon extra-virgin olive oil

Four 12-ounce brined ham shank steaks, ½ inch thick

2 cups Rich Pork Broth (page 548)

2 teaspoons all-purpose flour

1 teaspoon sugar

2 teaspoons Spanish smoked paprika (*pimentón*) or Hungarian paprika (see Sourcery, page 284)

½ cup freshly brewed coffee

2 tablespoons unsalted butter, cut into small pieces

1.   Preheat the oven to 250 degrees and place an ovenproof serving platter or large plate and an ovenproof gravy boat on the middle rack.

2.   Place the oil in a 12-inch cast-iron skillet and heat over medium-high heat until it shimmers. Add the ham steaks and fry in 2 batches, leaving about 1 inch of space between them. Turn each steak as it becomes golden brown in patches, about 4 minutes per side. Transfer the first 2 steaks to the serving platter and set it back in the oven to warm as you fry the second batch.

3.   When all 4 ham steaks are warming in the oven, reduce the heat to medium and add the broth to the skillet. When the sizzling subsides, stir with a wooden spoon, scraping up the browned bits from the bottom. Mix the flour, sugar, and paprika in a small bowl. When the broth comes to a simmer, sprinkle the flour mixture into it with one hand while whisking vigorously with the other, to prevent clumping. Add the coffee and continue to whisk occasionally until the gravy returns to a simmer. Turn the heat to low, and simmer, whisking occasionally, until the gravy has thickened to the consistency of melted ice cream, about 6 minutes. Turn off the heat and whisk in the butter until it melts.

4.   Remove the serving platter and gravy boat from the oven and fill the gravy boat with the gravy. Pass the gravy at the table.

Freelance Writers' Dream:
A Suite of Pork Picnic Shoulder Recipes

When people ask what advice we'd give to aspiring food writers, the first thing we say is, *Know how to cook a pork shoulder.* Without fail, they laugh at that advice, but we couldn't be more serious; our Sunday night shoulders have gotten us through the lean weeks with style.

Everyone who's ever been seriously low on cash and who loves good food knows the cut of pork called the picnic shoulder. It is the bottom part of the shoulder and encompasses much of the bone and joint, so it's perceived to be neither as meaty nor as choice as the top of the shoulder (called the Boston butt). Picnic shoulder is rarely more than a dollar and a half per pound and sometimes half that.

We adore the picnic shoulder. It's got unctuous dark-meat bits and also parts that are as sliceable and presentable as loin. Braise it and the fat just melts away. And the leftovers! Even though it feeds a great crowd, we cook one often on Sundays just to have some around for the workweek, because it keeps on giving and giving. Hence the number of variations and killer leftover suggestions we've provided here.

Chestnuts were once a significant source of nourishment for domestic hogs rambling through Southern woodlots, but in the early twentieth century a blight obliterated the East Coast's majestic stands of the tree. Those that remain have been interbred with resistant Asian or European species.

❈ OVEN BBQED PICNIC SHOULDER ❈

THIS PORK SHOULDER IS, HANDS DOWN, ONE OF OUR MOST POPULAR, AND IT CAME ABOUT FROM AN ATTEMPT TO RE-create in a Manhattan kitchen in midwinter the smoky, tender pulled pork you find in barbecue joints throughout the Carolinas. We seared the shoulder and made a smoky, fiery, tart braising liquid with tomatoes and onion, smoked paprika, and vinegar. It's not the sort of treatment that barbecue judges would allow—at no point do we actually treat the pork with woodsmoke—but when we cook this for guests, it disappears before you can say "academic."

❈

WHAT TO DRINK   *A creamy lager, like Pilsner Urquell from Czechoslovakia, Zywiec from Poland, or even Heineken from the Netherlands, would be a great complement to the pork and would complete the frugal-but-flavorful aspect of the meal.*

For 8 people

TIME: 4 hours

One 28-ounce can whole tomatoes, lightly
crushed, with juice

2 teaspoons Spanish smoked paprika
(*pimentón*) or 2 chipotles in adobo (see
Sourcery, page 276) plus more to taste

2 tablespoons sorghum molasses (see
Sourcery, page 447), cane syrup, or
honey, plus more to taste

½ cup white wine vinegar, champagne vinegar,
or cider vinegar, plus more to taste

One 6–8-pound pork picnic shoulder (or
Boston butt if you prefer)

2 teaspoons kosher salt, plus more to taste

1 teaspoon freshly ground black pepper, plus
more to taste

1½ tablespoons canola oil

4 large plum tomatoes, cored

1 medium yellow onion, trimmed, peeled, and
quartered

1. Preheat the oven to 400 degrees.

2. In a 6-quart enameled cast-iron stockpot or Dutch oven, bring the canned tomatoes, paprika, sorghum molasses, and 6 tablespoons vinegar to a simmer over medium-high heat.

3. Set the pork skin side up on your work surface. With a sharp knife, slice the skin from the shoulder with a gentle sawing motion, working back from the point diagonally across from the leg end where the skin forms a corner (asking your butcher to do this for you will save time). Leave a thin layer of fat on the shoulder. Season the pork with the salt and black pepper.

4. Pour the oil into a 12-inch skillet or sauté pan and heat over high heat. When the oil shimmers and just begins to smoke, place the pork in the pan, skinned side down, and sear until golden brown, about 3 minutes per side. Place the pork skinned side down in the pot with the tomato braising liquid.

5. Add the plum tomatoes and onion to the skillet and cook, turning every few minutes, until the skin of the tomatoes blisters and blackens and the onion is caramelized on all sides. Tuck the vegetables around the pork in the pot. Add the remaining 2 tablespoons vinegar to the skillet and stir with a wooden spoon, scraping up any caramelized pork, tomato, and onion bits from the bottom. Pour over the pork.

6. Cover the pot, transfer to the oven, and cook for 30 minutes. Baste the pork, then turn the heat down to 300 degrees and continue to cook, basting every 30 minutes, until the pork is very tender, about 2½ hours.

7. Remove the pork from the oven, transfer to a cutting board with a gutter, and let rest 10 minutes before carving. Season the sauce with molasses, vinegar, salt, pepper, and smoked paprika to taste.

THE DOWNTOWN TOUCH FOR THIS DISH IS TO PUREE THE COOKING LIQUID IN A BLENDER WHILE THE PORK IS RESTING AND SERVE IT AS A SAUCE WITH NEATLY CARVED SLICES OF PORK.

THE RUSTIC TOUCH IS TO COOK THE PORK IN THE OVEN 1 HOUR LONGER (3 1/2 HOURS TOTAL), SO IT FALLS FROM THE BONE, AND SERVE IT PULLED AND BATHED IN THE (UNPUREED) SAUCE.

KLO

KILLER LEFTOVERS: PULL ANY LEFTOVER PORK FROM THE BONE—YOU CAN ROAST THE BONES TO MAKE RICH PORK BROTH (PAGE 548)—AND REFRIGERATE IN A PLASTIC CONTAINER ALONG WITH ANY SAUCE. THE NEXT DAY, MAKE PORK TACOS BY HEATING 1/2 CUP (PER SERVING) OF PULLED PORK AND SAUCE (WHICH IS GELATINOUS WHEN COLD) IN A 9-INCH SKILLET. IN ANOTHER SKILLET, OVER LOW HEAT, TOAST CORN OR FLOUR TORTILLAS SINGLY, KEEPING THEM WARM BETWEEN TWO CLEAN DISH TOWELS. WHEN THE PORK AND SAUCE ARE BUBBLY AND HOT, FILL THE TORTILLAS, USING 1/4 CUP PORK AND SAUCE PER TACO. GARNISH WITH DICED RAW ONION AND CILANTRO OR YOUR FAVORITE SALSA.

IF YOU DON'T HAVE TORTILLAS ON HAND, LIGHTLY TOAST 2 SLICES OF WHITE BREAD OR A HAMBURGER BUN AND SLATHER WITH 1/3 CUP OF PULLED PORK AND SAUCE FOR PULLED PORK BBQ SANDWICHES. SERVE WITH COLESLAW (PAGE 195), ON THE SIDE OR, LIKE WESTERN NORTH CAROLINIANS WOULD, ON THE SANDWICH ITSELF.

FOR EACH SERVING OF QUICK PORK HASH, PUT 1/2 CUP PULLED PORK AND 1/4 CUP SAUCE IN THE FOOD PROCESSOR AND PULSE UNTIL SMOOTH. HEAT IN A SKILLET AND SERVE OVER HOT WHITE RICE, GARNISHED WITH FLAT-LEAF PARSLEY.

❋ LUAU-STYLE BBQED PORK SHOULDER ❋

WE'RE CONVINCED HAWAII IS ACTUALLY A CULTURAL PART OF THE SOUTH. THINK ABOUT IT: 1) ELVIS MADE IT BIG THERE, 2) boiled peanuts are big there, and 3) the trophy dish of the luau is a smoky, pit-cooked whole hog. Called kalua pig, the hog is wrapped in taro and banana leaves and set in an oven dug in the ground and lined with volcanic rock.

We developed this recipe for a smoky pork shoulder wrapped in collard greens when we were in Charleston and dreaming of the Aloha State. We were thrilled with the results. Like barbecue, kalua pig has a smoky pork flavor, but banana and taro leaves give it the herbal, stewed flavor of simmering greens. The collard greens in our recipe accomplish the same feat, and even if you've never been to Hawaii, you'll find this pork shoulder to be a revelation.

❋

WHAT TO DRINK   *A cold Jack and Ginger (page 51) cocktail would be a suave accompaniment to the earthy smokiness of this pork shoulder. A powerful red Zinfandel or Syrah, with some murky spice, would pair well too.*

EQUIPMENT

Butcher's string
Aluminum foil

One 6–8-pound pork picnic shoulder
1 tablespoon Spanish smoked paprika
 (*pimentón*)
2 tablespoons kosher salt

12 large collard leaves (about 1 large bunch;
 see "Sizing a Bunch of Collards,"
 page 212), stems trimmed

1. Preheat the oven to 500 degrees.

2. Set the pork skin side up on your work surface. With a sharp knife, slice the skin from the shoulder with a gentle sawing motion, working back from the point diagonally across from the leg end where the skin forms a corner (asking your butcher to do this for you will save time). Leave a thin layer of fat on the shoulder. Score the shoulder all over with cuts about 1½ inches apart. Mix the paprika and salt in a small bowl and rub the mixture all over the pork, making certain to rub it into all the crevices.

3. Cut six 3-foot lengths of string and lay four of them on your work surface in parallel lines about 3 inches apart. Center the remaining two, perpendicular to the others. Make a large rectangular blanket of collard greens over the strings by laying down 3 leaves in a line, their stems facing down and their edges overlapping 1 inch or more. Lay down 3 more leaves in the same way, with their stems facing up, and overlapping the stems of the row already on the work surface. At each end of this layer of leaves, position more leaves (2 at most), with their stem ends perpendicular to the stems already on the work surface. Lay the scored, seasoned pork in the center of the blanket and wrap the leaves around it, securing them with the string. Trim the ends of the string. Then wrap the pork in two layers of aluminum foil.

4. Pour ½ inch water in a 9-×-13-inch roasting pan. Place the pork on a rack in the pan and bake for 30 minutes. Turn the temperature down to 450 degrees and bake for 3 more hours, adding more water to the pan when it becomes dry.

5. Remove the pork from the oven and transfer to a work surface, still on the rack. Pour the water from the pan, return the rack and shoulder to the pan, and let rest for 10 minutes. Slice vents in the bottom of the aluminum foil so the juices drain into the pan. Transfer the pork to a cutting board and let cool. Unwrap the aluminum foil and cut the string. Unwrap the collard greens and discard.

6. Pull the pork from the bone and serve with spoonfuls of the pan juices and a cruet of Pepper Vinegar (page 518).

The lunchtime parking lot of one of a number of excellent barbecue restaurants in the Lexington, North Carolina, area, almost all of which feature a style of pepper-vinegar marinated pork served with a scoop of coleslaw on top.

⚜ EASY NORTH CAROLINA–STYLE ⚜ HALF PICNIC SHOULDER

THIS IS A GREAT MEAL TO COOK ON A THIRD DATE. ON THE FIRST DATE, YOU PROBABLY WENT TO A RESTAURANT AND learned that he or she didn't have any deal-breaking food hangups. The second may have been a dinner party at someone else's house that ran late and had one of various possible endings. On the third date, you're cooking dinner. It's the one that holds the most significance (and risk), because cooking for your quarry exposes more about your habits, priorities, talents, and background than you may realize. No one will admit it, but the third is the clincher date, and this dish is the perfect thing to make. It's designed for two, so it's intimate, but it's a challenge at the same time: spicy, with the darkly sweet edge of molasses. And it's rustic—half of this cut's weight is bone, which gives the flesh a deep pork flavor. You may learn a lot about your date from this dish. Make the menu simple: the half picnic shoulder, Best Family Farm Corn-Bread Salad (page 188), and a Sorghum Pecan Pie (page 449). If your date doesn't jump out of his or her clothes with gratitude, you were never meant to be together.

⚜

WHAT TO DRINK   *Uncorking a sparkling surprise, like a bottle of crisp Chateau Biltmore Methode Champenoise Brut, made in western North Carolina, would be appropriate with this soulful dish.*

For 2 people

TIME: 4 hours to marinate, 4 hours to cook

One 3–3½-pound half picnic pork shoulder,
    bone in, skin on
1 teaspoon canola oil
2 cups North Carolina–Style Barbecue Sauce
    (page 520)

1 tablespoon sorghum molasses (see Sourcery,
    page 447), cane syrup, or honey
½ cup Sunday Chicken Broth (page 532)
½ cup apple cider

1. Score the skin and fat on the picnic shoulder with a sharp knife, about ¾ inch deep. Place in a baking dish, pour the barbecue sauce over it, and marinate in the refrigerator for 4 hours. Remove from the refrigerator 2 hours before cooking so the meat comes to room temperature.

2. Preheat the oven to 325 degrees.

3. Remove the pork from the marinade and pat dry with paper towels. Reserve the marinade. In a Dutch oven or ovenproof baking dish large enough to hold the meat, heat the oil over medium-high heat. When you see the first wisp of smoke, add the pork, skin side down, and sear until the skin is golden brown, about 3 minutes. Turn and sear until the flesh on all sides is golden brown, about 3 minutes per side.

4. Pour the reserved marinade over the shoulder. Place the pork in the dish skin side up. Heat over medium-low heat on the stovetop until the marinade simmers. Transfer to the oven, cover, and bake, basting every 15 minutes, until a meat thermometer pressed into the middle of the shoulder registers 175 degrees and the pork is tender, about 3½ hours.

5. With a turkey baster, transfer ¼ cup of the cooking liquid to a small saucepan. Add the sorghum molasses, broth, and apple cider to the saucepan and bring to a simmer over high heat. Simmer vigorously until the liquid has reduced by one half, about 6 minutes. Reserve half the sauce in a gravy boat. Continue to simmer the liquid remaining in the saucepan until it has reduced again by three quarters and become a thick syrup, about 3 minutes. Baste the shoulder with the syrup, return to the oven, and turn the heat up to 425 degrees. Cook, uncovered, for 15 minutes more, until the skin has a shiny, lacquered appearance.

6. Remove the pork from the oven and let rest on a cutting board or rack set over a baking pan for 10 minutes. Discard the cooking liquid in the dish, or reserve for another use. Carve or pull the pork and serve with spoonfuls of the gravy.

❋ BRAISED OXTAILS ❋

LIKE PORK BELLIES AND PIG'S FEET, OXTAILS ARE EXPE-
RIENCING A STARTLING RENAISSANCE IN RESTAURANTS WITH THIRTY-
dollar entrées. Squeamishness and taboos about offal are fading; what was once considered French peasant food is now judged purely on its merits, as far as flavor is concerned. The best oxtails we've had in that setting were at Fiamma Osteria in Soho, where we inhaled an oxtail-filled ravioli, a single dollop of rich, braised oxtail between paper-thin sheets of fresh pasta. It was every bit as delicious as the oxtails you find for about a tenth the price in meat-and-threes throughout the South.

We've always loved oxtails, but they're about the richest thing we know. We tame them by cooking them until they're nearly spreadable and using them judiciously as a lusty gravy, over grits or a baked potato. We also add lemon juice and fresh ginger just a few minutes before turning off the heat, and plenty of flat-leaf parsley. These tonic elements seem to lighten the meaty flavor of the braising liquid.

A few of the nation's butchers sell whole oxtails, but they're unwieldy and take time and strength to cut up, so have your butcher do that work for you.

❋

WHAT TO DRINK   *A Cabernet Franc, Syrah, or Cabernet Sauvignon suits these deeply beefy oxtails and their spicy seasoning.*

357

For 6 people

TIME: 4 hours

3½ pounds oxtails, sliced into disks

1½ teaspoons kosher salt, plus more to taste

1 teaspoon freshly ground black pepper, plus more to taste

1 tablespoon canola oil

2 cups chopped yellow onions (about 3 medium onions)

2 cups finely diced carrots (about 6 medium carrots)

1½ cups robust red wine, such as Cabernet Sauvignon, Syrah, or a Bordeaux blend

1½ cups Sunday Chicken Broth (page 532)

1 teaspoon crushed red pepper

1 tablespoon plus 1 teaspoon chopped fresh thyme

A generous ½ teaspoon allspice berries, ground in a mortar or coffee grinder

2½ teaspoons grated fresh ginger

2 tablespoons lemon juice (from 1 large lemon)

1 bunch fresh flat-leaf parsley, stemmed, washed, and dried, for garnish

1. Season the oxtails all over with the salt and black pepper. Heat the oil in a 4- to 6-quart Dutch oven or enameled cast-iron pot over medium-high heat until it shimmers. Sear the oxtails in batches, turning them with tongs as each surface becomes golden brown, until they are browned all over, about 6 to 8 minutes per batch. When each batch is browned, remove them with tongs and reserve in a medium bowl.

2. Add the onions and carrots to the Dutch oven, and cook until softened, 2 to 3 minutes, stirring with a wooden spoon and scraping up any browned bits on the bottom. Add the wine, broth, chile, thyme, and allspice and bring to a simmer. Return the oxtails and any juices in the bowl to the Dutch oven, cover, and simmer gently until the meat is falling from the bone and the braising liquid has thickened, about 3 hours.

3. With tongs, transfer the oxtails to a medium bowl. When they are cool enough to handle, pick the meat from the bones and discard the bones and any cartilage. Chop the meat into pieces of roughly the same size. Skim some fat from the braising liquid.

4. Return the chopped oxtails to the Dutch oven and simmer over low heat, about 2 minutes. Add the ginger, lemon juice, and salt and black pepper to taste and heat through, stirring occasionally, about another 3 minutes.

5. Serve over grits, white rice, or a baked potato, and garnish with the parsley.

VARIATION—OXTAIL HASH: FOR A CHUNKY OXTAIL HASH THAT'S A STELLAR BRUNCH DISH WITH EGGS, WE COOK 2 CUPS DICED YUKON GOLD OR OTHER WAXY POTATOES FOR 15 MINUTES IN BOILING SALTED WATER, DRAIN, AND ADD THEM WITH THE CHOPPED BRAISED OXTAILS IN STEP 4.

❋ FRANCISCO'S TRACTOR-DISK WOK VENISON ❋

THERE'S AN ABUNDANCE OF DEER IN ST. MATTHEWS, SOUTH CAROLINA, AND THEY'RE A PARTICULAR NUISANCE TO THE folks at Wannamaker Seeds, where deer chow down on acres of precious soybean plants. So the Wannamakers hunt them as best they can and process the venison for their own consumption. Francisco Torres, the farm's foreman, has become famous locally for this dish, in which he cubes the venison and sears it with onions and fresh jalapeño chiles in a "wok" fashioned from the blade of a disk harrow, which is pulled behind a tractor to break up the earth. The genius of the tractor-disk wok is that it is so big around and its sides sloped so gently that Torres can warm the tortillas at the outer edge without disturbing the stir-fry action at the hot center.

We've adapted Francisco's dish for a conventional skillet or wok, but the simplicity and bold, zingy flavor of the original remains. The steam that rises from the peppers can be overpowering, but note that the flavor of the jalapeños is more fruity than fiery, and that that fruitiness, along with the caramelized sugar from the onions and the juices from the venison, makes a gravy that is out of this world. We've substituted lean beef for the venison in this dish with great success.

❋

WHAT TO DRINK   *The bubbles in a brisk Mexican lager like Pacifico are the perfect antidote to the fiery jalapeño and onion blend in this stir-fry.*

For 6 people

TIME: 45 minutes

4 tablespoons canola oil, plus more if needed

6 medium onions, chopped (4 cups)

2 teaspoons kosher salt, plus more to taste

2 pounds venison loin, cut into 1-inch dice
(about 5 cups)

12 fresh jalapeño peppers, stemmed, seeded,
and chopped (2 cups)

¼ cup lime juice, tequila, or Pepper Vinegar
(page 518)

18 soft corn tortillas

1 large lime, cut into small wedges

1. Preheat the oven to 200 degrees. Place a large ovenproof bowl on the bottom rack and a large ovenproof plate on the top rack.

2. Heat a large wok or 12-inch cast-iron skillet over high heat until water droplets dance and disappear readily. Stir-fry the ingredients in 4 batches: Pour 1 tablespoon oil into the wok, swirl it around so that it thinly coats the pan, then add 1 cup chopped onions and stir for 2 to 3 minutes, until they begin to brown and caramelize. Scatter ½ teaspoon salt lightly over the onions, then add 1¼ cups venison and sear for a few seconds. Turn the meat with a wooden spoon to brown all sides, about 3 minutes total. Add ½ cup jalapeños, stir-fry for another 2 minutes, and transfer the contents of the wok to the bowl in the oven. Deglaze the pan with 1 tablespoon lime juice and drizzle the pan juices over the meat. Repeat until all the ingredients except the lime wedges have been used.

3. In a 9- or 10-inch cast-iron skillet, warm each tortilla over medium-high heat, about 30 seconds per side, until it is fragrant and stiffening but not toasted. Add a few drops of canola oil to the skillet if the tortillas begin to scorch. Stack the tortillas on the plate in the oven and cover with a clean dish towel.

4. To serve, fold the tortillas in half and fill them with the venison, peppers, and onions. Serve with the lime wedges and your favorite mild salsa or sour cream, if desired.

VARIATION—TRACTOR-DISK WOK MUSHROOMS: THESE MAKE A TERRIFIC VEGETARIAN MAIN DISH. WOODSY FRESH MUSHROOMS LIKE CHANTERELLES, PORTOBELLOS, OR SHIITAKES PLAY THE ROLE OF THE GAMY VENISON BEAUTIFULLY. SIMPLY SUBSTITUTE 1 POUND MUSHROOMS FOR THE VENISON, AND ADD 2 TABLESPOONS WATER TO THE BROWNED ONIONS IN STEP 2 BEFORE ADDING THE MUSHROOMS TO THE WOK.

❊ HARLEM MEAT LOAF ❊

THE SUMMER OUR SISTER, CAROLINE, GRADUATED FROM COLLEGE, SHE MOVED INTO OUR HARLEM APARTMENT. THREE SIBlings in their twenties living together and sharing a kitchen sounds like a bad reality-TV show, but it worked out well. We gave Caroline some of our recipes, and she turned us on to a few of hers, like meat loaf, a dish we'd abandoned fifteen years earlier, in the cafeteria of our day school back in Charleston.

We never knew meat loaf could be anything more than a brick of hamburger (much less something wondrous), so we've borrowed her recipe, which has several noteworthy features. For the ground pork and veal commonly used along with ground beef, Caroline substitutes sweet Italian sausages cut from their casings—the more fennel seed, the better—which yields a more interesting and flavorful loaf. She also uses fresh sourdough bread crumbs to give it a lighter structure, and chopped sour dill pickles for a sassy flourish. A glaze of ketchup, Tabasco sauce, and Worcestershire sauce is lacquered across the top during the last fifteen minutes of cooking, and the meat loaf emerges from the oven resembling a photo from a cookbook much more than it does a brick.

We follow Caroline's recipe pretty much to the letter, but the one thing we don't do is wait a day before eating it. She claims meat loaf tastes so much better the next day that it's a waste to eat it the day it's made. While we're inclined to agree, we just don't have that much willpower.

❊

WHAT TO DRINK   *Lee Bros. Sweet Tea (page 23) or an easygoing red wine would be perfect partners for this meatloaf, whose kaleidoscope of flavors ranges from salty to sweet.*

362

For 4 people

TIME: 1¼ hours

1 pound ground beef, chuck or sirloin

½ pound sweet Italian sausages, cut from their casings

¾ cup ketchup

1 tablespoon plus 2 teaspoons Worcestershire sauce

1 tablespoon Tabasco sauce or Pepper Vinegar (page 518)

½ cup chopped sour dill pickles

1½ cups finely chopped yellow onion (about 1 large onion)

3 garlic cloves, peeled and minced

½ cup finely chopped fresh flat-leaf parsley

½ cup bread crumbs, preferably fresh, preferably sourdough

1 large egg, lightly beaten

½ teaspoon kosher salt

1. Preheat the oven to 350 degrees.

2. Break the beef and the sausage into golfball-sized hunks and place them in a large, wide bowl. In a second large bowl, whisk together ½ cup ketchup with 1 tablespoon Worcestershire sauce and 2 teaspoons Tabasco sauce. Pour evenly over the beef and sausage. In the same bowl, mix the pickles, onion, garlic, and parsley, then scatter the mixture over the beef and sausage. Sprinkle the bread crumbs evenly over the top, then add the egg and the salt. With your fingers spread wide apart, gently mix the ingredients together in 6 to 8 gathering motions, until the ingredients begin to be uniformly blended.

3. Transfer the mixture to a 9-×-13-inch roasting pan and pat it into a loaf shape. Bake for 35 minutes on the middle rack. The loaf will render some fat and the surface will begin to brown.

4. Whisk the remaining ¼ cup ketchup, 2 teaspoons Worcestershire sauce, and 1 teaspoon Tabasco sauce together in a small bowl. Brush the glaze generously over the top of the meat loaf. Continue to bake until the glaze stiffens and darkens slightly, about 15 minutes. Let rest for 10 minutes before slicing and serving.

5. For optimum flavor, let cool to room temperature, tent the roasting pan with aluminum foil, and refrigerate for 24 hours. The next day, reheat the loaf, covered with the foil, in a warm oven.

❋ CHICKEN-FRIED STEAK ❋ WITH VIDALIA CREAM GRAVY

WHOEVER FIRST HAD THE IDEA OF SUBJECTING A STEAK TO THE CRISPIFYING, CRUSTIFYING TREATMENT WE TYPICALLY GIVE chicken parts is unknown to food history, but that person deserves credit for a stroke of genius. It's a rare example of a recipe in which leaner, tougher, less exalted cuts of beef actually perform better than the fattier, tenderer rib eyes and strips. The crust adds a lusciousness to thin steaks, and they cook quite quickly. Serve this at the height of summer, with nothing more than fat slices of ripe tomato sprinkled with kosher salt.

❋

WHAT TO DRINK   *Roll out your best red Burgundy or Bordeaux for this downscale indulgence.*

For 4 people

TIME: 30 minutes

¼ cup peanut oil

1 large egg, beaten

½ cup whole or low-fat buttermilk (preferably whole)

1 recipe Lee Bros. All-Purpose Fry Dredge (page 552)

Four 6-ounce beef top round steaks, about ½ inch thick (often labeled "bracciole")

1 jumbo Vidalia onion (about 12 ounces), trimmed, peeled, and thinly sliced

2 tablespoons unsalted butter

Kosher salt to taste

1 teaspoon all-purpose flour

½ cup Sunday Chicken Broth (page 532)

¼ cup whole milk

1 teaspoon freshly ground black pepper, plus more to taste

1. Preheat the oven to 200 degrees. Place an ovenproof platter on the top rack. In a 12-inch cast-iron skillet or sauté pan with a candy thermometer clipped to it, heat the oil over medium-high heat to 350 degrees.

2. Whisk the egg with the buttermilk and pour into a shallow bowl. Place the fry dredge on a wide plate. Working with 1 steak at a time, envelop the steak in a single sheet of plastic wrap and pound several times with a wooden mallet to tenderize. Coat the steak in the dredge and shake off any excess. Dip in the egg wash to coat both sides. Allow the excess to drip off, then coat again in the dredge. Shake off the excess and place the steak immediately into the hot oil. Fry, checking the temperature of the oil and adjusting the heat as necessary to maintain the temperature at 350 degrees, until golden brown, about 2 minutes per side. Transfer to a plate lined with a double thickness of paper towels to drain excess oil, then transfer to the platter in the oven. Repeat with each steak, using fresh paper towels to drain each one.

3. When all the steaks have been fried and are warming in the oven, discard the oil in the skillet and return the skillet to the burner. Add the onion, the butter, and a pinch of salt and sauté over medium-high heat until the onion is soft and translucent, about 4 minutes. In a small bowl, vigorously whisk the flour into the broth until no lumps are left. Pour the broth and milk into the skillet and add the pepper. Bring to a simmer and simmer gently, stirring, until the gravy has thickened to the consistency of melted ice cream. Season to taste with salt and pepper.

4. To serve, place the steaks on large dinner plates and ladle a generous amount of gravy over each.

FISH, OYSTERS, CRABS, AND SHRIMP

THERE ARE EASIER WAYS TO PUT FRESH
FLOUNDER ON THE TABLE THAN WADING INTO

a creek at four o'clock in the morning with a flashlight and a gig (a broom-handle spear with a fierce-looking trident on the end). But that is exactly what Ted and his friend Charlie Geer used to do in Awendaw, a town on the Intracoastal Waterway about an hour north of downtown. Charlie's father, a Charleston doctor, taught us how. The fish are astoundingly flat, and they writhe into the sandy creek bottom at the first sign of danger, camouflaging themselves quite effectively. To catch one, you must shine the flashlight through the shallows and walk very slowly and lightly so as not to stir up the sand. When you see a shudder of movement, you drive the gig home and, if you are lucky, spear a flounder (and not, as was often the case, a blue crab).

In the coastal South, the line between sport and provisioning is blurry. Children in the Lowcountry are enlisted into culinary life at a very young age and taught how to toss a cast net, drop a line and lure a crab, cast a lure, and throw a gig. Mechanics and mayors alike perform the tasks of netting shrimp, reeling in red drum, and trolling for crabs on Saturday afternoons, with little of the air of competition that characterizes fishing elsewhere in the country. It's tough to say how much the joy of fishing is the sheer fun of the catch, or whether that pleasure is simply a dividend to filling the refrigerator (or the chest freezer, if you've caught a lot) with the freshest fish imaginable.

Believe it or not, fish is breakfast throughout the Lowcountry, and there are plenty of small roadside restaurants on the way back from Awendaw. One, Martha Lou's Kitchen, a pink cinder-block hut on Morrison Drive near the stevedores' union hall, is our favorite.

In this chapter we celebrate the fish and shellfish of our hometown with some classic Lowcountry recipes and a few that were simply inspired by our proximity to the great harvest of the coastal plain. Blue crabs, flounder, shrimp, spottail bass (a.k.a. red drum), whiting, and oysters are the building blocks of our most remarkable dishes, and they distinguish Lowcountry cuisine from other southern regional cuisines.

Even within the Lowcountry, however, culinary traditions differ from town to town, because they're loosely based on the variety of commercial fishing practiced in each place. For example, you can find shrimp burgers—cakes of chopped shrimp and seasonings—at a few roadside fish shacks in shrimping centers like Beaufort and St. Helena Island, but they're exceedingly rare elsewhere. Fried crab sandwiches are the lunch of choice in the McClellanville area. In Charleston, we use mullet only for bait, but in northern Florida, mullet is transformed into something sublime by smoking over hickory wood.

It's sometimes difficult to explain to someone not accustomed to coastal living how thoroughly the rhythms of the water affect daily life. At high tide and full moon, when the Ashley River covers Lockwood Boulevard in a half-foot of water, traffic slows to a crawl, and you can see minnows swimming by when you look out the car window. A small bridge over the causeway to Sullivan's Island opens every hour on the half-hour so that boats can go by. It's amazing how many times in a week—even in a day—we're brought to a standstill waiting for the bridge to open. The water humbles us, and the fact that it can literally stop us in our tracks seems like a small inconvenience for the amount of pleasure we get from living near it.

Often, when friends come for dinner, they'll bring along a share of whatever was caught most recently, whether it was sweet shrimp or an eight-pound red drum, cleaned and scaled.

❋ 83 EAST BAY STREET SHRIMP AND GRITS ❋

OUR TAKE ON THE QUINTESSENTIAL LOWCOUNTRY DISH IS NAMED FOR THE HOUSE WE GREW UP IN, WHERE WE FIRST EXPERimented with cooking. East Bay Street runs parallel to the harborfront, and no. 83, a tall, pastel yellow townhouse, is in the middle of a two-block stretch of faded pinks, yellows, greens, and blues that locals call Rainbow Row. In the eighteenth century, Rainbow Row was the mercantile center of the city (it faces the cobblestone wharves of the harbor), and until the 1920s most of the houses on our block were chandlers' shops, with a store on the ground floor, the owner's quarters and rooms to let above, and a warehouse out back.

Our kitchen was where the shop would have been, with two windows facing the street. It was a simple square, nearly taller than it was wide, equipped with an electric range from the 1950s, dark brown linoleum tile, and so many coats of beige paint on the cabinets that the doors always stuck in the humid months. But it worked. It was where we first boiled peanuts, first simmered veal kidneys in red wine, first cooked shrimp and grits, and first began to improvise. It was the center of our family universe until our parents sold the house and moved to Dallas.

Shrimp and grits is simply fresh, peeled shrimp cooked in a soupy gravy that often includes tomatoes (or some variant thereof, such as tomato paste or ketchup), bell peppers, and bacon. Traditionally the dish is served for breakfast, but these days we eat it around the clock. Each household in Charleston has its own recipe in much the way that Louisiana households hold gumbo recipes, which may be why shrimp and grits is the most celebrated of Charleston's iconic dishes (she-crab soup and benne wafers holding second and third place in the triumvirate).

Our household recipe draws out the tart flavor of tomatillos (or roasted green tomatoes) to play against the sweet essence of the shrimp. It's unconventional, for sure, but we think it does no harm to the reputation of the dish.

※

WHAT TO DRINK   *The lemony quality of a good Chablis, or any clean, steel-aged Chardonnay, pairs well with shrimp and with the note of smoky bacon in this dish.*

For 4 people

TIME: 70 minutes

FOR THE SHRIMP STOCK

1½ pounds headless large shrimp (26–30 per pound; see Sourcery, page 374), shells on

3 cups water

2 teaspoons Lee Bros. Shrimp Boil (page 553)

FOR THE GRITS

1½ cups stone-ground grits

1½ cups whole milk

3 cups water

2 pinches kosher salt, plus more to taste

Freshly ground black pepper to taste

FOR THE GRAVY

1 pound tomatillos, green tomatoes, or tomatoes (about 6 large tomatillos or 3 medium tomatoes)

1 tablespoon minced jalapeño pepper (about 1 jalapeño)

¼ pound slab bacon or 3 slices thick-cut bacon, diced

3 tablespoons unsalted butter

½ cup chopped green bell pepper

½ cup chopped yellow onion

1 tablespoon plus 1 teaspoon all-purpose flour

Kosher salt to taste

Freshly ground black pepper to taste

1.   Peel the shrimp, reserving the shells. In a medium saucepan, bring the water to a boil over high heat. Add the shells and the shrimp boil, reduce the heat to medium-low, and simmer for 20 minutes. Strain the broth (you should have about 1½ cups) and reserve. Discard the shells.

2.   While the broth simmers, stir the grits into a bowl of cold water and allow to settle. Corn hulls may float to the surface. Skim off the hulls and drain the grits. In a medium saucepan, bring the milk and the 3 cups water to a boil over high heat. Add the grits, stirring with a wooden spoon. Reduce the heat to medium, add the salt, and simmer, stirring occasionally. Once the grits thicken (about 10 minutes), reduce the heat to very low and cook, stirring frequently and adding water if the grits become too stiff. Cook until the grits are fluffy and creamy, 35 to 45 minutes. Season with salt and pepper and reserve.

3.   While the grits cook, remove the papery husks from the tomatillos and place them in a medium roasting pan or cast-iron skillet. Broil them about 3 inches from the flame or heating element, turning them as their skins blacken, until they're blackened all over, 7 to 10 minutes. Transfer the tomatillos to a food processor or blender and pulse to a soupy liquid, about three 5-second pulses (less for tomatoes). Press the liquid through a food mill or coarse strainer into a medium bowl (you should have about 2 cups). Add the jalapeño and reserve.

4.   Scatter the bacon in a 12-inch cast-iron skillet or sauté pan over medium-high heat. With a slotted spoon, move the pieces around until the bacon is firm and just golden brown, about 3 minutes. Transfer to a small bowl. Pour off all but 3 tablespoons of the fat and add the butter, bell pepper, and onion. Sauté until the pepper and onion just begin to soften, about 2 minutes.

5.   Pour 2 tablespoons of the shrimp broth into a small bowl, add the flour, and whisk until it becomes a smooth paste. Pour the remaining shrimp broth into the skillet with the pepper and onion. When the broth simmers, reduce the heat to medium. Simmer vigorously until the vegetables have softened, about 5 minutes. Add the flour paste to the pan, whisking vigorously to distribute the flour evenly throughout the broth. Add the sieved tomatillo and jalapeño mixture to the skillet, stirring, and return to a simmer. Cook until the gravy thickens enough to coat the back of a spoon heavily, 5 to 7 minutes more. Add the shrimp and continue cooking until they are pink and cooked through, 2 to 3 minutes. Season to taste with salt and pepper.

6.   To serve, divide the grits among 4 plates and ladle the shrimp and gravy on top.

VARIATION—83 EAST BAY STREET SHAD ROE AND GRITS: WE LOVE GIVING SHAD ROE THE 83 EAST BAY TREATMENT, BECAUSE THE TOMATILLO GRAVY LENDS SHAD ROE'S RICHNESS A PLAYFUL, TONIC EDGE. SUBSTITUTE 4 SETS OF SHAD ROE FOR THE SHRIMP AND 1 1/2 CUPS RICH FISH BROTH (PAGE 546) OR CLAM JUICE FOR THE SHRIMP BROTH. COOK THE ROE IN A SEPARATE SKILLET FROM THE GRAVY, AS FOLLOWS: PREHEAT THE OVEN TO 350 DEGREES. IN A SECOND 12-INCH CAST-IRON SKILLET OR SAUTÉ PAN, MELT 2 TABLESPOONS UNSALTED BUTTER OVER MEDIUM-HIGH HEAT. WHEN IT IS FROTHY, SAUTÉ THE ROE IN BATCHES, TAKING CARE NOT TO CROWD THE PAN, UNTIL IT IS GENTLY BROWN, ABOUT 3 MINUTES PER SIDE. WHEN ALL THE ROE IS COOKED, PLACE IT IN THE SKILLET AND BAKE FOR ABOUT 5 MINUTES, OR UNTIL THE ROE IS MEDIUM-RARE (SLICE ONE CROSSWISE; IT SHOULD HAVE A ROSY PINK MIDDLE ABOUT THE DIAMETER OF A NICKEL). TO SERVE, DIVIDE THE GRITS AMONG FOUR PLATES, REST 1 SET OF ROES ON EACH, AND LADLE THE GRAVY OVER THE TOP.

IN THIS BOOK, SHRIMP ALWAYS APPEAR IN THE INGRE-
dients list as "headless shrimp, shells on." That's for two reasons. First, fish markets and supermarkets most commonly sell fresh shrimp as such, so finding
them is easy. Second, keeping the shells on until you're ready to use the shrimp
keeps them from losing their natural moisture, which not only carries a great deal
of flavor but retains texture by keeping them from drying out. The shrimp shells
themselves bear a bounty of flavor, so we often use them to make Sunday Shrimp
Broth (page 536).

During shrimp season along the South Carolina coast, people sell shrimp
from trucks parked along coastal highway 17. Short of being on the dock when
the shrimp boats come in, this may be the most direct route to the freshest
shrimp available. You don't have to be intimidated if they're sold with the heads
on (they often are). Shrimp heads are easy to remove, requiring just a simple
pinch between thumb and forefinger, and they give wonderful flavor to broth.
When buying shrimp with heads, note that they spoil quicker and that the heads
constitute about 35 percent of the shrimp's weight. So if a recipe calls for 2
pounds of headless shrimp, shells on, buy almost 2¾ pounds whole shrimp with
shells to compensate.

Purchase shrimp only according to the count per pound and never by descriptions such as "large" or "medium." We've found these descriptions to fluctuate wildly from shop to shop (and even within the same shop!). A good fish market will always know the count per pound of each variety of shrimp it offers. These are average numbers, of course, which is why they are always expressed as a range. If the market does not know the piece count per pound, ask the fishmonger to place a dozen or so on a scale to see how much they weigh. The size we favor for most recipes is 26 to 30 shrimp per pound, generally considered large. Smaller ones tend to look measly on the plate and to require too much shelling labor. Jumbo shrimp, we find, become tough when cooked, and their texture flattens the flavor.

In some markets you can buy shrimp that are already peeled and deveined. These cost more, and often have been roughly handled. But having someone else peel your shrimp saves a great deal of time, so if that is a deciding factor in whether or not you make a recipe, by all means buy peeled shrimp. But keep in mind that a shrimp's shell and legs make up about 12 percent of its weight, so if you're using peeled shrimp in a recipe that calls for 2 pounds headless shrimp, shells on, you'll require only 88 percent of that weight, or about 1¾ pounds.

THE "VEIN" OF A SHRIMP IS ITS DIGESTIVE TRACT. IT IS flavorless, harmless to eat, and such a small proportion of a shrimp's weight that it doesn't pronouncedly affect its flavor or its texture; still, some eaters detect a certain grittiness when it hasn't been removed. Whether or not you devein shrimp is a matter of personal preference. We do it only when presentation is paramount. If you have the time and you want to do it, go for it.

You can devein raw shrimp with the shell on or off. Either way, the technique is the same: hold the shrimp between your thumb and forefinger one third of an inch behind where the head was cut off. Place the tip of a sharp paring knife *with the blade facing up* in the slight indentation at the top of the shrimp's body (which may or may not have a dark spot of vein marking it), and push the blade toward the tail, making a shallow incision the length of the shrimp's back. This cut will expose the dark vein, which you can then remove with the tip of the paring knife.

❈ CRAB CAKES ❈

ASIDE FROM PICKING APART A STEAMED CRAB ON THE SPOT AND SUCKING ON ITS SHELL, THE BEST WAY TO CONCENTRATE and savor the subtle flavor of crab is to mold the flaky meat into a crab cake.

By now most everyone agrees that the crab cake of the 1970s and 1980s, a browned puck more cake than crab, is behind us. Bread crumbs, garlic powder, and red bell pepper are all too overpowering for the precious, pearly white shards of meat. The modern crab cake is all about crab. It's at once richer and less filling. And more expensive. The briny, fishlike sweetness of crab is preserved and accentuated, and what do you know? People seem eager to pay for the luxury of actually tasting crab in their crab cakes.

That doesn't mean that a crab cake must be a monastic contemplation of pure, unadorned crab. We're not afraid to season a perfect pound of crabmeat, or even to add a few bread crumbs, but we take pains to ensure that the seasonings complement the crab and don't overpower it. We blend in seasonings cautiously, judiciously: ingredients like parsley and green onion can provide texture and heft to the cake without tipping the balance.

❈

WHAT TO DRINK   *A rich, buttery, browned crab cake calls for a wine with a little zest, like a Spanish Albariño or a tart Pinot Grigio.*

For 4 people (eight cakes)
TIME: 20 minutes to cook, 30 minutes to rest

377

¾ pound picked jumbo lump or lump backfin crabmeat (see Sourcery, page 70)

3 tablespoons high-quality store-bought mayonnaise, such as Duke's or Hellmann's

1 teaspoon Dijon mustard

1 tablespoon fresh bread crumbs

2 heaping tablespoons chopped fresh flat-leaf parsley

½ teaspoon minced garlic

2 tablespoons minced green onion

½ teaspoon kosher salt, plus more to taste

¼ teaspoon freshly ground black pepper, plus more to taste

1 large egg, beaten

1 tablespoon peanut oil or canola oil, plus more if needed

1 lemon, cut into wedges, for garnish

1. Place the crabmeat in a large bowl. Add the mayonnaise, mustard, bread crumbs, parsley, garlic, green onion, salt, and pepper and gently fold the ingredients together with a rubber spatula or wooden spoon until they're thoroughly incorporated. Season with more salt and pepper if desired. Add the egg and fold it into the mixture.

2. Using a 2¼-inch cookie cutter, mold the crab mixture into 8 cakes. Wrap them in plastic wrap, 2 at a time. Apply gentle pressure to flatten the cakes slightly, and let them rest in the refrigerator for 30 minutes.

3. Preheat the oven to 350 degrees.

4. Remove the crab cakes from the refrigerator and unwrap. Place the oil in a 12-inch cast-iron skillet or sauté pan and heat over medium-high heat. When it shimmers, transfer 4 of the cakes to the skillet, taking care not to crowd them in the pan. Sauté until gently browned on both sides, about 2 minutes per side. Transfer to a plate lined with a paper towel and repeat with the remaining 4 cakes, adding more oil to the pan if it is too dry. Place all the crab cakes in a medium baking pan and bake until warmed through, about 5 minutes.

5. Garnish with lemon wedges and serve with Summer-Herbed Grits (page 148) or a simple green salad. Pass around a ramekin of Lee Bros. Tartar Sauce (page 526).

THE DOWNTOWN TOUCH FOR THIS DISH IS TO SUBSTITUTE FRESH HERBS LIKE MINT, BASIL, OR SHISO AND 1/2 TEASPOON LEMON ZEST FOR THE PARSLEY.

⁂ BOBO-STYLE OYSTER PIE ⁂

MACARONI AND CHEESE HAS NOTHING ON OYSTER PIE, WHICH WE BELIEVE MIGHT BE THE ULTIMATE COMFORT FOOD: A warm, sloppy, buttery, nutmeg and chile-spiced gratin of loosely heaped oysters and bread. It's a perfect winter treat—the one baked oyster dish that seems to celebrate the flavor of oysters rather than mask it.

Our friend Bobo Lee (no relation, alas) is the chef and owner of a small all-you-care-to-eat southern buffet attached to a gas station on Edisto Island, an agricultural island about 40 miles south of Charleston that used to be the epicenter of Sea Island cotton production. It's a banner day when we pull up to his buffet and find oyster pie among the offerings. Bobo is an accomplished chef and a lifelong outdoorsman, the sort of gentleman who can wrestle a wild boar into submission and locate the best patch of woods for chanterelle mushroom picking. He and his wife, Pam, do a fine business catering weddings and sophisticated barbecues (yes, there is such a thing; the luxury travel-planning outfit Butterfield & Robinson use their services extensively). If Bobo's particularly proud of the results, extra dishes from a Friday night catering gig might turn up on the Saturday lunch buffet. Bobo introduced us to our first oyster pie this way.

Now, when we put on an oyster roast, we set aside the stubborn oysters, the shreds, the ones that refuse to slip their shell in one piece, and shuck them and their liquor into a container, which we refrigerate. Then we use them in the next day's oyster pie.

WHAT TO DRINK · *A mellow white Burgundy with a little age, or a German Gewurztraminer or Riesling with some spice would complement the faint nutmeg and brine of oyster pie.*

For 6 people

TIME: 1½ hours

2 cups shucked oysters (about 24 medium oysters), with liquor (see Sourcery, page 76)

4 tablespoons unsalted butter, plus more for greasing the pan

1½ cups roughly chopped white mushrooms (about ¼ pound)

½ cup chopped shallot or yellow onion (about 1 large shallot or 1 small onion)

1 cup chopped celery (about 2 stalks with tops)

1 teaspoon kosher salt, plus more to taste

½ teaspoon ground cayenne or other hot red chile

½ teaspoon ground nutmeg

¼ teaspoon yellow mustard seeds, smashed

¼ teaspoon freshly ground black pepper, plus more to taste

1¼ cups heavy cream

5 thin slices white bread, such as Pepperidge Farm, crusts cut off, toasted

2 tablespoons chopped chives or scallions

1 recipe Savory Pie Crust (page 510)

1. Preheat the oven to 425 degrees. Drain the oysters with a colander or strainer, reserving the liquor (you should have about ½ cup).

2. In a medium skillet, melt the butter over medium-low heat until frothy. Add the mushrooms, shallot, celery, and salt and sauté, stirring frequently, until thoroughly softened, 7 to 10 minutes. Add the cayenne, nutmeg, mustard seeds, black pepper, oyster liquor, and heavy cream and cook, stirring, until the cream has thickened slightly and turned a light buff color, about 5 minutes. Adjust the seasoning to taste with salt and pepper.

3. Butter a 9-inch-square baking pan and place the toasted bread in the bottom to cover in a single layer, cutting the slices if necessary. Using a slotted spoon, layer the oysters evenly over the bread, then scatter the chives over them. With the slotted spoon, distribute the vegetables from the skillet evenly over the oysters. Pour the liquid in the skillet over them and add a couple pinches of pepper.

4.   With a lightly floured pin, roll out the pie crust on a lightly floured surface to make a lid 9 inches square and about ⅛ inch thick. Lay the crust over the top of the pie filling, tucking any excess inside the edges of the pan. With a sharp knife, slice 3 inch-long vents at even intervals in the crust to allow steam to escape. Bake until the crust is lightly and evenly browned, 30 to 40 minutes. Let cool on a rack for 10 minutes.

5.   With a metal spatula, divide the pie into 6 servings. Serve with Tuesday Collards (page 208) or Stolen Tomato Bisque (page 291).

❊ SHRIMP BURGERS ❊

QUICK
KNOCKOUT

IN SHRIMPING TOWNS SUCH AS THUNDERBOLT, GEORGIA, MCCLELLANVILLE, SOUTH CAROLINA, AND MOREHEAD CITY, NORTH Carolina, you can find shrimp burgers, but every place that serves them has a different "secret" recipe. Some shrimp burgers are chunky with diced shrimp and herbs, loosely bound, and pan-fried. Others are like an enormous shrimp dumpling, with a smooth, shrimpy paste enrobed by a crunchy, deep-fried crust. We tested six shrimp burger recipes for a story and found the one Robert Stehling makes at Charleston's Hominy Grill to be the finest, to our tastes. It's the chunkier style of burger, and its genius is its use of lemon zest. When we developed our own shrimp burger recipe, we added corn for texture and a sweetness that draws out the shrimp flavor, and added fresh ginger to give it complexity.

Use a gentle hand when flipping the burgers in the skillet.

❊

WHAT TO DRINK   *A cold, hoppy American ale like a Dogfish Head I.P.A. or a white wine with a little oak are great sips with shrimp burgers.*

For 4 people

TIME: 20 minutes to cook, 30 minutes to rest

2 quarts water

1 recipe Lee Bros. Shrimp Boil (page 553)

1 pound headless large shrimp (26–30 per pound; see Sourcery, page 374), shells on

2 tablespoons chopped scallions

¼ cup fresh corn kernels, cut from the cob (about ½ ear)

2 tablespoons chopped fresh flat-leaf parsley

1 tablespoon grated fresh ginger

1½ teaspoons lemon zest (from 1 lemon)

3 tablespoons high-quality store-bought mayonnaise, such as Duke's or Hellmann's

1 cup bread crumbs, preferably fresh (from about 2 slices bread)

Kosher salt to taste

Freshly ground black pepper to taste

Pepper Vinegar to taste (optional; page 518)

1 egg, beaten

1½ tablespoons canola oil

1. In a 3-quart saucepan, bring the water and shrimp boil to a boil over high heat. Turn off the heat. Add the shrimp and let stand until they are just pink, about 2 minutes. Drain and run under cold water to stop the cooking. Peel the shrimp (and devein them if you wish; see "How To: Deveining Shrimp," page 376) and chop coarsely. You should have 1¾ cups chopped shrimp.

2. In a large bowl, mix the shrimp with the scallions, corn, parsley, ginger, and lemon zest. Stir in the mayonnaise and bread crumbs and season with salt, black pepper, and pepper vinegar. Add the egg and gently fold with a wooden spoon or rubber spatula until evenly distributed.

3. Form the shrimp mixture into 4 patties, each 3½ inches in diameter. Wrap the patties in plastic wrap and let stand in the refrigerator for 30 minutes.

4. Remove the burgers from the refrigerator and unwrap. Place the oil in a 12-inch skillet and heat over high heat. When it shimmers, add the burgers and sauté until both sides are gently browned, about 3 minutes per side. Drain on a dinner plate lined with a paper towel.

5. Serve on toasted hamburger buns with lettuce, tomato, and Lee Bros. Tartar Sauce (page 526).

❋ GRILLED MAHIMAHI ❋ WITH FRESH PEACH RELISH

QUICK KNOCKOUT

MAHIMAHI IS A DELICIOUSLY FATTY OCEAN FISH WITH DENSE FLESH THAT'S GREAT FOR GRILLING. ITS BUTTERY TEXTURE makes it perfect with playful sour/sweet/hot flavors. We love to pair a tropical fruit "relish" with mahimahi—not a true cooked relish, but a mixture more like a salsa, made of fruit, onion, olive oil, vinegar, and herbs. Since summer is prime grilling time, we typically use ripe peaches in our fresh relish.

If your cookout gets rained out, have no fear: dust the fillets with stone-ground cornmeal and sear them in a smoking hot cast-iron skillet with a tablespoon or two of a high-heat oil such as grapeseed or canola. The fish will have a crisp outside and a tender inside.

Mahimahi is quite plentiful in markets (and in most parts of the country is a sustainable choice), so you shouldn't have a difficult time finding it. If you do, some ocean-friendly alternatives that work well with this fresh peach relish are farmed cod and haddock.

Serve this dish with a summery salad, such as Coleslaw (page 195) or Best Family Farm Corn-Bread Salad (page 188).

❋

WHAT TO DRINK   *The cilantro and jalapeño in this relish argue for a bold white wine from Washington State or New Zealand.*

2 large ripe peaches (4–6 ounces each), washed, pitted, and finely diced

2 tablespoons seeded, minced fresh jalapeño pepper (about 1 small jalapeño)

½ cup diced red onion (1 small or ½ medium onion)

¼ cup coarsely chopped cilantro

1 large navel orange (about 8 ounces), supremed (see Technique, page 192), with juice

2 tablespoons white wine vinegar

½ cup extra-virgin olive oil

Kosher salt to taste

Freshly ground black pepper to taste

Four ¾-inch-thick mahimahi fillets (about 6 ounces each)

1. Prepare the relish by thoroughly mixing the peaches, jalapeño, onion, cilantro, orange, vinegar, and 6 tablespoons olive oil together in a large bowl. Season to taste with salt and pepper. Cover and let stand in the refrigerator until ready to serve, not more than 24 hours.

2. Build a banked fire of coals in your grill, or turn the flame on a gas grill to high. Lightly brush the surface of the fish fillets with olive oil and season them with salt and pepper. When the fire is very hot (you can hold your hand 5 inches above the grate no longer than 3 seconds), grill the fillets, taking care to flip them gently, until the centers are opaque, about 2 minutes per side. If they need further cooking, place them over the cooler side of the fire.

3. To serve, place the fillets on 4 plates and spoon the fresh peach relish liberally over them.

❊ FRIED WHITING ❊

IN CHARLESTON, FRIED FISH AND GRITS ARE OFTEN SERVED FOR BREAKFAST. IF WE'RE TOO LAZY TO START UP THE FRYER ON A groggy morning, we'll head to Martha Lou's Kitchen, a small pink restaurant near the stevedores' union hall and the port, where Martha Lou Gadsen (or her daughter, Deborah, or Deborah's daughter, Lisa) fries whiting to order. It always emerges with a thin, perfectly salty, crisp crust.

We adore whiting, and the fact that it is inexpensive makes its delicate sweetness all the more appealing. But you can use any variety of white-fleshed fish that has slender fillets (or fillets that can be cut down to manageable pieces); trout, mullet, porgy, and red drum are all delicious fried.

This isn't the heavily battered fried fish you find in the British Isles. Our fry dredge is typical of coastal South Carolina: it has just enough texture to give a thin, delectable crust, but it stands back and lets the fish shine through.

❊

WHAT TO DRINK   *For breakfast, fried whiting goes well with a cup of coffee or a Coca-Cola; for brunch, a Gran's Mimosa (page 34) is in order.*

For 6 people

TIME: 35 minutes

2–3 cups peanut oil or canola oil
1 recipe Lee Bros. All-Purpose Fry Dredge
    (page 552)

12 whiting fillets
1 lemon, cut into wedges, for garnish
1 recipe Lee Bros. Tartar Sauce (page 526)

1. Preheat the oven to 225 degrees.

2. Pour the oil into a large cast-iron skillet to a depth of about ½ inch (about 2 cups for a 10-inch skillet, 3 cups for a 12-inch skillet). Heat over medium-high heat until the temperature on a candy thermometer reads 365 degrees.

3. Scatter the dredge on a large dinner plate. Press each fillet into the dredge on both sides and shake off the excess. Once the oil reaches 365 degrees, add 2 dredged fillets, using tongs or a slotted spatula, and cover. Fry until the edges begin to turn golden and the side face down in the oil is golden brown, about 1½ minutes. Adjust the heat as necessary to maintain the temperature between 350 and 365 degrees. Flip each fillet, cover the skillet again, and fry, covered, until the side facing down is golden brown, about 30 seconds.

4. Transfer the fried fillets to a plate lined with a double thickness of paper towels. Test one end for doneness (beneath the crust, the flesh should be evenly opaque). If the fish needs more time to cook, adjust the time for succeeding batches. Place the plate in the oven to warm. Repeat, frying 2 fillets at a time and stacking the fried fish on the plate in the oven until all the fish is cooked.

5. Serve immediately, with the lemon wedges and tartar sauce. If serving for breakfast, Simple Grits (page 146) are a must.

Fishing boats tied up at the docks in Apalachicola, Florida, on the Gulf Coast.

❄ FRIED OYSTERS ❄

FRIED OYSTERS ARE AWESOME, BUT EVEN TEN YEARS AGO,
WE SAW THEM AS A RARE INDULGENCE. NOW THAT WE CAN GET A
nearly year-round supply of shucked oysters in pint-sized tubs, we eat them about once a month.

The dredge we use in these is the same as we use in our Tuesday Fried Chicken (page 333) and Fried Whiting (page 386): it yields a thin, nearly greaseless, crispy-salty-peppery crust. There are roughly 24 oysters in a pint, so we budget at least a dozen for each guest if we're serving them as the main event (see the two variations below). If the fried oysters are an hors d'oeuvre, serve them in brown wrapping paper folded into a cone and set into a silver cup or a pint glass.

As always, taste the oyster liquor as soon as you open the tub of shucked oysters (unless you're pregnant or have a compromised immune system); if the liquor isn't briny enough, scatter 1 teaspoon salt (per pint) and toss to distribute evenly.

❄

WHAT TO DRINK   *A cool lager or wheat beer is a refreshing chaser for fried oysters any time of year.*

For 6 people

TIME: 35 minutes

2–3 cups peanut oil or canola oil

1 cup Lee Bros. All-Purpose Fry Dredge (page 552)

72 shucked oysters (about 3 pints; see Sourcery, page 76), drained

1 recipe Zesty Cocktail Sauce (page 525)

1 recipe Lee Bros. Tartar Sauce (page 526)

1 lemon, cut into wedges, for garnish

1. Preheat the oven to 225 degrees.

2. Pour the oil into a large cast-iron skillet to a depth of about ½ inch (about 2 cups for a 10-inch skillet, 3 cups for a 12-inch skillet). Heat over medium-high heat until the temperature on a candy thermometer reads 365 degrees.

3. Scatter the dredge on a large dinner plate. Using your hands or 2 wooden spoons, gently toss the oysters in the dredge in batches, about a dozen at a time. Once the oil reaches 365 degrees, transfer the oysters to the skillet in batches, about a dozen at a time, using a slotted spoon. Agitate them in the oil until they're evenly browned, 30 to 45 seconds.

4. Transfer the fried oysters to a plate lined with a double thickness of paper towels and place the plate in the oven to warm. Repeat until all the oysters have been fried. Adjust the heat as necessary to maintain the temperature between 350 and 365 degrees.

5. Serve the oysters with cocktail sauce and tartar sauce, on plates garnished with plenty of lemon wedges. Appropriate accompaniments include Coleslaw (page 195) or Best Family Farm Corn-Bread Salad (page 188), or you can use the oysters as noted in the variations.

VARIATION—FRIED OYSTER SALAD: THIS IS A MAIN-COURSE SALAD FIT FOR DESERVING FRIENDS AND RELATIVES. PREPARE THE BEST FAMILY FARM CORN-BREAD SALAD ON PAGE 188, OMITTING THE CORN BREAD BUT FOLLOWING THE RECIPE TO THE END SO THE SALAD IS DRESSED AND READY TO GO. FRY THE OYSTERS. DIVIDE THE DRESSED SALAD AMONG 6 DINNER PLATES AND ARRANGE A DOZEN FRIED OYSTERS OVER EACH PLATE. PASS WITH LEMON WEDGES, SALT, AND FRESHLY GROUND BLACK PEPPER.

VARIATION—FRIED OYSTER SANDWICH: YOU MAY WONDER WHY WE CALL THIS A SANDWICH RATHER THAN A PO' BOY, THE LATTER BEING THE CORRECT TERM FOR THE FRIED OYSTER SANDWICHES SERVED ON LARGE ROLLS IN NEW ORLEANS (SINCE ADOPTED BY JUST ABOUT EVERY GREAT SEAFOOD SHACK FROM THE PEARL OYSTER BAR IN NEW YORK TO LOS ANGELES'S HUNGRY CAT). OUR REASONING IS THIS: OUTSIDE OUR OWN KITCHEN, WE'VE ALWAYS FOUND A PO' BOY TO BE, WELL, PO'—TOO LEAN ON OYSTERS AND OVERGENEROUS ON BREAD. WE ENCOURAGE YOU TO USE THINLY SLICED WHITE BREAD, PREFERABLY A HOMEMADE LOAF WITH A HINT OF SWEETNESS, SUCH AS SALLY LUNN (PAGE 500). FOR EACH SANDWICH, SPREAD 2 SLICES BREAD WITH TARTAR SAUCE. PLACE 1 SLICE ON A PLATE WITH THE TARTAR-SAUCED SIDE FACING UP. LAY A LEAF OF BUTTER LETTUCE ON THE BREAD AND A VERY THIN SLICE (OR TWO) OF TOMATO ON THE LETTUCE. THEN DO YOUR BEST TO STACK A DOZEN OYSTERS ON TOP OF THE TOMATO. TOP WITH THE SECOND TARTAR-SAUCED SLICE OF BREAD. GARNISH WITH A LEMON WEDGE AND SERVE WITH A SIDE PORTION OF COLESLAW (PAGE 195).

A basic sea island farm kitchen has the essentials for making simple meals from the fish, shrimp, oysters, and vegetables harvested from the property.

❋ FRIED SHRIMP ❋

THE SOUTH CAROLINA SHRIMP WE GET FOR SIX MONTHS OF THE YEAR, FROM MAY TO OCTOBER, ARE SWEET AND DELICIOUS and perfectly sized. They're large enough to make a generous mouthful, but not so large that they get too chewy the way the extra-large and jumbos tend to. Peeling them requires some effort, but we think you'll agree that crisp, cleanly fried shrimp are an incomparable culinary pleasure. Serve with a dab of cocktail sauce and a squeeze of lemon.

❋

WHAT TO DRINK   *The sweetness of shrimp and the crispy fried dredge argues for a racy white wine or a malty beer.*

For 6 people
TIME: 45 minutes

3 pounds headless large shrimp (26–30 per pound; see Sourcery, page 374), shells on

2–3 cups peanut oil or canola oil

1 cup Lee Bros. All-Purpose Fry Dredge (page 552)

1 lemon, cut into wedges, for garnish

391

1.   Peel the shrimp, leaving the tails on. Devein if you wish (in this recipe, deveining has the benefit of revealing more surface area for the dredge to cling to). Discard the shells or reserve them for Sunday Shrimp Broth (page 536).

2.   Preheat the oven to 225 degrees. Pour the oil into a large cast-iron skillet to a depth of about ½ inch (about 2 cups for a 10-inch skillet, 3 cups for a 12-inch skillet). Heat over medium-high heat until the temperature on a candy thermometer reads 365 degrees.

3.   Scatter the dredge on a large dinner plate. Using your hands or two wooden spoons, gently toss the shrimp in the dredge in batches, about a dozen at a time, until they're evenly coated. When the oil reaches 365 degrees, transfer the shrimp to the skillet in batches, about a dozen at a time, with a slotted spoon. Fry, turning the shrimp as they brown, until they're evenly golden brown, about 1½ minutes per side. Adjust the heat as necessary to maintain the temperature between 350 and 365 degrees.

4.   Transfer the fried shrimp to a plate lined with a double thickness of paper towels and place the plate in the oven to warm. Repeat until all the shrimp have been fried.

5.   To serve, place about a dozen shrimp on each of 6 plates. Serve with Coleslaw (page 195) or Crispy Fried Okra (page 217), and garnish with lemon wedges and liberal amounts of Zesty Cocktail Sauce (page 525).

☀ LOWCOUNTRY SEAFOOD PLATTER ☀
À LA WRECK

THE WRECK JUST MIGHT BE OUR FAVORITE RESTAURANT IN CHARLESTON. WHEN WE'RE UP FOR A DOSE OF CLASSIC SOUTH-ern food with sly contemporary twists, we'll head to Robert Stehling's Hominy Grill. But when we want straightforward fried seafood platters (and free boiled peanuts on the tables for snacking), we head to the Wreck of the Richard and Charlene, a fish shack known to locals simply as the Wreck. It's in the old part of Mt. Pleasant, on an inlet from Charleston Harbor called Shem Creek.

The restaurant overlooks the docks where the shrimp boats tie up, and it's a very personal place. Fred Scott, who owns it, is a guy who keeps his life (and the lives of his waitstaff) simple: no credit cards are accepted, you circle what you want on the menu with a thick marker, and the cost of each dish is calculated very precisely (seafood platter: $18.87) so that when the 6 percent South Carolina sales tax gets added, the bill is always a round number. (Cash or check only, please.) We adore the fried seafood platter they serve here, which comes with a strip of fried whit-ing, a handful of fried oysters, a scattering of fried shrimp, a hushpuppy, a small cake of fried, bacon-laced grits, and a generous spoonful of red rice.

With our humble cookbook, you can now attempt to recreate the Wreck's fried seafood plat-ter in the comfort of your own home, simply by following the recipes on previous pages. It may not be quick, but it is relatively simple, since you can fry the whiting, oysters, shrimp, and grits cakes in the same oil. We use a 3-quart enameled cast-iron saucepan filled with about a quart of oil, so we can virtually double the amount of protein that gets fried in each batch.

Assembling these platters is an unforgettable group event, so make sure you have plenty of friends around to lend a hand, take snapshots, and tell stories twenty years hence.

WHAT TO DRINK   *A fried food platter demands a light, tonic beverage—Lee Bros. Sweet Tea (page 23) or an effervescent, simple wine like Vouvray Brut, Spanish Cava, or Italian Prosecco*

For 6 people

TIME: 1 hour

3 pounds headless large shrimp (26–30 per
    pound; see Sourcery, page 374),
    shells on
1 quart peanut oil or canola oil
3 batches Lee Bros. All-Purpose Fry Dredge
    (page 552)
72 shucked oysters (about 3 pints; see
    Sourcery, page 76), drained
12 whiting fillets
1 batch Grits Croutons (page 157): follow the
    recipe for Deep-Fried Grits Cakes, but
    add chopped scallions and a tablespoon

of bacon grease to the grits to get them
    exactly like the Wreck's; cut them into
    2-inch cubes instead of ¾-inch cubes;
    and follow the recipe only up to the
    frying step.
1 batch Red Rice (page 172)
1 batch South Carolina–Style Hushpuppies
    (page 515)
3 lemons cut into wedges, for garnish
2 batches Lee Bros. Tartar Sauce (page 526)
2 batches Zesty Cocktail Sauce (page 525)

1.   Preheat the oven to 225 degrees.

2.   Peel the shrimp, leaving the tails on. Devein if you wish (in this recipe, deveining has the benefit of revealing more surface area for the dredge to cling to). Discard the shells or reserve them for Sunday Shrimp Broth (page 536).

3.   Pour the oil into a 3-quart enameled cast-iron saucepan and heat over medium heat until a candy thermometer reads 365 degrees. Place each batch of fry dredge in a separate 1-gallon plastic bag with a zipper lock. Place the shrimp in one bag, the oysters in the second, and the whiting in the third. Shake the bags until the fish and shellfish are evenly coated with dredge. Remove from the bags and shake off the excess dredge.

4. When the oil reaches 365 degrees, add the shrimp in batches, about 24 at a time, with a slotted spoon. Fry, turning them as they brown, until they are evenly golden brown, about 1½ minutes, adjusting the heat as necessary to maintain the temperature between 350 and 365 degrees. Transfer the fried shrimp to a plate lined with a double thickness of paper towels and place the plate in the oven to warm. Repeat until all the shrimp have been fried.

5. Using a slotted spoon, transfer the oysters to the oil, about 24 at a time, and agitate them until they are evenly browned, 30 to 45 seconds. Transfer to a second plate lined with a double thickness of paper towels and place the plate in the oven to warm. Repeat until all the oysters have been fried.

6. Using tongs or a slotted spatula, add 4 dredged whiting fillets to the oil and cover. Fry until the edges begin to turn golden and the sides that face the bottom of the pan are golden brown, about 1½ minutes. Flip each fillet, cover the saucepan again, and fry until the side facing down is golden brown, about 30 seconds. Transfer to a third plate lined with a double thickness of paper towels and place the plate in the oven to warm. Repeat until all the whiting have been fried.

7. Using a slotted spatula, transfer the croutons to the oil in one batch. Fry until evenly golden brown, about 2 minutes per side. Transfer to the plate with the whiting. Gather the red rice and prepare to assemble the platters.

8. To serve, place 2 fried whiting fillets, a dozen shrimp, and a dozen oysters on one half of each of 6 oval plates. On the other side, arrange the red rice, a couple hushpuppies, and a grits crouton. Garnish each plate with several lemon wedges and pass tartar sauce and cocktail sauce at the table.

❊ FLOUNDER WITH GRANNY SMITH APPLE ❊ AND GREEN TOMATO PAN GRAVY

QUICK
KNOCKOUT

ONE OF THE MANY MARVELS OF THE SOUTH CAROLINA AQUARIUM, A SCULPTURAL MODERN BUILDING THAT JUTS OUT OVER Charleston Harbor and affords a terrific view of the working port, is the flounder exhibit. Flounders are a perfectly flat, bottom-dwelling fish with both eyes facing up from one side of their head. They're extremely adaptable to their environment. At the aquarium, two flounders swim in a tank with a skid of beach sand at the bottom; when you approach the tank, the fish bury themselves in the sand, becoming so well camouflaged that they're nearly impossible to find (although the sign on the wall is quite helpful in this regard).

Flounder is a tasty white fish whose flavor gets amplified with a quick sauté in brown butter. We like to pair it with a sauce like this one, which has a lively triple dose of tartness, from roasted green tomato, lime juice, and a Granny Smith apple, whose sweetness bridges the acidity of the tomato and lime. But it's a lean sauce—as close as the Lee Bros. get to spa cuisine—so we like to add a touch of fat: once the fish are pan-fried and crisp, we transfer them to a plate and pour the sauce into the skillet and whisk it around so it picks up some of the brown butter in the bottom. Of course, you can skip that step and add olive oil, by teaspoonfuls, to taste, and warm the sauce in a pan on the stovetop or in a glass bowl in a microwave oven. Either way, it's delicious. If you can't find the chervil that provides the aromatic top note in the sauce, use stronger-tasting cilantro, but only half as much.

Makes 4 fillets

TIME: 30 minutes

1 large green tomato or 3 large tomatillos, cored

2 tablespoons lime juice (from 1 small lime)

1 large Granny Smith apple

2 cups chervil or 1 cup cilantro, washed and dried, stems trimmed (about 1 bunch chervil, ½ bunch cilantro)

½ small jalapeño pepper, trimmed, seeded, and finely diced

1 clove garlic, peeled and minced

Kosher salt to taste

Freshly ground black pepper to taste

2 tablespoons olive oil (optional)

1 batch Lee Bros. All-Purpose Fry Dredge (page 552)

4 flounder fillets (1–1¼ pounds total)

3 tablespoons unsalted butter

1.   Place the tomato in a small cast-iron skillet or ovenproof dish and slide it beneath the broiler, about 3 inches from the flame or heating element. Cook, turning when the skin becomes blackened, until the tomato is blackened all over, 6 to 8 minutes (4 to 6 minutes for tomatillos). Remove the pan from the broiler and let the tomato cool.

2.   While the tomato broils, pour the lime juice into a medium bowl. Grate the apple with a microplane or other fine-gauge grater, skin and all, into the bowl. Toss the apple in the lime juice several times as you work to keep it from turning brown.

3.   When the tomato has cooled enough to handle, peel it and place it in a food processor or blender. Add the apple-lime mixture, chervil, jalapeño, and garlic and pulse 2 or 3 times for about 2 seconds each, until the mixture is a chunky puree. Season to taste with salt and pepper, and olive oil, if using.

4. Spread the fry dredge evenly on a large dinner plate and press both sides of each fillet into it, making sure all surfaces are evenly coated. Melt the butter in a 12-inch skillet over medium heat until frothy but not yet browned. Fry the fillets in batches, 2 at a time, until lightly golden brown, about 3 minutes per side. Reserve the first batch on a plate lined with a double thickness of paper towels in a warm place (the oven may still be warm from broiling the tomato).

5. When all 4 fillets have been fried, pour the puree into the skillet, if not using olive oil, and whisk occasionally until it just comes to a simmer. Turn off the heat.

6. To serve, place a fillet on each of 4 plates and spoon the gravy on top. Serve with Crispy Fried Okra (page 217), Tuesday Collards (page 208), or simply with hot white rice.

A proud shellfish wholesaler in Apalachicola,
Florida, on the Gulf Coast.

❊ CRAB AND SHRIMP CUSTARDS ❊

THIS PLAY ON TRADITIONAL NINETEENTH-CENTURY "POTTED" SEAFOOD DISHES (BRITISH STAPLES BROUGHT TO OUR SHORES BY the colonists) works the sweetness of the two iconic Lowcountry shellfish, crab and shrimp, into a cheese-laden custard. It's essentially a miniature shellfish quiche, a nice comfort on rainy days and winter weekends, a great first course, or lunch on its own when paired with a leafy green salad.

❊

WHAT TO DRINK   *A glass of dry fino sherry would match well with the warm shellfish custard, especially on a rainy, London-like day.*

For 6 people
TIME: 45 minutes

1 tablespoon Lee Bros. Shrimp Boil (see page 553)

1 quart water

1 cup half-and-half

1 cup picked crabmeat (see Sourcery, page 70)

½ pound headless large shrimp (26–30 per pound; see Sourcery, page 374), shells on

1 large egg

3 large egg yolks

1 cup finely grated sharp cheddar cheese

1 teaspoon kosher salt

1½ teaspoons freshly ground pepper, preferably white

3 dashes Worcestershire sauce

1. Preheat the oven to 350 degrees. Set a 3-quart kettle full of water to boil over high heat.

2. In a medium-sized saucepan add the shrimp boil to the 1 quart water and bring to a vigorous boil over high heat.

3. In a 2-quart saucepan, bring the half-and-half to a simmer over medium-high heat. Add the crab and turn off the heat immediately; allow the crab to steep for 2 minutes. Drain the half-and-half into a small bowl, reserving the crab in another small bowl, and set the bowl of half-and-half in the freezer for 5 minutes to take the heat off.

4. When the water seasoned with shrimp boil has come to a boil, turn off the heat, add the shrimp, and cook until they are firm, about 2 minutes. Transfer the shrimp to a colander to drain and run them under cold water to stop the cooking. Peel, then chop them roughly.

5. In a large bowl, whisk the eggs, egg yolks, half-and-half, and cheese together until well blended. Add the shrimp, crab, salt, pepper, and Worcestershire sauce and stir to combine. Divide the mixture among six 4-ounce buttered ramekins.

6. Place a dish towel in a 9-×-13-inch roasting pan and set the ramekins on the towel. Carefully pour hot water from the kettle into the roasting pan until it reaches halfway up the sides of the ramekins. Bake until the custards are set, about 25 minutes.

7. Serve each ramekin on a plate, with a side of dressed salad greens.

❀ ROASTED WHOLE YELLOWTAIL SNAPPER ❀ WITH SWEET POTATOES AND SCALLIONS

QUICK
KNOCKOUT

EVERY KITCHEN SAGE KNOWS THAT FISH COOKED ON THE BONE JUST TASTES BETTER. SIMPLE REASON: THE FLESH, SAND-wiched as it is between the fatty skin and the gelatin-rich backbone, cooks in an environment with more moisture and fat, so it's sweeter and more luscious than filleted fish. Tasting a whole fish for the first time is as stunning as first tasting a genuinely fresh egg.

Whole fish is also quite simple to prepare, and this dish is the perfect weeknight supper, because the starch and protein are cooked in the same pan. All you need are some fresh salad greens and Sneaky Collards (page 205) or Crispy Fried Okra (page 217) and you're good to go.

Boning a cooked whole fish is easy. Three simple cuts enable you to lift the fillet cleanly from the spine, leaving most of the bones behind. The first cut is vertical, from the "shoulder" of the fish—a point just behind the top of the head—down toward the belly; the second is a short verti-cal cut through the body just in front of the tail fin; the third is a shallow incision that traces the top ridge and connects the first two cuts. Gentle pressure with a dull knife, a spatula, or even the back of a spoon will release portions of the fillet from the flat bone structure. After removing one side of the fish, gently lift the backbone, head, and tail, leaving the bottom fillet behind.

If yellowtail snapper isn't a sustainable choice in your area, try black bass or red drum.

❀

WHAT TO DRINK   *The heartiness of the snapper and its sweet potato accompaniment make this fish dish as good a pairing with a light red wine—a fruity Pinot Noir, for example—as with a white wine.*

For 2 people

TIME: 35 minutes

1½ pounds sweet potatoes, peeled and cut into
⅓-inch-thick disks

¼ cup extra-virgin olive oil

Juice of 1 lemon

1 teaspoon kosher salt

1 teaspoon freshly ground black pepper

1½ pounds whole yellowtail snapper, cleaned
and gutted, gills, fins, and scales
removed

2 bunches scallions

4 sprigs fresh thyme

1. Preheat the oven to 350 degrees.

2. Lay the sweet potatoes in a single layer in a 12-inch cast-iron skillet or other large ovenproof dish. Brush them with 2 tablespoons olive oil. Squeeze the lemon juice from half the lemon over them and season with ½ teaspoon salt and ½ teaspoon pepper. Roast until the potatoes are just tender when pierced with a fork, about 10 minutes.

3. Lay the fish flat on a clean cutting board and make two vertical, bone-deep cuts 2 inches apart into the thickest part of the body on each side. Brush both sides and the cavity with the remaining 2 tablespoons oil and season both sides of the fish and the cavity with the remaining ½ teaspoon salt and ½ teaspoon black pepper.

4. Trim the roots and any wilted leaves from the scallions and slice them thinly, on the bias, from the root end about 5 inches up their stalks. Reserve the tops. Press half the sliced scallions into the cuts on both sides of the fish. Double the tops over, squeeze tightly to bruise them and release their aromatic oils, and stuff them into the cavity of the fish, along with the thyme.

5. Lay the fish flat on the sweet potatoes in the skillet, squeeze the juice from the remaining half lemon over it, and scatter the remaining sliced scallions on top. Roast until the flesh of the fish nearest the bones is opaque, about 20 minutes. Remove from the oven and bone (see the headnote).

6. To serve, place each fillet on a plate with a few slices of sweet potato and a tangle of the scallion greens from the fish's cavity.

❋ OYSTER DRESSING ❋

THIS DRESSING (IN THE OLD-FASHIONED SENSE OF THE WORD) IS A GREAT STUFFING FOR POULTRY: TOASTED CUBES OF A tasty, homemade cornmeal and flour bread tossed with a soupy mixture of onions and celery cooked in butter and oyster liquor. We prepare it most often as a side dish for roast turkey, but it also makes a smashing lunch with poached eggs draped over the top or paired with a simple green salad. You could use Crispy Corn Bread (page 497) in this dish, but we prefer our dressing bread, a slight variation on our corn-bread recipe that lightens it with a touch of flour.

For 6 people
TIME: 45 minutes

1 recipe Dressing Bread (page 499)

1 pint shucked oysters (see Sourcery, page 76)

2 tablespoons unsalted butter

1 teaspoon kosher salt

½ teaspoon freshly ground black pepper

1¼ cups chopped celery (about two 12-inch-
     long stalks)

1¼ cups chopped yellow onion (about 1 large
     onion)

2 large eggs, beaten

½ cup dry, flavorful white wine, such as
     Sancerre or Chardonnay

½ cup Sunday Chicken Broth (page 532)

1. Preheat the oven to 350 degrees.

2. Cut the bread into 1-inch dice and place in an even layer in a 9-inch-square roasting pan. Toast on the top rack of the oven until gently browned, about 8 minutes. Remove and reserve in a large bowl.

3. Drain the oysters over a 12-inch skillet or sauté pan and reserve in a bowl. Add the butter, salt, and pepper to the oyster liquor and cook over medium heat until the butter has melted, about 2 minutes. Add the celery and onion and cook, stirring, until the vegetables have softened, about 10 minutes. Add the vegetables and oysters to the bowl of toasted bread and toss gently with a wooden spoon to distribute evenly.

4. In a small bowl, beat the eggs. Add the wine and broth and whisk to incorporate. Pour the mixture evenly, in a thin stream, over the contents of the oyster bowl and toss again with the wooden spoon. (At this point you may stuff the dressing into a chicken or turkey. This recipe will easily stuff an 18- to 20-pound turkey; if you are stuffing a smaller bird, bake the excess dressing in a small roasting pan, loaf pan, or skillet.) Transfer the dressing to the roasting pan and bake until the top is golden brown, about 35 minutes.

5. Serve immediately.

❃ SHRIMP POT PIES ❃

IT FIGURES THAT WE WOULD PUT A COASTAL SPIN ON CHICKEN POT PIE. THESE INDIVIDUAL SHRIMP POT PIES ARE FUN TO make. Guests are always fascinated when you serve them; most haven't had a pot pie since they left the high school cafeteria. To a spicy shrimp stock we add carrot and celery, then we thicken the gravy with a little flour and cream and spike it with white wine. The design challenge is to pack into every forkful of pie a shrimp, shards of crust, fresh peas, and some irresistible white wine gravy.

We consider shrimp pot pie the perfect autumn lunch.

❃

WHAT TO DRINK   *A glass of the crisp, citrusy, fruity Chardonnay, Sauvignon Blanc, or Riesling used in cooking the pot pie would be a fine accompaniment to the dish.*

For 4 people

TIME: 1½ hours

¾ pound headless large shrimp (26–30 per pound; see Sourcery, page 374), shells on

2 cups water

6 black peppercorns

1 bay leaf

½ teaspoon Lee Bros. Shrimp Boil (page 553), plus more to taste

2 stalks celery, 1 cut into 1-inch rods, 1 finely diced

1 recipe Savory Pie Crust (page 510)

3 ounces slab bacon or 2 strips thick-cut bacon, diced

2 tablespoons unsalted butter, plus more for greasing the ramekins

½ cup finely diced carrot (about 1 medium carrot)

¼ cup finely diced onion (about 1 small onion)

2 tablespoons all-purpose flour

¾ cup heavy cream

¼ cup crisp, citrusy, fruity white wine, such as steel-aged Chardonnay, Sauvignon Blanc, or Riesling

1 teaspoon chopped fresh thyme

Kosher salt to taste

Freshly ground black pepper to taste

½ cup shelled English peas, preferably fresh

4 stems fresh flat-leaf parsley, washed and dried

1. Preheat the oven to 425 degrees.

2. Peel the shrimp, reserving both shells and shrimp, and devein them if you wish. Place the water in a 2-quart saucepan and bring to a boil over high heat. Add the shrimp shells, peppercorns, bay leaf, shrimp boil, and celery rods. Reduce the heat to medium and simmer vigorously until the liquid has reduced by half, about 25 minutes. (Alternatively, you can discard the shells and substitute 1 cup clam juice for the shrimp stock.)

3. While the stock simmers, roll out the pie crust to a rough rectangle about ⅛ inch thick. Set an empty 8-ounce ramekin top side down on one quadrant of the dough. Dip the tip of a knife in flour and trace around the edge of the ramekin to cut a lid for 1 pie. Repeat on the other 3 quadrants. Cut three 1-inch-long slits, parallel to one another and about ¾ inch apart, into each lid, to let the steam vent during cooking. Place the lids in one layer on a sheet of waxed paper and refrigerate until needed. Wrap any extra dough in plastic and refrigerate or freeze for future use.

4. Scatter the diced bacon in a 12-inch cast-iron skillet or sauté pan over medium-high heat. With a slotted spoon, move the pieces around until the bacon is firm and just golden brown, about 3 minutes. Transfer to a small bowl. Add the butter to the skillet and heat until frothy. Add the diced celery, carrot, and onion and cook until just softening, 2 to 3 minutes. Scatter the flour over the vegetables and cook, stirring constantly, until the flour is well incorporated into the fat, about 2 minutes more. Whisk in the shrimp stock, cream, wine, and thyme and continue to cook until the mixture comes to a gentle simmer. Reduce the heat to low and simmer, stirring occasionally, until the bisque is thick enough to coat the back of a spoon, about 8 minutes. Season to taste with salt and pepper, adding shrimp boil if desired. Turn off the heat and add the peas and the reserved bacon.

5. Grease four 8-ounce ramekins with unsalted butter and divide the bisque among them, then divide the shrimp among them. Place 1 crust on top of each ramekin and bake on the top rack until the crusts are golden brown, about 20 to 25 minutes.

6. To serve, place each ramekin on a plate, and garnish with a stem of parsley. Serve with Lemon Grits (page 153) or Squash and Mushroom Hominy (page 219).

❋ SHAD ROE WITH MADEIRA AND ONION GRAVY ❋

QUICK
KNOCKOUT

SHAD ROE ARE THE EGG SACS OF AMERICAN SHAD, A FISH FOUND ALONG THE ATLANTIC COAST FROM QUEBEC TO THE Florida Keys. Shad are anadromous fish, which means that they live most of their lives in saltwater, but in the spring they migrate to freshwater rivers to spawn. Their roe look almost like two fresh sausage links laid side by side, and they have a meaty, almost livery flavor that we adore.

Shad roe are also a favorite in our family because their arrival in Charleston markets in March often accompanies the first signs of spring. When we were growing up, shad roe seemed to occupy the rarefied precincts of old country clubs like the Yeamans Hall Club in Moncks Corner, about fifteen miles north of Charleston, where the kitchen served a shot glass of ice-cold Red Cheek apple juice (or "chilled cider," according to the menu) between the main course and the dessert. But shad roe aren't stuffy at all; they're rustic, easy to prepare, and need little more than a wisp of bacon and lemon.

We add a touch of Madeira, too. While this recipe doesn't call for a great quantity, try to find a five-year-old or ten-year-old Madeira. These blends are available at most liquor stores, and they represent superb value for money (see "Madeira," page 41). You will be happy you made the effort, both for what it does to this dish and for what's left. It makes a great aperitif and a great wine to sip after dinner, with an assortment of cheeses.

WHAT TO DRINK   *Drinking a fine Madeira with shad roe is recommended, but for all occasions and budgets a good rosé would flatter this dish and get the spring season off to a stylish start—try our old standby, Chateau D'Aqueria's minerally Tavel.*

For 4 people

TIME: 30 minutes

4 sets medium shad roe (about 2 pounds)

2 tablespoons stone-ground cornmeal

Kosher salt

Freshly ground black pepper

¼ pound slab bacon or 4 strips thick-cut
    bacon, diced

2 tablespoons extra-virgin olive oil

¼ cup finely chopped green bell pepper (about
    ½ pepper)

2 medium yellow onions, 1 roughly chopped,
    1 finely chopped

¼ cup lemon juice (from 2 lemons)

½ cup water, at room temperature

1 tablespoon Madeira

½ teaspoon all-purpose flour

1 teaspoon sugar

4 tablespoons coarsely chopped fresh flat-leaf
    parsley

1 lemon, sliced very thin

1.   Preheat the oven to 350 degrees.

2.   Dust both sides of the roe with cornmeal and a pinch or two of salt and black pepper and shake off the excess.

3.   Scatter the bacon in a 12-inch cast-iron skillet or sauté pan over medium-high heat. With a slotted spoon, move the pieces around until the bacon is firm and just golden brown, about 3 minutes. Transfer to a small bowl and reserve. Pour off all but 1 tablespoon of the fat, add the olive oil, and turn the heat to high. When the oil shimmers, add the bell pepper and the roughly chopped onion and sauté, stirring occasionally, until they have softened slightly, about 3 minutes. With a slotted spoon, transfer to a second small bowl and reserve.

4. Place 2 roe sets in the skillet (taking care not to crowd them) and sauté until they are gently browned on both sides, 1 to 2 minutes per side. Remove and reserve on a plate, and repeat with the other 2 sets. When all the roe have been browned, transfer them to a small roasting pan. Pour ⅛ cup lemon juice over them and bake for 5 minutes.

5. Return the reserved onion and pepper to the skillet and pour the remaining ⅛ cup lemon juice over them. Add the finely chopped onion to the skillet and cook until it just begins to soften, about 2 minutes. Add the water, Madeira, flour, and sugar and bring to a simmer, stirring to scrape up any browned bits on the bottom of the pan. Reduce the heat to low and simmer gently, stirring, until the liquid thickly coats the back of a wooden spoon, 3 to 4 minutes. Season to taste with salt and black pepper.

6. To serve, separate two attached roe sacs in each set and nest them close together on each of 4 plates. Spoon the gravy over them, scatter the parsley and the reserved bacon on top, and garnish with slices of lemon.

OYSTER, SLAB BACON, AND TOASTED BENNE SKILLET STEW

THIS STEW IS AN INTERPRETATION OF A RECIPE FOR "BROWN OYSTER STEW" THAT APPEARS IN *CHARLESTON RECEIPTS*. When we first came across it years ago, the concept seemed appealing: a light, barely thickened oyster stew stiffened just slightly with crushed, toasted sesame seeds, served over rice or grits. When we actually got down to playing around with it, the stew became even more intriguing. Sesame seeds toasted in a dry skillet and crushed with a mortar and pestle release a beautifully smoky flavor that is quite similar to that of fried bacon, but with an unmistakably nutty nuance. They're a natural partner, it turns out, for oysters and onions, and the stew is divine served over Simple Grits (page 146) or hot white rice.

In this recipe, the oysters are added at the very end of cooking. If you cook them too long, they will release much of their water and thin the gravy—an event that may interfere with the other dishes on the plate. But whether the gravy is thick or thin, the flavor is out of this world.

WHAT TO DRINK   *This dish has "pint of Guinness" written all over it, but another stout, or a moderately-oaked white wine would pair equally well.*

For 4 people

TIME: 20 minutes

2 pints shucked oysters (see Sourcery, page 76), with their liquor

1 tablespoon benne (sesame) seeds

¼ pound slab bacon or 4 strips thick-cut bacon, diced

Olive oil, if needed

3 tablespoons all-purpose flour

3 tablespoons dry sherry, such as fino or amontillado

1 teaspoon lemon zest

Kosher salt to taste

Freshly ground black pepper to taste

1 bunch green onions, sliced into thin rounds, for garnish

1. If you are not pregnant and do not have a suppressed immune system, taste the raw oyster liquor to test the salinity. If the oysters aren't salty enough, add a few pinches of salt (about 1 teaspoon for a pint).

2. In a 9-inch skillet, toast the benne seeds over medium-low heat, agitating them constantly, until they are the color of unpopped popcorn, about 8 minutes. Remove and reserve. Scatter the bacon in the skillet and increase the heat to medium-high. With a slotted spoon, move the pieces around until the bacon is firm and just golden brown, about 3 to 5 minutes. You should have 3 tablespoons of fat. If you don't, add enough olive oil to make 3 tablespoons of fat. Turn the heat to low and add the flour, stirring constantly, until it turns the color of milky coffee, about 6 minutes.

3. In a small sauté pan, heat the oysters in their liquor just until the edges curl, 1 to 3 minutes, depending on the size of the oysters. Turn off the heat. With a sieve, drain the oysters thoroughly over the skillet with the bacon roux. Reserve the oysters.

4. Add the benne seeds, sherry, and lemon zest to the bacon gravy and continue to cook over low heat until the gravy is bubbly and thickly coats the back of a spoon, about 3 minutes. Turn off the heat. Add the oysters and stir to cook them very briefly. Season with salt and pepper.

5. Serve with grits or white rice, and garnish with the reserved bacon and green onions.

THE GREAT OUTDOORS

Along the South Carolina coast, many of life's great milestones—weddings, engagements, birthdays, anniversaries, graduations—are celebrated at large congregational meals served outdoors. Except for the whole-hog barbecue, most of these parties revolve around fish and shellfish: the oyster roast, the crab crack, the fish fry, the shrimp boil. It's more likely than not that these events take place in shady creekside groves or on docks that reach out into the marsh, and there's something poignant about them, because at the same time that we're toasting longevity or a particular achievement, we're also paying homage to the place where so much of our sustenance comes from.

In the Lowcountry, you can hire any number of catering teams to put on an oyster roast or a fish fry for fifteen or fifteen hundred people. They'll arrange the entire celebration, start to finish, and they might even provide a breathtaking site. It's so much more fun, though, and more meaningful, to make these outdoor meals potluck dinners. Assign each guest a dish to make or some piece of equipment to bring, so that everyone feels involved in the event, even if the occasion is nothing more than a great gathering of friends.

A source for exceptional southern comfort food and kitschy home decorations, Lynn's Paradise Café is a Louisville institution. We once built a fire in the parking lot not far from these plaster statues and roasted oysters, Lowcountry-style, for 150 people, as a tribute to our friend Ronni Lundy.

413

☀ LEGAREVILLE OYSTER ROAST ☀

SOUTH CAROLINA OYSTERS DON'T HAVE A RECOGNIZED TRADE NAME LIKE MAINE'S BELONS OR PRINCE EDWARD ISLAND'S Malpeques, but they deserve one. They're deliciously briny, slender, and concentrated, and during the chilly fall and winter months, the Lowcountry is alive with informal oyster roasts. Even if you're landlocked, you can have a great oyster roast if you have a source of raw oysters by the bushel and a halfway decent hardware store or handyman nearby.

Oysters were meant to be eaten amid clouds of salty steam and infused with woodsmoke from the fire. Put a cruet of Pepper Vinegar (page 518; we won't call it a mignonette, but you can) and some Zesty Cocktail Sauce (page 525) on the shucking table.

☀

WHAT TO DRINK   *A hydrating beverage, like a pale American lager (Budweiser and the like), suits an outdoor oyster roast, even as the weather turns sweatery. For a little more flavor, try to find a local brew in your area, like Charleston's Palmetto Lager.*

For 32 people
TIME: 2 hours

EQUIPMENT

4 cinder blocks

1 large sheet of steel, about 4 feet square

4 wheelbarrowfuls dry, split wood

Kindling or charcoal

1 burlap bag or 2 old towels

One 5-gallon pail water

1 metal shovel or pitchfork

10 pairs work gloves

12–16 oyster knives

2 bushels unshucked oysters (about 480–600 oysters)

4 recipes Zesty Cocktail Sauce (page 525)

4 cruets Pepper Vinegar (page 518)

1. Create a level, well-swept clearing on the ground and stand the cinder blocks end up so they form the corners of a rectangle to support the sheet of metal. Lay the metal over the cinder blocks and test it to make certain it is secure.

2. Remove the sheet of metal and build a fire in the center of the rectangle of ground defined by the cinder blocks. When the fire is roaring, place the piece of metal squarely on the cinder blocks. Dunk the burlap bags in the pail of water. When a handful of water tossed on the metal sizzles and dances, place 2 or 3 shovelfuls of oysters on it and blanket them with the soaked burlap. Let the oysters steam for about 5 minutes or until some (but not all) of them have opened, then remove the burlap and return it to the water bucket. Shovel the oysters off the metal and onto the shucking table (see "How to Shuck Oysters," page 417) and place the cocktail sauce and pepper vinegar on the table. When guests have nearly devoured the first batch of oysters, begin the second batch. When all the oysters have been steamed, you can douse the fire with any water left in the pail.

3. Serve with 6 recipes Fish Stew Man's Red Fish Stew (page 249), 4 recipes Red Rice (page 172) and 6 recipes Sunday Collards (page 205).

VARIATION—INDOOR OYSTER ROAST: SOMETIMES YOU JUST CAN'T BE OUTSIDE. OR MAYBE YOU LIVE IN CHICAGO, WHERE YOU CAN'T CLEAR A PATCH OF LAND AND START A ROARING FIRE ON IT. MAYBE

IT'S MINUS THIRTY OUTDOORS. NONE OF THESE CONCERNS SHOULD KEEP YOU FROM ROASTING OYSTERS WHEN YOU GET THE HANKERING.

THE KEY TO DOING AN INDOOR OYSTER ROAST SUCCESSFULLY—UNLESS YOUR BUDGET IS UNLIMITED—IS TO FIND A WHOLESALE FISH MARKET WHERE YOU CAN GET A GREAT PRICE ON UNSHUCKED OYSTERS. THIS IS NOT AS DIFFICULT AS YOU MIGHT THINK. WHOLESALE FISH MARKETS EXIST EVEN IN LANDLOCKED STATES; THEY'RE LISTED IN THE YELLOW PAGES, AND SINCE THEIR STOCK IS PERISHABLE, THEY ALWAYS WANT TO MOVE IT. YOU MAY HAVE TO PAY CASH, BUT YOU'LL ALWAYS GET A RECEIPT IF THE DEALER IS REPUTABLE.

YOU SHOULD PLAN ON BUYING ABOUT 15 TO 20 OYSTERS PER GUEST. SOME WHOLESALERS SELL OYSTERS IN 120-PIECE CARDBOARD BOXES, OTHERS BY BUSHEL BAG. THE SIZE OF THE OYSTERS DIFFERS DRAMATICALLY FROM VARIETY TO VARIETY, BUT 120 PIECES IN A BOX IS ROUGHLY EQUIVALENT TO HALF A BUSHEL BAG.

ALTHOUGH YOU WON'T NEED THE FIREWOOD, THE BUCKET OF WATER, THE BURLAP, OR THE CINDER BLOCKS, YOU WILL NEED OYSTER KNIVES AND WORK GLOVES FOR SHUCKING (SEE "HOW TO SHUCK OYSTERS," BELOW) AND A LONG TABLE THAT CAN TAKE A BEATING, OR AT LEAST ONE THAT CAN BE COVERED WITH A TARP OR MANY LAYERS OF NEWSPAPER.

THE TECHNIQUE FOR ROASTING OYSTERS IN THE OVEN IS SIMPLE. PREHEAT THE OVEN TO 475 DEGREES AND ARRANGE AS MANY OYSTERS AS POSSIBLE IN A SINGLE LAYER IN A 12-$\times$-16-INCH ROASTING PAN FITTED WITH A FLAT RACK. POUR 1/3 INCH OF HOT WATER INTO THE PAN AND BAKE FOR 7 MINUTES, OR UNTIL MOST (BUT NOT ALL) OF THE OYSTERS' SHELLS HAVE BEGUN TO OPEN (IF WE MISS THE OUTDOORS TERRIBLY, WE SCATTER A FEW WOOD CHIPS IN THE BOTTOM OF THE OVEN TO GENERATE WOODSMOKE). USING GLOVES OR TONGS, TRANSFER THE OYSTERS TO A TABLE COVERED IN NEWSPAPER FOR GUESTS TO SHUCK, GARNISH, AND EAT WHILE THE NEXT BATCH COOKS. REPEAT UNTIL ALL THE OYSTERS HAVE BEEN SERVED, ABOUT 45 MINUTES FOR 120 OYSTERS. SERVE WITH HOT SAUCE AND LEMON WEDGES AND WITH ANY OR ALL THE SIDE DISHES IN THE RECIPE ABOVE, MODIFYING THE QUANTITIES ACCORDING TO HOW MANY GUESTS YOU'VE INVITED.

DOWNTOWN TOUCH: GIVE ANY OYSTER ROAST THE DOWNTOWN TOUCH BY SERVING SOUR ORANGE SAUCE (PAGE 528) AS A CONDIMENT.

HOW TO SHUCK OYSTERS

TO SHUCK AN OYSTER, LAY THE UNOPENED OYSTER IN your palm with the tapered hinge end pointing toward you (be sure to wear a work glove on the hand holding the oyster). Ease the tip of an oyster knife into the hinge, applying steady pressure, and wiggle it left and right in the joint. Once the hinge has slackened, you can slide the knife around the edge of the oyster enough to open it. Scrape the edge of the knife under the body of the oyster to separate it from the bottom shell. Dress it with condiments if you desire, then slurp it down. If the oyster is impossible to open, throw it back beneath the steaming burlap or back in the oven for a few minutes. Clams and mussels get steamed until they open up, but if you do that with an oyster, you'll wait an age to eat the driest, toughest little nuggets of oyster muscle you've ever encountered.

⚜ RURAL MISSION CRAB CRACK AND FISH FRY ⚜

THE SUMMER BEFORE TED'S SENIOR YEAR IN HIGH SCHOOL, HE WORKED AS A TEACHER'S ASSISTANT IN A SCHOOL FOR THE children of the many migrants who work the farms on Johns Island during the summer. The school is one outreach project of the Rural Mission, an ecumenical, nonprofit group of women working to alleviate the stresses of poverty on the lives of Johns Island residents. On most Tuesday nights, the Rural Mission hosts a feast—a crab crack and fish fry—as a gesture of thanks to all the volunteers who work in its various service programs.

When we were growing up, the Rural Mission fish fry was without question our favorite food experience, the truest of true Lowcountry gatherings. The meal begins with enormous stockpots of blue crabs harvested from the creek behind the mission, steamed in a chile-laced boil and dumped onto picnic tables for picking. When you've had your fill of fresh crabmeat, you proceed to the buffet of whiting (and sometimes shark) fresh from the fryer, red rice, macaroni and cheese, coleslaw, and banana pudding. The evening is capped off with a performance by the Johns Island praying band, a choir that uses their hands, their feet, and their voices to create the most mesmerizing music—at times joyous, occasionally mournful—you've ever heard.

⚜

WHAT TO DRINK   *A boatload of crabs argues for having on hand a large quantity of good crisp, mild beer to allow the delicate crab flavor to shine through. A jelly jar of a quiet, less fruity, more minerally Chardonnay (a Chablis, for example) or a Gavi would be terrific too.*

For 24 people

TIME: 4–6 hours

EQUIPMENT

Work gloves
4 cinder blocks
1 sheet of steel about 4 feet square
OR an outdoor tripod gas cooker
One 8-gallon enameled tin cauldron

4 wheelbarrowfuls dry, split wood
Kindling or charcoal
1 metal shovel
1 long-handled slotted dipper or small
    pitchfork

4 gallons water
1 recipe Lee Bros. Shrimp Boil (page 553)
72 live blue crabs (about a bushel basket of crabs)

1. Create a level, well-swept clearing on the ground and stand the cinder blocks end up so they form the corners of a rectangle to support the sheet of metal. Lay the metal over the cinder blocks and test it to make certain it is secure. (Alternately, set up a trestle for a gas cooker, if you are using one.)

2. Remove the sheet of metal and build a three-log fire in the center of the rectangle of ground defined by the cinder blocks. (Alternately, turn the control knob on the gas cooker to high.) When the fire is roaring, place the piece of metal squarely on the cinder blocks. Fill an 8-gallon enameled tin cauldron with 4 gallons water and add the shrimp boil. Place the pot on the metal or the gas burner and bring to a low boil (if using live fire, control the heat by pushing logs around the fire with the shovel, but take care not to disturb the sheet of metal). Add a third of the crabs to the pot and boil for 3 minutes, until their shells turn a deep orange. With the slotted dipper, transfer the crabs to a table covered with layers of newspaper for guests to pick with their hands (see "How to Pick and Eat Whole Crabs," below).

3. Serve the crabs as an appetizer with 4 recipes Fried Whiting (page 386), 2 recipes Macaroni and Cheese (page 235), 3 recipes Red Rice (page 172), 3 recipes Coleslaw (page 195), and 4 recipes Banana Pudding Ice Cream (page 432).

WHEN THE HOT CRABS HIT THE TABLE AT A LOWCOUN-try crab crack, a rush typically ensues (among those with asbestos fingers) to find the crabs with the largest claws.

1.   To pick the crab, begin by removing the whole claws and arms attached to them. Guard them carefully, but do not eat just yet.

2.   Peel the orange top shell off the crab as follows: Hold the crab in one open palm, facing away from you. Close your other hand over it so your fingertips are touching and drive both thumbs into the slight gap between the back edge of the crab shell and the white body, then pull the two apart. Discard the top shell.

3.   Snap the crab body in half down the middle, separating the two sets of legs.

4.   Do your best to pluck, suck, disassemble, and prod the white meat out of its cartilaginous framework, using the sharp end of one claw as a picking tool.

5.   When you've picked the crab clean, reward yourself by cracking open the claws and helping yourself to the sweet dark meat inside. Then on to the next crab!

❋ LOWCOUNTRY SHRIMP BOIL ❋

"SHRIMP BOIL" REFERS TO NO FEWER THAN THREE THINGS.
FIRST, IT IS THE TERM FOR THE SEASONING MIXTURE OF CAYENNE
pepper, kosher salt, freshly ground black pepper, and bay leaf that we often use when cooking
shrimp in water and making shrimp stock.

"Shrimp boil" is also another name for Frogmore Stew (page 255), and it is the term we use
for a large event where an enormous Frogmore Stew is cooked outdoors over a wood fire.

This recipe is fundamentally our Frogmore Stew recipe, adapted for twice the crowd and an
outdoor setting. It tastes most delicious served this way, because the smell of woodsmoke seems
to add a layer of flavor and festivity.

❦

WHAT TO DRINK   *The seriously fishy, spicy, and flavorful shrimp boil would be well served by a beer
with a little more oomph, like an amber English-style ale. Samuel Smith's Brewery in Yorkshire makes
several worthy examples, distributed widely in the U.S.*

For 24 people

TIME: 3 hours

EQUIPMENT

Work gloves

4 cinder blocks

1 sheet of steel, about 4 feet square

OR an outdoor tripod gas cooker

4 wheelbarrowfuls dry, split wood

Kindling or charcoal

One 6-gallon stockpot, preferably with a wide bottom

1 metal shovel

Oven mitts

Sturdy long-handled tongs

1 long-handled slotted spoon

1 long-handled wooden spoon

1 long-handled ladle

¼ cup extra-virgin olive oil, peanut oil, or canola oil

8 serrano, pasilla, or other dried red chiles, trimmed, slit down their sides, seeded, and flattened

6 pounds smoked pork sausage, Cajun andouille, or kielbasa (see Sourcery, page 258), cut on the bias into 1¼-inch-thick pieces

4 cups chopped celery (about 8 stalks)

8 cups chopped yellow onions (about 12 large onions)

8 quarts (32 cups) Sunday Shrimp Broth (page 536)

3 tablespoons Lee Bros. Shrimp Boil (page 553)

1 tablespoon kosher salt, plus more to taste

3 bay leaves

24 blue crabs, cooked and cleaned, or 2 pounds lump crabmeat (see Sourcery, page 70)

6 pounds peeled Yukon Gold or other waxy potatoes (about 12 large potatoes), cut into 1-inch dice

12 ears fresh corn, cut into 24 pieces

Two 28-ounce cans whole plum tomatoes, drained and crushed

8 pounds headless large shrimp (26–30 per pound; see Sourcery, page 374), shells on

4 medium lemons, thinly sliced, for garnish

1. Create a level, well-swept clearing on the ground and stand the cinder blocks end up so they form the corners of a rectangle to support the sheet of metal. Lay the metal over the cinder blocks and test it to make certain it is secure. (Alternately, set up the trestle for a gas cooker if you are using one.)

422

2.   Remove the sheet of metal and build a three-log fire in the center of the rectangle of ground defined by the cinder blocks. (Alternately, turn the control knob on the gas cooker to high.) Stoke the fire with more logs, and when the fire is roaring, place the steel squarely on the cinder blocks. Pour the oil into the stockpot and set the pot on the metal or the cooker. (If using live fire, control the heat by pushing logs around the fire with the shovel, but take care not to disturb the sheet of metal). When the oil shimmers, add the chiles to the pot and gently toast them until they discolor and release some of their fragrance, about 30 seconds. Add the sausage, and move it around with the tongs until all the pieces are browned on most of their surfaces, 10 to 12 minutes. Using the slotted spoon, remove the chiles and sausage and reserve in a large bowl. Add the celery and onion to the stockpot and cook until softened, about 6 minutes.

3.   Add 8 cups broth to the pot. Using the wooden spoon, stir in tight circles, scraping up any browned bits from the bottom. Bring the broth to a boil and boil until reduced by one quarter, about 12 minutes. Pour the remaining broth into the pot, add the shrimp boil, salt, and bay leaves, and cover. When the broth boils, uncover, and simmer vigorously until the broth has reduced by one sixth, about 12 more minutes.

4.   Add the crabs and potatoes and cook until they have softened a bit but are not yet fork-tender, about 10 minutes. Add the corn, tomatoes, and reserved sausage and any juices they may have released, cover, and bring the stew to a vigorous simmer. Tamp the fire down and simmer the stew gently, uncovered, for 10 minutes, or until the tine of a fork easily pierces the potatoes.

5.   Add the shrimp, stir to distribute them evenly, and simmer about 3 minutes more, or until the shrimp are pink and cooked through.

6.   Serve in large bowls, garnished with the lemon slices. Serve with 4 recipes Coleslaw (page 195).

❋ DESSERTS ❋

SOUTHERNERS TEND TO TAKE THEIR SWEETS SERIOUSLY, BUT THEY BRING TO THE

last chapter of the meal a bristling creative energy that could easily be confused with fun. The sheer number and variety of desserts invented in the South boggles the mind—everything from tender, ethereal cakes studded with exotic nuts and embellished with elaborate frostings to almost immaterial gelatinous fruit salads seasoned with ginger ale.

We have tackled many of the desserts in the southern culinary canon and can attest to their seriousness. Some are a challenge for home cooks like us to prepare. Still, the fun factor must prevail, so we've selected and honed recipes that work consistently, with great results. In other cases we've picked a target—sweet potato pie, for example—and played around with the formula until something slightly different takes shape and the result pleases us. If you've read this far, you may recognize a pattern to our kitchen play: much of what we do in freshening up recipes begins with a simple transposition of technique or ingredients from one culinary idiom to another. That cafeteria banana pudding with vanilla wafers—why not refashion it as an ice cream? Did you notice that corn syrup is the main ingredient in pecan pie? Why not try sorghum syrup, which is similar but much more flavorful? We once were flabbergasted by an amazing chocolate truffle with chili powder, a combination that tasted delicious and delivered heat in a subtle way. Why not introduce chili powder into bourbon balls?

These subtle (and not-so-subtle) tweaks of the classics—keeping the idea of the dish alive but introducing a new layer of meaning, and breaking a rule or two in the process—are our bread and butter. It's what we've learned from hanging around talented home cooks and chefs, and it's the result of a simple quest for novelty once you're comfortable with the basics of cooking.

Experimenting, and even cutting corners, is a large part of keeping life in the kitchen fresh and exciting, being resourceful and personalizing your everyday cooking and entertaining. We hope you've caught the bug. If you have, you may consider yourself southern, no matter where you're from.

ICE CREAMS

A small, inexpensive Donvier ice cream maker was one of very few gadgets in the kitchen at 83 East Bay Street. A squat plastic cube with a hand crank on the top, it looked like a toy, but the peach-buttermilk ice cream our mom made with it seemed very grown up—annoyingly so from our perspectives, as it was only lightly sweetened and had the yogurty tang of something good for you. Only when our palates had matured did we get hip to its refreshing brilliance.

Homemade ice cream is an impressive dessert, and that's only one advantage of doing it yourself. Another is that you get to personalize your flavors. Of course there are many ice creams on the market these days, but few of them are free of junk—stabilizers, artificial flavorings, and whatnot, to allow them to sit in the store for weeks on end—and fewer still are truly delicious *and* exciting. Against the unchanging backdrop of anything-goes flavors with peanut butter cup pieces, caramel chips, and streaks of marshmallow fluff, a flavor as simply intriguing as our Chocolate Grits Ice Cream (page 438) seems like the future of the medium.

The ice creams in the pages that follow are ones we've developed over the past ten years, using the ingredients we grew up with. It would be difficult to find as southern a selection of ice creams as these elsewhere.

Despite what those glossy kitchen catalogues would have you believe, you don't need a fancy Italian ice cream maker to create deliciously rich, wonderful ice creams that are fun to serve (and terrific to give as gifts, by the way). Whether you use a $900 Nemox, a $40 Cuisinart, or an old-fashioned barrel with a dasher, making ice cream is simple, as long as you stay attentive to the temperature of the custard.

Most ice creams are made in a four-step process. First you prepare a custard in a double boiler or saucepan on the stovetop. Then you chill it, either in the freezer for a short time or in the refrigerator for a longer time, until the custard is very cold but not frozen. Next you churn it in an ice cream maker until it is the consistency of a very thick milk shake. Finally you chill it in the freezer for several hours until it completes the final stage of hardening (called "tempering"), so it forms tight round balls that hold their shape when you scoop it.

During the first step, when you're cooking the custard on the stovetop, keep a candy thermometer close at hand so you can regulate the heat and maintain the temperature at 170 degrees, so the custard thickens but does not boil. (If it boils, you may be left with scrambled eggs, which doesn't make for appealing ice cream.)

During the second stage, chilling the ice cream base, plan to refrigerate the custard for at least four hours, and overnight if possible. The colder your custard is when it goes into the ice cream maker, the quicker it will freeze, and the creamier the resulting texture will be.

Another reason to plan: all ice cream machines freeze ice cream only until it is thick and holds its shape. But it still won't be hard enough to scoop into perfect round balls. For that, ice cream requires about two hours of further hardening in the freezer. So if you're making ice cream on the day of a party at which you plan to serve it, factor the time it takes to temper it into your preparation schedule.

❊ BOILED PEANUT AND SORGHUM SWIRL ❊
ICE CREAM

WE LOVE FINDING INNOVATIVE USES FOR SORGHUM SYRUP, WHICH IS EMPLOYED ON MANY SOUTHERN TABLES AS A CONDIMENT for morning biscuits (see Sorghum Butter, page 529), evening corn bread, and most things in between. It has a sweet, tangy flavor, like dried fruit mixed with caramel.

About twelve years ago, Ben & Jerry's canvassed America soliciting ideas for new flavors of ice cream, and we submitted this recipe for vanilla ice cream studded with shelled boiled peanuts and stripes of sorghum. We doubted that many Vermonters had ever tasted either boiled peanuts or sorghum, much less both, and thus were not entirely surprised to receive no response whatsoever from those enterprising guys. But even the most avid boiled peanut fanatics and sorghum lovers may be shocked by this one. Boiled peanuts are never a dessert food in the South, and sorghum is only if it's baked into a cake.

Peanuts, remember, are actually legumes—beans—so this ice cream takes its inspiration as much from the red bean ice cream found in many Japanese restaurants as from the popular nut-and-fudge-swirl category. Like those desserts, the key to this recipe's success is the balance of salty and sweet, cream and bean (or nut, as the case may be).

Makes about 1 quart; enough for 6 people

TIME: 7 hours, including chilling and freezing

2 large egg yolks

½ cup sugar

1 cup whole milk

2 cups heavy cream

2 teaspoons natural vanilla extract

½ cup shelled Boiled Peanuts, chilled (page 58)

½ cup pure sorghum syrup (see Sourcery, page 447) or cane syrup

Benne Wafers (page 485), for garnish (optional)

1. In a medium bowl, beat the egg yolks lightly with a whisk, then add the sugar and beat until the mixture is a milky lemon-yellow color, about 1½ minutes. In a medium saucepan, warm the milk over medium heat, stirring occasionally, until a candy thermometer reads 150 degrees, 6 to 8 minutes (you may see steam rising from the pan, but the milk should not start to boil). Pour the warm milk into the egg mixture in a slow stream, whisking constantly. The resulting custard will be thin but lustrous and smooth.

2. Return the custard to the saucepan or, preferably, the top of a double boiler and cook slowly over very, very low heat, stirring constantly with a wooden spoon. When it reaches 170 degrees on a candy thermometer (8 to 10 minutes; it should be thick enough to coat the back of the spoon), turn off the heat and let cool to room temperature. Add the cream and vanilla, stir to incorporate thoroughly, transfer to a pitcher or other container, and refrigerate for 4 hours or overnight, until the custard is very cold.

3. Pour the chilled custard into an ice cream maker, add the peanuts, and churn according to the manufacturer's instructions, until the ice cream becomes very thick and holds its shape. It should be the consistency of a very thick milk shake; depending on how cold your custard is and the type of ice cream maker you have, this will take 15 to 30 minutes. Transfer to a container with a tight-fitting lid and cut several channels through the ice cream with a wooden spoon. Pour the sorghum syrup evenly into them, then gently fold the ice cream in swirling patterns until the sorghum is evenly distributed. If there is any space between the surface of the ice cream and the container's lid, press plastic wrap onto the surface.

4. Freeze the ice cream until it has hardened, at least 2 hours. Remove from the freezer 10 minutes before serving.

5. Serve small scoops of the ice cream in bowls and garnish with Benne Wafers.

A sorghum cane field on the Ellis family farm, Stoney Creek, Tennessee. Juice pressed from the cane is boiled down to make sorghum syrup.

❊ BANANA PUDDING ICE CREAM ❊

WHEN SOUTHERNERS DON'T HAVE TIME TO PUT TOGETHER A BANANA CREAM PIE, THEY MAKE BANANA PUDDING BY LAYERING vanilla pudding with banana slices and vanilla wafers. Banana pudding is always a popular potluck dessert, and in theory we love all the ingredients that go into it. But in reality, it's often a disaster. The bananas go brown, the wafers get soggy, and the pudding is almost always artificial.

We thought it might be fun to turn banana pudding upside-down a bit: to make a puree of caramelized bananas, brown sugar, and rum, whisk it into a sweet egg custard, churn the custard in an ice cream maker, and fold crushed vanilla wafers into the ice cream toward the end of the churn. We did just that, and we think you'll be as thrilled as we are with the result.

Makes about 1 quart; enough for 6 people

TIME: 7 hours, including chilling and freezing

2 tablespoons unsalted butter

¼ cup tightly packed dark brown sugar

2 ripe bananas, sliced in half crosswise and lengthwise

2 tablespoons dark rum, such as Mount Gay or Myers's

2 large egg yolks

⅓ cup sugar

1½ cups whole milk

2 cups heavy cream

Eight 2-inch vanilla wafers, roughly chopped into bite-sized pieces, plus 6 whole vanilla wafers for garnish

1. In a medium skillet over medium-high heat, melt the butter until frothy. Add the brown sugar and spread it with a wooden spoon. Sauté the sugar until it becomes a flat, bubbling mass, about 1½ minutes. Add the bananas and stir, turning them in the sugar for about 1½ minutes, until they are well coated and softening.

2. Pour the rum over the contents of the skillet (it will hiss and pop but soon subside). Let it bubble for a minute or two to burn off the alcohol (which would inhibit freezing). Transfer the contents of the skillet to a food processor or blender.

3. In a medium bowl, beat the egg yolks lightly with a whisk, then add the sugar and beat until the mixture is a milky lemon-yellow color, about 1½ minutes. In a medium saucepan, warm the milk over medium heat, stirring occasionally, until a candy thermometer reads 150 degrees, 6 to 8 minutes (you may see steam rising from the pan, but the milk should not start to boil). Pour ½ cup of the hot milk into the banana mixture in the food processor and puree until smooth, about 1 minute. Reserve and let cool.

4. Add the remaining 1 cup hot milk slowly and in a thin stream into the egg and sugar mixture, whisking constantly as you pour. Pour the custard back into the saucepan or, preferably, the top of a double boiler, and cook slowly over low heat, stirring constantly with a wooden spoon. When the custard reaches 170 degrees on a candy thermometer (8 to 10 minutes; it should be thick enough to coat the back of the spoon), turn off the heat. Add the banana puree to the custard (don't be alarmed if the puree has solidified to a gel-like consistency as it cooled) and gently whisk to incorporate it completely, about 1½ minutes. Let the custard cool to room temperature, and whisk in the cream. Transfer to a pitcher or other container and refrigerate for 4 hours or overnight, until the custard is very cold but not frozen.

5.   Pour the custard into an ice cream maker and churn according to the manufacturer's instructions, until the ice cream becomes stiff and holds its shape. It should be the consistency of a very thick milk shake; depending on how cold your custard is and the type of ice cream maker you have, this will take 15 to 30 minutes. Transfer to a container with a tight-fitting lid and scatter the cookie pieces over the top. Fold them into the ice cream until they're evenly incorporated. Pat a sheet of plastic wrap onto the surface and cover the container.

6.   Freeze the ice cream until it has hardened, at least 2 hours. Remove from the freezer 10 minutes before serving and remove the plastic wrap.

7.   Serve small scoops of ice cream in bowls, and garnish with a whole vanilla wafer.

TEXAS RED-BRAISED BEEF SHORT RIBS, PAGE 320, WITH
SIMPLE GRITS, PAGE 146

LUAU-STYLE BBQED PORK SHOULDER, PAGE 352, *first step:* scored pork before seasoning with kosher salt, freshly ground black pepper, and smoked paprika (*pimentón*)

LUAU-STYLE BBQED PORK SHOULDER, PAGE 352, *second step:* seasoned pork shoulder on a bed of fresh collard green leaves

LUAU-STYLE BBQED PORK SHOULDER, PAGE 352, *third step:* seasoned
pork shoulder wrapped in fresh collard green leaves and tied with butcher's twine,
before being wrapped in aluminum foil and baked at a high temperature

COOKED LUAU-STYLE BBQED PORK SHOULDER, PAGE 352, pulled from
the bone and served on a bun, WITH PEPPER VINEGAR, PAGE 518

BOILED PEANUT AND SORGHUM SWIRL ICE CREAM, PAGE 429,
WITH BENNE WAFERS, PAGE 485

FOUR-LAYER RED VELVET CAKE, PAGE 466,
WITH CREAM CHEESE ICING, PAGE 467

SWEET POTATO BUTTERMILK PIE, PAGE 442, with whipped cream

❋ BUTTERMILK ICE CREAM ❋

GROWING UP, WE USED BUTTERMILK FOR BAKING AND OCCASIONALLY IN ICE CREAM BUT NOT MUCH ELSE. IT SEEMS strange in retrospect: buttermilk tastes like a drinkable yogurt, and it has so many wonderful uses. In fact, a quick, terrific breakfast or snack is to whisk a tablespoonful of sweet preserves like strawberry or peach into a cold cup of buttermilk. Delicious!

It was Kathy Starr, a caterer in the Mississippi Delta and the author of the book *The Soul of Southern Cooking*, who opened our eyes to buttermilk's possibilities. When she was young, she writes, her favorite after-school snack was corn bread crumbled up in a bowl, sprinkled with sugar, doused with buttermilk, and eaten with a spoon.

Reading Kathy's book, we were inspired to create Buttermilk Ice Cream and Corn-Bread Parfaits (see Downtown Touch, below), and in the process, buttermilk ice cream became our house ice cream flavor. It is deliciously creamy, with the sweetness balanced perfectly by a faint, refreshing sourness. Buttermilk ice cream goes with just about any cake or pie you can imagine, or with a scattering of fresh berries on top.

Makes about 1 quart; enough for 6 people

TIME: 7 hours, including chilling and freezing

4 large egg yolks

½ cup sugar

2 cups heavy cream

1½ cups cold whole or lowfat buttermilk
(preferably whole)

Benne Wafers (page 485), for garnish
(optional)

Fresh berries, for garnish (optional)

1. In a medium bowl, beat the egg yolks lightly with a whisk, then add the sugar and beat until the mixture is a milky lemon-yellow color, about 1 minute.

2. In a small saucepan, heat the cream and 1 cup buttermilk over medium-low heat, stirring, until a candy thermometer reads 150 degrees, 6 to 8 minutes (you may see steam rising from the pan, but the milk should not start to boil). Pour the cream and buttermilk mixture in a thin stream into the egg mixture, whisking constantly, until the liquids are completely incorporated. Transfer to a pitcher or other container and refrigerate for 4 hours or overnight, until the custard is very cold but not frozen. Add the remaining ½ cup buttermilk and stir gently with a wooden spoon to incorporate thoroughly.

3. Pour the chilled buttermilk custard into an ice cream maker and churn according to the manufacturer's instructions, until the ice cream becomes very thick and holds its shape. It should be the consistency of a very thick milk shake; depending on how cold your custard is and the type of ice cream maker you have, this will take 15 to 35 minutes. Transfer to a container with a tight-fitting lid. If there is any space between the surface of the ice cream and the container's lid, pat a sheet of plastic wrap onto the surface. Cover the container.

4. Freeze the ice cream until it has hardened, at least 2 hours. Remove from the freezer 10 minutes before serving and remove the plastic wrap.

5. Serve small scoops of ice cream in bowls, and garnish with Benne Wafers or fresh berries.

VARIATION—PEACH BUTTERMILK ICE CREAM: PEEL 2 RIPE PEACHES, PIT THEM, AND CHOP THEM ROUGHLY. PLACE THE PEACHES AND 1/2 CUP SUGAR IN A SMALL SAUCEPAN AND COOK OVER MEDIUM HEAT ABOUT 15 MINUTES, STIRRING, UNTIL THE SUGAR HAS COMPLETELY DISSOLVED AND THE SYRUP IS A LUMINOUS ORANGE COLOR. CAREFULLY PUREE THE HOT MIXTURE IN A FOOD PROCESSOR OR BLENDER. LET COOL TO ROOM TEMPERATURE. FOLLOW THE RECIPE ABOVE, SUBSTITUTING THE FRUIT PUREE FOR THE SUGAR IN STEP 2.

DOWNTOWN TOUCH—BUTTERMILK ICE CREAM AND CORN-BREAD PARFAITS: PREPARE A SKILLET OF CRISPY CORN BREAD (PAGE 497), ADDING AN EXTRA 1 TABLESPOON SUGAR TO THE DRY INGREDIENTS. IN TALL PINT GLASSES, LAYER SQUARES OF THE HOT CORN BREAD WITH SCOOPS OF BUTTERMILK ICE CREAM. A PINT OF JUICY, SLIGHTLY TART FRUIT LIKE DICED PEACHES OR BLUEBERRIES OR STRAWBER-RIES, COOKED DOWN WITH 1/4 CUP SUGAR, ROUNDS OUT THIS PARFAIT NICELY, BUT WE'RE JUST AS LIKELY SIMPLY TO DRIZZLE SOME SORGHUM SYRUP OR CANE SYRUP OVER THE PARFAIT. SERVES 6 TO 8 PEOPLE.

❊ CHOCOLATE GRITS ICE CREAM ❊

HEAR US OUT ON THIS ONE. IN THE LATE NINETIES, WE ATE A CHOCOLATE GRITS SOUFFLÉ AT THE ESTEEMED (NOW SADLY defunct) four-star restaurant Lutèce in New York City. Eberhard Mueller was the chef at the time, and his dessert made innovative use of stone-ground grits to give fine-grained texture to an otherwise airy, decadent chocolate soufflé. But we admit that we were apprehensive about submitting this recipe to our editor, Maria Guarnaschelli. She might think we'd gone round the bend.

In fact, she'd eaten the same soufflé at Lutèce, and had even encouraged one of her authors, the cooking star Lynne Rosetto Kasper, author of the groundbreaking, best-selling cookbook *The Splendid Table* (and host of the radio show of the same name), to develop a chocolate polenta pudding cake recipe for her book *The Italian Country Table*. That cake became one of the most popular and most talked-about recipes in Kasper's book.

We can't say whether this will be our most popular recipe, but the speed at which this ice cream disappears from our freezer is a promising indication.

Makes about 1 quart; enough for 6 people

TIME: 7 hours, including chilling and freezing

4 large egg yolks

¾ cup Dutch-process cocoa powder

½ cup sugar

1½ cups plus 2 tablespoons whole milk

1½ cups heavy cream

½ vanilla bean or ½ teaspoon natural vanilla
extract

¼ cup stone-ground grits, plus more for
garnish (optional)

½ cup dark semisweet chocolate, chopped
(3 ounces)

Shaved chocolate, for garnish (optional)

1. In a large bowl, beat the egg yolks lightly with a whisk or an electric hand mixer, about 30 seconds. Add the cocoa, sugar, and 2 tablespoons of the milk and beat until thickened and dark, glossy brown in color, about 3 minutes.

2. In a small saucepan, heat the remaining 1½ cups milk and the cream over medium-low heat until a candy thermometer reads 150 degrees (you may see steam rising from the pan, but the milk and cream should not start to boil). With a sharp knife, slice the vanilla bean lengthwise, scrape the tiny black seeds into the milk, and add the vanilla bean to the pan (or add the vanilla extract, if using). Add the grits and continue to cook, stirring occasionally and maintaining the temperature around 150 degrees, until the grits swell and the mixture thickens to the consistency of a thin porridge, about 10 to 20 minutes, depending on the freshness of the grits and the coarseness of the grind. Remove the vanilla bean and discard.

3. Whisk 1 cup of the milk and grits mixture slowly into the cocoa mixture, stirring constantly with a wooden spoon or heatproof rubber spatula until the liquids are thoroughly incorporated. Add the chopped chocolate to the grits mixture remaining in the saucepan and stir until it dissolves, 2 to 3 minutes. Stir the cocoa mixture into the grits and chocolate mixture and cook over low heat, stirring occasionally to prevent scorching, until the custard thickens to the texture of a thick, liquid pudding, 8 to 12 minutes. Let cool to room temperature and transfer to a container. Press plastic wrap onto the surface of the custard and refrigerate for 4 hours or overnight, until the custard is very cold but not frozen.

4. The cold custard may not be pourable, depending on how long your grits cooked to become soft; if it is not pourable, simply put the custard in the freezer to temper it to firmness, then go to Step 5. If it is pourable, pour the custard into an ice cream maker and churn according to the manufacturer's instructions until the ice cream becomes very thick and holds its shape. Quickly transfer the ice cream to a container with a tight-fitting lid. If there is any space between the surface of the ice cream and the lid, pat a sheet of plastic wrap on the surface. Cover the container.

5. Freeze the ice cream until it has hardened, at least 2 hours. Remove from the freezer 10 minutes before serving and remove the plastic wrap.

6. Serve small scoops of ice cream in bowls, and garnish with shaved chocolate or—for fun—a pinch of dry, raw grits.

We love pie, and we especially love tweaking the formulas for ubiquitous southern pies. Fortunately, our tailorings don't make these pies any more baroque than the ones they're modeled on. Whether you're making our grape hull pie or our pecan pie, the only challenge you may face is making the pastry, so use our handy tips on making pie crust from scratch in Chapter 10: The Bread Basket and the Pantry. The recipes themselves are easy as . . . well, you know.

A couple notes about our pie recipes in general. These recipes are all for standard 9-inch pie pans, but if you've ever compared the volume of one of those painted ceramic deep-dish pans from Williams-Sonoma to the inexpensive tin pie pans you find at vintage kitchenware stores, then you know they can differ by as much as 6 liquid ounces. As a result, we've calibrated our pie and crust recipes to the largest of 9-inch pie pans.

And about pie yields: yes, you can get eight servings from a 9-inch pie, but you can't get a crumb more, and nobody gets seconds if you have a group of eight. You know best whether your crowd will stand for that. We say that all these recipes serve six. That way, everyone gets an ample serving. And if we have eight for dinner, we make two pies!

❊ SWEET POTATO BUTTERMILK PIE ❊

THIS IS A LEE BROS. ORIGINAL, BORN OF OUR BOREDOM WITH CONVENTIONAL SWEET POTATO PIES, WHICH WE FIND OFTEN to be leaden and dull. (One notable exception is a sweet potato pie we ate at the home of the Texas sweet potato farmers Rona and Dale Smith, which had a fabulous crunchy Rice Krispies, brown sugar, and butter topping.) We wanted our pie to resemble the light, tangy buttermilk pie Robert Stehling of the Hominy Grill makes. So we whisked sweet potato puree into a filling we adapted from Stehling's recipe for buttermilk pie, and the result was astonishing. Some have compared it to a cross between sweet potato pie and cheesecake, which rings true when you taste it. But we'd like to note that it doesn't weigh on you the way cheesecake does. It's ethereal, frothy, and divine, and it just may be our most crowd-pleasing dessert.

For 6 people
TIME: 1 hour, 10 minutes

1½ pounds sweet potatoes (about 2 medium potatoes), peeled and chopped into ½-inch dice

4 tablespoons unsalted butter, melted

2 tablespoons fresh lemon juice

½ teaspoon freshly grated nutmeg

½ teaspoon ground cinnamon

½ teaspoon kosher salt

3 large eggs, separated

½ cup sugar

2 tablespoons all-purpose flour

¾ cup whole or lowfat buttermilk (preferably whole)

1 Sweet Pie Crust (page 508), prebaked

1. Preheat the oven to 375 degrees.

2. Pour 1½ inches of water into a 3-quart stockpot with a strainer basket and bring to a boil over medium-high heat. Add the sweet potatoes, cover, and steam until fork-tender, about 20 minutes. Strain the sweet potatoes, place in a large bowl, and let cool to room temperature. Mash them to a smooth puree with a fork or a potato masher. You should have 1¼ cups puree; discard any excess. Add the butter, lemon juice, nutmeg, cinnamon, and salt, mixing thoroughly with a wooden spoon or rubber spatula after each addition.

3. In a small bowl, beat the egg yolks lightly with a whisk, about 30 seconds. Add the sugar and beat until they're a creamy lemon-yellow color, about 1½ minutes. Add the egg mixture to the sweet potato mixture and stir with a wooden spoon or rubber spatula until the eggs are thoroughly incorporated and the filling is a consistent bright orange color. Add the flour a little at a time, stirring after each addition, until thoroughly incorporated. Add the buttermilk and stir to incorporate.

4. Wash the whisk in a stream of hot water to wash away any butter residue, then rinse in cold water to cool it down and dry with a paper towel. In a separate bowl, whisk the egg whites to soft peaks, about 1½ minutes. With a wooden spoon or rubber spatula, gently fold the egg whites into the sweet potato–buttermilk mixture until thoroughly combined. Pour the mixture into the prepared pie crust and bake on the middle rack until the center is firm and set, 35 to 40 minutes.

5. Remove the pie from the oven and cool completely on a rack. Serve at room temperature (or cover with plastic wrap, chill in the refrigerator, and serve cold), with a dollop of whipped cream and a mint leaf on top.

❋ SOUR ORANGE PIE ❋

WE DO LOVE KEY LIME PIE, AND WE FIND THE ONE SIMMONS SEAFOOD SELLS AT THEIR MARKET ON THE CAUSEWAY TO Sullivan's Island to be irresistible. Trying to get out of there with a few pounds of shrimp and no pie requires tremendous willpower. But after we tasted super-tart sour oranges on a trip to Florida, we developed this refreshing twist on the pie, and at least in our own kitchen, we've never gone back to Key limes.

Along Florida's Gulf Coast, where sour orange trees grow wild, the blotchy, bumpy-skinned fruit is a backyard nuisance. Too tart to eat and packed with seeds, most sour oranges are left to rot on lawns.

They shouldn't be. Their juice, which has the perfume of a sweet orange and the acidity of a lemon or lime, is superb, and as versatile as vinegar. (You can make an easy, delicious substitute by mixing 1 part grapefruit juice with 1 part lemon juice and 1 part orange juice). True Key limes shipped from the Gulf cost almost a dollar apiece; sour oranges are four for a dollar, and sometimes less. You just have to try both and find out which you prefer.

Outside of Florida and New York City, sour oranges can be found in almost every American town with a sizable community of people of Latin American descent, who know sour oranges as *naranjas agrías* (pronounced nah-*rahn*-hahs ah-*gree*-ahs). Look in the yellow pages for a produce wholesaler who specializes in what the trade refers to as "tropicals." If the wholesaler is reluctant to make a retail sale (we've yet to find one who refuses cold cash), ask him or her to give you the names of some greengrocer customers in the area. And if you absolutely cannot find sour oranges, we repeat: 1 part grapefruit juice, 1 part lemon juice, 1 part orange juice.

The zest of most varieties of sour orange is a pale yellow, so we add the more vivid zest of a conventional navel orange when garnishing this pie.

For 6 people

TIME: 45 minutes

FOR THE CRUST

1½ cups store-bought graham cracker crumbs
     or 8 graham crackers pulsed 10 times in
     a food processor to make fine crumbs

3 tablespoons sugar
6 tablespoons unsalted butter, melted (warm
     or cool)

FOR THE FILLING

5 large egg yolks
One 14-ounce can sweetened condensed
     whole milk
2 cups plus 2 tablespoons heavy cream
½ cup plus 1 tablespoon strained sour orange
     juice

1 tablespoon sour orange zest
1½ tablespoons navel orange zest
1 teaspoon confectioners' sugar
8 fresh mint leaves (about 2 sprigs), for
     garnish (optional)

1. Preheat the oven to 350 degrees.

2. In a large mixing bowl, combine the graham cracker crumbs and the sugar. Add the melted butter and toss thoroughly with a wooden spoon or rubber spatula until the butter is evenly incorporated, about 1 minute. Using the bottom of a sturdy juice glass, press the mixture firmly into a 9-inch pie pan, creating an even layer on the bottom and sides. Bake on the middle rack until the crumb mixture has darkened from a reddish brown to the brown of a pecan shell and the sugar and butter have fused with the crumbs to form a crust, 10 to 15 minutes. Remove from the oven and let cool completely on a rack. Reduce the oven temperature to 325 degrees.

3. In a large mixing bowl, beat the egg yolks well with a hand mixer or a whisk until they have lightened in color, about 1 minute. Add the condensed milk and 2 tablespoons cream and stir with a wooden spoon to incorporate. Add the sour orange juice, sour orange zest, and 4 teaspoons navel orange zest and stir until the filling is consistently creamy and light yellow in color, about 1 minute.

4. Pour the filling into the crust and bake on the middle rack until the surface is quivery, like gelatin, 14 to 16 minutes. Transfer to a rack and cool for 30 minutes, by which time the pie will have set firmly. Transfer to the refrigerator to cool completely, about 4 hours (cover in plastic if keeping for more than 24 hours; we recommend eating the pie within 24 hours).

5. Before serving, whip the remaining 2 cups cream with the confectioners' sugar. Spread the whipped cream over the top of the pie and sprinkle the remaining 1½ teaspoons navel orange zest over the whipped cream. Slice into portions and serve, with a mint leaf stuck in the whipped cream on top of each slice if desired.

VARIATION—TRADITIONAL KEY LIME PIE: MAKE A WONDERFUL, CLASSIC KEY LIME PIE BY SUBSTITUTING KEY LIME JUICE OR CONVENTIONAL LIME JUICE FOR THE SOUR ORANGE JUICE AND 1 1/2 TABLESPOONS KEY LIME OR CONVENTIONAL LIME ZEST FOR THE ORANGE ZESTS. STIR ALL BUT 1 TEASPOON ZEST INTO THE PIE FILLING, RESERVING THE REMAINING 1 TEASPOON FOR GARNISH.

MAPLE SYRUP HAS A SOUTHERN COUSIN IN SWEET sorghum, a ruby-tinged molasses extracted and boiled down from the twelve-foot-tall stalks of *Sorghum vulgare saccharatum*, a plant that resembles earless corn. If you thought all molasses was the same, then you've got some learnin' to do. Sorghum's flavor is as distinct from sugarcane molasses (the grocery-store staple) as maple syrup is from corn syrup. In fact, in many parts of the South, sorghum appreciation is a sign of affiliation. Some folks consider themselves sorghum people, and others are cane syrup people, and if you confuse the two, you're likely to be excused from the dinner table. Central southern families have used sorghum as a condiment for nearly two centuries now, deploying it on breakfast biscuits, with a turkey supper, and for everything in between.

A host of people from Pennsylvania to Texas still boil sorghum, but the center of the cottage industry is Tennessee, where the early fall air carries the malty aroma of sorghum sap boiling in open pans. Bob and Zedia Ellis, of Stoney Creek, are sorghum people. At their farm, on the west bank of the Wautauga River, they process about 400 Mason jars a year on the cast-iron 1891 sorghum press they've hitched between their orange tractor and a custom-built, stainless steel, wood-fired evaporating pan.

Sorghum, like wine, is a sensitive concentrate—the weather, soil, variety, and handling that go into its creation all affect the flavor of the finished syrup. When we last visited the Ellises, in 1999, they had skillfully negotiated the challenges of a dry year to produce a sorghum that might have been the vintage of the century: perfectly smooth, full of the dried fruit and caramel elements that are at the heart of the molasses's flavor, but with a wheaty, grassy note—"very close to the grain," as Mr. Ellis says. The 1999 Ellis vintage had no trace of the burnt-sugar flavor that's the mark of a hastily boiled batch. The house style is a thinner syrup than most we've sampled, with a peachy tint and a slightly gelatinous bead as it drizzles off a spoon. Mr. Ellis got the seed for his sorghum variety thirty years ago from a fellow farmer, whose family had cultivated it in eastern Tennessee for three generations.

From the enormous mahogany pile of discarded seed tassels that sat in the Ellises' yard, they would replant the crop the next year. But they spoke of the future with a tone of resignation. Advancing age makes the task of harvesting, pressing and boiling more difficult, and their son, who owns a successful car stereo business in nearby Elizabethton, showed no signs of turning down the volume, and pitching in to cut cane or feed the mill the next year.

Still, the Ellises weren't giving up. Eight buckets of corn were pickling under the eaves of their garage and there was a whole season's worth of heirloom apples in the orchard ready to be pressed for Zedia's famous cider vinegar. As another sorghum purchaser pulled into their driveway, Zedia sweetened the conversation, remarking, "We do what we can—we're just blessed to be surrounded by good food."

Our Lee Bros. Boiled Peanuts Catalogue sells undiluted Tennessee sorghum year-round. P.O. Box 315, Charleston, SC 29401; 843-720-8890; www.boiled peanuts.com.

❋ SORGHUM PECAN PIE ❋

THE SECRET TO THE MOST DELICIOUS PECAN PIE YOU'VE EVER TASTED IS TO RETIRE THAT BOTTLE OF PALLID CORN SYRUP AND replace it with sorghum molasses (see "Sourcery: Sorghum Molasses," page 447) or cane syrup, whose deeply nuanced flavors, with notes of dried fruit, caramel, and nuts, are a superb match for the richness of pecans. Honestly, using anything less than a great syrup would be an insult to your pecans. Serve this pie warm, with scoops of buttermilk ice cream.

For 6 people

TIME: 1 hour

⅓ cup tightly packed dark brown sugar

3 large eggs, beaten

4 tablespoons unsalted butter, melted

1 tablespoon cornstarch

¼ teaspoon kosher salt

¾ cup pure sorghum molasses, cane syrup, or molasses

1½ cups chopped pecans

1 Sweet Pie Crust (page 508), prebaked

1. Preheat the oven to 375 degrees.

2. In a large bowl, beat the brown sugar with the eggs using a hand mixer or a whisk until they're just incorporated, about 1½ minutes. Add the butter, the cornstarch, and the salt and mix until thoroughly combined, about 1½ minutes. Pour the sorghum and pecans into the bowl and stir to incorporate (the pecans will float on the surface of the filling, which is fine).

3. Pour the filling into the pie shell and bake on the middle rack until the center has risen and is quivery, like gelatin, 35 to 40 minutes. Remove from the oven and cool on a rack for 1 hour.

4. Serve warm, topped with lightly sweetened whipped cream or with a scoop of Buttermilk Ice Cream (page 435). Alternately, let the pie cool to room temperature, about another 30 minutes, then cover with plastic wrap and store it in the refrigerator (if you do, heat it in a warm oven for 15 to 20 minutes before serving). It will keep for several days.

KLO

KILLER LEFTOVER—PIE-SHAKES: IT WAS NOT ANYWHERE IN THE SOUTH BUT AT THE HAMBURG INN NO. 2, A DINER IN IOWA CITY, THAT WE ENCOUNTERED OUR FIRST PIE-SHAKE, WHEN WE WERE ON ASSIGNMENT FOR THE TRAVEL SECTION OF THE *NEW YORK TIMES*. WE WROTE IN THE STORY THAT WE FOUND THE HAMBURG'S PIE-SHAKE TO BE "A SIGN OF MIDWESTERN INGENUITY," BUT A FEW PROMINENT MIDWESTERNERS DENIED THE CLAIM, SO WE'VE RECLASSIFIED THE RESOURCEFUL GENIUS OF THE PIE-SHAKE AS SOUTHERN IN ORIGIN.

A PIE-SHAKE IS A PORTABLE PIE À LA MODE, A SHAKE SHOT THROUGH WITH PIE, MADE SIMPLY BY WHIPPING 2 SCOOPS ICE CREAM WITH 1/2 CUP MILK IN A BLENDER AND THEN DROPPING A SLICE OF PIE INTO IT WHILE THE BLENDER IS ON. YOU CAN MIX AND MATCH ICE CREAM FLAVORS AND KINDS OF PIE TO SUIT YOUR TASTE. OUR FAVORITES ARE VANILLA AND SOUR ORANGE PIE-SHAKE, BUTTER PECAN AND PECAN PIE-SHAKE, AND BUTTERMILK AND GRAPE HULL PIE-SHAKE.

❉ CLOVER PEACH FRIED PIES ❉

GEORGIA IS KNOWN AS "THE PEACH STATE," BUT EVEN SOME GEORGIANS WE KNOW WILL ADMIT THAT THE SWEETEST peaches come from York County, South Carolina, and in particular from the small town of Clover, about four hours' drive north of Charleston.

The peach—summer's essence, blushing red and orange—is so sublime that being choosy about the type seems absurd. And yet to us, July's Sunhighs, Red Havens, and Georgia Belles are the most flavorful, with a flowery, rosy peachiness that we prefer to June's understated cling varieties (better for canning and cobblers) and August's treacly Blakes, Monroes, and Elbertas.

The Sanders Peach Stand, in tiny Filbert, between Clover and York, is a spartan shed just south of the North Carolina border; it sells all those varieties plus ten others. Dori Sanders, who works the farm's fifty acres with her sister, Virginia, and their brothers, Orestus and Jarvis, may be the only peach farmer in America who has written a novel—*Clover*, set on a peach farm, of course—that has been translated into eight languages and appeared on bestseller lists in Japan. While there are always a starstruck few making the pilgrimage to buy signed copies of her books, locals visit the open-air woodshed for the quality of her ripe peaches.

Though the Sanderses keep trying out new varieties and rotating tree crops every ten to twelve years, they maintain an old orchard, too, for longtime customers who prefer classics like Elbertas and Starlights. And since the stand has no refrigeration (it's the only one in York County without electricity), the peaches are picked twice a day. If you arrive in the late afternoon and they've sold out of your beloved Sunhighs, Dori might ask you to sit a spell beneath a shade tree while she fires up the Massey-Ferguson tractor, drives out to the orchard, and picks you some to order.

These peach fried pies are scrumptious little pastry envelopes of velvety filling, cooked down from rehydrated dried peaches with just a hint of spice and a splash of bourbon, but not enough to obscure the ripe flavor of summer peaches. We dehydrate Sanders's July peaches ourselves, and they are wonderful, but any high-quality dried peaches from a reputable market will suffice.

Makes 12 pies; enough for 6 people

TIME: 1½ hours

2¾ cups plus one tablespoon sifted cake flour or 2½ cups sifted bleached all-purpose flour, plus more for dusting surfaces and hands

1 teaspoon kosher salt

½ teaspoon baking powder

4 tablespoons cold butter, cut into ¼-inch dice

4 tablespoons cold lard, cut into ¼-inch dice

¾ cup cold whole milk

2 cups dried peaches (about 4½ ounces)

¼ cup packed light brown sugar

¼ cup Tennessee whiskey or Kentucky bourbon

½ teaspoon cinnamon

2 whole cloves

2½ cups peanut oil

1 tablespoon confectioners' sugar, for garnish

1. Sift the flour, salt, and baking powder together twice. Add the butter and lard and work the mixture with a pastry blender or your fingertips until it resembles coarse crumbs with pea-sized pieces scattered throughout. Add the milk and toss with a fork until the dough comes together when you pinch a small amount between your thumb and forefinger. With floured hands, knead the dough a couple of times. Roll it into 12 equal balls and refrigerate for 30 minutes.

2. In a medium saucepan, bring the peaches and 4 cups water to a boil over high heat. Turn the heat down to low, cover, and simmer vigorously until the peaches have reconstituted and are very soft, about 30 minutes. Strain, discard the cooking water, and return the peaches to the pan. Mash with a fork or potato masher. Add the brown sugar, bourbon, cinnamon, and cloves, stir to combine, and simmer over very low heat for 15 minutes more, stirring every 3 minutes, until the peaches are as thick as jam. Remove the cloves and discard.

3. On a floured board, flatten the balls of dough and roll with a floured pin into rounds about 6 inches in diameter and ⅛-inch thick. Place 2 tablespoons peach mixture in the center of each round and brush cold water around the perimeter. Fold the dough over the peach mixture and seal the pie by pressing gently with a fork around the seam. Trim any excess dough.

4. Preheat the oven to 225 degrees. Line a baking sheet or large platter with paper towels.

5. Pour the oil into a 9-inch skillet to a depth of ½ inch. Heat over high heat until the oil reaches 375 degrees on a candy thermometer. Place 4 pies in the skillet and fry, turning them once, for 3 minutes total, until the crusts are golden brown. Transfer the fried pies to the baking sheet lined with paper towels and place in the oven to warm. Repeat with two more batches of pies. When all the pies have been fried, dust them with confectioners' sugar.

6. Serve each guest 2 warm pies, with scoops of Buttermilk Ice Cream (page 435).

❊ GRAPE HULL PIE ❊

THIS DOUBLE-CRUST PIE MAY BE OUR FAVORITE PIE OF LATE SUMMER, AN INDULGENCE THAT CELEBRATES THE SOUTHERN grape harvest. Since we proselytize about the fruit so extensively in the recipe for Scuppernong Preserves (page 132), we won't belabor the point here, except to say this: make this pie. It is distinctive and delicious, and it gets great texture from cooking the skins and adding them to the filling.

If you don't have muscadine grapes in your area, try to find local native grapes, which may be Concords, Niagaras, or Nortons. They are available at most farmers' markets in the Northeast and the Midwest from mid-September to mid-October, and they have that wonderful fox-grape flavor that makes outstanding pie.

For 6 people
TIME: 1½ hours

1¾ pounds (about 5 cups) stemmed, washed scuppernongs or other muscadine grapes, or labrusca varieties such as Concord or Niagara

⅓ cup plus 2 tablespoons sugar

⅔ cup all-purpose flour

1 tablespoon fresh lemon juice

1 tablespoon orange zest

2 recipes Sweet Pie Crust (page 508), 1 pie shell and 1 top, unbaked, the pie shell brushed with 1 beaten egg yolk

1 tablespoon unsalted butter

1. Preheat the oven to 400 degrees.

2. Set 2 large bowls on the kitchen counter. Separate the grape pulps from their skins by pointing a grape's stem scar toward the bowl and pinching the opposite side. The pulp and seeds will squirt into the bowl, along with some juice; rub the skin to extract the intensely fruity nectar that clings to the inside. Reserve the skins in the other bowl. When all the pulps have been separated, roughly chop the skins in a food processor, using a few short pulses (alternately, use a very sharp chef's knife to chop the skins on a board). Reserve.

3. Place the pulps and juice in a medium saucepan and bring to a simmer over low heat. Simmer, stirring occasionally, uncovered, until the pulps dissolve and the seeds float free, about 10 minutes. Remove the pan from the heat and cool slightly on a rack, about 10 minutes. Place a wire-mesh strainer over a bowl and strain the grape mixture to remove the seeds, stirring and pressing the pulp through the mesh. Discard the seeds.

4. In a large saucepan, combine the pulp and the reserved grape skins and place over low heat. Simmer, uncovered, stirring occasionally, for 10 minutes, or until the skins soften. Add the sugar, flour, lemon juice, and orange zest and blend with a whisk.

5. Pour the mixture into the pie shell. Cut the butter into 4 pats and place on top of the filling. Add the top crust and crimp the edges to seal the bottom and top crusts together. Cut 3 or 4 slits in the top crust to vent. Place the pie on the middle rack and bake until the top crust is golden brown, 35 to 40 minutes. Remove from the oven and transfer to a rack to cool, about 1 hour.

6. Serve immediately, warm, with dollops of lightly sweetened whipped cream or scoops of Buttermilk Ice Cream (page 435). Alternately, let the pie cool to room temperature, another 30 minutes, then cover with plastic wrap and store it in the refrigerator (if you do, heat the pie in a warm oven for 15 to 20 minutes before serving). It will keep for several days.

❊ COCONUT CREAM PIE ❊

THIS PIE MAY HAVE CARIBBEAN ROOTS, BUT NOWADAYS IT'S SOUTHERN TO THE CORE, FOUND YEAR-ROUND AT COUNTLESS cafeterias and restaurants. It's simple, cool, creamy, and fabulous. Our recipe lets the coconut provide more weight than in most pies, because we love the rich, almost flanlike density it gives the custard filling.

For 6 people

TIME: 30 minutes

FOR THE CRUST

1½ cups store-bought graham cracker crumbs
    or 8 graham crackers pulsed 10 times in
    a food processor to make fine crumbs

3 tablespoons sugar
6 tablespoons unsalted butter, melted (warm
    or cool)

FOR THE FILLING

2 cups heavy cream
4 egg yolks, well beaten
2 teaspoons natural vanilla extract

2 tablespoons cornstarch
2 cups shredded coconut, preferably
    unsweetened

1.   Preheat the oven to 350 degrees.

2.   In a large mixing bowl, combine the graham cracker crumbs and sugar. Add the melted butter and toss thoroughly with a wooden spoon or rubber spatula until the butter is evenly incorporated, about 1 minute. Using the bottom of a sturdy juice or pint glass, press the mixture firmly into a 9-inch pie pan, creating an even layer on the bottom and sides. Bake on the middle rack until the crumb mixture has darkened from a reddish brown to the brown of a pecan shell and the sugar and butter have fused with the crumbs to form a crust, 10 to 15 minutes. Remove from the oven and cool completely on a rack. Reduce the oven temperature to 325 degrees.

3.   In a medium saucepan over low heat, whisk the cream, egg yolks, vanilla, cornstarch, and coconut together. Stirring constantly, simmer until the mixture is thick enough to coat the back of a spoon, about 8 minutes (use a candy thermometer, and take care not to let temperature of the custard rise above 170 degrees).

4.   Pour the coconut custard into the pie crust and bake for 10 minutes on the middle rack. Remove the pie from the oven, cool on a rack to room temperature, and transfer to the refrigerator to chill completely, at least 4 hours and preferably overnight.

5.   Serve the pie cold, topped with whipped cream flavored with a little rum. Alongside it, serve a shot of dark Caribbean rum like Mount Gay, Barbancourt, or Appleton twenty-one-year old.

CAKES

Charleston's resident cake, a nut-and-spice cake that has chopped morsels of dried fruit in its white vanilla frosting, is called Lady Baltimore. It emerged from the pages of fiction, invented by the novelist Owen Wister for his roman à clef *Lady Baltimore*, set in Charleston.

Curiously, Lady Baltimore cake isn't the only southern dessert to become famous through fiction. Red velvet cake was invented in the kitchen of New York City's Waldorf-Astoria Hotel, according to folk legend (and the Waldorf's publicists, of course), but people have thought of it as a southern dessert ever since the 1986 movie *Steel Magnolias* (an ur-southern drama set in a beauty parlor) made it a star.

Cakes and storytelling seem intertwined in the South, and in fact we have our own cake tale, which is set, if you can believe it, in New York. A college friend asked us to bake her wedding cake. Since we had no reputation at the time for baking, we figured it was an informal affair—the kind where each friend chips in a skill or talent, like bartending or flower arranging. Long after accepting the challenge, we learned that the event had become (as most weddings do) an exquisitely planned affair, in this case for 250 people.

We'd never baked a wedding cake in our lives, so we decided to consult two friends who bake wedding cakes for a living (each of whom has lifetime's worth of cake stories of her own to tell). One, Rosaleen Poole, lives in an apartment above our office; the other, Margaret Braun, is a pastry artist who works out of a studio in the West Village.

They both let us in on some wonderful baking tips and a few hard-won insights. Most importantly, though, they gave us the confidence to bake a fondant-covered, five-tiered cake that weighed more than 50 pounds. The cake was Margaret's lemon butter cake, from her gorgeous book, *Cakewalk*, but we slipped in a few layers of dark red velvet cake beneath the fondant to surprise the bride and groom. The fondant decoration was pretty-girl primitive—polka dots of pastel pink and blue—but to maintain our self-respect, we added a Mad Hatter figurine on top—the Goth-metal rocker Alice Cooper, frozen in a menacing plastic grimace that in this context could only be interpreted as comedy.

We love the madcap diversity of southern cakes. Beyond layer cakes like Lady Baltimore and red velvet, there are light and tender loaf cakes, like the versatile buttermilk pound cake that's the foundation for many desserts we serve, and fig preserve and black walnut cake—

a real rarity, and a sophisticated dessert we serve warm, with hard sauce. The stack cake we first tasted on a trip through the mountains of eastern Kentucky is an architectural marvel, alternating pencil-thin sheets of spice cake and an intensely sweet and tart apple-butter filling. Recipes for stack cakes in community cookbooks in the Appalachians call for as many as twelve layers, but a fork falling cleanly through our six-layer stack gives a single, sensational impression.

HERE ARE SOME TIPS WE'VE LEARNED ALONG THE WAY, acquired in the process of making mistakes, as well as through the generous, patient guidance of experts like Margaret Braun and Rosaleen Poole.

Make your kitchen as cool as you can. All the ingredients for these cakes—with the exception of stack cake, which is more a quick bread and whose batter is more like biscuit dough—should be at room temperature, 70 to 73 degrees Fahrenheit. Chances are if your oven is on and it's a hot day, the air is going to be well above room temperature, so do whatever it takes—crank up the AC, turn the ceiling fans to high and open the windows and the doors—to keep the room as cool and as dry as possible. A cool, dry room makes every task—icing, mixing, and baking—easier and more successful.

Preparing cake pans for baking. Margaret uses a thin film of grease and flour on her pans; Rosaleen uses a product made by Wilton, a baking supplies company, called Cake Release. Some people prefer to use greased, floured waxed paper. We've had success with every one of these methods, and we encourage you to choose the one that best fits your cooking style.

Use cake flour. Like most southerners, we favor flours like White Lily, milled from soft red winter wheat, for our cakes. Soft winter wheat contains less protein than all-purpose flour (it's the variety of wheat used in branded cake flours such as Softasilk and Swans Down) and tends to form less gluten, which can toughen a cake. We seem to have more and more difficulty finding cake flour in both conventional and gourmet markets. If you can't find cake flour, substitute *bleached* all-purpose flour, but use less of it: for each cup of cake flour a recipe calls for, use only ¾ cup plus 2 tablespoons sifted *bleached* all-purpose flour.

Avoid overmixing the batter. When you add flour to a batter, it comes into contact with liquid, and the proteins bond with one another to form a sticky substance called gluten, which gives cakes structure but can also make them tough, especially if you are using all-purpose flour. The more you mix the flour and liquid together and the more gluten you create in the batter, the tougher your cake will be. So whenever you add flour—alternating with liquids in the recipes that follow—hand-mix the batter with a wooden spoon or rubber spatula, and mix only as long as it takes just to incorporate the added ingredient. Once all ingredients have been incorporated, beat the batter 10–12 strokes with your wooden spoon (or rubber spatula) if using cake flour, 2–3 strokes if using bleached all-purpose flour.

Inverting cakes from their pans. When the cake has cooled in its pan on a rack for about 10 minutes, run the tip of a very thin knife around the edge of the pan, taking care not to cut into the cake at all (it shouldn't be necessary unless your pan was not properly prepared and the cake has stuck to its sides). Rest a baking sheet on top of the pan, then gently flip it and set it down on the counter so the upside-down pan is resting on the sheet. Tap the top and sides of the cake pan several times with your fingertips and lift it away from the cake. Transfer the cake to a rack to cool by sliding it off the baking sheet and onto the rack.

❋ LADY BALTIMORE CAKE ❋

IMAGINE THAT YOU ARE A NOVELIST AND A CAKE RECIPE YOU INVENT FOR YOUR MAGNUM OPUS BECOMES KNOWN WORLD- wide and is baked by thousands of people for centuries, while the novel, though successful upon publication, fades into memory. Owen Wister is that novelist. In *Lady Baltimore*, set in Charleston in the years just after the end of the Civil War, a character bakes the eponymous cake. Has anyone ever read *Lady Baltimore*? We'd wager that 99 percent of the people who make this cake have never even heard of the book.

Wister's Lady Baltimore (the cake, that is) is laced with dried figs and raisins, but we've revised the recipe to use dried apricots and golden raisins, because we think they give the cake a fruitier, brighter flavor and an altogether sunnier look. Whether you use pecans or walnuts matters little, as long as they are fresh and tasty.

Our first experience with Lady Baltimore cake was when our friend Owen Lee made one for Matt's twenty-first birthday. It's a sophisticated departure from the usual birthday cake.

Makes one 2-layer 9-inch cake; enough for 12 people

TIME: 1¼ hours, plus 4 hours to marinate the fruit

FOR THE CAKE

½ cup chopped dried apricots or dried figs

½ cup chopped golden raisins

2 tablespoons lemon juice (juice of ½ lemon)

1 cup dark Caribbean rum, such as Mount Gay or Myers's, or dry sherry, such as fino or amontillado

3½ cups sifted cake flour or 3 cups plus 1 tablespoon sifted bleached all-purpose flour, plus more for flouring the pans

1 tablespoon baking powder

1 teaspoon salt

2 cups walnuts, 1 cup finely chopped, 1 cup coarsely chopped

1 cup (2 sticks) unsalted butter, softened, plus more for greasing the pans

1 teaspoon natural vanilla extract

2 cups sugar

2 large egg yolks

1 cup whole milk

6 large egg whites

FOR THE ICING

1¼ cups (2½ sticks) unsalted butter, softened

1 pound sifted confectioners' sugar

¼ teaspoon salt

1 teaspoon vanilla extract

1. Place the apricots and raisins in a medium bowl and pour the lemon juice and rum over them. Cover with plastic wrap and let stand at room temperature for 4 hours or overnight. Strain the fruit and reserve; discard all but 1 tablespoon of the liquid.

2. Preheat the oven to 350 degrees. Grease and flour two 9-×-2-inch cake pans, or line their bottoms with greased and floured waxed paper.

3. Sift the flour, baking powder, and 1 teaspoon salt together twice. Add the finely chopped nuts and stir with a wooden spoon until the nuts are evenly mixed throughout, about 30 seconds.

4. In a large mixing bowl, beat 1 cup butter with an electric mixer until creamy, about 30 seconds. Add 1 teaspoon vanilla extract, the reserved tablespoon of the lemon juice and rum mixture, and 1¾ cups granulated sugar ¼ cup at a time, beating about 15 seconds after each addition (and scraping down the sides of the bowl with a rubber spatula, if necessary), until the mixture has lightened in color and become fluffy.

5. Add the egg yolks one at a time, beating about 15 seconds after each addition, until the mixture becomes smooth and a consistent cream color, about 2 minutes. Wash the blades of the mixer well and dry them.

6. Add the dry ingredients to the butter and egg mixture in thirds, alternating with two ½-cup additions of the milk. After each addition, gently mix with the wooden spoon or rubber spatula just until the ingredient is incorporated into the batter.

7. In another large bowl, beat the egg whites with the mixer on slow speed, 30 seconds to 1 minute. As the eggs get foamy, gradually increase the speed to medium, then to medium-high, until soft peaks form, about 3 minutes. Slowly add the remaining ¼ cup granulated sugar and beat until the peaks are stiff but not dry, about 2 to 4 minutes more. Using the wooden spoon or spatula, fold the egg whites into the batter in thirds.

8. Divide the batter between the cake pans and spread the tops evenly with the spatula or the back of the wooden spoon. Bake on the middle rack until a cake tester or toothpick emerges clean, 40 to 45 minutes. Remove from the oven and let the cakes cool in their pans on a rack for 10 minutes, then slide a thin paring knife around the edge of the pans and invert the cakes (see "Cake Tips," page 460). Lift away the waxed paper, if using. Cool the cakes completely on a rack with their tops facing up.

9. With an electric mixer, beat the butter on medium speed until creamy, about 30 seconds. Add the confectioners' sugar, the salt, and the vanilla extract and beat, scraping down the sides of the bowl if necessary, until the sugar is thoroughly incorporated into the butter. Add the rum-soaked fruit and the coarsely chopped walnuts to the icing and mix with a wooden spoon or rubber spatula until evenly incorporated.

10. Spoon ½ to ¾ cup of icing in the center of the cake layer. Working an icing or rubber spatula in gentle swirling motions, spread the icing from the center toward the edges of the cake until it forms an even layer ¼ to ⅓ inch thick (if you need to add more icing, add it to the center and work it out toward the sides).

11. Carefully set the second cake layer on top of the first and ice the second layer in the same manner, beginning with a dollop in the center and working it out to the sides. Then ice the sides of the cake. (If you prepared your pans well, the sides of the cake should have pulled away from the pan and baked to a firm, flat surface. But if the sides are crumbly, brush excess crumbs away and place a thin layer of icing on the cake to seal the crumbs in, then apply another, thicker layer on top of the first.)

12. Store the cake at room temperature, beneath a cake cover. If you don't plan to eat it for 24 hours, put it on a plate, tent it with plastic wrap, and store it in the refrigerator for up to 3 days. Remember to remove the cake from the refrigerator 1 hour or more before serving to take the chill off. Serve with shot glasses of Madeira.

❋ RED VELVET CAKE ❋

RED VELVET CAKE IS A MELLOW CHOCOLATE CAKE WITH
AN INTENSE RED COLOR. A WHITE CREAM CHEESE ICING IS TRADI-
tional, preferably applied with such care that when you cut it, the cake's redness is a surprise.

We've tasted plenty of red velvet cakes that were somewhat bland—cocoa in search of a focus.
Then we tasted a red velvet cake so laden with orange extract that its chocolate flavor was barely
perceptible. But the marriage of cocoa and orange was alluring—like candied orange peel dipped
in chocolate—so we developed this rich butter cake spiked with cocoa and orange zest and colored a vivid red.

Makes one 2-layer, 9-inch cake; enough for 12 people

TIME: 1½ hours

FOR THE CAKE

2¾ cups plus 1 tablespoon sifted cake flour or
    2½ cups sifted bleached all-purpose
    flour, plus more for flouring the pans
2 teaspoons salt
2 teaspoons baking powder
¼ teaspoon baking soda
¼ cup natural cocoa powder such as Hershey's
1 ounce red food coloring

1½ tablespoons water
1 cup (2 sticks) unsalted butter, softened, plus
    more for greasing the pans
2 cups sugar
3 large eggs
1½ teaspoons natural vanilla extract
1 tablespoon orange zest (from 1–2 oranges)
1 cup whole or lowfat buttermilk

¾ cup (1½ sticks) unsalted butter
1 pound cream cheese (2 packages), softened
1 pound (4 cups) sifted confectioners' sugar
2 tablespoons whole milk, if needed

1. Preheat the oven to 350 degrees. Grease and flour two 9-×-2-inch cake pans or line their bottoms with greased, floured waxed paper.

2. Sift the flour, salt, baking powder, and baking soda together twice. In a small mixing bowl, whisk the cocoa, red food coloring, and water to a smooth paste, about 1 minute, and reserve.

3. In a large mixing bowl, beat 1 cup butter with an electric mixer until creamy, about 30 seconds. Add the sugar, ¼ cup at a time, beating about 15 seconds after each addition and scraping down the sides of the bowl if necessary, until the mixture has lightened in color and become fluffy, about 2 minutes. Add eggs, 1 at a time, the vanilla, and orange zest, beating for 15 seconds after each addition. Add the red cocoa paste and mix until evenly incorporated.

4. Add the flour mixture to the butter and egg mixture in thirds, alternating with 2 additions of half the buttermilk. To avoid overworking the batter, gently mix with a wooden spoon or rubber spatula after each addition, until the ingredient is just incorporated. Once all ingredients are incorporated, beat the batter 10 to 12 strokes with your spoon or spatula if using cake flour, 2 to 3 strokes if using bleached all-purpose flour.

5. Divide the batter between the cake pans and spread the tops evenly with the wooden spoon or spatula. Bake until a cake tester or toothpick emerges clean, about 30 minutes. Remove from the oven and let the cakes cool in their pans on a rack for 10 minutes, then slide a thin paring knife around the edge of the pans and invert the cakes (see "Cake Tips," page 460). Lift away the waxed paper, if using. Cool the cakes completely on a rack, with their tops facing up.

6. In a large bowl, beat ¾ cup butter with the mixer until creamy, about 30 seconds. Add the cream cheese and beat until the mixture is fluffy, white, and very smooth, about 1 minute. Add the confectioners' sugar 1 cup at a time, beating for 30 seconds after each addition, until the mixture is creamy, fluffy, and smooth. If the frosting is too stiff, beat the milk into it to loosen it.

7. Gently ice the cake layers generously. Spoon 1 cup of icing in the center of the first cake layer. Working an icing or rubber spatula in gentle swirling motions, spread the icing from the center toward the edges of the cake until it forms an even layer ⅓ to ½ inch thick (if you need to add more icing, add it to the center and work it out toward the sides).

8. Carefully set the second cake layer on top of the first and ice the second layer in the same manner, beginning with a dollop in the center and working it out to the sides. Then ice the sides of the cake. (If you prepared your pans well, the sides of the cake should have pulled away from the pan and baked to a firm, flat surface. But if the sides are crumbly, brush excess crumbs away and place a thin layer of icing on the cake to seal the crumbs in. Refrigerate for 30 minutes, then apply another, thicker layer on top of the first.)

9. Store the cake at room temperature, beneath a cake cover. If you don't plan to eat it for 24 hours, put it on a plate, tent it with plastic wrap, and store it in the refrigerator for up to 3 days. Remember to remove the cake from the refrigerator 1 hour or more before serving to take the chill off. Serve with glasses of cold milk.

❊ KENTUCKY APPLE STACK CAKE ❊

WHEN WE WERE TRAVELING THROUGH EASTERN KENTUCKY, A HOME COOK AND ARTISAN NAMED HAZEL MIRACLE GAVE US A taste of a two-year-old dried apple so flavorful it seemed to contain the concentrate of an entire orchard. We discovered that drying apples not only makes them last, it can subtly transform their flavors in mysterious and thrilling ways. This may be why apple butter, a cooked jam made from reconstituted dried apples, is one of the most popular roadside attractions we found in eastern Kentucky.

We also tasted our first Kentucky stack cake along those country roads, and it was a marvel, made of a dough that was somewhere between a quick bread and a true cake. In our version, you divide the dough into six balls and roll them out into thin pastry rounds, which you pat into a skillet and bake one by one. (The more skillets you have, the quicker this recipe goes.) Once you have six or more cakes, you slather a layer with sweet apple butter, place the next cake on top, and repeat until you've used up all your cakes. The finishing touch is to "marinate" the cake—to store it, covered, at room temperature for several hours, so the layers absorb some of the apple butter spread between them. When you're ready to serve it, you top the stack cake with spiked whipped cream and invite your best friends over.

Makes one 6-layer, 9-inch cake; enough for 9 to 12 people

TIME: 2 hours, plus 3 hours to "marinate"

1¼ pounds dried apples (about 7 cups)

2 quarts cold water

1 teaspoon ground cinnamon, plus more for dusting

½ teaspoon ground nutmeg

½ cup tightly packed brown sugar

⅓ cup plus 1 tablespoon dark Caribbean rum, such as Mount Gay or Myers's

7 cups (26 ounces) sifted cake flour or 6 cups plus 2 tablespoons sifted bleached all-purpose flour, plus more for flouring the pans and dusting

½ teaspoon salt

1 teaspoon baking soda

1 cup (2 sticks) unsalted butter

1 cup plus 2 teaspoons sugar

1 cup sorghum molasses (see Sourcery, page 447) or cane syrup

2 large eggs, beaten

1 cup whole or lowfat buttermilk (preferably whole)

1 cup heavy cream

1. Place the apples in a 6-quart stockpot and add the water to cover. Cover the pot and bring to a boil over medium-high heat. When the water boils vigorously, reduce the heat to medium-low, uncover, and simmer vigorously, stirring continuously, until the apples are very soft and the liquid has reduced by three quarters, about 1 hour.

2. In a food processor, puree the apples with their cooking liquid in batches and return them to the pot. Add the cinnamon, nutmeg, and brown sugar, and stir until blended. Cook gently over low heat, stirring continuously, for 30 minutes, until the apples have become a thick puree. Add the rum, stir, and simmer for a few minutes more to let the alcohol burn off. Turn off the heat and set the pot on a trivet to cool.

3. Grease and flour one or two 9-inch skillets or 9-×-2-inch cake pans, or line their bottoms with greased, floured waxed paper.

4. In a medium bowl, sift the flour, salt, and baking soda together twice. In a large bowl, beat the butter with an electric mixer until creamy, about 30 seconds. Add 1 cup of the sugar ¼ cup at a time, beating for 15 seconds after each addition and scraping the sides of the bowl if necessary, until the mixture has lightened in color and become fluffy. Add the sorghum molasses and beat until completely incorporated and the mixture is a consistent warm buff color, about 1 minute. Add the eggs, 1 at a time, beating after each addition just until the egg is incorporated, about 15 seconds.

5. Add the flour mixture to the butter and egg mixture in thirds, alternating with 2 additions of half the buttermilk. After each addition, gently mix and pat the dough with a wooden spoon or rubber spatula only until the ingredient is incorporated. The "batter" will have a texture somewhere between that of cake batter and biscuit dough. Divide the dough into 6 roughly equal balls and refrigerate for 30 minutes.

6. Preheat the oven to 350 degrees.

7. Take as many dough balls as you have 9-inch skillets and cake pans out of the refrigerator. On a lightly floured surface, flatten each ball of dough with the heel of your palm. Sprinkle a little flour on top of each disk and scatter it around. With a lightly floured rolling pin, roll each disk into an 8-inch round about ¼ inch thick. Pat each round into a 9-inch skillet or cake pan and bake on the middle rack until a cake tester or toothpick emerges clean, 8 to 10 minutes. (If you are using 2 pans, place 1 on the lower rack.) Remove from the oven and let the cakes cool on a rack in their pans for about 5 minutes, then slide a thin paring knife around the edge of the pans and invert the cakes (see "Cake Tips," page 460). Cool the cakes completely on a rack, with their tops facing up. Repeat until all the cakes have been baked.

8. Spread 1 cake layer with ¼ inch of the apple filling and place another layer on top. Repeat until all the cake layers and all the apple butter have been used. Cover with a cake cover and let stand 3 hours or overnight at room temperature. Thereafter, you can transfer the cake to a plate, tent it with plastic wrap, and store it in the refrigerator for up to 3 days. Remember to remove the cake from the refrigerator 1 hour or more before serving to take the chill off.

9. Just before serving, whip the cream with the remaining 2 teaspoons sugar and the remaining tablespoon rum until fluffy and stiff. Spread it in an even layer over the top of the stack cake. Dust the whipped cream with ground cinnamon and serve.

❋ FIG PRESERVE AND BLACK WALNUT CAKE ❋

THIS RICH LOAF CAKE COMBINES TWO OF OUR FAVORITE INDULGENCES, BLACK WALNUTS AND FIG PRESERVES. IT'S A FESTIVE holiday treat and an easy cake to bake, and—after boiled peanuts, of course—it's the recipe our customers request most. We serve the cake warm, with hard sauce, a decadent blend of butter, sugar, and rum that melts into the crumbly cake. You can forget fruitcake this year, or the trouble of a steamed pudding. But if you don't have a local source for black walnuts, factor procurement time into your holiday schedule, because most folks have to mail-order them. We'd be happy to ship them to you: phone 843-720-8890; www.boiledpeanuts.com.

Makes 1 cake; enough for 8 people

TIME: 1½ hours

FOR THE CAKE

2¼ cups sifted cake flour or 2 cups sifted bleached all-purpose flour, plus more for flouring the pan

1 teaspoon baking soda

1 teaspoon ground cinnamon

1 teaspoon ground nutmeg

1 cup (2 sticks) unsalted butter, plus more for greasing the pan

1¾ cups granulated sugar

3 large eggs, beaten

1 cup whole or low-fat buttermilk (preferably whole)

1 cup Fig Preserves (page 128), with syrup

1 cup black walnut pieces

½ cup (1 stick) unsalted butter
1 cup sifted confectioners' sugar
2 tablespoons dark Caribbean rum, such as Mount Gay or Myers's

1. In a medium bowl, sift the flour, baking soda, cinnamon, and nutmeg together twice. Thoroughly grease and flour a 2-quart Bundt pan. Preheat the oven to 350 degrees.

2. In a large bowl, beat 1 cup butter with an electric mixer until creamy, about 30 seconds. Add the sugar and beat until the mixture is fluffy and lighter in color, about 1 minute. Add the eggs, one at a time, and beat until they are thoroughly incorporated.

3. Add the flour mixture in thirds to the butter and egg mixture, alternating with 2 additions of ½ cup buttermilk, ½ cup fig preserves, and ½ cup walnuts. To avoid overworking the batter, gently mix with a wooden spoon or rubber spatula after each addition, until the ingredient is just incorporated. The batter should be pourable; add a small quantity of buttermilk if it is too stiff.

4. Pour the batter into the Bundt pan and bake on the middle rack until a cake tester or toothpick emerges clean, about 50 minutes.

5. While the cake is baking, prepare the hard sauce. In a large bowl, beat the ½ cup butter with an electric mixer until creamy, about 30 seconds. Add the confectioners' sugar and rum and beat until smooth and fluffy, about 2 minutes. With a wooden spoon or rubber spatula, gather the mixture into a log. Transfer it to a small plate, cover with plastic wrap, and refrigerate until 10 minutes before you are ready to serve.

6. Remove the cake from the oven and let cool in its pan on a rack for 15 minutes, then slide a thin paring knife around the edge of the pan and invert the cake (see "Cake Tips," page 460).

7. Place the cake on a plate and serve immediately, with pats of the slightly chilled hard sauce. Alternately, store it beneath a cake cover for up to 24 hours and reheat it, covered in aluminum foil, in a 225-degree oven for 15 minutes before serving. If storing for longer than 24 hours, transfer the cake to a plate, tent it with plastic wrap, and store it in the refrigerator for up to 3 days. Remember to remove the cake from the refrigerator 1 hour or more before serving to take the chill off.

❋ BUTTERMILK POUND CAKE ❋

IN THIS VERSATILE POUND CAKE, WE USE A COMBINATION OF THREE SUGARS. THOUGH IT MAY SEEM LIKE ONE INGREDIENT too many, it's worth it. If you must choose one brown sugar, however, use light brown, so as not to overwhelm the delicious tang of the buttermilk.

We often turn to this cake as a bed for other desserts, like Fried Apples with Bourbon Caramel (page 479). If we have a pint of fruit going just beyond ripe, we'll create a quick syrup by heating the fruit in a saucepan with a little sugar and water and spooning it over a scoop of Buttermilk Ice Cream (page 435) we've set atop a thin slice of buttermilk pound cake.

Makes 1 loaf cake; enough for 6 to 8 people
TIME: 1½ hours

2 cups sifted cake flour or 1¾ cups sifted
    bleached all-purpose flour, plus more
    for flouring the pan
¼ teaspoon baking soda
½ teaspoon salt
¼ teaspoon ground mace
4 whole eggs, lightly beaten
1¼ teaspoons natural vanilla extract

1¼ cups (2½ sticks) unsalted butter, softened,
    plus more for greasing the pan
½ cup tightly packed light brown sugar
¼ cup tightly packed dark brown sugar
2 tablespoons granulated sugar
½ cup whole or lowfat buttermilk (preferably
    whole) or sour cream

1. Preheat the oven to 325 degrees. Lightly grease and flour an 8½-×-4½-inch (6 cup) loaf pan, or line the bottom with greased, floured waxed paper.

2. In a medium bowl, sift the flour, baking powder, salt, and mace together twice.

3. In a measuring cup, whisk the eggs and vanilla together until thoroughly combined, about 1 minute.

4. In another large bowl, beat the butter with an electric mixer until creamy, about 30 seconds. Add the light brown sugar, dark brown sugar, and granulated sugar and beat on high speed until the mixture is a maple-cream color and has a fluffy texture, about 2 minutes. Add the egg mixture in a thin stream and mix on slow speed about 2 minutes until it has been incorporated and the mixture has lightened in color and become smooth (it may look curdy, which is fine). Turn off the mixer and scrape down any batter clinging to the sides of the bowl.

5. Add the flour mixture in thirds, alternating them with two ¼ cup additions of the buttermilk. To avoid overworking the batter, gently mix with a wooden spoon or rubber spatula after each addition until the ingredient is just incorporated.

6. Pour the batter into the pan and bake on the middle rack until a cake tester or toothpick inserted into the cake's center emerges clean, about 1 hour. Remove the cake from the oven and let cool in its pan on a rack for about 15 minutes. Then slide a thin paring knife around the edge of the pan and invert the cake (see "Cake Tips," page 460).

7. Serve the cake immediately, warm, or let it cool completely on the rack, cover tightly with plastic wrap, and store at room temperature up to 24 hours. If storing for longer, refrigerate for up to 3 days. Remember to remove the cake from the refrigerator 1 hour or more before serving to take the chill off.

❉ ROLLINS FAMILY GENUINE APPLE FLOAT ❉

WE NEVER UNDERSTOOD WHY OUR FRIEND CONLEY RAVED ABOUT APPLE FLOAT, A DESSERT HE CLAIMED HIS GRANDMOTHER made by whisking Mott's applesauce with CoolWhip and floating it in a pool of Jell-O instant vanilla pudding. It sounded to us like a sloppy eight-year-old's dream dessert, so we avoided it.

Then Conley got married, and at the rehearsal dinner thrown by his mother and father, apple float was served. We asked Conley's father, Tommy, about Grandma Rollins's apple float, and he revealed that hers was a homemade vanilla custard with a homemade sauce of June apples she'd picked from her own trees and real whipped cream.

Conley had been throwing us a line. From a real, delicious southern recipe, he'd fabricated a horrendous shortcut and claimed the latter to be the original, just to get our goat.

In our own apple float, everything's as Grandma Rollins would want it to be. We don't know if she'd approve of the liquor we spike the whipped cream with, but as long as she's not around to protest, no harm done.

For 6 people

TIME: 45 minutes

3 Granny Smith apples, peeled, cored, and cut
  into chunks
3 Macoun, McIntosh, or Gala apples, peeled,
  cored, and cut into chunks
1 teaspoon ground cinnamon
¼ teaspoon ground nutmeg
¼ teaspoon ground mace
¼ cup dark Caribbean rum, such as Mount
  Gay or Myers's

4 large eggs, separated
¼ cup plus 1 teaspoon sugar
2 cups whole milk
1 vanilla bean
¼ teaspoon salt
1 cup heavy cream

1. Place a medium stainless steel bowl in the freezer. In a food processor, puree the apples until smooth (about two 1-minute pulses). Transfer to a medium saucepan and add the cinnamon, nutmeg, mace, and 2 tablespoons of the rum. Cook over low heat until the puree is thick and most of the liquid has evaporated. Pour in a large bowl and let cool to room temperature, about 30 minutes.

2. In a small bowl, beat the egg yolks with a whisk or electric mixer on medium speed until they are a creamy yellow color, about 1 minute. Add ¼ cup sugar and beat until it has dissolved and the yolks have lightened in color, about 1 minute.

3. In a small saucepan heat the milk over medium-high heat until a candy thermometer registers 150 degrees (the surface of the milk may steam, but the milk should not start to boil). Remove the pan from the heat. Split the vanilla bean lengthwise with a small paring knife, and with the knife's point, scrape the seeds into the milk. Cut the bean in half crosswise and add to the milk, along with the salt. Stir a few times to distribute the flavor throughout the milk.

4. Slowly pour ½ cup of the hot milk into the egg-yolk mixture in a thin stream, whisking constantly. Pour the mixture into the pan with the remaining hot milk (or, preferably, the top of a double boiler), whisking constantly. Heat the custard over the lowest possible heat, stirring constantly, until it is thick enough to coat the back of a spoon, 8 to 10 minutes.

5. Using an electric mixer, beat the egg whites to stiff peaks. Gently fold into the apple puree.

6. In the chilled stainless steel bowl, whisk the cream, the remaining 1 teaspoon sugar, and the remaining rum together and whip until the cream is thick and holds its shape.

7. To serve, ladle ⅓ cup custard into each of 6 shallow bowls. Mound ½ cup puree in the center of the custard and spoon dollops of whipped cream on top.

❋ FRIED APPLES ❋
WITH BOURBON CARAMEL

FRIED APPLES ARE AMONG THE SIMPLEST FRUIT PREPA-
RATIONS TO MAKE, AND IN THE MOUNTAIN SOUTH THEY'RE CON-
sumed most often alongside a savory main course. Here we make fried apples a dessert, with a
quick caramel sauce made with bourbon or Tennessee whiskey (rye is a great alternate too). One
good thing about fried apples is that you can whip them up while someone's clearing the dinner
plates. If they seem too easy for a dinner party, you can give them the Downtown Touch by spooning them over Buttermilk Pound Cake (page 474) or topping them with Buttermilk Ice Cream
(page 435). Although you might be tempted to spice them up with plenty of allspice, cinnamon,
and clove, we think whiskey and brown sugar flatter the concentrated apple flavor perfectly.

For 6 people
TIME: 15–20 minutes

3 tablespoons unsalted butter
6 Granny Smith apples, peeled, cored, and
    sliced into ⅛-inch-thick half-moons
½ cup water

¼ cup plus 2 tablespoons dark brown sugar
½ teaspoon ground cinnamon
¾ cup heavy cream
¼ cup Tennessee whiskey or Kentucky bourbon

1.   In a 12-inch skillet, heat the butter over medium-high heat until frothy. Add the apples, cover, and cook, stirring occasionally, until the apples have begun to soften, about 3 minutes. Stir in the water, brown sugar, and cinnamon and cook, covered, stirring occasionally, for about 5 minutes, until the syrup is thick, the apples are soft, and the pan is almost dry. Add the cream and cook, uncovered, until the juice is syrupy, 1 to 2 minutes. Turn off the heat. Stir in the bourbon and let stand for another minute to let the alcohol evaporate.

2.   Spoon the apples over pound cake or serve in bowls, with a scoop of ice cream or a dollop of whipped cream on top.

❈ TEA CUSTARD ❈

IRONICALLY, PERUSING OLD COOKBOOKS—TRULY OLD
ONES, FROM THE NINETEENTH CENTURY—IS AN EXCELLENT WAY TO
find fresh ideas in cooking. One ancient pamphlet in our collection, a southern tract on winemaking, moves quickly from grapes to fruits like plum and prickly pear (the magenta-colored fruit of the prickly pear cactus) and even includes a recipe for "Tea Wine." The odd notion of treating tea, the stuff of porcelain English afternoons, like just another sack of fruit was liberating. We're not so sure about its potential as wine (we never attempted it), but it gave us the courage to try tea as a flavoring, in a basic custard—an idea we found in another old cookbook. The jasmine tea–scented custard is subtle and delicious, and wouldn't be out of place at Claridge's Hotel in London.

In the eighteenth century, tea was grown experimentally around Summerville, South Carolina, and it continues to be grown at a farm on Wadmalaw Island. Aromatic teas like Orange Pekoe, of the sort in the Lipton tea bag, work perfectly in this elegant dessert. Serve it cool or cold in the summer and warm in the fall and winter.

Makes six 6-ounce custards

TIME: 20 minutes preparation, 30 minutes cooling down, 40 minutes cooking

2 cups half-and-half
1 ounce fragrant loose tea such as jasmine or
    1½ tea bags
3 tablespoons plus 2 teaspoons sugar, plus
    more for dusting

2 large eggs
2 large egg yolks
2 tablespoons unsalted butter, for greasing
    ramekins
Light brown sugar, for garnish

1. Prepare a kettle of boiling water. Pour the half-and-half into a small saucepan and bring it almost to a boil over medium heat, stirring frequently.

2. Place the loose tea or the tea bags in the bottom of a small saucepan and pour on a splash of boiling water—just enough to soften the leaves. Add the sugar and stir.

3. When the half-and-half begins to froth and simmer, remove it from the heat and pour it over the sugar and tea. Stir twice, cover the pan, and place it in the refrigerator or freezer to cool to room temperature, about 30 minutes. Strain the loose tea from the mixture or remove the tea bags.

4. Preheat the oven to 325 degrees. Grease six 6-ounce ramekins with butter and dust them with sugar.

5. When the tea mixture has cooled, whisk the 2 whole eggs and 2 egg yolks briskly in a medium bowl, until uniformly lemon-yellow in color. Stir into the tea mixture just until blended.

6. Strain the mixture through a fine-mesh strainer and pour into the ramekins. Place the ramekins in a large baking pan and carefully pour hot water into the pan to reach halfway up their sides. Bake for 40 minutes, until the custards appear firm and a knife or toothpick inserted in the centers comes away clean.

7. Remove the pan from the oven and the ramekins from the pan. Dust the tops of the custards with a few pinches of brown sugar and serve immediately, or refrigerate until cool.

❋ PICKLED PEACH FRUIT SALAD GELÉE ❋

NOW THAT GELÉES HAVE BECOME ALL THE RAGE AMONG THE MOST FORWARD-THINKING CHEFS OF SPAIN, FRANCE, AND North America, it's safe for southerners to dust off our congealed fruit salads and let them out on the town.

A gelatin done right has an alluringly smooth and yielding texture, like an Italian panna cotta. Clumsily done, it can be rubbery.

This is our rendition of the pickled peach and ginger ale salad that is a familiar Christmastime buffet item. We give it a goose in a number of ways. First, we call it dessert. Second, we add real ginger and a little sherry to amplify the flavors of the salad and make it irresistible. Then we add diced apple and chopped crystallized ginger for some textural contrasts. It's a refreshing, satisfying finish to a meal, and visually stunning, too.

¾ pound Pickled Peaches (page 105), strained (about 5 small peaches, or 1 cup), syrup reserved

1 cup peeled, diced Granny Smith apple (about 1 apple)

½ cup chopped pecans

½ teaspoon kosher salt

12 ounces cold water

12 ounces ginger ale (1½ cups, or 1 can)

1 tablespoon cold lemon juice

1 tablespoon cold sherry

2 envelopes unflavored gelatin

2 teaspoons lemon zest (from 1 large lemon)

1 teaspoon grated fresh ginger

2 tablespoons finely chopped crystallized ginger

2 cups whipped cream

1. Shred the peaches with your hands or chop them with a knife. Mix the peaches, apple, nuts, and salt in a mixing bowl and then pat the mixture into the bottom of eight 4-ounce ramekins or a 4½-cup ring mold.

2. Combine the water and ginger ale in a medium saucepan and bring to a boil over high heat. In a small bowl, combine the lemon juice and sherry, add the gelatin, and stir with a fork to dissolve; let stand for 1 minute. Add the gelatin mixture, lemon zest, grated ginger, and crystallized ginger to the hot ginger ale mixture and return to a simmer. Simmer vigorously for 2 minutes more. Pour the hot liquid into the ramekins or ring mold and refrigerate for 4 hours, or until the gelatin jiggles stiffly when the mold is gently shaken.

3. To unmold, run the tip of a knife about ¼ inch deep around the edge of the gelée where it meets the ramekin, or around both outer and inner edges of the gelée if using a ring mold. Fill a bowl with hot water and dip each ramekin or the ring mold into it for 15 seconds. Hold a small serving plate face down on top of each ramekin or a large plate or serving platter on top of the mold and invert in a single swift motion. If the gelée doesn't immediately release, alternately dab the ramekin or mold with a clean dish towel soaked in hot water and tap it with your fingers until it releases.

4. Cut the gelée into slices with a sharp knife. Serve on plates with dollops of whipped cream.

❈ BENNE WAFERS ❈

LIKE SHRIMP AND GRITS OR SHE-CRAB SOUP, BENNE WAFERS ARE A CULINARY ICON OF THE LOWCOUNTRY. BAKERIES IN Charleston sell these tiny, quarter-sized sesame-seed cookies by the tubful. We offer benne wafers in our Boiled Peanuts Catalogue because they're a ready-to-eat hit. They're delicate, too, so we have to stamp "Fragile" on every box that goes out.

A Lowcountry staple since the turn of the eighteenth century, benne wafers taste even better when freshly baked. Their toasted sesame flavor makes them insanely addictive, and they're ideal with tea or after dinner, with coffee or dessert wine. Their crispness contrasts nicely with soft, creamy desserts, so use them as a garnish for ice cream or Tea Custard (page 481).

Makes 120 quarter-sized cookies

TIME: 45 minutes

⅓ cup benne (sesame) seeds

¼ cup plus 1 tablespoon (1 ounce) sifted bleached all-purpose flour, plus more for flouring cookie sheet

½ cup sugar

¼ cup light brown sugar

½ teaspoon salt

¼ teaspoon baking soda

2 tablespoons cold unsalted butter, plus more for greasing cookie sheets

1 large egg white

½ teaspoon natural vanilla extract

1. Preheat the oven to 375 degrees. Thoroughly grease and flour two cookie sheets or spray them with a vegetable-oil based cooking spray.

2. In a 9-inch cast-iron skillet, toast the seeds over medium-low heat, agitating them frequently in the pan, until they are the color of unpopped popcorn, about 5 minutes.

3. Sift the flour with the sugar, brown sugar, salt, and baking soda twice. Cut the butter into the dry ingredients with punching strokes of a pastry blender or with your fingertips until the mixture resembles coarse crumbs.

4. Using an electric mixer, beat the egg white on medium speed to medium-stiff peaks. Add the dry ingredients in quarters, beating until the batter is consistently smooth and lustrous, about 2 minutes. Add the toasted seeds and vanilla and beat on low speed just until the seeds are evenly incorporated. Transfer the batter to a pastry bag fitted with a round tip or to a plastic bag with a zipper seal with a tiny piece of its corner cut out.

5. Working in batches of 30, pipe the batter in ¼-teaspoon-sized drops about 2 inches apart onto the cookie sheets and bake until the cookies just begin to turn from blond to auburn, about 4 to 6 minutes. Transfer the cookie sheets to a rack and cool until the cookies have stiffened, about 5 minutes. Transfer with a spatula to a container with a tight-fitting lid. Repeat until all the cookies are baked, and let them cool completely before sealing the container.

6. The cookies will keep in the container for 3 or 4 days.

ALWAYS A STEP AHEAD, MARY JO WANNAMAKER, OF WANnamaker Seeds in St. Matthews, South Carolina, is now growing sesame, a plant imported from Africa whose seeds are a popular ingredient and garnish in Japan and in sushi restaurants throughout the world. She led us into her fields recently to show off her first fifty-acre plot of black sesame. In the middle of a drought-stricken summer, it was a sight to behold: a lush, blemish-free, radiantly green field, shoulder high with sprays of light lavender flowers (only the seeds of this variety are black). The crop was grown entirely without irrigation, and the deer hate it, so it's as close to a perfect southern crop as can be devised. Conventional sesame was grown in the Carolinas before, and in fact, the seeds were popular as early as the eighteenth century. Today they can be found in cookies, candies, and our toasty, crisp Benne Wafers (page 485).

Sesame, like okra, was brought from Northern Africa to North America with the slave trade. The drought-tolerant plant looks healthy even after a parched August, and is unappetizing to deer—as close to a perfect crop as you could want in South Carolina.

❊ SORGHUM POPCORN BALLS ❊

WE USE A HALF-AND-HALF MIXTURE OF SORGHUM
MOLASSES AND SUGAR WHEN MAKING THE BUTTERY CARAMEL FOR
our popcorn balls. And we season the sweetness with a little bit of heat, in the form of ½ teaspoon
cayenne pepper. The result is a flavorful, easy spin on caramel popcorn balls. These are fun set out
in a silver bowl for a holiday party, but they're also quite portable, so we pack them to take along
on canoe trips and car rides.

There's a trick to this recipe, since it requires forming the syrup-covered popcorn into balls
when the syrup is still very warm. Wear kitchen gloves that have been sterilized in boiling water
and greased with butter to protect your hands as you form the balls.

Makes about twenty 2½-inch balls

TIME: 25 minutes

EQUIPMENT

1 candy thermometer
Kitchen gloves, sterilized, greased with a little butter

12 cups popped corn (about 3 ounces), popped from ½ cup popcorn kernels

¾ cup sugar

¾ cup sorghum molasses (see Sourcery, page 447) or cane syrup

1 teaspoon salt

½ cup water, at room temperature

½ teaspoon natural vanilla extract

4 tablespoons unsalted butter

½ teaspoon cayenne pepper or other hot ground chile powder (optional)

1. Place the popped popcorn in a large mixing bowl.

2. In a medium saucepan, heat the sugar, sorghum molasses, salt, water, and vanilla over medium heat, stirring occasionally with a wooden spoon or heat-resistant spatula, until the syrup reaches the hard-ball stage (260 degrees on a candy thermometer), 12 to 15 minutes. Take care not to let the hot syrup foam over the sides of the pan.

3. Add the butter to the syrup, stir until thoroughly incorporated, and then turn off the heat. Immediately pour about a quarter of the syrup in a thin stream over the popcorn in the bowl and toss with a wooden spoon or heatproof rubber spatula. Add another quarter of the syrup and toss again. Repeat until all the syrup has been poured, and toss to distribute evenly (this step is much easier with a helper on hand, either to toss the popcorn or to pour the syrup).

4. Put on the clean, greased kitchen gloves and shape the popcorn into balls about 2 to 2½ inches in diameter (a little larger than a golfball). If the popcorn does not stick together, wait 30 seconds for the syrup to cool slightly and try again. Transfer the balls to a sheet of waxed paper to cool completely.

5. Serve the cooled popcorn balls immediately, or store at room temperature in a container with a tight-fitting lid. They will keep for 3 or 4 days.

❧ HOT-SPICED BOURBON BALLS ❧

QUICK
KNOCKOUT

IN CHARLESTON, WE SEE BOURBON BALLS ONLY AT COCK-
TAIL PARTIES DURING THE HOLIDAYS. BUT THEY'RE A SWOON-
worthy treat anytime—with afternoon tea, with morning coffee, or even as a small dessert at the
end of a filling meal. Moreover, they're a breeze to make.

We've noticed that in the past several years, pastry chefs have become hip to chile and chocolate (a common pairing in Mexico). We love the combination, too, and it's what inspired us to add
the kicky heat of cayenne pepper to these bourbon balls. The cayenne is optional, of course, but
how could you resist?

Makes about thirty 1-inch balls; enough for 12 to 16 people

TIME: 15 minutes

1¼ cups sifted confectioners' sugar

2 tablespoons natural or Dutch-process cocoa
    powder

½ teaspoon ground cayenne pepper (optional)

¼ teaspoon ground mace

¼ teaspoon ground cinnamon

½ teaspoon salt

¼ cup bourbon

2 tablespoons sorghum syrup (see Sourcery,
    page 447), cane syrup, molasses, or
    honey

10 ounces vanilla wafers (about 60)

1 cup coarsely chopped pecans

1. In a large bowl, sift 1 cup confectioners' sugar and the cocoa, cayenne, mace, cinnamon, and salt together. In a small bowl, whisk the bourbon and sorghum syrup until well blended. Stir the bourbon syrup into the dry ingredients with a wooden spoon or rubber spatula until the mixture is a dark, glossy paste.

2. In a food processor, pulse the vanilla wafers to fine crumbs, about ten 5-second pulses. Mix the crumbs with the pecans. Stir the pecan and cookie mixture into the cocoa mixture until it becomes consistently doughy and workable, about 2 minutes.

3. Roll the dough into 1-inch balls between your palms. Roll each ball in the remaining ¼ cup confectioners' sugar and place on a sheet of waxed paper. Refrigerate in a container with a tight-fitting lid, with a sheet of waxed paper between each layer of bourbon balls, not more than 4 days.

❄ OWEN'S PRALINES ❄

OUR NEIGHBOR OWEN LEE, WHO HAS A BIT OF A SWEET TOOTH, MAKES THESE CLASSIC, SIMPLE CANDIES. WE LOVE THEM for their intriguingly soft texture and fabulous pecan flavor.

Makes twelve 2-inch pralines; enough for 6 people

TIME: 30 minutes

1 cup sugar
½ cup tightly packed light brown sugar
2 pinches salt
½ cup half-and-half

1 cup chopped pecans
1 tablespoon unsalted butter
1 teaspoon natural vanilla extract

1. In a 3- to 4-quart saucepan with a heavy bottom, combine the sugar, brown sugar, salt, and half-and-half. Cook over medium-high heat, stirring with a wooden spoon or heatproof rubber spatula, until the sugars have dissolved and the liquid just begins to simmer, about 10 minutes.

2. Add the pecans and butter and simmer, stirring, until the temperature reads 230 degrees on a candy thermometer. Add the vanilla, turn off the heat, and continue stirring with a wooden spoon until the mixture thickens perceptibly, to about the viscosity of beaten egg yolks, 4 to 8 minutes.

3. Ladle or spoon a little less than 1 tablespoon of the syrup onto greased wax paper, creating a puddle that is approximately 2 inches in diameter. Repeat until all the syrup has been used. Cool the pralines for 10 minutes, until they harden and are cool enough to handle.

4. Transfer to a container with a tight-fitting lid, separating each layer with a sheet of waxed paper. The pralines will keep at room temperature for 3 or 4 days.

✺ THE BREAD BASKET AND THE PANTRY ✺

The baking chapters of southern cookbooks tend to begin with a lament about how we've lost the tradition of daily bread. This lament usually takes shape from the author's memory of watching a relative make biscuits or corn bread *without using measuring spoons.*

The implication is clear: if you have to use measuring spoons, your baking isn't southern enough. These homilies rarely take into account the leagues of southerners who bake happily with measuring cups and spoons, make unholy messes, and run out of ingredients often. So the southern baking memory we'll share here is of waking up on Sullivan's Island to the most wonderful smell of baking biscuits and our friend Jo announcing she had made the best batch she'd ever made in her life—a claim we did not take lightly, since Jo is a lifelong Charlestonian and has made a few biscuits in her time.

Those were astounding biscuits, but they were entirely a mistake: Jo had run out of buttermilk and used yogurt instead. They were dense, crinkled, slightly sour, moist, and undeniably delicious. And she said she would never make biscuits the old way again.

Another friend, Ginny, once ran out of butter when she was baking chocolate cupcakes, so she used lard instead, and they were scrumptious. Even though she might not produce lard cupcakes again—as much as we encourage her—we relate these memories because they may inspire you to get into the kitchen and make baking a fearless daily routine, the kind of ritual that will evolve as you do. It might even get you to that baking nirvana in which you measure your flour, your butter, and your milk *without measuring spoons.*

✺ CRISPY CORN BREAD ✺

*Fine with me if someone puts a half-teaspoon of sugar in her corn bread. As long as she calls it "cake,"
not "corn bread."*
—RONNI LUNDY

SOUTHERNERS ARE PARTICULAR—TOUCIIY, EVEN—ABOUT
THEIR CORN BREAD. AT THE SOUTHERN FOODWAYS SYMPOSIUM, IN
Oxford, Mississippi, a tall woman collared Ted, shouting, "I've got a bone to pick with you!" We'd
recently published a recipe in the *New York Times* for corn bread and chestnut dressing which
used—gasp!—yellow cornmeal. "You gotta use *white* meal if you're gonna make *real* corn bread!"
she hollered. Then, in a quieter voice: "Hi, I'm Mindy Merrell."

For twelve years, Mindy worked in the test kitchen of the Nashville milling company Martha
White. She's made thousands of batches of corn bread, and she knows a lot about how southerners bake. As is often the case with folks who are zealous about their food, we became fast friends,
and she told us she would bake us a proper corn bread the next time we were in Nashville. A year
later we passed through Music City and took her up on the offer. Our expectations were high, and
of course she exceeded them, and forever changed the way we cook corn bread.

Mindy's version has an emphatic corn flavor and the textbook caramelized crust, but its
genius lies in the way it manages to double the crispiness of the bread while remaining perfectly
moist. And it has nothing to do with chemistry (or color of the meal) but everything to do with
skillet size. Mindy bakes a single six-serving batch in a 12-inch skillet instead of a 9-incher, so the
batter lies thinner in the pan. The bread bakes up only about a half-inch thick, which means the

crust-to-crumb ratio is quite high. It's a thin, elegant flatbread, and if you start baking it daily, you just might make up for all those thick, Sahara-dry corn-bread bricks you've eaten.

You can use white cornmeal if you wish. We use yellow more often than not.

For 6 people

TIME: 30 minutes

1 tablespoon lard or unsalted butter
1½ cups stone-ground cornmeal
1 teaspoon baking powder
1 teaspoon baking soda
½ teaspoon salt

1 teaspoon sugar
1 large egg
1½ cups whole or lowfat buttermilk
    (preferably whole)
2 tablespoons unsalted butter

1. Preheat the oven to 450 degrees. Grease a 12-inch skillet with the lard, leaving any excess in the pan, and place it in the oven.

2. In a large bowl, sift the dry ingredients together. In a medium bowl, whisk the egg until frothy and then whisk in the buttermilk. Add the wet ingredients to the dry ones and mix thoroughly. Melt the butter in a small skillet over low heat, and whisk the butter into the batter.

3. When the fat in the large skillet is smoking, carefully remove the skillet from the oven and swirl the fat around to coat the bottom and sides evenly. Pour the batter into the skillet; it should sizzle alluringly. Bake for 15 minutes, or until the top of the bread is golden brown and the edge has pulled away from the side of the skillet. Remove from the oven.

4. Cut the corn bread into 6 wedges in the skillet and serve hot, with Sorghum Butter (page 529).

❈ DRESSING BREAD ❈

WHEN A STUFFING, OR DRESSING, LIKE OUR OYSTER DRESSING (PAGE 403), HAS A MEDLEY OF SAVORY FLAVORS, WE USE this bread recipe, a variant of Crispy Corn Bread that substitutes flour for a portion of the cornmeal. The result is a deliciously crisp bread with a toned-down corn taste that adds structure without overwhelming the other wonderful flavors that go into those dishes. To make Dressing Bread, follow the recipe for Crispy Corn Bread, but substitute ¾ cup all-purpose flour for an equal quantity of stone-ground cornmeal, so you've got a half-and-half ratio of stone-ground cornmeal to flour.

❊ SALLY LUNN ❊

SALLY LUNN IS THE SOUTH'S CHALLAH, A FAINTLY SWEET, ALMOST CHEWY MOIST WHITE BREAD WITH A CRISP GOLDEN CRUST that's delicious spread with Pimento Cheese (page 89), Ham Relish (page 94), Butterbean Pâté (page 73), or butter and Scuppernong Preserves (page 132). It makes out-of-this-world French toast, too.

Stories about how Sally Lunn got its curious name are akin to hoppin' John stories—unconvincing and uncorroboratable. Some historians maintain there was a baker in Bath, England, named Sally Lunn who invented this loaf, others that the name was a British mispronunciation of *soleil et lune*, the French term for a similar bread made across the Channel. We rarely take sides in these academic quarrels, but for some inexplicable reason we find it more fun to tell stories involving mispronunciations.

Sally Lunn isn't as simple to make as corn bread, so it's not our household's daily bread, but it's worth making it a part of your week.

Makes one 8½-×-4½-inch loaf; enough for 6 sandwiches

TIME: 1½ hours

1 cup whole milk

1 package (¼ ounce, or 2¼ teaspoons) active dry yeast, at room temperature

8 tablespoons butter (1 stick), softened

⅓ cup sorghum molasses (see Sourcery, page 447), cane syrup, or honey

3 large eggs, at room temperature

4 cups (16 ounces) sifted unbleached all-purpose flour, at room temperature

1 teaspoon salt

1. In a small saucepan, heat the milk over medium heat, stirring occasionally, until the temperature reads 105 degrees on a candy thermometer. Turn off the heat. Pour the yeast into the milk, whisk gently with a fork to dissolve (some of the yeast may not dissolve immediately), and let stand until tiny bubbles form on the surface of the milk, 5 to 10 minutes.

2. With an electric mixer, cream 7 tablespoons butter with the molasses in a large bowl until smooth, glossy, and slightly fluffy, about 2 minutes. Add the eggs, 1 at a time and beat until café-au-lait in color (if you use honey, it will be creamy light yellow).

3. In a medium bowl, sift the flour with the salt. Add the flour mixture and the milk and yeast mixture to the egg mixture alternately, one fourth at a time, mixing well with a wooden spoon after each addition, until all the flour is incorporated and the dough comes together. Stir for a few minutes to ensure a smooth consistency.

4. Mark the level of the top of the dough on the outside of the bowl with a dab of butter or flour. Cover the dough with a clean dish towel and let it rest in a warm place. When the dough has doubled in size, about 35 minutes, transfer it to a clean, flat surface and punch it down. Beat it with your fist 30 times.

5. Butter an 8½-×-4½-inch loaf pan with the remaining 1 tablespoon butter. Transfer the dough to the loaf pan and pat it evenly into place. Mark the level of the top of the dough on the outside of the pan with another dab of butter or flour. Set in a warm place to rest.

6. Preheat the oven to 350 degrees. When the dough has doubled in size again (about 12 minutes), bake on the middle rack for 35 minutes, or until the top is golden brown. Cool the bread in its pan on a rack for 10 minutes, then invert the pan and remove the loaf. Slice with a serrated bread knife while warm, or let cool completely on the rack.

LARD IS NOTHING MORE THAN RENDERED PIG FAT, North America's primary grease from the time European explorers introduced hogs to this continent until the middle of the twentieth century. Pig fat proved to be excellent for making soap, lubricating moving parts, fueling lamps—and cooking.

But lard has come to be perceived as sinister, the ringleader of a gang of dietary ills associated with rural poverty: overdependence on fried foods, over-salting, too few fruits and vegetables. In the mid-1950s, just as more rural Americans were moving to the cities, the first studies linking the consumption of animal fats to high levels of cholesterol in the blood were published. Subsequent studies indicated that high cholesterol levels were a significant risk factor for heart disease. Throughout the 1970s and 1980s, as groups of doctors and nutritionists popularized the findings, the public developed a stubborn prejudice against lard, so that today most Americans would sooner smoke unfiltered Camels while riding a motorcycle without a helmet than eat it.

But recent studies differentiating between saturated and unsaturated fats put lard in a better light, particularly as the emphasis has shifted away from avoiding fat altogether and toward choosing the type of fat you consume carefully. According to the Agriculture Department's Nutrition Database, lard is composed of 42 percent saturated fat (which may increase cholesterol levels in the blood) and 54 percent unsaturated fat (which may decrease cholesterol in the blood). By comparison, butter is 43 percent saturated fat and 30 percent unsaturated, while olive oil is 14 percent saturated and 83 percent unsaturated. Thus, lard is no worse for you than butter, and they're both a heck of a lot healthier than any of the processed, hydrogenated margarines and spreads.

Lard is nearly 100 percent fat (by comparison, the fat rendered from beef is 92 percent fat, and butter is 81 percent fat, the balance made up with water and other solids). Cooks around the world, particularly in Mexico and eastern Europe, still rely on it.

While most nutritionists continue to discourage regular use of lard, not everyone agrees. "Lard's not a big deal," says Dr. John M. Dietschy, who conducts studies of cholesterol metabolism as director of the department of gastroenterology at the University of Texas Southwestern Medical School in Dallas. "The real danger in the human diet is in total calories consumed. All oils are extremely rich, about nine calories per gram."

We like lard. We perceive it to be a special fat, like butter. We don't use it every day, but when we do, we use it without guilt and with great results. One claim about lard that is undisputed is that it gives biscuits and pie crusts an appealing flakiness. But we use it in combination with butter, because while we like the texture that lard provides, we also crave the unmistakable sweet-cream flavor that butter gives our biscuits and pie crusts.

In supermarkets, lard is sometimes labeled by its Spanish name, *Manteca*, and it's often whipped up with the preservative BHT (butylated hydroxytoluene) to keep it shelf-stable. BHT adds off flavors to it, so whenever possible, buy lard directly from a butcher, and ask at the meat counter of a supermarket. Fresh lard is inexpensive and worth seeking out. One excellent source is Faicco's Pork Store, 260 Bleecker St., New York, NY, 10014; 212-243-1974.

Kentucky native James Miracle holds one of his hand-hewn bowls. Its insulating properties encourage leavened bread dough to rise.

❋ BIRD–HEAD BUTTERMILK BISCUITS ❋

BUTTERMILK BISCUITS ARE OUR PREFERRED VEHICLE FOR SALTY SHARDS OF COUNTRY HAM, BUT THESE BISCUITS ARE also a favorite for breakfast, with pats of butter and dollops of Fig Preserves (page 128). They have moderate rise and an airy flakiness that's caused by using lard and a layered technique during rolling that encourages the biscuits to break apart in sheets, the way the ones we grew up with did.

In the South, there seems to be a fetish for large biscuits, called "cat-head biscuits" because they're the size of a cat's head. We like smaller biscuits, so we call them bird-head biscuits.

Makes about sixteen 2-inch round biscuits

TIME: 30 minutes

2¼ cups sifted cake flour or 2 cups sifted bleached all-purpose flour, plus more for your work surface and hands
1 tablespoon baking powder
1 tablespoon plus 1 teaspoon sugar
1 teaspoon salt

4 tablespoons cold unsalted butter, cut into several pieces
2 tablespoons cold lard or vegetable shortening, cut into several pieces
¾ cup cold whole or lowfat buttermilk (preferably whole)

1.   Preheat the oven to 400 degrees.

2.   In a medium bowl, mix the dry ingredients thoroughly with a fork. Transfer to a food processor fitted with the chopping blade. Add the butter and lard and pulse the mixture in 2-second increments until the mixture resembles coarse crumbs with a few pea-sized pieces, about 5 pulses. (If you don't have a food processor, cut the fats into the dry ingredients in a bowl by mashing with a fork, a whisk, or a pastry blender; it will take about 3 minutes.)

3.   Transfer the mixture back to the bowl, pour the buttermilk over it, and mix with the fork for about 1 minute, until the dough just comes together. Turn the dough out onto a floured board, knead with floured fingers once or twice, and pat it into a rectangle about 6 × 10 inches and 1 inch thick.

4.   Fold the rightmost third of the rectangle over the center third and fold the left third on top. Turn the dough a quarter turn, pat it into a 6-×-10-inch rectangle, and fold it upon itself in thirds again. Repeat one more time, then pat the dough into a 6-×-10-inch rectangle about 1 inch thick.

5.   Using a floured 2-inch biscuit cutter (or an upside-down shot glass), cut the biscuits from the dough and place them about 1½ inches apart on an ungreased baking sheet. Bake for 15 to 20 minutes, until the tops just begin to brown.

6.   Serve the biscuits warm, with Sorghum Butter (page 529), with eggs and bacon, or with a dollop of Jerusalem Artichoke Relish (page 112) and a sliver of country ham.

CRACKLIN' BUTTERMILK BISCUITS: ADD 1/4 CUP VERY FINELY DICED PORK CRACKLINGS, COOKED BACON, OR COUNTRY HAM, OR JUST ABOUT ANY CURED MEAT THAT IS DELICIOUS EATEN OUT OF HAND, AFTER YOU ADD THE BUTTERMILK IN STEP 3.

BUTTERMILK CHEESE BISCUITS: ADD 1/3 CUP GRATED EXTRA-SHARP CHEDDAR CHEESE ALONG WITH THE FATS TO THE DRY INGREDIENTS IN STEP 2.

LEMON BUTTERMILK BISCUITS OR LIME BUTTERMILK BISCUITS: WITH A FORK OR PASTRY BLENDER, MIX 2 TEASPOONS LEMON OR LIME ZEST INTO THE DRY INGREDIENTS IN STEP 2, BEFORE CUTTING IN THE FATS.

HERBED BUTTERMILK BISCUITS: WITH A FORK OR PASTRY BLENDER, MIX 2 TABLESPOONS FINELY CHOPPED LEMON THYME, BASIL, OR DILL INTO THE DRY INGREDIENTS IN STEP 2, BEFORE CUTTING IN THE FATS. BECAUSE ROSEMARY HAS SUCH AN ASSERTIVE FLAVOR, FOR ROSEMARY BUTTERMILK BISCUITS, USE ONLY 1 TABLESPOON OF THE HERB, FINELY CHOPPED.

VANILLA BUTTERMILK BISCUITS: THESE MAKE TERRIFIC QUICK DESSERTS IF YOU SERVE THEM WITH A SCOOP OF BUTTERMILK ICE CREAM (PAGE 435) AND A DOLLOP OF FRUIT PRESERVES, STEWED FRUIT, CANE SYRUP, OR SORGHUM. ADD 1 TABLESPOON MORE SUGAR TO THE RECIPE, FOR A TOTAL AMOUNT OF 2 TABLESPOONS PLUS ONE TEASPOON. WITH A PASTRY BLENDER OR FORK, MIX THE SEEDS FROM ONE WHOLE VANILLA BEAN INTO THE DRY INGREDIENTS IN STEP 2. (ALTERNATELY, ADD 1 TEASPOON NATURAL VANILLA EXTRACT TO THE BUTTERMILK BEFORE POURING IT OVER THE BUTTER AND FLOUR MIXTURE.)

❈ SWEET PIE CRUST ❈

THIS PIE CRUST WORKS WELL FOR ALL KINDS OF DESSERT PIES. THE TRICK TO GETTING IT TO BAKE UP NICE AND FLAKY IS TO chill all your ingredients ahead of time in the bowl you're going to be working in. if it's really warm out, we even put our rolling pin in the freezer while the ingredients are chilling. Although some people like to use cake flour in their pie crusts, we like the flavor of all-purpose better.

Makes 1 pie shell or 1 top (for a double-crust pie)
TIME: 1 hour to chill, 5–8 minutes to prepare, 25 minutes to bake

1½ cups sifted bleached all-purpose flour, plus more for dusting
1 tablespoon sugar
1 teaspoon salt

4 tablespoons cold lard, cut into small pieces
4 tablespoons cold butter, cut into small pieces
¼ cup ice water

1. Sift the dry ingredients together in a medium bowl. Sprinkle the pieces of lard and butter over them and place the bowl in the refrigerator for 30 minutes. Dust your work surface with flour. If prebaking, preheat the oven to 325 degrees.

2. Using a pastry blender or your fingertips, cut the lard and butter into the dry ingredients until the mixture resembles coarse crumbs, with a scattering of pea-sized pieces throughout. Add ice water a tablespoon at a time, and toss with a fork to combine after each addition, until the pastry holds together when pinched (you may not use all the ice water).

3. Gather the pastry together into a round disk, wrap tightly in plastic wrap, and refrigerate for 15 minutes or until ready to use.

4. With a floured pin, roll out the dough on the floured surface to a 12-inch round. To make a pie shell, transfer to a 9-inch pie pan. Fold any excess dough that hangs below the rim of the pan on top of the rim so you have enough material to crimp. Cut off any egregious excess and use it to patch any holes or tears. Refrigerate for 15 minutes before filling or prebaking.

5. To prebake the crust for Sorghum Pecan Pie (page 449) or Sweet Potato Buttermilk Pie (page 442), lay a sheet of aluminum foil over the dough and carefully scatter pie weights, dried beans, or pennies in the pan. Bake on the middle rack for 12 to 15 minutes. Remove the pie weights and the foil, prick the bottom of the crust with a fork, and bake for 10 minutes more, or until the bottom of the crust appears dry.

Note: To make the top of a double-crust pie such as Grape Hull Pie (page 454), simply slide a baking sheet under the 12-inch round and refrigerate for 15 minutes or until ready to use.

❋ SAVORY PIE CRUST ❋

THIS PIE CRUST, WHICH HAS A TOUCH OF BUTTERMILK AND MORE BUTTERY BROWNING ABILITY THAN SWEET PIE CRUST, is perfect for savory pies. It works equally well as a 9-inch square lid for Bobo-Style Oyster Pie (page 379) and as toppers for individual Shrimp Pot Pies (page 405).

Makes 1 pie shell or 1 top (for a double-crust pie)
TIME: 1 hour to chill, 5–8 minutes to prepare

1 cup sifted bleached all-purpose flour
1 teaspoon salt
3 tablespoons cold butter, cut into pieces

1 tablespoon cold lard, cut into pieces
6 tablespoons cold whole or lowfat buttermilk
   (preferably whole)

1.   Sift the flour and salt together in a large bowl. Add the butter and lard, and place the bowl in the refrigerator to chill for 30 minutes. Place your rolling pin in the freezer, too, if there's room. Dust your work surface with flour.

2.   With a pastry blender or your fingertips, cut the butter and lard into the flour until the mixture resembles coarse crumbs with pea-sized pieces throughout. Add the buttermilk and toss with a fork to combine. Gather the pastry together into a disk. Cover tightly with plastic wrap and refrigerate for 30 minutes.

3. Dust the rolling pin with flour and roll out the dough on the floured surface to a 9-inch square if you are making Bobo-Style Oyster Pie (page 379), or to a circle 13 inches in diameter if you are making Shrimp Pot Pies (page 405). Slide a rimless baking sheet under the pastry, cover with plastic wrap, and refrigerate until required.

A handsome frame building in White Springs, Florida, that was once the Adams Country Store.

HUSHPUPPIES TWO WAYS

The hushpuppies we grew up eating with fried fish, red rice, and coleslaw were tablespoon-sized footballs of seasoned cornmeal batter, with a golden brown crust that you crunch through to reach the hot, onion-spiked bread. We've yet to find a better hushpuppy, but we found a keen challenger in the hushpuppies at Fuller's Barbecue in Lumberton, North Carolina, along Interstate 95 a few miles north of the South Carolina border.

When we were in college and began traveling I-95 frequently—a journey that we still make about eight times a year—Fuller's was a convenient dinner stop on the way down (if we left at the crack of dawn) or a lunch stop on the way up (if we left by 9 A.M.). The Locklears, who own the place, are Lumbee Indians, and the trophy of their barbecue buffet is a finely minced, dry style of pulled pork to which you add a bracing hot-pepper vinegar. But we think their hushpuppies—gumdrop-sized, pillowy, and a soft, cereal yellow—are equally praiseworthy. We developed our North Carolina hushpuppy recipe from our memories of theirs.

Which hushpuppy recipe we use depends on what we're cooking. We serve the lighter, more "poppable" North Carolina–style hushpuppies with pulled pork or fried chicken. The richer, denser, crustier ones we grew up with are terrific with Fried Whiting (page 386) or Fried Oysters (page 388).

✻ NORTH CAROLINA–STYLE HUSHPUPPIES ✻

Makes 60 gumball-sized hushpuppies

TIME: 30 minutes

1 cup stone-ground cornmeal

1 cup all-purpose flour

1 teaspoon baking soda

1 teaspoon baking powder

½ teaspoon salt

2 teaspoons sugar

¼ cup finely minced scallions

1 teaspoon lemon zest

1 large egg

1 cup plus 2 tablespoons whole or lowfat
        buttermilk (preferably whole)

2 cups peanut oil, canola oil, or lard

1.   Preheat the oven to 225 degrees. Set a large ovenproof plate lined with paper towels on the middle rack.

2.   Sift the cornmeal and flour into a mixing bowl. Add the baking soda, baking powder, salt, sugar, scallions, and lemon zest and stir with a fork to distribute evenly. In a small bowl, beat the egg, and add it to the dry ingredients. Slowly add 1 cup buttermilk, mixing with a spoon. Add more buttermilk as needed until the batter is flexible and tacky.

3.   In a 9-inch skillet, heat the oil over high heat until a candy thermometer reads 375 degrees. Drop the batter by teaspoonfuls into the oil taking care not to crowd them in the skillet, and fry in batches of 15 until golden brown, about 3 minutes, agitating to cook evenly. Adjust the heat as necessary to maintain the temperature of the oil between 350 and 375 degrees. Using a slotted spoon, transfer the hushpuppies to the warming plate, and repeat until all the batter has been used.

4. Serve warm, with Sunday Fried Chicken (page 335) or Oven BBQed Picnic Shoulder (page 349).

☀ SOUTH CAROLINA–STYLE HUSHPUPPIES ☀

Makes 30 hushpuppies

TIME: 45 minutes

1¼ cups stone-ground cornmeal
½ cup all-purpose flour
½ teaspoon baking soda
½ teapoon baking powder
1½ tablespoons sugar
½ teaspoon salt
½ teaspoon freshly ground black pepper

3 tablespoons plus 2 teaspoons minced
    scallions
1 large egg
½ cup plus 2 tablespoons whole or lowfat
    buttermilk (preferably whole)
2 cups canola oil, peanut oil, or lard

1. Preheat the oven to 225 degrees. Set a large ovenproof plate lined with paper towels on the middle rack.

2. Sift the cornmeal and flour into a mixing bowl. Add the baking soda, baking powder, sugar, salt, pepper, and scallions and stir with a fork to distribute evenly. In a small bowl, beat the egg, and add it to the dry ingredients. Slowly add ½ cup buttermilk, mixing with a spoon. Add more buttermilk as needed until the batter is flexible and tacky.

3. In a 9-inch skillet, heat the oil until a candy thermometer reads 375 degrees. Using a lozenge-shaped tablespoon, ease a spoonful of dough into the oil with the back of a second spoon. Add 5 more spoonfuls and fry until golden brown, about 5 minutes, agitating to cook evenly. Adjust the heat as necessary to maintain the temperature of the oil between 350 and 375 degrees. With a slotted spoon, transfer the hushpuppies from the oil to the warming plate, and repeat, frying in batches of 6, until all the batter has been used.

4. Serve warm, with Fried Shrimp (page 391), Fried Oysters (page 388), or Fried Whiting (page 386).

The Pantry

Pantry staples are cooking catalysts. If you have on hand the broths, spices, sauces, and condiments that get you excited about cooking, you inevitably cook more often, and with greater confidence. We know these recipes by heart, since we have to replenish them so frequently.

⁂ PEPPER VINEGAR ⁂

WE ALWAYS BRING A CRUET OF PEPPER VINEGAR TO THE TABLE ALONG WITH THE SALT AND PEPPER. IT'S A GREAT HOT SAUCE to shake on everything from a fried oyster to a morsel of pork shoulder. It's also a superb tenderizer for meats and an easy way to gussy up a favorite salad dressing. Best of all, making it is very, very easy. You can use fresh or dried hot peppers, but fresh ones give the vinegar kick for longer. Just keep topping up your cruet with vinegar until the peppers no longer give it heat. You'll be surprised how long-lasting hot peppers are. Some cruets we've had are on their third year, and the vinegar seems as fiery as the first day we made it.

Makes 2 cups
TIME: 2 minutes to prepare, 24 hours to chill

1 cup white wine vinegar
2 Thai, serrano, or bird's-eye chiles, fresh or dried

With a funnel, pour the vinegar into a cruet. Add the chiles and use a chopstick or the handle of a wooden spoon to submerge them, if necessary. Cap the cruet and place it in the refrigerator. The vinegar will be well infused in 24 hours and will keep for months in the refrigerator.

❋ BUTTERMILK-LIME DRESSING ❋

THIS CREAMY HERB DRESSING IS REFRESHING AND GREEN, GREEN, GREEN. BUT IT'S NOT AS HEAVY AS A TRADITIONAL GREEN Goddess dressing, and the small amount of honey rounds out the acidity in the lime and buttermilk. It is wonderful not only on salad but as a dip (see the variation) for anything fried: okra, green tomatoes, oysters, hushpuppies, you name it.

Makes 1¼ cups

TIME: 5 minutes

¾ cups whole or lowfat buttermilk (preferably whole)

5 tablespoons freshly squeezed lime juice (from 3–4 limes)

2 tablespoons extra-virgin olive oil

1 tablespoon honey

¼ cup finely minced fresh basil

¼ cup finely minced green onions

¼ cup finely minced fresh flat-leaf parsley

½ teaspoon salt, plus more to taste

In a small bowl, whisk the ingredients together until thoroughly combined. Cover tightly and store in the refrigerator not more than 2 days.

VARIATION—BUTTERMILK DIP: WHISK 1/3 CUP SOUR CREAM OR CRÈME FRAÎCHE AND 1/4 TEASPOON SALT WITH THE ABOVE INGREDIENTS.

❋ NORTH CAROLINA–STYLE BBQ SAUCE ❋

NORTH CAROLINA'S DISTINCTIVE STYLE OF BARBECUE IS
A FAVORITE OF OURS. THE SAUCE IS ALMOST ENTIRELY VINEGAR, SO
it has the same consistency as water and seems thin compared to the gloppy, ketchup-thick sauces
of the mid-South, the Deep South, and Texas. But what this sauce is designed to do better than
any other is to saturate pork; smoky, slow-cooked tufts of succulent pulled pork shoulder absorb
it like a sponge. The acidity in the vinegar and the heat of red pepper in the sauce cuts the richness
of the meat perfectly. The sauce is most often used as a condiment, but we find it's a delicious
marinade for a variety of meats, from pork tenderloin to fatty chicken thighs.

Makes 2 cups
TIME: 5 minutes

2 cups white vinegar

2 tablespoons ground red chile (New Mexico
    chile, if available)

1 teaspoon freshly ground black pepper

1 tablespoon salt

1 teaspoon sugar

In a medium bowl, whisk the ingredients together until thoroughly combined. Decant into a
bottle or cruet. Stored in the refrigerator, this sauce will keep a month or more.

❊ SOUTH CAROLINA–STYLE BBQ SAUCE ❊

CAN YOU HEAR THE PROTESTS IN ORANGEBURG? YES, TO IMPOSE A SINGLE SAUCE ON THE PALMETTO STATE IS TO INVITE hate mail. But a mustard-based sauce represents the broad consensus of South Carolina's barbecue tastes. Our version is very similar to one that you'll find in most barbecue temples in the central part of the state, especially in Florence and Columbia (the state capital). Besides its robust mustard and black pepper flavor, this barbecue sauce is famous for its clinging ability, so use it as a basting sauce as you cook, or warm it slightly and serve in a sauceboat for use as a condiment.

To quell the voices from Orangeburg, and because their unique orange sauce is so damn good, we've included that recipe, too (page 523). It's a mild mustard variation that features pickle juice and mayonnaise (Duke's Mayonnaise, of course).

Makes 2 cups

TIME: 25 minutes

2 cups prepared yellow mustard

¼ cup lemon juice (from 1 lemon)

½ cup brown sugar, or less, to taste

2 tablespoons ketchup

2 tablespoons olive oil

2 teaspoons freshly ground black pepper

2 teaspoons dried oregano (optional)

2 teaspoons Worcestershire sauce

Salt to taste

In a 1- or 2-quart saucepan over medium heat, whisk the ingredients together until thoroughly combined. When the mixture begins to bubble and spit, reduce the heat to low and simmer, stirring frequently, for 10 minutes. Turn off the heat and allow to rest for 10 minutes. Decant into a bottle or jar. Stored in the refrigerator, this sauce will keep for a month or more.

❧ ORANGEBURG COUNTY–STYLE BBQ SAUCE ❧

Makes 1¾ cups

TIME: 5 minutes

1 cup prepared yellow mustard
½ cup high-quality store-bought mayonnaise
    such as Duke's or Hellmann's
¼ cup pickle juice, drained from a jar of any of
    the pickle recipes on pages 105–127 or
    from a store-bought jar

2 tablespoons ketchup
½ teaspoon freshly ground black pepper

Whisk the ingredients together in a medium bowl until thoroughly combined. Decant into a bottle or jar, cover tightly, and store in the refrigerator for up to 2 days. Use as a condiment with any of the Freelance Writers' Dream recipes (page 348).

❋ LEMONY MAYONNAISE ❋

DUKE'S MAYONNAISE IS THE SOUTHEASTERN UNITED STATES' HOUSE BRAND. IT'S TANGY AND TASTES HOMEMADE, BECAUSE unlike most commercial brands, it has no sweetener in it. But when we run out of Duke's, we substitute this flavorful mayonnaise, which is perfect for sandwiches, Roasted Tomato Aspic (page 83), and Deviled Eggs (page 87).

Makes 1 cup

TIME: 5 minutes

2 large egg yolks

2 tablespoons freshly squeezed lemon juice (from 1 lemon)

½ cup vegetable oil

½ cup extra-virgin olive oil

1 teaspoon white vinegar, white wine vinegar, champagne vinegar, red wine vinegar, or sherry vinegar

¼ teaspoon kosher salt

¼ teaspoon finely ground black pepper

In a small bowl, whisk the egg yolks with the lemon juice. Add the oils in a thin stream, whisking constantly to emulsify. When the mayonnaise is thick and consistent, add the vinegar, salt, and pepper and whisk vigorously to incorporate. Store in a container with a tight-fitting lid in the refrigerator. The mayonnaise will keep for up to 2 days.

☀ ZESTY COCKTAIL SAUCE ☀

ORANGE ZEST IS THE SURPRISE INGREDIENT IN THIS COCKTAIL SAUCE, AN ESSENTIAL CONDIMENT FOR FRIED OYSTERS (page 388), Fried Shrimp (page 391), or shrimp steamed in their shells.

Makes 1 cup

TIME: 5 minutes

One 15-ounce can crushed Italian tomatoes

2 tablespoons tomato paste

2 tablespoons plus 2 teaspoons prepared horseradish, drained

1 tablespoon plus 1 teaspoon lemon juice

2 teaspoons kosher salt

2 teaspoons sugar

1 teaspoon orange zest

Place the ingredients in a food processor or a blender and pulse 3 or 4 times, until the mixture is a smooth puree. Transfer to a container, cover tightly, and store in the refrigerator. The cocktail sauce will keep for up to 4 days.

❦ LEE BROS. TARTAR SAUCE ❦

A TARTAR SAUCE WITH A LITTLE SOMETHING EXTRA CAN REALLY MAKE THE DIFFERENCE BETWEEN A SENSATIONAL FRIED Whiting (page 386), Fried Oysters (page 388), or Shrimp Burgers (page 382) experience and a merely excellent one. Most tartar sauces call for store-bought sweet pickle relish; we use our own pickles and relishes, because they tend to have more flavor than the grocery-store brands.

We first drain the relish (or chop the pickles, if we're using, for example, Pickled Okra), but we keep some of the brine on hand. Then, after we've combined the mayonnaise and the relish or chopped pickle, we add some brine to the sauce until we get the consistency we want.

It'll be hard to go back to ho-hum tartar sauce once you've had Jerusalem Artichoke Tartar Sauce or Pickled Scallion Tartar Sauce!

Makes 1 cup

TIME: 5 minutes

½ cup Chowchow (page 108), Jerusalem Artichoke Relish (page 112), or Pickled Corn
(page 122), drained, or chopped Pickled
Okra (page 118), or chopped Pickled
Scallions (page 124), drained

½ cup Lemony Mayonnaise (page 524) or
high-quality store-bought mayonnaise
such as Duke's or Hellmann's

In a medium bowl, fold the relish into the mayonnaise until thoroughly combined. If you prefer
your tartar sauce thinner, add pickling brine by half-teaspoonfuls, whisking to incorporate. Transfer to a container, cover tightly, and store in the refrigerator. The tartar sauce will keep for up to
2 days.

☀ SOUR ORANGE SAUCE ☀

THIS ALL-PURPOSE TONIC MAKES A TERRIFIC MARINADE FOR PORK, AND A FEW TABLESPOONS MAKE A QUICK SHORTCUT TO a knockout dressing when used in place of vinegar in a vinaigrette.

Makes 2 cups

TIME: 10 minutes to prepare, 2 days to steep

5 stems fresh cilantro

5 stems fresh mint

2 cups sour orange juice, strained (from about 24 oranges), or substitute three equal parts fresh grapefruit, lemon, and orange juice

2 garlic cloves, peeled and crushed

1 serrano chile, roasted, peeled, seeded, and minced

1 slice large yellow onion

1. Place the cilantro and mint on a cutting board and roll a rolling pin over them once, to bruise them and release their oils.

2. Pour the juice into a 1-quart Mason jar. Add the herbs and remaining ingredients and refrigerate. Steep for 2 days in the refrigerator before using as a marinade for pork, chicken, or fish. The sauce will keep in the refrigerator for 2 weeks.

VARIATION—EASIER SOUR ORANGE SAUCE: ADD 4 STEMS FRESH OREGANO AND 2 SMASHED CLOVES GARLIC TO 2 CUPS STRAINED SOUR ORANGE JUICE. LET STEEP FOR 2 DAYS IN THE REFRIGERATOR.

❋ SORGHUM BUTTER ❋

PERHAPS THE QUICKEST WAY TO GET A JAR OF SORGHUM
TO DISAPPEAR FROM YOUR PANTRY IS TO SERVE HOT BISCUITS WITH
sorghum butter. Other ways include Buttermilk Ice Cream and Corn-Bread Parfaits (page 437),
Boiled Peanut and Sorghum Swirl Ice Cream (page 429), Sorghum Pecan Pie (page 449), or simply over your favorite ice cream.

Makes 1 cup

TIME: 2–3 minutes

8 tablespoons (1 stick) unsalted butter, softened
½ cup pure sorghum molasses (see Sourcery, page 447)

Using a spatula or an electric mixer, cream the butter with the molasses in a medium bowl. Transfer the sorghum butter to two 4-ounce ramekins, cover with plastic wrap, and refrigerate.
Sorghum butter keeps in the refrigerator for about 1 week.

Broths

We simmer up tasty broths from bones and trimmings, herbs and aromatic vegetables, to give a foundation of flavor and body to our favorite soups, stews, and sauces. We store them by the pint in the freezer, or in the refrigerator if we intend to use them soon.

These broths aren't "stocks" in the classic French culinary sense of the word. First, we don't take the time to scrub the bones; in fact, in the case of our pork, chicken, and beef broths, we use bones, meat, and even a small proportion of fat—any part of the animal we think will add flavor. Also, we simmer our broths only as long as we can, which may be just forty-five minutes or an hour (the eight hours required for a correct *fond de boeuf* rarely fits with our daily schedules).

Here's an example of the way the broth develops. Say we've made a whole snapper with sweet potatoes for dinner. Once we've filleted the fish, we save the head, tail, and bones in a plastic bag with a zipper lock. After the meal, one of us will do the dishes while the other prepares the broth. And if we simply don't have time to prepare the bones, we stash them in the freezer until we do.

As gratifying as it is to make homemade broths—which, according to our tendency, we call "Sunday broths"—there are occasions when we run out of the broths we use most often (shrimp and chicken) and don't have time to cook one up from scratch. So in this section we also offer "Tuesday broths"—simple recipes for torquing up our preferred canned broths with a quick sauté of dried herbs, vegetables, and wine.

KLO

KILLER LEFTOVER—SIMPLE BROTH SOUP WITH POACHED EGGS: ANY OF THE BROTHS IN THIS CHAPTER MAKE A GOOD QUICK LUNCH ON A WINTRY DAY, ESPECIALLY PAIRED WITH A SLICE OF TOASTED, BUTTERED SALLY LUNN (PAGE 500). BUDGET 1 1/2 TO 2 CUPS BROTH AND 2 EGGS PER SERVING. POUR THE BROTH INTO A MEDIUM SAUCEPAN AND BRING TO A BOIL OVER HIGH HEAT. TURN THE HEAT DOWN VERY LOW, SO THAT THE LIQUID SIMMERS EVER SO GENTLY. POACH THE EGGS BY CRACKING EACH ONE INTO THE BOWL OF A LARGE LADLE WITH A DROP OF VINEGAR IN IT. LOWER THE LADLE GENTLY INTO THE BROTH AND RELEASE THE EGG. REPEAT UNTIL ALL THE EGGS ARE IN THE BROTH, AND SIMMER UNTIL THE EGGS HAVE POACHED (2 TO 3 MINUTES FOR SOFT YOLKS; 4 TO 5 MINUTES FOR FIRM YOLKS). SERVE IN BOWLS, AND FLOAT STEMS OF FLAT-LEAF PARSLEY ON THE SURFACE OF THE SOUP.

OUR FAVORITE COMMERCIAL BRANDS ARE (IN ORDER of preference, because many markets don't carry all brands) Swanson, College Inn, and Campbell's Original Red and White Label, and we find our preferences to be consistent across chicken, beef, and vegetable varieties. We tend to buy the reduced-sodium versions, because we can always add salt if we want to. If you don't have a favorite commercial broth, do a taste test to find the one you like best. When you're tasting, be alert to any off flavors; strangely enough, a great many brands on the market, even ones labeled organic, taste like the ingredients came from an unnatural place. In our experience, the most expensive commercial broths often taste the worst.

☀ SUNDAY CHICKEN BROTH ☀

THIS BROTH IS THE BASE OF MANY OF THE STEWS AND
SOUPS IN THIS BOOK. IT IS A FLAVORFUL BUT MILD BROTH, AKIN TO
a white chicken stock. If you have the time and you prefer a darker, more robust chicken broth,
roast the bones and trimmings in a small roasting pan or skillet on the top rack of a 425-degree
oven for 30 minutes before preparing the broth.

Makes about 1 quart

TIME: 1¼ hours

Bones and trimmings (but not giblets) of one
    3½–4½-pound chicken, or 12–14 ounces
    chicken bones and trimmings
1 large onion, trimmed, peeled, and cut into
    eighths
6 large stems fresh flat-leaf parsley
1 stalk celery, cut into 2-inch lengths

2 large bay leaves
5 cups cold water
1 cup crisp dry white wine, such as Pinot
    Grigio or Sauvignon Blanc
Lee Bros. Shrimp Boil (page 553) to taste, or
    salt and freshly ground black pepper to
    taste

1.   Place the bones in a medium stockpot and add the onion, parsley, celery, and bay leaves. Pour
the water and wine into the pot (the liquid should cover all the ingredients; if it doesn't, add more

water). Bring to a vigorous simmer over high heat, then turn down the heat and simmer gently for 45 minutes to 1 hour, skimming any scum or fat that rises to the surface with a slotted spoon.

2. Strain the broth into a bowl through a fine-mesh strainer. Discard the solids. Measure the amount of broth you're left with. Taste it: if you don't plan to reduce it further, season it gently with shrimp boil or salt and pepper (start with ¼ teaspoon shrimp boil or ⅛ teaspoon salt and ⅛ teaspoon pepper per 1 cup broth).

3. Pour the broth into a container with a tight-fitting lid and store in the refrigerator until the fat congeals on its surface. Scrape the fat from the broth with a spoon. If you plan to use the broth within 2 days, reseal the container and store it in the refrigerator. If you don't plan to use it within 2 days, place it in the freezer, where it will keep for 1 month or more.

❋ TUESDAY CHICKEN BROTH ❋

SUPER-EASY AND VERY TASTY.

Makes 2½–3 cups

TIME: 30 minutes

1 tablespoon unsalted butter or olive oil
½ cup finely diced yellow onion (about 1 medium onion)
⅓ cup grated carrot (about 1 large carrot)
½ cup finely diced celery (about 1 large stalk)
6 stems fresh flat-leaf parsley

1 quart (4 cups) low-sodium canned chicken broth (see Sourcery, page 531)
Lee Bros. Shrimp Boil (page 553) to taste, or salt and freshly ground black pepper to taste (optional)

1.   In a medium stockpot, heat the butter over medium-high heat until frothy. Add the onion, carrot, celery, and parsley and sauté until softened and very fragrant but not browned, about 6 minutes.

2.   Pour the chicken broth into the pot and turn the heat to high. When the broth simmers vigorously, turn the heat down to low and keep at a lively simmer for 15 minutes.

3. Strain the broth into a bowl through a fine-mesh strainer. Discard the solids. Measure the amount of broth you're left with. Taste the broth: if you don't plan to reduce it further, season it gently with shrimp boil or salt and pepper (start with ¼ teaspoon shrimp boil or ⅛ teaspoon salt and ⅛ teaspoon pepper per 1 cup broth).

4. Pour the broth into a container (or two) with a tight-fitting lid and store in the refrigerator until the fat congeals on its surface. Scrape the fat from the broth with a spoon. If you plan to use the broth within 2 days, reseal the container and store it in the refrigerator. If you don't plan to use it within 2 days, place it in the freezer, where it will keep for 1 month or more.

❊ SUNDAY SHRIMP BROTH ❊

Makes 3–4 cups

TIME: 45 minutes

3–4 ounces shrimp shells (shells from 1
    pound headless shrimp)
1 large onion, trimmed, peeled, and cut into
    eighths
2 stalks celery, greens and stem ends trimmed,
    cut into 2-inch-long pieces
6 stems fresh flat-leaf parsley

3 bay leaves
6 cups water
½ cup crisp dry white wine, such as Pinot
    Grigio or Sauvignon Blanc
Lee Bros. Shrimp Boil (page 553) to taste, or
    salt and freshly ground black pepper to
    taste

1. Place the shrimp shells, onion, celery, parsley, and bay leaves in a medium stockpot. Add the water and wine and bring to a vigorous simmer over high heat. Turn the heat to low and simmer gently for 45 minutes.

2. Strain the broth into a bowl through a fine-mesh strainer. Discard the solids. Measure the amount of broth you're left with. Taste the broth: if you don't plan to reduce it further, season it gently with shrimp boil or salt and pepper (start with ¼ teaspoon shrimp boil or ⅛ teaspoon salt and ⅛ teaspoon pepper per 1 cup broth).

3. Store the broth in the refrigerator if you plan to use it within 2 days. If you don't plan to use it within 2 days, store the broth in the freezer, where it will keep for 1 month or more.

❋ TUESDAY "SHRIMP" BROTH ❋

THIS BROTH ACTUALLY HAS NO SHRIMP IN IT AT ALL—
IT'S A VEGETABLE SAUTÉ WITH A SPLASH OF WINE THAT GETS
reduced and gives oomph to store-bought clam juice. We love the fresh marine flavor of clam juice,
and we think it's a great, quick substitute in any recipe that calls for shrimp broth. We like the Bar
Harbor and Atlantic brands, which are all-natural and inexpensive and have a fresh-from-the-sea
flavor.

Makes 2½–3 cups

TIME: 30 minutes

1 tablespoon unsalted butter
½ cup finely diced yellow onion (about 1
 medium onion)
½ cup finely diced celery (about 1 large stalk)
⅓ cup grated carrot (about 1 large carrot)
6 stems fresh flat-leaf parsley

½ cup crisp dry white wine, such as Pinot
 Grigio or Sauvignon Blanc
4 cups (1 quart) clam juice
Lee Bros. Shrimp Boil (page 553) to taste, or
 salt and freshly ground black pepper to
 taste (optional)

1.   In a medium stockpot, melt the butter over medium-high heat until frothy. Add the onion, celery, carrot and parsley and sauté until softened but not browned, about 6 minutes. Add the wine. Turn the heat to high and simmer vigorously until the wine is reduced by one half, about 6 minutes more.

2.   Add the clam juice. When the broth comes to a vigorous simmer, reduce the heat to low and simmer gently for 15 minutes. The vegetables will be completely softened and the broth will be very fragrant.

3.   Strain the broth into a bowl through a fine-mesh strainer. Discard the solids. Measure the amount of broth you're left with. Taste the broth: if you don't plan to reduce it further, season it gently with shrimp boil or salt and pepper (start with ¼ teaspoon shrimp boil or ⅛ teaspoon salt and ⅛ teaspoon pepper per 1 cup broth).

✺ SUNDAY VEGETABLE BROTH ✺

Makes 3–4 cups

TIME: 1¼ hours

2 large yellow onions, trimmed, peeled, and
    cut into eighths
2 carrots, peeled and diced
3 stalks celery, cut into 2-inch pieces
4 cloves garlic, peeled and crushed

12 stems fresh flat-leaf parsley
6 cups cold water
Lee Bros. Shrimp Boil (page 553) to taste, or
    salt and freshly ground black pepper to
    taste

1. Place all the ingredients except the seasonings in a medium stockpot and bring to a simmer over high heat. Turn the heat down to low and simmer gently for 1 hour.

2. Strain the broth into a bowl through a fine-mesh strainer. Discard the solids. Measure the amount of broth you're left with. Taste the broth: if you don't plan to reduce it further, season it gently with shrimp boil or salt and pepper (start with ¼ teaspoon shrimp boil or ⅛ teaspoon salt and ⅛ teaspoon pepper per 1 cup broth).

3. Pour the broth into a container with a tight-fitting lid and store in the refrigerator if you plan to use it within 2 days. If you don't plan to use the broth within 2 days, place the container in the freezer, where the broth will keep for 1 month or more.

☀ TUESDAY VEGETABLE BROTH ☀

Makes 2½–3 cups

TIME: 30 minutes

1 tablespoon unsalted butter

½ cup finely diced yellow onion (about 1 medium onion)

½ cup finely diced celery (about 1 large stalk)

⅓ cup grated carrot (about 1 large carrot)

6 stems fresh flat-leaf parsley

3 cloves garlic, peeled and crushed

½ cup crisp dry white wine, such as Pinot Grigio or Sauvignon Blanc

4 cups (1 quart) canned vegetable broth

Lee Bros. Shrimp Boil (page 553) to taste, or salt and freshly ground black pepper to taste (optional)

1. In a medium stockpot, melt the butter over medium-high heat until frothy. Add the onion, celery, carrot, parsley, and garlic and sauté until softened but not browned, about 6 minutes. Add the wine. Turn the heat to high and simmer vigorously until the wine is reduced by one half, about 6 minutes more.

2. Add the broth. When the liquid comes to a vigorous simmer, reduce the heat to low and simmer gently for 15 minutes. The vegetables will be completely softened and the broth will be very fragrant.

3. Strain the broth into a bowl through a fine-mesh strainer. Discard the solids. Measure the amount of broth you're left with. Taste the broth: if you don't plan to reduce it further, season it gently with shrimp boil or salt and pepper (start with ¼ teaspoon shrimp boil or ⅛ teaspoon salt and ⅛ teaspoon pepper per 1 cup broth).

❧ SUNDAY BEEF BROTH ❧

THIS RECIPE USES OXTAILS, ONE OF OUR FAVORITE CUTS OF THE COW, TO MAKE A RICH, SILKY BEEF BROTH. THESE BONES are filled with gelatin and flavor, and we coax the most out of them by searing them in the stockpot before preparing the broth.

Makes 3–4 cups

TIME: 70 minutes

1 tablespoon canola oil
1 pound oxtails
½ cup diced yellow onion (about 1 medium onion)
½ cup diced carrot (about 1 large carrot)

3 large bay leaves
¼ cup full-bodied red wine
6 cups cold water
Salt and freshly ground black pepper to taste

1.   Heat the oil in a medium stockpot over high heat until it shimmers. Add the oxtails in 2 batches and sear, turning them with tongs as each surface becomes golden brown, until they are browned all over, about 10 minutes per batch. Remove and reserve in a medium bowl.

2.   Add the onion, carrot, and bay leaves to the pot and cook, stirring, until softened, 2 to 3 minutes. Add the wine and stir with a wooden spoon, scraping up any browned bits on the bottom. Simmer the wine until it is reduced by one half, about 3 minutes.

3.   Return the browned oxtails to the stockpot and add the water. Bring to a vigorous simmer over high heat, then turn the heat to low and simmer gently for 45 minutes to 1 hour, skimming any scum or fat that rises to the surface with a slotted spoon.

4.   Strain the broth into a bowl through a fine-mesh strainer. Discard the solids. Measure the amount of broth you're left with. Taste the broth: if you don't plan to reduce it further, season it gently with salt and pepper (start with ⅛ teaspoon salt and ⅛ teaspoon pepper per 1 cup broth).

5.   Pour the broth into a container with a tight-fitting lid and store in the refrigerator until the fat congeals on its surface. Scrape the fat from the broth with a spoon. If you plan to use within 2 days, reseal the container and store it in the refrigerator. If you don't plan to use it within 2 days, place it in the freezer, where the broth will keep for 1 month or more.

❊ TUESDAY BEEF BROTH ❊

THIS SHORTCUT DRESSES UP CANNED BEEF BROTH IN LESS THAN HALF THE TIME IT TAKES TO MAKE OUR SUNDAY BEEF Broth.

Makes 3 cups

TIME: 30 minutes

1 tablespoon unsalted butter

½ cup finely diced yellow onion (about 1 medium onion)

½ cup finely diced celery (about 1 large stalk)

⅓ cup grated carrot (about 1 large carrot)

3 cloves garlic, peeled and crushed

2 large bay leaves

4 cups low-sodium canned beef broth (see Sourcery, page 531)

Salt and freshly ground black pepper to taste

1.   Melt the butter in a medium stockpot over medium-high heat until frothy. Add the onion, celery, carrot, garlic, and bay leaves. Sauté, stirring, until softened and the onion has turned translucent, 5 to 6 minutes.

2.   Add the beef broth and bring to a vigorous simmer over high heat. Turn the heat to low and simmer gently for 15 minutes.

3. Strain the broth into a bowl through a fine-mesh strainer. Discard the solids. Measure the amount of broth you're left with. Taste the broth: if you don't plan to reduce it further, season it gently with salt and pepper (start with ⅛ teaspoon salt and ⅛ teaspoon pepper per 1 cup broth).

4. Pour the broth into a container with a tight-fitting lid. If you plan to use the broth within 2 days, seal it and store it in the refrigerator. If you don't plan to use it within 2 days, place it in the freezer, where the broth will keep for 1 month or more.

❈ RICH FISH BROTH ❈

THE BONES AND TRIMMINGS OF MOST NON-OILY,
WHITE-FLESHED FISH, SUCH AS SNAPPER, BASS, AND WHITING, ARE
great for making fish broth. Some fish markets keep a supply of bones and trimmings (carefully
separated from any scales, guts, fins, or gills) on hand, but you can also use small whole fish that
have been freshly scaled, gutted, gilled, and cleaned.

Makes 3–4 cups

TIME: 1 hour

2 tablespoons unsalted butter
½ cup finely diced yellow onion (about 1
    medium onion)
½ cup finely diced celery (about 1 large stalk)
3 large bay leaves
1½ pounds fish bones and trimmings or whole
    small, non-oily fish, such as snapper,
    bass, or whiting

½ cup crisp dry white wine, such as Pinot
    Grigio or Sauvignon Blanc
6 cups cold water
Lee Bros. Shrimp Boil (page 553) to taste, or
    salt and freshly ground black pepper to
    taste

1. Melt the butter in a medium stockpot over medium-high heat until frothy. Add the onion,
celery, and bay leaves and sauté until the vegetables have softened and the onions are completely

translucent, about 6 minutes. Add the fish bones and trimmings and the wine and bring to a simmer. Simmer vigorously until the wine is reduced by one half, about 6 minutes more.

2. Add the water and bring to a vigorous simmer over high heat. Turn the heat to low and simmer gently for 45 minutes.

3. Strain the broth into a bowl through a fine-mesh strainer. Discard the solids. Measure the amount of broth you're left with. Taste the broth: if you don't plan to reduce it further, season it gently with shrimp boil or salt and pepper (start with ¼ teaspoon shrimp boil or ⅛ teaspoon salt and ⅛ teaspoon pepper per 1 cup broth).

4. Pour the broth into a container with a tight-fitting lid. If you plan to use it within 2 days, seal it and store it in the refrigerator. If you don't plan to use it within 2 days, place it in the freezer, where the broth will keep for 1 month or more.

❧ RICH PORK BROTH ❧

WE USE THIS BROTH IN OUR HOPPIN' JOHN, BECAUSE IT
DRAWS OUT THE FLAVOR OF THE SEASONING MEAT. WE MAKE IT
from pork bones and trimmings left over from Oven BBQed Picnic Shoulder (page 349) and
Luau-Style BBQed Pork Shoulder (page 352). Of all our broths, this may be the one that is most
like a French stock, because gelatin in the shoulder bones readily dissolves into to the simmering
broth, resulting in a particularly silky body.

    As with our chicken broth, if you have the time and are looking for super-robust pork flavor,
roast the bones and trimmings on the top rack of a 425-degree oven until the bones are gently
browned, 35 to 40 minutes, before simmering them with the vegetables and water.

Shoulder bones from a bone-in pork shoulder
   or 1 pound pork shank bones and
   trimmings
1 large onion, trimmed, peeled, and cut into
   eighths

2 large stalks celery, greens and stem end
   trimmed, cut into 2-inch pieces
4 bay leaves
6 cups cold water
Salt and freshly ground black pepper to taste

1.   Place the bones, onion, celery, and bay leaves in a medium stockpot and cover with the cold water. Bring to a vigorous simmer over medium-high heat, then turn the heat to low and simmer gently for 1 hour.

2.   Strain the broth into a bowl through a fine-mesh strainer. Discard the solids. Measure the amount of broth you're left with. Taste the broth: if you don't plan to reduce it further, season it gently with salt and pepper (start with ⅛ teaspoon salt and ⅛ teaspoon pepper per 1 cup broth).

3.   Pour the broth into a container with a tight-fitting lid. If you plan to use the broth within 2 days, store it in the refrigerator. If you don't plan to use it within 2 days, place the broth in the freezer, where it will keep for 1 month or more.

❄ WILD MUSHROOM BROTH ❄

THIS DELICIOUS BROTH USES BOTH DRIED MUSHROOMS AND FRESH MUSHROOMS. WE LIKE TO USE A MIXTURE OF WILD mushrooms, such as the chicken mushrooms and chanterelles we find growing on the Sea Islands near Charleston. But if you don't have a source for these, cultivated button mushrooms work fine.

Makes 3–4 cups

TIME: 45 minutes

6 cups cold Sunday Chicken Broth (page 532), Tuesday Chicken Broth (page 534), Sunday Vegetable Broth (page 539), or Tuesday Vegetable Broth (page 540)
1 ounce dried porcini or morel mushrooms
2 tablespoons unsalted butter

6 ounces fresh wild mushrooms, such as sulfur shelfs, chanterelles, or hens-of-the-woods, or cultivated button mushrooms, sliced
¼ cup finely diced yellow onion (about 1 small onion)
¼ cup dry sherry, such as fino or amontillado
1 large bay leaf

1. In a small saucepan, heat 1 cup broth over high heat until it simmers vigorously. Turn off the heat. Add the dried mushrooms and steep for 5 minutes, or until soft. Chop the reconstituted mushrooms and strain the broth through a fine-mesh strainer, a coffee filter, or a double thickness of clean paper towels.

2. In a medium stockpot, melt the butter over medium heat until frothy. Add the fresh mushrooms and onion. Sauté until the onion has softened and turned translucent and the mushrooms have absorbed the butter and released their own juices, about 6 minutes. When the pot is virtually dry but before the onions have browned, add the sherry and simmer until it is reduced by one half, about 3 minutes.

3. Add the reconstituted mushrooms and their soaking liquid and the remaining 5 cups broth to the pot. Bring to a simmer over medium-high heat. Turn the heat to low and simmer gently for 20 minutes, until the mushrooms are very soft and have released all their flavor into the broth.

4. Strain the broth into a bowl through a fine-mesh strainer. Discard the solids. Measure the amount of broth you're left with. Taste the broth: if you don't plan to reduce it further, season it gently with salt and pepper (start with ⅛ teaspoon salt and ⅛ teaspoon pepper per 1 cup broth).

5. Pour the broth into a container with a tight-fitting lid. If you plan to use it within 2 days, store it in the refrigerator. If you don't plan to use it within 2 days, place it in the freezer, where the broth will keep for 1 month or more.

❧ LEE BROS. ALL-PURPOSE FRY DREDGE ❧

THIS MIXTURE OF FLOUR, CORNMEAL, AND SEASONINGS IS WHAT WE USE TO FRY ALMOST EVERYTHING, FROM FISH TO green tomatoes. There's enough cornmeal to add flavor and texture, but not so much that it obscures a delicate flavor like that of flaky whiting, a popular local fish. The dredge has a modest amount of salt, enough pepper, and a scattering of bread crumbs to give it a nice color. It stands back and lets the flavor of the food shine through. We recommend frying in peanut oil or a mixture of peanut and canola.

Makes ¾ cup

TIME: 5 minutes

½ cup all-purpose flour
3 tablespoons stone-ground cornmeal
2 teaspoons salt

1½ teaspoons freshly ground black pepper
A sprinkling of bread crumbs for quick browning, if dredging fish or oysters

In a medium bowl, sift the flour, cornmeal, salt, and pepper together twice. Stir and turn out onto a flat surface. Press fish or green tomatoes or oysters or chicken or clams into the mixture on all sides and shake the excess loose.

Milled grains should be treated as perishable products, so if you're not using this dredge immediately, transfer it to a quart-sized plastic bag with a zipper lock and store in the freezer not longer than 4 weeks. Remove the dredge 1 hour before using so it can come to room temperature.

❋ LEE BROS. SHRIMP BOIL ❋

A SHRIMP BOIL IS A SPICE BLEND THAT COMBINES WITH WATER TO MAKE AN INSTANTLY SPICY AND AROMATIC BROTH, A PERfect medium for boiling all sorts of fish and shellfish. This recipe makes enough to season 4 gallons of water. Budget 1 tablespoon per 1 quart water.

Makes 1 scant cup

TIME: 5 minutes

1 tablespoon peppercorns
1 tablespoon celery seeds
6 bay leaves, shredded with scissors

½ cup kosher salt
3 tablespoons ground cayenne pepper

Pound the peppercorns, celery seeds, and bay leaf with the salt in a mortar, in batches if necessary. Place in a small bowl and stir in the cayenne. Stored in an airtight container, it will keep for up to 2 months.

❋ INDEX ❋

Note: Page numbers in **boldface** refer to recipes themselves.

❋ *ABOUT THE AUTHORS* ❋

Matt Lee and Ted Lee grew up in Charleston, South Carolina, and in 1994 founded the Lee Bros. Boiled Peanuts Catalogue, a mail-order source for southern pantry staples (843-720-8890; www.boiledpeanuts.com). They currently write about food for the *New York Times* and are the wine columnists for *Martha Stewart Living*. Since 2001, they have been contributing editors at *Travel + Leisure*. Their radio show, *The Lee Bros. Boiled Peanut Hour*, the only national radio show devoted exclusively to Southern food, is broadcast on Martha Stewart Living Radio, Sirius Channel 112.